AF840562

Gender, Development and Social Change

Series Editors

Wendy Harcourt
Associate Professor in Critical Development and Feminist Studies
The International Institute of Social Studies
Erasmus University
The Netherlands

Series Committee

Lydia Alpizar
Feminist activist and consultant
São Paulo, Brazil

Srilatha Batliwala
India-based feminist activist and Scholar
Associate with the Association for Women's Rights in Development
Bangalore, India

Yvonne Underhill-Sem
Associate Professor of Development Studies
University of Auckland
New Zealand

The 'Gender, Development and Social Change' series brings together path-breaking writing from gender scholars and activist researchers who are engaged in development as a process of transformation and change. The series pinpoints where gender and development analysis and practice are creating major 'change moments'. Multidisciplinary in scope, it features some of the most important and innovative gender perspectives on development knowledge, policy and social change. The distinctive feature of the series is its dual nature: to publish both scholarly research on key issues informing the gender and development agenda as well as featuring young scholars and activists' accounts of how gender analysis and practice are shaping political and social development processes. The authors aim to capture innovative thinking on a range of hot spot gender and development debates from women's lives on the margins to high level global politics. Each book pivots around a key 'social change' moment or process conceptually envisaged from an intersectional, gender and rights based approach to development.

More information about this series at
http://www.springer.com/gp/series/14999

Zohra Khan • Nalini Burn
Editors

Financing for Gender Equality

Realising Women's Rights through Gender Responsive Budgeting

palgrave
macmillan

Editors
Zohra Khan
United Nations
New York, USA

Nalini Burn
Flic en Flac
Mauritius

Gender, Development and Social Change
ISBN 978-1-137-46100-1   ISBN 978-1-137-46101-8 (eBook)
DOI 10.1057/978-1-137-46101-8

Library of Congress Control Number: 2016957784

© The Editor(s) (if applicable) and The Author(s) 2017
The author(s) has/have asserted their right(s) to be identified as the author(s) of this work in accordance with the Copyright, Designs and Patents Act 1988.
This work is subject to copyright. All rights are solely and exclusively licensed by the Publisher, whether the whole or part of the material is concerned, specifically the rights of translation, reprinting, reuse of illustrations, recitation, broadcasting, reproduction on microfilms or in any other physical way, and transmission or information storage and retrieval, electronic adaptation, computer software, or by similar or dissimilar methodology now known or hereafter developed.
The use of general descriptive names, registered names, trademarks, service marks, etc. in this publication does not imply, even in the absence of a specific statement, that such names are exempt from the relevant protective laws and regulations and therefore free for general use.
The publisher, the authors and the editors are safe to assume that the advice and information in this book are believed to be true and accurate at the date of publication. Neither the publisher nor the authors or the editors give a warranty, express or implied, with respect to the material contained herein or for any errors or omissions that may have been made. The publisher remains neutral with regard to jurisdictional claims in published maps and institutional affiliations.

Cover image © Serena Dinelli
Cover design by Jenny Vong

Printed on acid-free paper

This Palgrave Macmillan imprint is published by Springer Nature
The registered company is Macmillan Publishers Ltd.
The registered company address is: The Campus, 4 Crinan Street, London, N1 9XW, United Kingdom

Series Editor's Preface

Financing for Gender Equality: Realizing Women's Rights through Gender-Responsive Budgeting

This is an exciting collection to include in the 'Gender, Development and Social Change' series. It has been one of the first volumes we were discussing for the series back in late 2012. One of the editors Zohra Khan and I have worked together since the mid-2000s when we both served on the board of Women in Development Europe Network. Different jobs and different countries later, we are still good friends and still committed to changing development discourse and practice to include gender equality. Zohra has brought together leaders in the field who are well known and highly respected.

What is personally very rewarding for me about this book is that the contributors have produced a volume that brings together the best of feminist scholarship, knowledge and policy insight. In the three years it took to come to fruition, I was privileged to see what a unique and important collection it was, not only because of the content but also because of the process. The book is truly a feminist project that has high policy relevance, original evidence-based material and the conviction of all the authors to use gender-responsive budgeting as a strategic lever for transformative change. The depth of the contributions speaks for itself. But what is less visible is the way in which its long gestation is due to the politics of producing an excellent-quality academic publication within the framework of an international policy arena. In this, I congratulate the editors, contributions, UN Women and Palgrave Macmillan for producing this pioneering book.

Although it has been a long time in production, the book comes at a very timely moment with the announcement of the Sustainable Development Goals (SDGs) and the 2030 sustainable development agenda in September 2015. The collection provides compelling evidence for why gender-based budgeting (GRB) needs to be part of new fiscal policy and other public policy instruments to ensure the success of the SDGs. The chapters illustrate the importance of understanding how gender power relations are embedded in structures of economic, social and political power. Although addressing the technocratic policy debate, the chapters also underline that the budget process is very much a political one. The chapters do not flinch in looking at gendered structures of power and at the link between the distribution of power and the distribution of resources.

The book, in short, documents a feminist project that aims to impact on the next years of fiscal policy in the context of the SDGs. Made up of 12 chapters, including a comprehensive introduction, it helps us to understand financing for gender equality in the context of the 2030 Agenda for Sustainable Development and the Financing for Development. From first-hand experience, the chapters map out the key milestones of GRB concepts, methodologies and approaches in different country contexts. The chapters give the history of GRB from the mid-2000s chronicling programmatic GRB knowledge management, scholarly investigation and feminist and women's rights advocacy. In this, the book corrects the blindness of current policy histories by carefully looking at the implications of the (too often gender blind) fiscal discipline of over 20 years of economic liberalization.

It perhaps comes as no surprise that many of the chapters show that though in words governments are committed to the Beijing Framework of gender equality, women's rights and empowerment there are few resources for policies and programmes provided. This lack, the authors show, will pose major challenges for the achievement of the SDGs. As Khan suggests in her chapter, 'transformative financing' is required based on gender-responsive planning and budgeting, to increase financing for gender equality and women's rights. The book gives convincing historical, theoretical and evidence-based arguments about the economic and social importance of financing gender equality across the board. The chapters consequently focus on a large array of concerns—gender equality programmes, development aid, peacebuilding, women's rights organizations and movements and climate funding. The examples come from around the world—Africa, Asia Pacific, Latin America and Andalusia. The breadth of critique is deeply impressive, from finance, to neo-liberal macroeconomics, public policy, development policy and women's rights. The wealth of knowledge of the authors and their own engagement in the strategies they comment on and propose make this a very important book for hands-on research, teaching, policy making and advocacy.

I am confident that this is going to be a landmark collection with important ramifications in many fields.

Wendy Harcourt
The Hague, January 2016

Acknowledgements

We would like to thank Wendy Harcourt, Series Editor, for giving us the space to reflect on an area of feminist investigation so close to our hearts.

We owe a debt of gratitude to the authors, the women and men who have shaped this book and who made it possible in some form or other. We especially thank the dedicated colleagues and friends we have worked with over the years in a number of countries and organizations, who continue to search for ways and means to finance gender equality and who blend spirited and inspired public action with professionalism in ministries, local councils, NGOs and UN and other international agencies.

To Sheraz and Rudi who share my life and who gently nudge me to keep a better balance among its many rhythms, I hope you will not baulk at such public acknowledgement, when I do put words to paper in my own name.

To Hawa and Ahmed who continually inspire and motivate me, your unconditional love and support made it all worthwhile.

Contents

Notes on Contributors

Buenaventura Aguilera, M.A is Strategic Advisor to the Secretary General for Finance in the Andalusian Government, Spain. His research interests include budgeting, finance and fiscal policy and gender-responsive budgeting.

Lorena Barba Albuja, M.A is Programme Specialist on Gender Responsive Budgeting for the Americas and Caribbean for UN Women. She provides technical assistance and training on gender-responsive planning and budgeting to Parliaments, Ministries of Finance, Women's Machineries, international organizations and women's organizations.

Angelika Arutyunova, M.A is Program Director for Feminist Movement Building Program at the Association for Women's Rights in Development (AWID). Prior to this, she was Manager for Resourcing Women's Rights and the Strategic Initiative 'Where is the Money for Women's Rights?'. Angelika previously worked for the Global Fund for Women as Program Director for Europe and CIS.

Nalini Burn, M.Sc is an independent researcher, who has worked for over 20 years as a hands-on practitioner of gender-responsive policy planning and budgeting in a wide number of countries. She has held academic posts at the University of Mauritius and the University of Brighton, Sussex, UK.

Raquel Coello Cremades, Ph.D is Associated Researcher of the Gender Area at the Complutense Institute for International Studies (ICEI-UCM). She works as a consultant and adviser to International Organizations, Development Agencies and Public Institutions on Gender and Economy, Fiscal Policies and Gender Responsive Budgeting.

Paula Cirujano Campano, Ph.D is Gender Budgeting Program Coordinator at IEHPA Foundation (Seville, Spain). Her research interests include feminist economics, women's political participation and women's rights mobilization.

Sarah Douglas, M.Sc is Policy Specialist to the UN Women's Peace and Security Section in New York. She specializes in gender-responsive peacebuilding, security sector reform and disarmament, demobilization and reintegration. She was a finalist in the 2004 UNDP Administrator's Innovation and Commitment award.

Diane Elson, Ph.D is Professor Emerita at the University of Essex, UK, and recipient of the 2016 Leontief Prize for Advancing the Frontiers of Economic Thought. She is also Chair of the UK Women's Budget Group. Her research interests are gender equality, economic policy and human rights.

Emily Esplen, M.A leads the work on gender equality in the OECD Development Co-operation Directorate, where she co-ordinates the DAC Network on Gender Equality (GENDERNET). Prior to this, Emily has worked at Womankind Worldwide, One World Action and the Institute of Development Studies, leading policy and research across a range of women's rights issues including financing for gender equality.

Alicia del Olmo Garrudo, M.A is the Head of the Gender Budgeting Program at IEHPA Foundation (Seville, Spain). Her research interests include feminist economics, gender institutionalization in administration and public policies and gender-responsive budgeting.

Zohra Khan, M.A is Policy Advisor to the United Nations Entity for Gender Equality and the Empowerment of Women (UN Women). She has over 15 years' experience in international and non-governmental organizations providing policy advice and technical assistance on gender-responsive planning and budgeting.

Cécile Mazzacurati, M.A heads the Secretariat (joint United Nations Population Fund/Peacebuilding Support Office) that supports the development of the Security Council–mandated progress study on youth, peace and security. Cécile has worked for over 10 years at the United Nations on youth and gender in peacebuilding and humanitarian settings.

Yamini Mishra, M.A is Regional Gender Responsive Budgeting Specialist for Asia Pacific for UN Women. She provides technical support to various stakeholders in Asia Pacific including member states, regional bodies, UN Agencies and CSOs. She sits on the Feminist Economist Committee set up by the Planning Commission of India. Before joining UN Women, Yamini was the Executive Director at the Centre for Budget and Governance Accountability (CBGA) in Delhi, India.

Patti O'Neill, M.A headed the Global Partnerships and Policies Division of the Development Co-operation Directorate of the Organization for Economic Co-operation and Development (OECD) at the time of her retirement in late 2015. She had previously worked on gender equality and women's rights with both New Zealand's aid agency and the Ministry of Women's Affairs.

Stephanie Seguino, Ph.D is Professor of Economics at the University of Vermont, USA. Her research explores the relationship between inequality, growth and development. She is former president of the International Association for Feminist Economics (IAFFE), an instructor in the African Program for Rethinking Development Economics (APORDE) and Associate Editor of *Feminist Economics* and *Journal of Human Development and Capabilities*.

Navanita Sinha, M.Phil is Programme Specialist (Governance) for the UN Women Office for India, Bhutan, Maldives and Sri Lanka. Prior to joining UN Women, Navanita worked with different civil society organizations. Her areas of interest include women's rights and public policy.

Mariama Williams, Ph.D is Senior Researcher/Programme Officer at the South Centre. Her research interests include climate change, gender and climate finance, economic development, gender and trade, international monetary and finance institutions and sovereign cross-border debt.

List of Figures

List of Tables

List of Boxes

CHAPTER 1

Introduction

Zohra Khan and Nalini Burn

This collection of essays focuses on financing for gender equality and women's rights, drawing on over a decade of scholarly analysis and practice on gender-responsive budgeting (GRB). The purpose of this collection is to position GRB as a means of realizing women's rights in the debates over framing, defining, financing, implementing and monitoring the new Sustainable Development Goals (SDGs), especially SDG 5, and the gender targets across the other SDGs. The universal character of the goals and the emphasis on addressing the systemic and structural dimensions of gender inequality represent a significant advance over the Millennium Development Goals (MDGs). The stand-alone goal to "achieve gender equality and empower all women and girls"—SDG 5—includes targets on ending violence and harmful practices against women, addressing women's unpaid care work, as well as addressing women's sexual and reproductive health and rights, amongst others. The full implementation of

Z. Khan
United Nations, New York, NY, USA

N. Burn
Wolmar, Flic en Flac, Mauritius

© The Author(s) 2017
Z. Khan, N. Burn (eds.), *Financing for Gender Equality*,
DOI 10.1057/978-1-137-46101-8_1

these goals would substantially reduce gender inequality in these areas, but that will only happen with adequate resourcing. The book therefore offers some ideas on financing for gender equality, drawing on over two decades of GRB policy and practice. It does not present GRB as a silver bullet but rather grapples with some of the tensions of this work and asks important questions about future direction.

The overall stance of the book stems from a conviction that GRB can be a strategic lever for transformative change and that fiscal policy, as well as other public policy instruments, must be harnessed to achieve this goal. It lays claim for a particular position, which is to understand gender as a relation of power, embedded in other structures and hierarchies of economic, social and political power. An important aspect of positioning GRB in the sustainable development discourse, which interlinks the economic, social and environmental dimension, is to reclaim the early understanding of GRB that the budget is as much a political as a technical process. There is the interplay between the distribution of power and the distribution of resources.[1] There are various overlays of resistances to institutional and organizational change, which will be explicitly brought out in different chapters, in particular when transformation is also about challenging the gendered structures of power.

The book charts the key GRB milestones and trajectories, the evolving concepts, methodologies and approaches and how they have been used in different country contexts. The chapters in this volume underscore the importance of a retrospective view of GRB stretching before the 2007–08 crises. The capacity for effective GRB has been undermined well before the crises by the very dynamics in which these crises are bound. However, programmatic GRB knowledge management, scholarly investigation and feminist and women's rights advocacy may not have focused their lens sufficiently to illuminate these multiple facets. For instance, the Beijing+ 20 National Reports ask about the implications of austerity measures on the 12 critical areas of action of the Platform, but not about the implications of fiscal discipline embedded in over 20 years of economic liberalization.

The book also maps GRB in relation to the trajectories of economic liberalization building on key milestones and critical events:

1995 as the year of the Beijing Platform of Action, but also the creation of the WTO;

2001 as the year of the important GRB Conference in Belgium which triggered a second wave of GRB initiatives, building on the experiences of the first wave stimulated by the Beijing Platform of Action, but also the launching of the Public Expenditure and Financial Accountability Programme (PEFA) to orient and track public financial management reform (PFM);

2008 as a watershed year for Finance for Development, and the Commission of the Status of Women (CSW) 52nd Meeting with Financing for Gender Equality as the priority theme, and the bubbling of the systemic and interlocking crises later unfolding into financial crisis.

The authors present arguments for shaping the future trajectory of GRB through deploying a rights-based approach. This involves re-envisioning macroeconomic and sectoral policies, the conduct of public policy processes, the restructuring of systems and structures steeped in patriarchy as well as the accountability and financing frameworks for realizing women's rights and achieving gender justice. The book aims to capture the state of feminist and GRB scholarship, practice and advocacy albeit not in a comprehensive systematic way, but in an illustrative, context-driven and thought-provoking way. It will give a sense of the gap between the expectations for the SDGs to meet human rights obligations, norms and standards on the one hand and, on the other hand, the available financing for development and gender equality, including resourcing women's organizations and feminist movements. It will present inspiring as well as sobering and sometimes frustrating examples and facets of GRB practices.

The book features an edited collection of 11 essays by prominent scholars, practitioners and policy experts engaged in GRB policy and programming at the global, regional, national and local levels. It will also generate insight into GRB practice as action research, as learning by doing, on knowledge gained, such as understanding where the power and influence lies, and about the formal and informal structures of power. The book therefore has three interrelated objectives:

The **first objective** is to map the conceptual, normative, political and economic pathways of GRB over the past two decades and locate it within the financing for development landscape, specifically as shaped by the trajectories of economic liberalization.

The **second objective** is to highlight the role of women's rights organizations, feminist scholars and activists, and gender equality champions in enabling, supporting as well as influencing GRB at global, national and local levels.

The **third objective** is to document how GRB has been understood and applied in different country/regional contexts and policy environments, teasing out what has been achieved and learned and how this knowledge can contribute to positioning GRB as a lever of public action and finance for realizing women's rights in the implementation of SDGs.

The country and regional chapters locate GRB experiences and trajectories within the three periods of GRB practice applying both a retrospective, reflexive lens as well as a forward-looking lens. It grapples with the key issues of unequal distribution of resources, power, and accountability at all levels.

Each chapter in this volume concludes with a reflection on emerging trends, highlighting the gaps in knowledge and experience and proposing areas for further investigation.

Note

1. Norton, Andy and Diane Elson (2002) *What's behind the budget? Politics, rights and accountability in the budget process.* Overseas Development Institute, London.

CHAPTER 2

Financing for Gender Equality: Reframing and Prioritizing Public Expenditures to Promote Gender Equality

Stephanie Seguino

Introduction

The United Nations (UN) has advocated for a holistic approach to financing for development, one that emphasizes finance for sustainable, gender-sensitive, inclusive development. There is a growing consensus that inequality is unsustainable as evidenced by the global financial crisis that began in 2008, whose cause is widely linked to the growth of inequality within and between countries since the 1970s (Stiglitz 2012). Moreover, gender equality is increasingly understood not only as an end in itself but also as a means to raise society-wide living standards.

Investment in women's economic empowerment is an important measure of governments' commitment to achieving gender equality and pro-poor policy objectives. At the Fourth World Conference on Women in 1995, governments made commitments on financing for gender equality and women's empowerment and reiterated these commitments in a number

S. Seguino (✉)
University of Vermont, Burlington, VT, USA

© The Author(s) 2017

Z. Khan, N. Burn (eds.), *Financing for Gender Equality*,
DOI 10.1057/978-1-137-46101-8_2

of subsequent UN summits and conferences. At regional and national levels, most governments have made similar or greater commitments.

And yet, it is often argued that governments simply cannot afford the expenditures needed to reduce poverty and inequality. Some political leaders have stated that gender equality is a luxury expenditure that must take a back seat while other more urgent problems are dealt with. That said, under the UN Human Rights Declaration, signatory states have an obligation to take appropriate legislative, administrative, budgetary and other measures to progressively realize economic rights, to use maximum resources to do so and to avoid retrogression. With regard to the latter, states are required to demonstrate no deliberate retrogression and must show they have considered all alternatives (Elson 2012).

Government budgets are indeed constrained by the global economic downturn, declining foreign assistance and rising needs in the face of the global food, fuel and jobs crises. Research shows, however, that well-targeted public investments that reduce inequality can be self-sustaining insofar as they raise the productive capacity of the economy and thereby stimulate growth. With growth come higher incomes, generating the tax base to fund future public investment expenditures. The astute reader will discern a key underlying tenet of this body of work: the state, far from being superfluous, has a key role to play in facilitating a development strategy that is characterized by greater equality and economic stability.

This chapter explores these issues as they regard gender equality, first considering the main macroeconomic challenges for financing for gender equality. I then identify crucial linkages between expenditures to promote gender equality and fiscal space, providing some empirical evidence on the beneficial effects of inclusive and equitable policies in a variety of developing countries. In so doing, I underscore key alternative policies and measures in relation to financing for gender equality that deserve policymakers' attention. An added benefit is that in many cases, public investment that contributes to gender equality can also reduce other forms of intergroup inequality.

Macroeconomic Constraints to Funding Gender Equality

The fiscal space to fund programmes and policies that improve human development and gender equality has come under severe strain in recent years. The global economic crisis that began in 2008 led to dramatic increases in joblessness and falling incomes and squeezed public sector budgets. The food price crisis has reduced the purchasing power of already severely constrained household budgets.

These crises have increased the degree of need, and at the same time, constrained government resources with which to address the material stress families have experienced. While some countries have been able to maintain their expenditures during the financial crisis, a number of countries have made plans to cut budgets. In a survey of 56 developing countries, Kyrili and Martin (2010) found that two-thirds were cutting budget allocations in 2010 to sectors that have significant effects on gender equality, including education, health, social protection, as well as subsidies on food, fuel and basic items.

The fiscal impact of the most recent crisis is merely an extension of over 20 years of pressure on government budgets. The macroeconomic policy framework adopted in many countries has contributed to constraints on public sector spending needed to spur equitable growth. The contours of those policies and their link to equity are discussed below.[1]

Macroeconomic Policy Constraints

International financial institutions (IFIs) have contributed to developing country budget woes with loan conditionalities that require the reduction of budget deficits through fiscal austerity. The emphasis then has been on *fiscal prudence* rather than *development goals,* negatively impacting on public sector expenditures. In Africa, for example, public expenditures fell from 9% of gross domestic product (GDP) in 1980 to 6% of GDP in 2005, rebounding somewhat by 2010, but still lower than in 1980.[2] In Mexico and Argentina, those percentages fell from roughly 12% to 2% of GDP during the same time period (Roy et al. 2009). Public spending has rebounded to some extent in Latin America, due to the commodity price boom in the 2000s (Cornia 2012), but the same cannot be said of Africa. Of particular concern in that region is the decline in public expenditures on agriculture (Fan and Rao 2003). The critical problem with the fiscal austerity approach to resolving budget imbalances is that it implies an excessive focus on the short run, and too little emphasis on longer run goals—and as such, represents a timeframe mismatch between fiduciary concerns and development.

Public sector deficits have deteriorated due to a variety of other causes. One is trade liberalization policies which contribute to a decline in tariff revenues, a major source of public sector revenue in developing countries (Khattry and Rao 2002). Tariff reductions were intended to stimulate the import of cheaper intermediate inputs, and spur exports, thereby promoting economic growth. The predicted increase in growth rates would in turn generate tax revenues to offset losses from tariff reductions. For many regions of the world, trade liberalization did not have the intended effect. The rapid growth of the global supply of inexpensive export goods was not matched by a growth in demand from rich countries. Instead, overproduction worsened joblessness in a number of developing countries while growth has stagnated and public sector budgets have been squeezed. Growth rates of GDP since 1980 have on average been lower than in the period 1960–80 for most developing regions (Seguino 2011).

Slow growth (and therefore pressure on public sector budgets) is also in part attributable to financial liberalization. Wealth holders are now free to seek the highest inflation-adjusted rate of return on their financial investments. In this global competition for finance, made more necessary than ever as foreign aid declines, developing countries are under pressure to maintain high interest rates and keep inflation rates low. Both of these effects are deflationary, contributing to higher unemployment and slower growth.

Higher interest rates, for example, make it more costly for businesses to borrow, and as a result, dampen business spending that could otherwise both raise productivity and expand output and employment. The pressure to keep inflation rates low has led to inflation targeting policies with central banks using contractionary monetary policies to slow aggregate spending. The problem with this approach is that it contributes to slow growth, reducing public revenues available for public spending which could otherwise 'crowd in' private investment and stimulate growth. And of course, it also directly slows growth through the negative effect of higher real (inflation-adjusted) interest rates on business spending and thus job creation.

A second impact of financial liberalization is that it has led to the selling off of a number of developing country banks to foreign ownership, with some disturbing effects. Stein (2010), for example, finds evidence in sub-Saharan Africa that this has resulted in poor financial development, higher costs of financial intermediation, a decline in lending to the private sector and increased capital flight as foreign banks invest more of their assets abroad. All of these contribute to slow economic and job growth.

A third problem that emerges from financial liberalization is the increased vulnerability of countries to financial crisis. A series of banking and financial crises since the onset of the most recent wave of global financial deregulation in the early 1980s has had harmful effects, especially on low-income households and women. In addition, severe economic crises reduce government coffers as incomes fall, and increase funding needs to maintain social safety nets. Most recently, for example, a number of developing countries are responding to budget imbalances that have emerged as a result of the financial crisis by austerity measures that lead to lower social spending (Ortiz et al. 2011).

IFIs have responded to the increased risk of financial crisis by requiring countries to maintain larger foreign exchange reserves in order to hedge against potential crisis from financial panics, bankruptcies and competitive devaluations. Specifically, borrowing countries are required to place a significant portion of foreign aid into foreign exchange reserve accounts or use these funds to reduce debt. Reserves held by low-income countries now amount to 8 months of imports and almost 30% of GDP (Rodrik 2006). The cost of holding such large reserves is the interest that could be earned from investing funds in higher-yielding financial assets, at an estimated loss of approximately 1% of GDP. Second, the opportunity cost of holding such reserves is the potential for public investment to 'crowd in' private investments and reduce inequality.[3] An antidote to the vulnerability resulting from financial liberalization would be capital management techniques to reduce the volatility of financial flows, a policy stance that until now has faced objections from the IMF.

Gender Equality and Public Investment

The public sector has a key role to play in creating the conditions for gender equality. Through its budget allocations, the state has the potential to redress inequalities and discrimination in the household, in asset ownership and in labour and credit markets. This can be achieved through various measures including spending on education and training that close gender gaps, investments in access to health care and expenditures that reduce women's care burden.

For example, improved water and sanitation facilities decrease illness and time spent fetching water. The latter, considered a 'female' task, is a major factor adding to women's unpaid labour burden in a number of developing countries. Transportation improvements reduce the time women spend in marketing goods, and they also improve women's ability to access medical care. Insofar as these public infrastructure investments reduce women's unpaid labour burden, they expand opportunities to perform remunerative work. A large body of evidence indicates that improvements in women's access to income result in more resources invested in children's health, education and development. This is due in part to women's greater propensity to spend their income on children than men (Folbre 2001; Xu 2007). Further, improvements in mothers' health have been found to affect children's health *in utero*, with long-term positive effects on children's cognitive skills and thus productivity (Agénor et al. 2010).

These linkages imply that physical infrastructure investments to reduce women's care burden and improve their health have long-term economic benefits in the form of a healthier, more educated and productive workforce, and can thereby stimulate economic growth. An added advantage is they contribute to greater gender equality.

Given the potential for public sector spending to close gender gaps, austerity measures of recent years are particularly worrisome. In addition to cuts in social spending, fiscal austerity measures have led to underinvestment in physical infrastructure (roads, bridges, irrigation) (Roy et al. 2009). For example, for the period 2001–08, the share of public infrastructure spending in GDP averaged 0.64% across sub-Saharan Africa (Briceño-Garmendia et al. 2008; World Bank 2012). And yet, infrastructure needs for the region for 2010–15 have been estimated to be 9–14% of GDP. South Asia faces similar gaps (Estache 2010). In Latin America, actual public infrastructure expenditures were 2% of GDP in 2005, compared to an estimated need of 3% of GDP (Griffith-Jones and Ocampo 2008).

Constraints on public sector expenditures also limit funding for agriculture (such as credit and extension services), leading to increased reliance on imported food. Pressures on public sector budgets have a particularly negative effect on women as farmers who provide the bulk of food in sub-Saharan Africa. Studies have shown, for example, that were there equitable distribution of assets to females, on-farm productivity and output would increase substantially. Evidence from Burkina Faso, Kenya and Zambia shows a 10–20% increase in output is possible with equalization of female access to agricultural inputs (Saito 1994; Udry 1996).

Women's lack of access to agricultural inputs is in part due to restrictions on women's right to own land in a number of countries (Jütting et al. 2008). As a result, women lack the collateral to access credit needed to purchase inputs. Women's share of small farmer credit in sub-Saharan Africa, for example, is estimated to be 10%, and for all agriculture, 1% (Doss 2011). Use of public sector spending to equalize access to credit and agricultural inputs could have a profound positive effect on women's well-being, on children's well-being and on overall agricultural output, but fiscal austerity (and gender-blind budgeting) has made this option more difficult to implement.

A Rethinking of Fiscal Space: The Investment Character of Expenditures Geared Towards Achieving Gender Equality

Many countries might be construed as lacking sufficient *fiscal space* to undertake public investment, even if economically desirable. The degree of space is circumscribed by limits placed on a country's debt to GDP ratio as noted above. The problem with the current approach to establishing debt ceilings is that it does not factor in the growth-expanding potential of public investments which, by their very nature, yield benefits in the longer term. This is particularly the case for public expenditures that help to promote gender equality.

The challenge is for governments to reframe their thinking on public expenditures that could contribute to greater gender equality by recognizing the investment character of such expenditures. We can disaggregate such expenditures into two categories: physical infrastructure spending (to reduce women's care burden) and social infrastructure spending, which improves the productivity of labour. Some of those benefits are more immediate, but many are evident only in the longer run and manifest as higher economy-wide productivity. Key here is to identify the link between such spending and long-run growth.

It may be more immediately clear to the reader that spending on *physical infrastructure* has a public goods quality because it produces spillover benefits to society as a whole, with the stream of returns accruing over many years. Less clearly understood is that some forms of social spending are not only for social welfare or social protection but also improve *social infrastructure*. This is because, by raising labour productivity, such expenditures raise incomes, generating tax revenues with which to pay down the debt incurred to finance the original investment. In the past, we have merely considered such spending as consumption spending, without any feedback effects on labour productivity and thus economic growth.

The timeframe for generating measurable returns to this type of spending (and thus in many cases borrowing) may be as long as five to ten years.

By that time, appropriate public investments will have begun to expand the productive base of the economy, generating (taxable) incomes with which to pay down the debt. Such investments then are both fiscally sound and sustainable. Key here is that gender-responsive investment itself *creates* fiscal space by adding to the productive base of the economy (Seguino et al. 2010).

In the case of education and employment, the growth stimulus of expenditures and policies that close gender gaps has been widely documented (Klasen and Lamanna 2009; Bandara 2012). Moreover, an expanding body of research demonstrates the linkages between physical infrastructure spending and gender equality in health, education and income (Agénor et al. 2010). For example, Seguino and Were (2014) provide empirical evidence of a positive effect of infrastructure investments on gender equality in employment rates, using a sample of 38 sub-Saharan African economies for the period 1991–2010.

Using data from Tanzanian time use surveys, Fontana and Natali (2008) are able to simulate the benefits of targeted public sector infrastructure investments that reduce time spent on unpaid care activities for gender equality. They demonstrate that the such investments, by reducing the time spent on fetching water, fuel and other unpaid household maintenance activities, reduce the care burden and as a result, raise the earnings potential of both women and men. Their results show that women benefit disproportionately from such investments. Based on their results, Fontana and Natali (2008) estimate that the time released from unpaid work would raise women's income by 17.7% relative to the economy-wide average income, and men's by 1.6% annually.

Framework for Prioritizing Expenditures to Promote Gender Equality

Financing for gender equality requires a well-targeted approach that strategically uses resources capable of leveraging change in multiple domains. In order to do this, we need to be clear about what our precise gender equality goals are. Over the last several years, a conceptual framework has emerged that identifies three domains of gender (in)equality: *capabilities, economic opportunities* (access to and control over resources) and *empowerment* (or voice in decision-making).

Indicators of *capabilities* include: education, access to health care, reproductive care and support for care work. *Economic opportunities* can be measured by wage equality, share of paid employment, access to credit and technical assistance and women's land ownership rights and access to land. *Empowerment/voice* is illustrated by women's share of political and civil government positions, and their share of professional, managerial and supervisory jobs.

For governments to effectively allocate financing to promote gender equality, it will be essential to begin by prioritizing among the many alternative potential budget allocations. How do we do that? While the priorities will depend on country-specific conditions, those goals that can leverage change in other domains should be prioritized. There is no one-size-fits-all rule on gender equality priorities. This will vary by country and context. In some cases, prioritizing the closure of employment gaps can be the key to leveraging changes in other domains. For example, underinvestment in girls' education may be linked to women's lack of viable job opportunities.

Gender-responsive budgeting (GRB) is a tool to promote gender equality by assessing the effect of government revenue and expenditure policies on both women and men (Budlender and Hewitt 2003). GRB is premised on the notion that implementation of gender equality commitments requires translation of those commitments into programmes, services and measures that should be reflected in sector and local plans and budgets. In its simplest form, GRB is an approach built around five steps (Budlender and Hewitt 2003; Sharp 2003):

1. Gender analysis of the situation of men, women, girls and boys in a particular sector;
2. Analysis of how policies address the identified gender issues;
3. Analysis of whether the assigned budget allocations are sufficient to implement gender-responsive policy;
4. Monitoring of expenditures and implementation of policies (which requires assessing whether public expenditure was spent as intended); and
5. Evaluation of outcomes (which requires assessing the impact of policy and expenditure and checking how it has contributed to the government gender equality commitments).

Each of the above steps corresponds to stages of public policy making from planning, to budgeting, implementation, monitoring and evaluation. Applying GRB entails utilizing a range of tools and methodologies at each of those stages. At the planning stage, gender analysis, audit and policy assessment are useful for identifying needs, and ensuring that gender equality priorities are integrated into national and sector development plans. At the sector planning stages, it is important to identify effective interventions and programmes that should be provided by the sector ministries, and the necessary budgets and monitoring budget performance from a gender perspective (these include budget analysis, beneficiary incidence analysis and citizen report cards).

We still have work to do in thinking through how to prioritize and sequence budgeting recommendations that contribute to greater gender equality. That said, gender budgeting processes should have a clear sense of their priorities. To give an example, for a number of sub-Saharan African countries, the major constraints on gender equality are attributable to women's unpaid care burden and lack of resources to improve their agricultural productivity. In that environment, it makes sense to prioritize several goals: public investments in electricity, clean water, rural health clinics and roads to reduce women's care burden; expansion of credit to small farmers, especially women, using government loan guarantees to overcome lack of collateral; and the implementation of quotas for women's representation in relevant bodies (such as have been adopted in Rwanda and Uganda) to help to ensure that public investment priorities reflect women's needs.

In other contexts, such as those where gender disparities in education are minimal but unemployment gaps between men and women are very large, the focus would be on employment generation in general, as well as specific policies to promote gender equality in access to paid work and in sharing the care burden.

The macroeconomic constraints to gender equality and human development that we have observed in the last two decades underscore the need to develop alternative macroeconomic policies at the country level. Ministries of finance and central banks must also develop greater capacity to effectively assess the costs of shrinking public sector spending in all areas, but particularly as regards gender. This implies that ministries of finance and central banks are some of the most important government entities to 'engender'.

In addition to gender budgeting then, financing for gender equality requires gender-equitable monetary and fiscal policies. This is a daunting task because the technical skills of policymakers and experts at this level are often not matched with a skilled gender analysis. Nevertheless, although macro-level policies that promote gender equality may not on their surface be gender-focused, they can be essential for gender equality.

To take an example, a reorientation of central bank policy from a narrow focus on keeping inflation low to one of employment generation can stimulate job opportunities. Inflation targeting has become the dominant focus of most central banks, which address inflationary pressures by raising interest rates, thus discouraging borrowing and spending. This approach attempts to solve the problem of inflation by reducing aggregate demand but at the cost of slower growth and higher unemployment. For many countries, however, the problem of inflationary pressures is related to low productivity due to widespread health problems such as HIV/AIDS, poor transportation networks and constrained food supplies.

This implies that inflation might be more efficiently addressed with public investment rather than monetary policy. Studies show that inflation rates under 20% a year are not harmful to a country's growth (Pollin and Zhu 2006). In an alternative framework that emphasizes inclusive monetary policy, the central bank would identify a 'real' target, that is, one that identifies the key social and economic problem to be addressed by policy.

As noted above, an obvious one is employment. Under this scenario, the central bank's policy goal would shift to employment targeting in place of inflation targeting. If a country has a particular problem with generating good jobs for women, or more jobs in a particular region of the country, then the real targeting approach can accommodate such needs. An example of a policy to reach employment targets would be for the central bank to identify priority sectors or groups, and provide loan guarantees to banks that extend loans in these areas. In agricultural economies where women are subsistence farmers, small-scale agriculture is an obvious choice. Priority might also be given to small- and medium-sized firms.

To take a second example, capital controls, widely agreed to be a solution to excessive exchange rate and economic volatility, is a gender issue, not just a macroeconomic or balance of payments issue. Capital account liberalization is costly, not only because of the potential for economic crisis but also because countries are required to hold foreign exchange reserves to protect against volatility. Capital controls would permit countries to reduce the size of their foreign reserves, thus freeing up revenue for public expenditures. Investing those additional resources, even if just 1% of GDP, on expenditures that promote gender equality could induce further economic growth. And the resulting reduced economic volatility would decrease the drain on public coffers for social safety net expenditures.

To summarize, to be successful, financing for gender equality must move into the domain of macroeconomic policy formulation. The technical skills required for this are not insignificant. That said, a fundamentally important step is to address the macro-level constraints and analyse the downside gender costs of public sector contraction as well as various policies that deregulate capital flows and trade.

Examples of Gender-Equitable Policies and Public Expenditures

These observations suggest some changes in the way we think about the goals of financing for gender equality. The work carried out by gender equality advocates the past five years has demonstrated that despite national commitments and policy guidelines from donors and national partners, gender equality as a development priority is often absent from development and aid management processes and instruments.[4] Gender equality goals are absent from direct budget support coordination groups, system-wide action plan (SWAP) technical teams, country strategy papers and performance monitoring indicators. Further, spaces for shaping strategic policies are not adequately inclusive of GE issues or gender equality advocates.

There is ample evidence of how integrating a gender perspective contributes to the achievement of aspired development results. The opportunity cost of the lack of attention to gender inequalities and women's empowerment has also been demonstrated in numerous studies. Donor and partner countries should ensure that development approaches that are inclusive of women's priorities are rights based and address the root causes of gender inequality and discrimination. Effective and inclusive development approaches should aim at integrating a gender perspective in mainstream policies and processes and put an end to the marginalization of women and girls in development processes. Applying this approach requires opening spaces for gender advocates and experts to engage in policy dialogue that shapes the systems and instruments, and defines priorities for action, budget allocations and accountability measures.

More generally, the financing for gender equality agenda should include efforts to analyse the relationships between macroeconomic policies and human development (of which gender equality is a component). Several examples of macro-level policies that support greater gender equality are explored below.

Social Spending in Latin America

Coincident with the ascendance of left-of-centre and social democratic governments in Latin America in recent years, countries have raised minimum wages, increased public investment and expanded social protection programmes. These have contributed to a marked decrease in class inequality in the region, measured as decreases in the Gini coefficient (Birdsall et al. 2011; Cornia 2012). These policies have also increased female and male employment rates, and because the effect on women is larger, they have narrowed gender employment gaps (Braunstein and Seguino 2012). This is significant since the most acute areas of gender inequality in Latin America are employment, wages, occupational segregation and incomes.[5]

Examples of social protection programmes adopted at either the national or provincial level include a primary care programme in Brazil and conditional cash transfer (CCT) programmes such as *Bolsa Familia* in Brazil and *Oportunidades* in Mexico. Each of these programmes aims to improve human development by focusing on education, nutrition and health of poor families, particularly children and their mothers. As such, they should be categorized as social infrastructure spending. With regard to CCTs, funds are transferred to mothers, conditional on mothers ensuring children meet the goals of the programme with regard to health check-ups and school attendance, as well as mothers' attendance at workshops.

Molyneux (2007: 2) claims, 'The recently developed antipoverty programmes (in Latin America) are … still premised on a gendered construction of social need and, indeed, have the effect of retraditionalizing gendered roles and responsibilities'. Indeed, one potential outcome of CCTs is that women would withdraw or reduce time spent in paid labour in order to carry out their obligations under the rules of CCTs. Though they do not have specific data on CCTs, Braunstein and Seguino (2012) find that as social spending in Latin America has risen, women's relative employment rates have also increased. It would appear then that programmes such as CCTs are beneficial not only for children but also because they improve women's access to jobs.[6]

Gender Budgeting Innovations in Ecuador, Nepal and Cambodia to Promote Gender Equality

The identification and implementation of gender-equalizing and growth-stimulating public investment require institutions that are up to the job and have the mandate to pursue such goals. Ecuador, Nepal and Cambodia have made strides in effecting institutional change to this end.

In the case of Ecuador, GRB has been adopted via collaboration between the country's national women's machinery and the Ministry of Finance. A major focus of this effort has been capacity building so that government personnel can view budgets through a gendered lens. As of 2011, the government has mandated that the national budget include a report detailing spending to address equity gaps. To support this effort, a new tool, the Classifier K, was developed that permits the Ministry of Finance to identify spending towards gender equality.[7] Though developed earlier, this tool is an example of a response to the post-Busan monitoring framework that includes a commitment for governments to develop indicators to track and make public allocations for gender equality and women's empowerment. Such gender indicators can help to focus governments' efforts to establish and implement systems that effectively track and make public allocations for gender equality to inform policy decisions and investments.

The Classifier K is applied to capital and current allocations and expenditures that fund activities implementing gender-related policies and laws, including those focused on women's social, economic and political rights, violence, access to justice, and sexual and reproductive health. The data generated through this system facilitates analyses of government spending towards gender equality, and allows for comparison in trends across fiscal years. This data also facilitates the distinction between budget allocations and spending.

The data generated from this has revealed that financing for gender equality in sectors beyond sexual and reproductive health is very weak. As an example, the Ministry of Agriculture, Livestock, Aquaculture and Fishing allocated only 2.54% of its 2011 budget to expenditures for achieving gender equality (Almeida 2012). The ability to make visible the gendered nature of expenditures is itself major progress, and generates the evidence on which to base public debates over allocation decisions.

In Nepal, the Ministry of Finance has formally introduced a system for sectoral ministries to categorize their programme budgets based on the extent to which they support gender equality. Allocations are evaluated by the benefit incidence of public expenditures, the extent of support to women's employment and income generation and the impact on women's time use. From this analysis, allocations are categorized into three groups: (a) directly responsive to gender equality (more than 50% of the allocation directly benefits women), (b) indirectly responsive (20–50% of the allocation directly benefits women), or (c) neutral (less than 20% of the allocation benefits women). Additionally, the Ministry of Finance requires all programmes or projects with a budget exceeding 50 million Nepali Rupees to have a gender audit report attached. In 2009/2010, approximately 17.3% of the national budget was identified as allocation for programmes directly benefiting women, and 36.4% of the total budget indirectly benefiting women (Baskota 2010).

Cambodia has also made institutional reforms to ensure that gender concerns are a priority in the early stages of planning and budgeting. This is facilitated by Gender Mainstreaming Action Groups (GMAGs) that are active in 26 sectoral ministries. Of critical importance, the Ministry of Finance and Economy was among the first ministries to establish a GMAG. Cambodia has recorded significant progress in women's health, in closing educational gaps and in women's political representation. The government is now aiming to improve women's share of formal sector employment, where their proportion is currently only 30% in contrast to their 82% share of informal sector employment (Ing 2012).

Increasing Financing for Women's Priorities at the Local Level

UN Women and UNCDF established the Gender Equitable Local Development (GELD) programme in 2009 to support local governments in five African countries (Mozambique, Rwanda, Senegal, Sierra Leone and Tanzania) to improve women's access to resources and services. Under the GELD programme, Local development funds (LDFs), administered by local councils, provide funding for initiatives responding to priorities identified by women in those communities.

For instance, in Tanzania, the LDF is improving access to clean water by reducing the distance to water supply sources. An electricity project is being implemented in Muembe district in Mozambique that will use solar energy to provide lighting to the central area of the district. Women from Muembe district will implement the project and receive training in automotive electricity and mechanics. In Gicumbi district in Rwanda, the LDF is supporting the construction of a health centre that will improve women's and girls' access to health and reproductive services, including ante-natal care, vaccination and voluntary counselling and HIV/AIDS testing. The LDF in Kenema district in Sierra Leone is providing funding for the construction of an early childhood and adult learning centre. The centre will give priority to single parents or young parents who would like to continue their education and low-income families who cannot afford to send their children to private pre-schools (UN Women 2011).

Employer of Last Resort Programme in India

In 2005, the Indian government passed a rural job guarantee programme, now renamed the National Rural Employment Guarantee Act (NREGA). This act establishes a legal job guarantee for 100 days of employment every year to adult members of any rural household willing to do public work (mainly unskilled) at the statutory minimum wage. The overall effect is to improve the incomes of rural people by providing primarily semi- or unskilled work opportunities, whether or not workers are below the poverty line. This programme differs from the *Plan Jefes* job guarantee programme in Argentina, where only one member of a household was eligible for this work, thus creating gender competition for slots. In India, women's participation rate in the programme is double their participation rate in the casual labour market, and in 2009–10 women comprised about 48 % of those employed by this job guarantee scheme (Dutta et al. 2012).

Conclusion

Expenditures that contribute to gender equality can 'crowd in' private investment, stimulate growth and generate a stream of revenues in the future to pay down the costs of the initial investment. This approach helps us to avoid the erroneous argument that governments lack fiscal space to fund physical and social infrastructure investments that promote gender equality.

More work is needed to create a robust gender analytical framework for policymakers as well as empirical research that would allow us to quantify the impacts of public sector spending to promote gender equality. In particular, countries will benefit by investing more resources into identifying the investment character of gender expenditures and measuring their contribution to productivity growth. This provides the data for a cost-benefit analysis on which to base public expenditure/investment decisions.

These observations suggest some changes in the way we think about the goals of financing for gender equality. Specifically, it is recommended that countries develop country-specific priorities on gender equality or match their existing policies and plans to achieve gender equality with adequate budget allocations. Secondly, countries should develop policy priorities that address macroeconomic constraints—slow growth, unemployment, macroeconomic and exchange rate volatility and link macroeconomic policies to gender equality goals. This two-pronged approach can create the framework for financing for gender equality that is sustainable.

Notes

1. For a comprehensive discussion of the gendered employment effects of neoliberal macroeconomic policies, see Braunstein (2012).
2. Author's calculations, using *African Development Indicators*, online (accessed October 15, 2012).
3. Public expenditures that 'crowd in' private investment do so by reducing the costs of business production (through, for example, better roads, communications and education) and thus stimulate private investment.
4. For example, see Gender Responsive Budgeting and Aid Effectiveness Knowledge Briefs, 2010, UNIFEM (now UN Women). http://www.gender-budgets.org/index.php?option=com_joomdoc&task=cat_view&gid=277&Itemid=189
5. In contrast, gender disparities in education are minimal, and indeed, in a number of countries, women's educational attainment exceeds men's on average (Ñopo 2012).
6. This may be because CCT funds helped women improve their health status, and covered the costs of child care so that they could then take a paid job.
7. The origins of the Classifier K date to 2007 in response to efforts by the National Women's Machinery (CONAMU) to promote strengthening of systems for gender-responsive planning and budgeting.

References

Agénor, P.-R., O. Canuto, and L. P. da Silva. (2010). "On Gender and Growth: The Role of Intergenerational Health Externalities and Women's Occupational Constraints." World Bank Policy Research Working Paper No. 5492.

Almeida, M. (2012). *Ecuador's gender-sensitive budget tracking methodology*. Presentation at UN Commission on the Status of Women panel "National experiences in implementing the agreed conclusions on financing for gender equality and the empowerment of women", New York, NY.

Bandara, A. (2012). *Economic cost of gender gaps in effective labor: Africa's missing growth reserve*. New York/Dar-es-Salaam: Mimeo/UNDP Tanzania.

Baskota, K. H. (2010). Gender responsive budget: The Nepalese Experience. (English translation of article in *Kathmandu Post*). *UN Women*. http://www.gender-budgets.org/index.php?option=com_content&view=article&id=719&catid=51&Itemid=215.

Birdsall, N., Lustig, N., & McLeod, D. (2011). *Declining inequality in Latin America: Some economics, some politics,* Working paper 251, Washington, DC: Center for Global Development.

Braunstein, E. (2012). *Neoliberal development macroeconomics. A consideration of its gendered employment effects,* UNRISD Gender and Development Programme paper No. 14.

Braunstein, E., & Seguino, S. (2012). *The impact of economic policy and structural change on gender inequality in economic opportunity in Latin America, 1990–2010,* MPRA working paper 43261. http://mpra.ub.uni-muenchen.de/43261/

Briceño-Garmendia, C., Smits, K., & Foster, V. (2008). *Financing public infrastructure in sub-Saharan Africa: Patterns and emerging issues.* AICD, Background Paper 15 (Phase I).

Budlender, D., & Hewitt, G. (2003). *Engendering budgets: A practitioners' guide to understanding and implementing gender-responsive budgets.* London: Commonwealth Secretariat.

Cornia, G. A. (2012). *Inequality trends and their determinants. Latin America over 1990*–2010, UNU-WIDER working paper No. 2012/09.

Doss, C. 2011. "The Role of Women in Agriculture." Agricultural Development Economics Division. Food and Agriculture Organization, ESA Working Paper No. 11–02.

Dutta, P., Murgai, R., Ravallion, M., & van de Walle, D. (2012). *Does India's employment guarantee scheme guarantee employment?* World Bank Policy Research Working Paper 6003.

Elson, D. (2012). *Human rights and budget decisions.* Presentation at the UN women high level conference on gender responsive budgeting, Marrakech.

Estache, A. (2010). *Infrastructure policy for shared growth post-2008: More and better, or simply more complex?,* ECARES working paper 2010-032.

Fan, S., & Rao, N. (2003). *Public spending in developing countries: Trends, determination, and impact,* EPTD discussion paper No. 99. IFPRI.

Folbre, N. 2001. *The Invisible Heart: Economics and Family Values.* New York: The New Press.

Fontana, M., & Natali, L. (2008). *Gendered patterns of time use in Tanzania: Public investment in infrastructure can help.* Paper prepared for the IFPRI Project on *Evaluating the Long-Term Impact of Gender-focused Policy Interventions.*

Griffith-Jones, S., & Ocampo, J. A. (2008). *Sovereign wealth funds: A developing country perspective.* Paper presented at Sovereign Wealth Funds workshop, London.

Ing, K. P. (2012). *Financing the implementation of national priorities for the empowerment of women*. Presentation at UN Commission on the Status of Women panel "National experiences in implementing the agreed conclusions on financing for gender equality and the empowerment of women".

Jütting, J., Dayton-Johnson, J., Dreschler, D., & Morrisson, C. (2008). Measuring gender inequality. *Journal of Human Development, 9*(1), 65–86.

Khattry, B., & Rao, M. (2002). Fiscal faux pas?: An analysis of the revenue implications of trade liberalization. *World Development, 30*(8), 1431–1444.

Klasen, S., & Lamanna, F. (2009). The impact of gender inequality in education and employment on economic growth: New evidence for a panel of countries. *Feminist Economics, 15*(3), 91–132.

Kyrili, K., & Martin, M. (2010). *The impact of the global economic crisis on the budgets of low-income countries*. Oxford: Oxfam International.

Molyneux, M. (2007). *Change and continuity in social protection in Latin America. Mothers at the Service of the State?* Gender and Development Programme paper No 1. Geneva: UNRISD.

Ñopo, E. (2012). *New century, old disparities: Gender and ethnic earnings gaps in Latin America and the Caribbean*. Washington, DC: Inter-American Development Bank.

Ortiz, I., Chai, J., & Cummins, M. (2011). *Identifying fiscal space: Options for social and economic development for children and poor households in 182 countries*. UNICEF Social and Economic Policy working paper.

Pollin, R., & Zhu, A. (2006). Inflation and economic growth: A cross-country non-linear analysis. *Journal of Post Keynesian Economics, 4*, 593–614.

Rodrik, D. (2006). *The social cost of foreign exchange reserves*, National Bureau of Economic Research working paper 11952.

Roy, R., A. Heuty, and E. Letouzé. 2009. "Fiscal Space for Public Investment: Towards a Human Development Approach." In R. Roy and A. Heuty (eds), *Fiscal Space: Policy Options for Financing Human Development*. London: Earthscan Publications, pp. 67–92.

Saito, K. (1994). *Raising the productivity of women farmers in sub-Saharan Africa*, Discussion paper No. 230. Washington, DC: World Bank.

Seguino, S. (2011). 'Rebooting' is not an option: Toward equitable social and economic development. In D. Jain & D. Elson (Eds.), *From crisis to equality: Harvesting feminist knowledge for public policy*. Thousand Oaks: IDRC/Sage Publishers.

Seguino, S., & Were, M. (2014). Gender, development, and growth in sub-Saharan Africa. *Journal of African Economies, 23*(supplement 1), i18–i61.

Seguino, S., Berik, G., & Rodgers, Y. (2010). *An investment that pays off: Promoting gender equality as a means to finance development*. Friedrich-Ebert-Stiftung occasional paper.

Sharp, R. (2003). *Budgeting for equity: Gender budget initiatives within a framework of performance oriented budgeting*. UNIFEM (UN Women).

Singh, A. (2003). Capital account liberalisation, free long-term capital flows, financial crises and economic development. *Eastern Economic Journal, 29*(2), 191–216.

Stein, H. (2010). Financial liberalisation, institutional transformation and credit allocation in developing countries: The World Bank and the internationalisation of banking. *Cambridge Journal of Economics, 3*, 257–273.

Stiglitz, J. (2012). Macroeconomic fluctuations, inequality, and human development. *Journal of Human Development and Capabilities, 13*(1), 32–58.

Udry, C. (1996). Gender, agricultural production, and theory of the household. *Journal of Political Economy, 104*(5), 1010–1046.

UN Women. (2011). *GELD program profile.* http://www.uncdf.org/en/gender-equitable-local-dev

World Bank. (2012). *Africa Infrastructure Country Diagnostic (AICD).* Online database. Accessed 8 Dec 2012.

CHAPTER 3

Financing for Gender Equality: How to Budget in Compliance with Human Rights Standards

Diane Elson

Introduction

The ultimate objective of financing for gender equality is to promote the realization of women's rights, as set out in the Universal Declaration of Human Rights and subsequent human rights treaties, such as the International Covenant on Economic, Social and Cultural Rights (ICESCR) and the Convention on the Elimination of All Discrimination Against Women (CEDAW). The latter prohibits discrimination against women in all its forms and obligates States to condemn such discrimination and take steps 'by all appropriate means and without delay' to pursue a policy of eliminating such discrimination (Article 2), including adopting appropriate legislative and other measures. It is clear that CEDAW does not only mean the absence of a discriminatory legal framework, but also means that policies must not be discriminatory in effect. CEDAW is part of a comprehensive framework of human rights treatise that together set out the substantive content of the human rights of all, and the obligations

D. Elson (✉)
Emeritus Professor, University of Essex, Colchester, UK

© The Author(s) 2017

Z. Khan, N. Burn (eds.), *Financing for Gender Equality*,
DOI 10.1057/978-1-137-46101-8_3

of governments to realize them. All human rights require governments to allocate resources towards their realization. More detailed guidance on financing realization of rights is provided in some of these treaties, such as ICESCR.[1]

This chapter discusses the obligations of governments to finance the realization of women's rights and the guidance this provides for gender-responsive budgeting, with particular reference to CEDAW and ICESCR. It considers not only the distribution of public expenditure between women and men, girls and boys, but also the adequacy of expenditure allocations in relation to what is required for realization of rights. It further considers human rights obligations for the mobilization of finance and for managing government budgets so as to avoid deterioration in the enjoyment of rights, even in the context of economic crises. Finally, it discusses the opportunities that the human rights system provides for pressing governments to meet their obligations to finance the realization of women's rights.

What Do Human Rights Treaties and Treaty-Bodies Say About Government Budgets?

The text of CEDAW makes no specific reference to the financial resources required for its implementation, but it does impose the general obligation on States parties to take 'all appropriate measures' to eliminate discrimination against women. Moreover, the CEDAW Committee[2] has indicated that States do have obligations to use budgetary measures to fulfil women's rights. For example, the Committee has explained that the duty to fulfil Article 12 of the Convention (relating to women and health) involves an obligation on States parties to take, inter alia, budgetary measures to the maximum of available resources to ensure that women realise their right to equality in health care (General Recommendation 24, para. 17).[3]

The text of ICESCR has specific reference to resource allocation in Article 2.1:

> Each State Party to the present Covenant undertakes to take steps, individually and through international assistance and co-operation, especially economic and technical, to the maximum of its available resources, with a view to achieving progressively the full realization of the rights recognized in the present Covenant by all appropriate means, including particularly the adoption of legislative measures.

The reference to 'progressive realization' recognizes that that the resources at the disposition of a government are not unlimited, and that fulfilling economic and social rights will take time. Thus, it is not true that a human rights perspective ignores resource constraints. At the same time, it requires continued progress towards the realization of rights: Resource constraints are not an excuse for doing nothing, as had been made clear by the Committee on Economic, Social and Cultural Rights (CESCR).[4] Moreover, CESCR has clarified that realization of equality in enjoyment of rights is an immediate obligation.[5] This means that women's equality must always be a priority in the progressive realisation of economic, social and cultural rights and that any steps that a State takes to progressively realise such rights must be non-discriminatory in both policy and effect.

Moreover, States that are parties to the ICESCR are also under a 'minimum core' obligation to ensure the satisfaction of, at the very least, 'minimum essential levels of each of the rights' in the ICESCR. This means that a State party in which any 'significant number' of persons is 'deprived of essential foodstuffs, of essential primary health care etc is prima facie failing to meet obligations' under the Covenant.[6] CESCR has begun to identify the content of the minimum core obligations with respect to the rights to food, education, health and water.[7]

There is a strong presumption that retrogressive measures on the part of a State are not permitted. An example of a potentially retrogressive measure would be cuts to expenditures on public services that are critical for realization of economic and social rights. If such retrogressive measures are deliberate, then the State has to show that they have been introduced after consideration of all alternatives and are fully justifiable by reference to totality of rights provided for in the Covenant and in context of the full use of the maximum of available resources.[8] For example, cutting government spending on health and education, while not cutting expenditure on arms, will likely violate the principle of non-retrogression. An important way to avoid retrogression is to ensure that the government makes every effort to mobilize resources for the realization of human rights.

Both CEDAW and ICESCR have important implications for participation and accountability with respect to resource allocation. CEDAW requires that women be able to participate on equal terms with men in decision-making about the budget. Article 7(a) calls for women to participate equally in the formulation of government policy and its implementation and to hold public office and perform all public functions; and Article 7(b) calls for women to participate in non-governmental organisations and associations which address the state's public and political life (e.g. as members of budget watchdog groups).[9] CESCR has indicated that the right of individuals to participate must be an 'integral component' of any policy or practice that seeks to meet the State obligation to ensure the equal right of men and women to the enjoyment of all human rights.[10] It has also emphasized that:

> rights and obligation demand accountability ....whatever the mechanisms of accountability, they must be accessible, transparent and effective.' (United Nations, Committee on Economic, Social and Cultural Rights, 2001, para. 14. UN Doc. E/C.12.2001/10)

In addition to obligations to their own citizens and to all the people living in their country, states also have extra-territorial obligations not to harm the human rights of people in other countries, and to assist the governments of other countries in fulfilling their human rights obligations, as is made clear in the United Nations (UN) Charter Articles 55 and 56.

Obligations with respect to international development cooperation between governments are explicitly referred to in Article 2 ICESCR, and are underlined in specific provisions in Article 11 (right to an adequate standard of living). Articles 22 and 23 specifically refer to the need for international measures. In 1990, CESCR General Comment 3 explicitly stated that 'international co-operation for development ... is an obligation of all States'.

States enjoy a margin of discretion in selecting the means to carry out their human rights obligations, but in discharging their obligations, states must pay regard to the following key principles : the immediate obligation for non-discrimination and promotion of substantive equality; the immediate obligation for the satisfaction of minimum essential levels of economic and social rights; the requirement for progressive realization; the avoidance of retrogression; the use of maximum available resources; the requirement for participation, transparency and accountability; and compliance with their extra-territorial obligations. These principles can be applied to the analysis of financing for gender equality to ascertain whether governments are fully meeting their obligations towards women's rights, and can be used as principles to guide gender-responsive budgeting.

Maximum Available Resources and Government Budgets

It is particularly important to clarify further the obligation to use maximum available resources, as this encompasses all dimensions of the budget. CESCR made a statement in 2007 entitled 'An Evaluation of the Obligation to Take Steps To the "Maximum of Available Resources" Under an Optional Protocol to the Covenant', reemphasising this obligation and stating that it refers 'both the resources existing within a state as well as those available from the international community through international cooperation and assistance' (E/C.12/2007/1).

Governments clearly have an obligation to ensure that they spend these resources in ways that are compliant with human rights norms. In addition, several UN Special Rapporteurs have also referred to obligations with respect to taxation. For instance, the former Special Rapporteur on the Realization of Economic, Social and Cultural Rights Danilo Türk noted that:

> Progressive (as opposed to regressive) measures of taxation can, if supported by adequate administrative machinery and enforcement mechanisms, lead to gentle and gradual forms of income redistribution within States without threatening economic stability or patterns of growth, thereby creating conditions that enable a larger proportion of society to enjoy economic, social and cultural rights. (Türk 1992)

Olivier de Schutter, the former Special Rapporteur on the Right to Food, in his 2009 report on Brazil, drew attention to the role of taxes in fulfilling the obligation to use the maximum available resources:

> The tax structure in Brazil remains highly regressive. Tax rates are high for goods and services and low for income and property, bringing about very inequitable outcomes. [...] while the social programmes developed under the "Zero Hunger" strategy are impressive in scope, they are essentially funded by the very persons whom they seek to benefit, as the regressive system of taxation seriously limits the redistributive aspect of the programmes. Only by introducing a tax reform that would reverse the current situation could Brazil claim to be seeking to realize the right to adequate food by taking steps to the maximum of its available resources. (De Schutter 2009: para 36)

Thus, the human rights system has recognized the importance of sources of finance, such as taxation and official development assistance, to the use of maximum available resources.

Building on this, human rights oriented economists have suggested that it is also necessary to take into account government borrowing, and monetary policy and financial regulation (which can constrict or expand the available resources, as explained further below) (Balakrishnan et al. 2011; Elson et al. 2013). This can be summarized as the five point MAR STAR: the extent to which a government is making use of maximum available resources for the progressive realization of economic and social rights depends on how it spends money, how it raises revenue, the development assistance it receives, the extent to which it borrows and how it invests the loans, and the type of monetary policy and financial regulation it operates (Balakrishnan et al. 2011; Elson et al. 2013). Each of these dimensions is discussed below, drawing out the implications for financing for gender equality and gender-responsive budgeting to realise women's rights.

Human Rights Principles and Public Expenditure

There have been quite a lot of studies of public expenditure from a human rights perspective (see for instance, Elson 2006; Balakrishnan and Elson 2011; Harvey et al. 2013). Here, we focus on some key issues in relation to the allocation of public expenditure so as to achieve substantive equality for women.

Many exercises in gender-responsive budgeting have emphasized increasing allocations for programmes specifically targeted to women (such as training or credit specifically for women). Such programmes do not violate the principle of non-discrimination, even if they exclude men, provided that the programmes are 'temporary special measures' aimed at overcoming past discrimination and achieving substantive equality. CEDAW specifically allows such measures—Article 4.1. However, allocations for such programmes are only ever a very small proportion of total government expenditure, so it is important to examine the rest of government expenditure to see whether it is contributing sufficiently to the achievement of substantive equality for women.

One way to do this (though by no means the only way) is to examine the distribution of benefits of the expenditure between women and men (or girls and boys) in relation to particular rights. Often it is hard to quantify the benefits directly, and the distribution of expenditure is taken as a proxy (see, e.g., Demery 2002; Glick et al. 2004; Sabir 2002). For example, a study of the distribution of educational expenditure in Timor Leste in 2007 found that the share of boys was higher than of girls (Austen et al. 2013). The disparity was particularly pronounced in the case of rural girls at secondary education level: the share of rural girls was 12 per cent, of rural boys, 16.7 per cent, of urban girls 35.3 per cent and of urban boys, 36.0 per cent. This reflects disparities in enrolment in school, not deliberate discrimination against girls. The schools are open to both boys and girls. The inequality in the distribution of expenditure is because families are not sending girls to school at the same rate as boys. Nevertheless, it indicates that the government is not fully meeting its obligation with respect to equality in the right to education. Article 10 of CEDAW requires that 'States Parties shall take all appropriate measures to eliminate discrimination against women in order to ensure them equal rights with men in the field of education'; and in subsection 10(a) requires states to ensure: 'the same conditions for career and vocational guidance, for access to studies and for the achievement of diplomas in educational establishments of all categories in rural as well as in urban areas'. The state has a responsibility here because there are measures it is required to take under CEDAW to persuade and enable families to send girls to school at the same rate as boys. Such measures include those provided for in Article 10 of CEDAW and temporary special measures that can be adopted under Article 4(1) to accelerate the achievement of substantive equality. These measures can include: providing scholarships for girls, providing separate school toilet facilities for girls and boys and providing more women teachers. This could be funded by redistributing existing education funding, redistributing to the education sector from other sectors, raising more revenue (for instance from the recently discovered fossil fuel resources) and allocating it to the implement the measures.

As well as the immediate obligation to ensure non-discrimination and gender equality, there is also the immediate obligation for the satisfaction of minimum essential levels of economic and social rights. One such right is the right to water, which had been identified by CESCR as a right implied by ICESCR.[11] States formally recognized as the human right to water during the 64th session of the UN General Assembly in a resolution adopted in July 2010. The resolution recognized 'the right to safe and clean drinking water and sanitation as a human right that is essential for the full enjoyment of life and all human rights' and called 'upon States and international organizations to provide financial resources, capacity-building and technology transfer, through international assistance and cooperation, in particular to developing countries, in order to scale up efforts to provide safe, clean, accessible and affordable drinking water and sanitation for all'. (A/64/64/292). The Human Rights Council reaffirmed this decision with a resolution adopted by consensus on 30 September 2010.

However, many poor rural households in developing countries still lack access to clean piped water, and the women and girls in these households have to spend a lot of time collecting and purifying water for domestic use (Fontana and Elson 2014). Moreover, a disproportionate level of funding is still directed to extending services in urban areas, and many countries have not mobilized the funding required to meet the Millennium Development Goal for safe drinking water and basic sanitation (halve by 2015 the proportion of the population without sustainable access to these facilities). Total international aid commitment to water and sanitation is only around 5 per cent of all reported international aid (Fontana and Elson 2014).

A further issue is *affordable* access to clean water, identified as critical by UN Special Rapporteur on the human right to safe drinking water and sanitation (de Albuquerque 2012). Connection charges are often a significant barrier for those living in poverty. Recent research suggests that the average connection cost paid by each household to utilities was USD 186 in Africa and USD 169 in Asia, equivalent to an entire year's income of a poor household (Franceys 2005). The Special Rapporteur notes that governments can apply subsidies or rebates to assist low-income populations who cannot afford to pay the full price for water services. One possibility is to make the subsidy universally available, as in South Africa, where the government makes a fixed basic amount of water available to all households regardless of status, while those who use more pay a rising tariff. An alternative approach is to target benefits at particular individuals or groups, and apply conditions that need to be met to receive this benefit, whether based on income such as in Chile, or location such as in Colombia.

The evidence suggests that the expenditure being committed to provide clean water is too small and too badly distributed in many countries for the government to fulfil its human rights obligation to ensure all women enjoy a basic level of access to clean water. This could be remedied by a combination of measures, such as redistributing existing water expenditure to low-income rural areas; redistributing expenditure from other uses that are less important for achieving essential levels of economic and social rights; mobilizing more tax revenue in equitable ways and allocating this to investment in water; donors proving more aid for water and borrowing to invest in clean water (which has multiple pay-off in terms of improvements in health, better schooling outcomes for girls and more time for women to engage in income earning activities (Fontana and Elson 2014).

Financial crisis has often been followed by cuts to types of public expenditure that are important for realization of women's rights (Elson 2013). This runs the risk of being retrogressive. In May 2012, this was drawn to the attention of States Parties to the ICESCR in a letter from the Chair of CESCR, which says that any proposed policies to adjust the implementation of Covenant rights, in context of financial and economic crisis, must meet the following requirements:

> First, the policy is a temporary measure covering the period of crisis only; second the policy is necessary and proportionate, in the sense that the adoption of any other policy, or failure to act, would be more detrimental to economic, social and cultural rights; third, the policy is not discriminatory and comprises all possible measures, including tax measures, to support social transfers to mitigate inequalities that can grow in times of crisis and to ensure that the rights of disadvantaged and marginalised individuals and groups are not disproportionately affected; fourth, the policy identifies the minimum core content of rights, or a social protection floor, as developed by the International Labour Organisation, and ensures the protection of this core content at all times.[12]

There is certainly cause for concern that the deep cuts to expenditure on social security (benefits and public services adopted in the UK since 2010) are retrogressive with respect to women's rights (Elson 2012). The measures are not temporary, and they reduce the incomes and access to public services of households comprising single women more than of household comprising single men and couples (Pearson and Elson 2015). Social transfers to poor women have been particularly subject to cuts, as have services for migrant women and for Black, Asian and Ethnic Minority[13] women (Lonergan 2015; Sandhu and Stephenson 2015). The government that introduced these cuts argued that they were essential in order to reduce the budget deficit and government borrowing, but it made little use of tax increases to reduce the deficit via an increase in government revenue. In the UK, fiscal consolidation since 2010 has comprised 82 per cent expenditure cuts and 18 per cent tax revenue increases (Institute for Fiscal Studies 2015: 10). Moreover, the main tax measure was an increase in Value Added Tax (VAT), which takes away more, in proportion to their income, from low-income than from high-income people. In add, the attempts to reduce the budget deficit and government borrowing stifled the recovery of the economy from the impact of the 2008 financial crisis that was underway in early 2010; output fell and unemployment rose. It is estimated that resources worth around 5 per cent of GDP will have been lost for ever by delaying the recovery, equivalent to about £100 billion, or £1500 for each adult and child in the UK (Wren-Lewis 2015).

Human Rights Principles and Taxation

States are unable to fulfil their human rights obligations without raising revenue from taxation.[14] They must raise sufficient revenue to fulfil these obligations, and they must design and implement taxes in compliance with human rights principles; in particular, the tax regime should comply with the principle of non-discrimination and equality.

The average tax to GDP ratio in OECD countries rose from 30.1 per cent in 1970 to 35.5 per cent in 2000. In developing countries, the average tax ratio did not change very much, rising from 16.2 per cent in the 1970s to 17.0 per cent in 2000 (Bird 2010). It is easier to mobilize tax revenue in high-income countries, where the informal economy is a much smaller share than in low-income countries, but it is possible to improve tax effort in all countries. Tax effort can be measured by comparing actual tax revenue to potential tax revenues, which can be measured as the total value of tax revenue which would be raised under the prevailing tax code if 100 per cent of taxes were actually collected. Tax effort has been increasing in some low-income countries. For example, in a number of sub-Saharan African countries, the amount of revenue collected has been enhanced through institutional reforms in the way that taxes are administered and collected, independent of changes in tax policy (OECD and ADB 2010).

However, the efforts of many governments to raise more revenue are frustrated by tax avoidance and evasion. The existence of tax havens, with very low taxes, facilitates tax avoidance and evasion. Multinational corporations take measures to show their profits as accruing in tax havens to avoid paying taxes. One way of doing this is through mispricing goods and services that are transferred between different branches of the same company operating in different countries. By setting up a branch in a tax haven and then manipulating the price of imports purchased from and exports shipped to other divisions and affiliates of the same company operating in different countries, corporations can show their profits as accruing to the branch in a tax haven rather than in a country with higher taxes. Estimates of the annual tax revenue lost to developing countries due to trade mispricing amount to USD 98 to 106 billion (Hollingshead 2010). This compares to total overseas development assistance (ODA) in 2009 from the countries in the OECD's Development Assistance Committee of USD 83.5 billion.[15] Tax havens are created by the tax laws of some governments, which thereby make it more difficult for other governments to mobilize tax revenue (and could be seen as an infringement of extra-territorial obligations). Cooperation among states is vital to reduce the scope for cross-border tax avoidance strategies.

The structure of tax revenue varies with the level of national income (Barnett and Grown 2004: 12–13). In low-income countries, about two-thirds of tax revenue is raised through indirect taxes, including trade taxes (such as tariffs on imports), excise taxes (such as taxes on alcohol and cigarettes) and broad-based taxes on goods and services, such as General Sales Tax and VAT. In high-income countries, indirect taxes account for only about one-third of tax revenue. The other two-thirds is raised through direct taxes. The share of trade taxes in tax revenue is much higher in low-income countries than in high-income countries: over one-third, compared to less than one-hundredth. In low-income countries, income tax accounts for just over a quarter of tax revenue, while in high-income countries, it accounts for over a third of tax revenue.

CEDAW does not contain any explicit reference to taxation. However, the principles of non-discrimination and substantive equality can be brought to bear upon taxation. Women must be treated as equal to men in tax laws; as individual, autonomous, citizens, rather than as dependents of men. Moreover, the impact of tax laws, in terms of incidence of taxation on income (i.e. the share of a person's income that is paid in tax), and incentives/disincentives for particular kinds of behaviour, should promote substantive, and not merely formal, equality between women and men, including egalitarian family relations (Elson 2006: 77).

The case of personal income tax (PIT) provides a good example. When joint taxation is the rule, tax liability is assessed on the combined income of both partners and they file a joint tax return. In these cases, the partner with the lower income (mostly women) might effectively pay more tax than they would if they were taxed as separate individuals. This happens if aggregating the income of the two partners takes the joint income into a higher tax bracket than the bracket in which the lower earner would fall if filing as an individual. De Villota (2003) demonstrates how joint filing in PIT might create disincentives to female labour market participation. Considering the same issue, Himmelweit (2002: 16) argues that separate taxation of each person in a couple (individual filing) 'can be seen as a step towards gender equality in employment............ Separate taxation also improves women's bargaining power within their households; as women usually earn less than their husbands, wives will generally gain from being taxed at an individual, rather than a joint, rate'.

Poor women, especially in developing countries, are likely to be outside the direct scope of PIT, since there is generally a minimum income below which there is no liability to pay income tax. However, all women are affected by broad-based indirect taxes like VAT, sales tax and excise duties.

Grown and Valodia (2010) provide an internationally comparative review of gender aspects of tax systems, covering Argentina, India, Mexico, Ghana, Morocco, South Africa, Uganda and the UK. The research covers both PIT and selected indirect taxes, namely VAT, excise taxes and fuel taxes. The research uncovered implicit biases in the PIT systems in all the countries. These are mainly the result of the nature and structure of exemptions and deductions provided by the particular tax regime, and the manner in which these relate to the distribution of employment and income. In many of the countries, for example, contributions to pension funds attract generous tax exemptions or deductions, which benefit men more than women, because men's higher incomes, and higher likelihood of formal sector employment, mean that they are more likely to contribute to pension funds.

It is not possible to empirically investigate the incidence of indirect taxes on the income of men as compared to women because there is no data in household surveys on individual incomes and expenditures. In many of the countries, in the study, there was not even data on household income, only data on household expenditure, in total and on particular items. The study therefore investigated the incidence of VAT, excise duties and fuel tax on total household expenditure for households differentiated by their gender characteristics.[16] Unfortunately, this means that the regressive character of indirect taxes, in terms of their incidence on household income, was obscured.

A study of the rise in VAT in the UK in 2010 used the same approach of differentiating households by their gender characteristics, and examined incidence of the rise in VAT on income rather than expenditure (De Henau and Santos 2011). This found that the group that faced the largest increase in VAT payment as a share of their income was one of the most vulnerable groups in the UK, lone mothers. The incidence of the increase in VAT payment was highest for the poorest groups of households where 60 per cent of adult household members were women.

It is possible for the unequal gender and poverty impact of VAT on household incomes to be offset if tax revenue funds public services and social security for low-income women, as is the case in some countries.[17] This indicates that we need to consider taxation and public expenditure together. One way of making a tighter link between the two is by earmarking the revenue from certain taxes to fund services and social security payments that are critical for realizing the rights of women, especially low-income women. Economists and public finance managers are not generally in favour of earmarking taxes, but earmarking can help to improve the transparency of government budgets and the accountability of governments to their citizens, which in turn may lead to greater willingness to pay taxes.

Higher tax revenues increase the resources available to a government, but it is not the only determinant of maximum available resources. Development assistance and borrowing also augment resources.

Human Rights Principles and Overseas Development Assistance

Governments have human rights obligations to provide development assistance, as set out above. In judging the extra resources ODA provides to recipients, it is important to recognise that ODA takes the form of loans, as well as grants. Interest has to be paid on loans, and the loan has eventually to be repaid. These payments of debt service and amortization of loans mean that not all of the ODA that flows into a country any one year is a net addition to the resources available to the government. It is important to distinguish between gross inflows of ODA and net inflows of ODA. Even the net inflows can overstate the amount of new resources being made available, since debt relief is counted as part of the new ODA. However, debt forgiveness simply writes off debt; it does not make any new resources available.

The impact of ODA on available resources in recipient countries will be reduced if ODA is tied to purchases of imports from donor countries that cost more than goods and services available locally or on the international market. The proportion of bilateral aid that is formally untied rose from

46 per cent in 1999–2000 to 76 per cent in 2007; however, research has found that in most investment projects, the main contract and technical assistance is still procured from donor countries, so some of the ODA that has flowed into a recipient country almost immediately flows back out again to the donor (Clay et al. 2009).

The Office of the High Commission for Human Rights has stated that human rights must be taken into account in the Poverty Reduction Strategies that governments have to agree with the World Bank before loans are provided; they have also issued guidelines on how this may be done (Office of the High Commissioner for Human Rights 2006). Bilateral donors have increasingly promoted a rights-based approach to development, including the Governments of the UK, Sweden, Switzerland, Canada and Germany (Piron 2001).

However, there is concern that there may be drawbacks to a rights-based approach to development, if it becomes another set of conditions that rich countries impose on poorer countries, without any reciprocal understanding of obligations. Some of the donor governments that press aid recipients to adopt a rights-based approach to development are themselves engaged in activities (such as the promotion of arms sales and the failure to adequately regulate banks) that may undermine the capability of recipient governments to fulfil their obligations.

The best way to use ODA to build the capacity of recipient governments to fulfil their human rights obligations is to assist with the transparent use of funds, and the development of processes by which citizens and their elected representatives can participate in budget decision-making and implementation, track the use of funds and their impact, and hold governments to account. If ODA is to contribute effectively to achievement of gender equality and fulfilment of women's rights, it is vital that women should be equal players in such processes, and that a comprehensive system of gender-responsive budgeting is in place to provide women with the necessary information.

Human Rights Principles and Government Borrowing

Borrowing makes more resources available to a government in the short run, but it creates a future charge on government budgets, as debt has to be serviced and repaid. In deciding whether borrowing can contribute to or hinder the realisation of women's rights, it is critical to consider whether the government is using the debt to finance the creation of assets that will both help in the realisation of women's rights and generate future streams of revenue with which the debt can be serviced and repaid. Well-chosen, gender-equitable public investments in education, health, nutrition, care services, water and sanitation, clean energy, safe public transport and good quality housing can help to realise women's rights, and can generate future revenues via raising women's productivity. It can also promote an increase in private investment, by women themselves, and by businesses attracted by a healthy, well-educated female work force. Enhanced productivity and investment support faster growth and higher incomes which, in turn, increase tax revenues and allow governments to pay back the initial borrowing over time.

Unfortunately, governments have often misused borrowing and left behind a large accumulation of debt that reduces the resources available for the realisation of human rights. The UN Independent Expert on the Effects of Foreign Debt on Human Rights has developed the concepts of onerous, odious and illegitimate debt to provide tools with which to analyse the implications of accumulated debt.[18] Onerous debt generally refers to a situation in which the obligations attached to the debt—for example, debt servicing payments—significantly exceed the benefits which have been derived from taking on the debt. In these circumstances, the cost of servicing the debt can greatly limit the ability of the state to progressively realise rights. Odious and illegitimate debt refers to situations in which debt was incurred by a government and used for purposes that do not serve the interests of the people. For example, borrowed funds were invested in ways that served only to enrich an elite who secreted their gains in overseas tax havens, or was used to finance war or repression. When money is borrowed and used in ways that do not advance women's rights, the interest that has to be paid on this accumulated debt also hinders progress towards realizing such rights in the future Public debt audit commissions have been created in some countries that have accumulated very high levels of debt to assess the legitimacy of a country's accumulated debt and consider if there is a case for repudiation (or forgiveness) of some of the debt.[19]

Governments borrow by taking loans from other governments, commercial banks and international financial institutions like the IMF and World Bank; and by selling bonds[20] to a wide range of private sector investors. The payments that governments have to make to service their debts vary with prevailing interest rates and exchange rates, which can be very variable. Borrowing by issuing bonds thus opens governments to the risks of national and international financial markets. These risks depend on the way in which financial markets are regulated, and the types of monetary policies adopted, especially by the biggest and most powerful high-income countries. Austerity measures that some European governments have been forced to undertake in 2010/11, as a result of pressure from the EU and the IMF, are part of an attempt to restore the confidence of bondholders in order to convince them to continue holding the bonds. Nevertheless, bondholders have been demanding higher rates of return in exchange for agreeing to hold the debt of some governments (including Ireland, Portugal, Greece and Spain). This raises the payments governments must make to service the debt. In the context of an economic downturn, when government revenues are already under pressure, higher debt servicing payments squeeze other areas of spending. There is a danger that obligations to creditors overwhelm the obligation to progressively realise human rights. International cooperation is necessary to deal with a crisis of this kind, which has its roots in inadequate financial regulation. To ensure that government borrowing can safely augment the resources available for progressive realization of women's rights, we need more effective regulation of international financial markets and international financial sector companies, so that finance can support rather than undermine the realization of women's rights.[21]

Gender-responsive budgeting has tended to ignore government borrowing, but a comprehensive approach to gender-responsive budgeting would examine how much of the budget is devoted to paying interest on government loans, and how the loans have been used. It would ensure that women participate fully in debates about how much new borrowing a government should undertake, and how it should use the borrowed funds; and ensure that any debt audit commission examined the implications of accumulated debt for women's rights.

Human Rights Principles and Monetary Policy

Thus far, we have been considering the implications of fiscal policy (expenditure, taxation and borrowing) for realization of women's rights. However, monetary policy, conducted by central banks, also matters, as it directly affects the resources available for the realisation of economic and social rights. It does this by influencing interest rates, exchange rates and the amount of credit available in the economy, which in turn influences investment, output and employment. Thus, it has implications for the whole range of women's economic and social rights, most directly the right to work and the right to an adequate standard of living.

Today, central banks are, in most countries, quasi-independent institutions, free to make their own decisions on interest rates and exchange rates provided they meet objectives set by the government that appoints the governor of the bank. Several central banks have a strict mandate under law to maintain the rate of inflation at a specified low rate; for example, the European Central Bank. Those that are not bound by statute have, nevertheless, in many cases formally adopted a policy of 'inflation-targeting' and announced the target rate. The extent to which the mandate and practices of the central bank are consistent with human rights obligations is rarely considered. However, there is no reason why central banks should not be held accountable to the same human rights principles as other government agencies.

A key issue in relation to maximum available resources is the impact of central bank policy on the level of output and employment. If a low rate of inflation is the only objective, this is likely to lead to higher rates on interest than would otherwise be the case, as central banks raise interest rates to depress demand, guided by neoclassical economic theory which considers inflation as primarily caused by excessive aggregate demand. The result is to keep unemployment higher than it otherwise would be.

However, inflation is not necessarily the result of a monetary policy which is too lax. In many countries, inflation is not a problem of excessive credit leading to too much demand, but rather a problem of poor infrastructure, low productivity and/or the monopoly power of some businesses which have sufficient market power to raise prices. Increasing prices in global markets for essential goods, such as food and energy, can also contribute to inflation through the cost of imports. Monetary policy could do more to mobilize resources in countries where there is high unemployment and underemployment if central banks had regard to job creation as well as to inflation. This is particularly important for women's right to work, as there is evidence that when central banks try to control inflation by raising interest rates, it has more adverse impact in developing countries on jobs for women than for men (Braunstein and Heintz 2011). Thus, a comprehensive approach to financing for gender equality and women's rights would look at the policies of central banks as well as of Ministries of Finance, and at monetary policy as well as government budgets.

Can a Human Rights Perspective Help to Leverage More Finance for Gender Equality and Women's Rights?

Reminding governments that they have human rights obligations to provide finance for gender equality and realization of women's rights is not guaranteed to bring about improvements. However, it does open up another arena in which governments can be held to account: the UN system through which governments must report periodically to UN treaty bodies on their progress in implementing treaty obligations. For instance, governments that have ratified CEDAW (which is almost all governments) must report periodically to the CEDAW Committee, and the Committee holds hearings in Geneva to discuss the report and issues Concluding Comments that identify good practice, but also identify shortcomings and what needs to be done to sustain progress. NGOs are able to submit Shadow Reports to the Committee and attend the hearings as observers. Many women's organizations have used this opportunity to provide additional information to the CEDAW Committee, especially on areas of government weakness in fulfilling obligations. They have also publicised the Concluding Comments and used them in campaigning for more progress in realizing women's rights.

The CEDAW Committee has made several references to the need for gender-responsive budgeting in Concluding Comments. For instance, in reference to Luxembourg in 2000, the Committee 'welcome[d] the [Women's] Ministry's interest in, and support for, proposals to conduct a gender analysis of the entire State budget. This will contribute to a better understanding of the way in which women and men benefit from governmental expenditures in all areas' (United Nations, Committee on the Elimination of Discrimination Against Women 2000: para. 393). In 2002, when reviewing Fiji's report, the Committee 'commend[ed] the efforts of the State party to strengthen gender mainstreaming and monitoring through the gender budget initiative, and a gender audit project' (United Nations, Committee on the Elimination of Discrimination Against Women 2002: para. 43). Some governments have also made references to gender equality and government budgets in their reports, such as South Africa in its initial report in 1997, and France in its report in 2002 (Elson 2006: 36).

In the context of cutbacks in public expenditure in some European countries since 2010, concerns have been raised that governments have been adopting retrogressive measures that reduce women's enjoyment of human rights. For example, in relation to the UK, the CEDAW Committee commented in 2013:

> 20. The Committee is concerned that the austerity measures introduced by the State party have resulted in serious cuts in funding for organizations that provide social services to women, including those that provide services for women only. The Committee is concerned that the cuts have had a negative impact on women with disabilities and older women. It is also concerned that the State party does not provide direct funding for these services but resorts to commissioning them, which allegedly risks undermining the provision of the services. The Committee is further concerned that budgetary cuts in the public sector disproportionately affect women, owing to their concentration in this sector.
>
> 21. The Committee urges the State party to mitigate the impact of austerity measures on women and the services provided to women, especially women with disabilities and older women. It should also ensure that spending reviews continuously focus on measuring and balancing the impact of austerity measures on women's rights. It should further review the policy of commissioning services wherever this may undermine the provision of specialized services for women. (United Nations, Committee on the Elimination of Discrimination Against Women 2013).

In reaching these conclusions, the CEDAW Committee was informed by the Shadow Report submitted by UK women's organizations (Women's Resource Centre 2013), and these organisations subsequently used the Concluding Comments in campaigning against the retrogressive measures. Several UK political parties pledged to reverse some of the retrogressive measures in their manifestos for the UK general election in spring 2014.

Conclusions

Human rights standards do provide guidance to governments on how they can make progress in providing finance for gender equality and manage their budgets so as to realize women's rights. This guidance does take into account the fact that resources are limited, but also provides guidance on how to augment the resources available for expenditure to realize women's rights, through appropriate taxation, ODA and borrowing, and through appropriate financial regulation and monetary policy. The guidance also notes the ways in which the policies open to governments depend not only on their own efforts but also on cooperation with other governments. As well as human rights obligations towards the people in their own jurisdiction, governments have extra-territorial obligations not to harm the human rights of people in other jurisdictions, and to assist other governments in meeting their human rights obligations. It remains to be seen whether governments will do more to meet their obligations, but in pressing them to do this, women's organizations can frame finance for gender equality not only in terms of money, but also in terms of rights, and make use of the resources of the UN human rights system to promote comprehensive gender-responsive budgeting.

Notes

1. There is also mention of resources in the Convention on the Rights of the Child, Article 4, but for reasons of space, this chapter will not make reference to this Convention.
2. The CEDAW Committee is the UN body that monitors the implementation of CEDAW and considers the periodic reports that states that have ratified CEDAW are required to submit.
3. General Recommendations are issued from time to time by the CEDAW Committee to clarify the implications of CEDAW for particular issues.
4. CESCR is the UN body that monitors the implementation of ICESCR and considers the periodic reports that states that have ratified ICESCR are required to submit. In a series of General Comments, CESCR has clarified that concept of 'progressive realization' is not intended to take away all 'meaningful content' of a State's obligation to realize economic, social and cultural rights (CESCR, General Comment 3, para. 9). Progressive realization imposes a 'specific and continuing' (CESCR General Comment 12, para. 44) or 'constant and continuing' (CESCR, General Comment 15, para. 18) duty to move as 'expeditiously and effectively as possible' (CESCR, General Comment 3, para. 9; CESCR, General Comment 12, para. 44; CESCR, General Comment 15, para. 18) towards full realization of rights. These steps towards full realization of rights must be 'taken within a reasonable short time after the Covenant's entry into force for the States concerned', and such steps should be 'deliberate, concrete and targeted as clearly as possible' in order to meet the obligations of States (CESCR, General Comment 3, para. 2; CESCR, General Comment 12, para. 43; CESCR, General Comment 14, para. 30; CESCR, General Comment 15, para 17).
5. Article 2(2) of ICESCR; CESCR, General Comment 3, para. 2; CESCR, General Comment 12, para. 43; CESCR, General Comment 14, para. 31; CESCR, General Comment 15, para 17.

6. CESCR, General Comment 3, para. 10.
7. General Comments Nos. 11, 13, 14 and 15 respectively.
8. (CESCR, General Comment 3, para. 9; CESCR, General Comment 12, para. 45; CESCR, General Comment 14, para. 32; CESCR, General Comment 15, para. 19).
9. There are numerous other declarations and conventions that emphasize the importance of the principle of participation of women (see e.g. the list contained in CEDAW, General Recommendation 23 at para. 4).
10. General Comment 16, para. 37. See further General Comment 14, para. 54; General Comment 15, paras. 16(a) and 48.
11. Committee on Economic, Social and Cultural Rights: General Comment No. 15, The right to water (arts. 11 and 12 of the International Covenant on Economic, Social and Cultural Rights), UN Doc. E/C.12/2002/11, 20 January 2003
12. Committee on Economic, Social and Cultural Rights, 'Letter from CESCR Chairperson to States Parties in the context of the economic and financial crisis', CESCR/48th/SP/MAB/SW, 16 May 2012: www2.ohchr.org/english/bodies/cescr/docs/LetterCESCRtoSP16.05.12.pdf.
13. This is the terminology in general use in the UK.
14. States may have other revenue sources, such as royalties from extraction of oil or other mineral, but here we focus specifically on taxation.
15. Estimates are from OECD data (http://stats.oecd.org).
16. Households were not only differentiated into male and female-headed households, but also by employment status of adults (male-breadwinner households, female-breadwinner households, dual-earner households and non-employed households); and number of adults by sex (male-majority households, female-majority households and equal-number households).
17. This is not what happened in the UK after 2010, where the increase in VAT was accompanied by cuts to public services and social security that were important to economic and social rights of low-income women. However in Nordic countries, a high rate of VAT is used to generate revenues that fund a welfare state in which there is a high level of fulfilment of women's rights compared to most other countries
18. For more information, see the reports of the UN Independent Expert on the Effects of Foreign Debt on Human Rights: www2.ohchr.org/english/issues/development/debt/index.htm.
19. A commission to audit Greek debt along these lines was set up by the Greek parliament in 2015.
20. A bond specifies the size of the payments to the bondholders and the length of time over which the bond must be repaid. These conditions of repayment are fixed for each bond. Short-term bonds are paid back quickly, often within a few months, while long-term bonds are repaid over a much longer

period, often many years. Bonds are bought and sold in the bond market, and once the government issues a bond, it can be traded among investors in global markets. The price of the bonds varies with conditions in the bond market. If a government has difficulty finding investors willing to hold its bonds, the price of the bonds falls until they are sold. From the government's point of view, lower bond prices mean that borrowing has become more expensive (the implicit rate of interest is higher), since the sale of bonds generates fewer resources. From the investor's point of view, lower prices mean a higher rate of return, since the investor has to pay less money initially in exchange for the future payments the government must make as stipulated by the bond. The price of the bonds is influenced by the ratings they are given by international credit rating agencies (which are private firms): the lower the rating, the lower the price of the bond and the higher the implied rate of interest.

21. For more discussion of financial governance and gender equality, see Young et al. 2011.

References

Austen, S., Costa, M., Sharp, R., & Elson, D. (2013). Expenditure incidence analysis: A gender-responsive budgeting tool for educational expenditure in timor-leste? *Feminist Economics, 19*(4), 1–24.

Balakrishnan, R., & Elson, D. (2011). *Economic policy and human rights obligations.* London: Zed Press.

Balakrishnan, R., Elson, D., Heintz, J., & Lusani, N. (2011). *Maximum available resources and human rights, analytical report.* New Brunswick: Center for Women's Global Leadership, Rutgers University.

Barnett, K., & Grown, C. (2004). *Gender impacts of government revenue collection: The case of taxation, economic paper 62.* London: Commonwealth Secretariat.

Bird, R. (2010). *Taxation and development* (Economic Premise, No 34). Washington, DC: World Bank.

Braunstein, E., & Heintz, J. (2011). Central Banks, employment and gender in developing countries. In B. Young, I. Bakker, & D. Elson (Eds.), *Financial governance from a feminist perspective.* London: Routledge.

Clay, E., Geddes, M., & Natali, L. (2009). *Aid untying: Is it working?* London: Overseas Development Institute.

de Albuquerque, C. (2012). *On the right track: Good practices in realising the rights to water and sanitation, Report of the UN Special Rapporteur.* New York: United Nations.

de Henau, J., & Santos, C. (2011). Gender analysis of the changes in indirect taxes introduced by the coalition government, 2010–2011. http://wbg.org.uk/wp-content/uploads/2013/10/Indirect_tax_Budget_2011_final_report_June_20.pdf de Schutter, O. (2009). Report of the special Rapporteur on the right to food, mission to Brazil (A/HRC/13/33/Add.6). http://www.srfood.org/images/stories/pdf/officialreports/20100305_a-hrc-13-33-add6_country-mission-brazil_en.pdf

de Villota, P. (2003). Aproximación desde una perspectiva de género a la política presupuestaria desde la vertiente impositiva. El caso de España. In P. de Villota (Ed.), *Economía y Género. Macroeconomía, política fiscal y liberalización. Análisis de su impacto sobre las mujeres.* Barcelona: Icaria Editorial.

Demery, L. (2002). Gender and public spending: Insights from benefit incidence. In United Nations Development Fund for Women (UNIFEM) (Ed.), *Gender budget initiatives. Strategies, concepts and experiences.* New York: UNIFEM.

Elson, D. (2006). *Budgeting for women's rights; Monitoring government budgets for compliance with CEDAW.* New York: UNIFEM.

Elson, D. (2012). The reduction of the UK budget deficit: A human rights perspective. *International Review of Applied Economics, 26*(2), 1771–1901.

Elson, D. (2013). Economic crises from the 1980s to the 2010s: A gender analysis. In G. Waylen & S. Rai (Eds.), *New frontiers in feminist political economy.* London: Routledge.

Elson, D., Balakrishnan, R., & Heintz, J. (2013). Public finance, maximum available resources and human rights. In C. Harvey, A. Nolan, & R. O'Connell (Eds.), *Human rights and public finance: Budget analysis and the advancement of economic and social rights.* Oxford: Hart Publishing.

Fontana, M., & Elson, D. (2014). Public policies on water provision and Early Childhood Education and Care (ECEC): Do they reduce and redistribute unpaid work? *Gender and Development, 22*(3), 459–474.

Franceys, R. (2005) Charging to enter the water shop? The cost of urban water connection for the poor. Water Science and Technology: Water Supply *5*(6), 209–15.

Glick, P., Rumki, S., & Younger, S. (2004). *Integrating gender into benefit incidence and demand analysis. Food and nutrition policy program report.* Ithaca: Cornell University.

Grown, C., & Valodia, I. (Eds.). (2010). *Taxation and gender equity. A comparative analysis of direct and indirect taxes in developing and developed countries.* New York: Routledge.

Harvey, C., A. Nolan, & R. O'Connell (Eds.) (2013). Human Rights and Public Finance: Budget analysis and the advancement of economic and social rights. Oxford: Hart Publishing.

Himmelweit, S. (2002). Making visible the hidden economy: The case for gender-impact analysis of economic policy. *Feminist Economics, 8*(1), 49–70.

Hollingshead, A. (2010). *The implied tax revenue loss from trade mispricing.* Washington, DC: Global Financial Integrity.

Institute for Fiscal Studies. (2015). Green budget. http://www.ifs.org.uk/publications/7530

Lonergan, G. (2015). Migrant women and social reproduction under austerity. *Feminist Review, 109*, 124–145.

OECD and ADB. (2010). *African economic outlook 2010*. Paris: Organisation for Economic Co-operation and Development and African Development Bank.

Office of the High Commissioner for Human Rights. (2006). *Principles and guidelines for a human rights based approach to poverty reduction strategies*. Geneva: UNOHCHR.

Pearson, R., & Elson, D. (2015). Transcending the impact of the financial crisis in the United Kingdom: Towards plan F- a feminist economic strategy. *Feminist Review, 109*, 8–30.

Piron, L. H. (2001). Rights-based approaches and bilateral aid agencies: More than a metaphor? *IDS Bulletin, 36*(1), 19.

Sabir, M. (2002). Gender and public spending on education in Pakistan: A case study of disaggregated benefit incidence. *Pakistan Development Review, 41*(4), 477–493.

Sandhu, K., & Stephenson, M.-A. (2015). Layers of inequality-a human rights and equality impact assessment of the public spending cuts on black. Asian and Minority Ethnic Women in Coventry, *Feminist Review, 109*, 169–179.

Türk, D. (1992). *The realization of economic, social and cultural rights*, Special Rapporteur on Economic and Social Rights (E/CN.4/Sub.2/1992/16). http://www.unhchr.ch/huridocda/huridoca.nsf/%28Symbol%29/E.CN.4.Sub.2.1992.16.En?Opendocument

United Nations, Committee on Economic, Social and Cultural Rights (2001) Poverty and the International Covenant on Economic, Social and Cultural Rights. UN Doc E/C.12/2001/10.

United Nations, Committee on the Elimination of Discrimination Against Women. (2000). *Concluding comments of the Committee on the Elimination of Discrimination Against Women: Luxembourg*, UN Doc.A/55/38.

United Nations, Committee on the Elimination of Discrimination Against Women. (2002). *Concluding comments of the Committee on the Elimination of Discrimination Against Women: Fiji*, UN Doc.A/57/38.

United Nations, Committee on the Elimination of Discrimination Against Women. (2013). *Concluding observations on the seventh periodic report of the United Kingdom of Great Britain and Northern Ireland*, CEDAW/C/GBR/CO/7.

Women's Resource Centre. (2013). *Women's equality in the UK—A health check*. Shadow report from the UK CEDAW Working Group assessing the United Kingdom Government's progress in implementing the United Nations Convention on the Elimination of all Forms of Discrimination Against Women (CEDAW). London: Women's Resource Centre.

Wren-Lewis, S. (2015). The Austerity Con. *London Review of Books, 37*(4). http://www.lrb.co.uk/v37/n04/simon-wren-lewis/the-austerity-con.

Young, B., Bakker, I., & Elson, D. (Eds.). (2011). *Financial governance from a feminist perspective*. London: Routledge.

CHAPTER 4

Gender-Responsive Budgeting in Africa: Chequered Trajectories, Enduring Pathways

Nalini Burn

Introduction

Gender-responsive budgeting (GRB) has been initiated in Africa in the immediate aftermath of the Beijing Platform for Action but in an institutional arena increasingly fashioned by a dominant economic liberalisation agenda. The chapter explores some facets of the tensions and dynamics which underpin the trajectories and pathways of GRB initiatives in Africa in this unfolding setting over the last 20 years.

Specifically, it focuses on how the Public Financial Management (PFM) reform agenda accompanying economic liberalisation can, in principle, support but also thwart the flourishing of GRB, check its trajectory and limit its impacts so far, as indeed the realisation of the broader agenda of sustainable development goals as underpinned by human rights.

The chapter is not a comprehensive survey of all GRB initiatives, some of which such as in Rwanda have made important strides. It rather gives a practitioner's insight into specific GRB experiences—Morocco, Mauritius, Senegal, as well as a perspective from the tracking of iconic initiatives,

N. Burn (✉)
Independent researcher, Wolmar, Flic en Flac, Mauritius

© The Author(s) 2017

Z. Khan, N. Burn (eds.), *Financing for Gender Equality*,
DOI 10.1057/978-1-137-46101-8_4

such as in South Africa, Tanzania, Uganda—to tease out the politics as well as the economic dimensions of liberalisation. [1]As such, it brings into the frame the broader contextual variables pertinent for making any assessments of GRB, given the increasing scrutiny of its reach and impacts, as aid agencies and financial institutions weigh up options for combining effective financing for gender equality with the pursuit of policies underpinning the global fiscal squeeze since the systemic crises (see Combaz 2013 for the UK's Department for International Development (DFID) and the International Monetary Fund's regional surveys of gender budgeting efforts, and for Sub-Saharan Africa, within the broad assessment of macroeconomic policy in low-income countries (Stotsky et al. 2016). Part of this emerging interest in GRB is lodged in the broader policy stance of making the macroeconomic case for gender equality as a means to economic growth. The chapter puts the case for a more thorough assessment of the impacts of PFM reform on prospects for GRB as a transformative lever to achieve gender equality.

- The chapter is in two parts. Part 1 sets out the elements to the context of GRB on the African continent and the knowledge gained over time through pioneering practice in Africa as well as through feminist innovation, which can be used as a frame to describe and assess GRB experiences.
- Part 2 covers country case studies of varying lengths of selected GRB experiences, focusing more on sifting out and illuminating pathways and trajectories in the context of economic liberalisation in South Africa, Uganda, Mauritius, Morocco, Senegal and Tanzania.
- The concluding section draws out the strands from the analysis and proposes some broad directions for the future of GRB in Africa.

Part 1: A Prism for Situating and Framing GRB Experiences

Policy and Sustainable Development Context

GRB in Africa needs to gain traction in a context where the dominant policy narrative even more so now tends to be economic growth to catch up with and attain higher global income groupings. African countries are

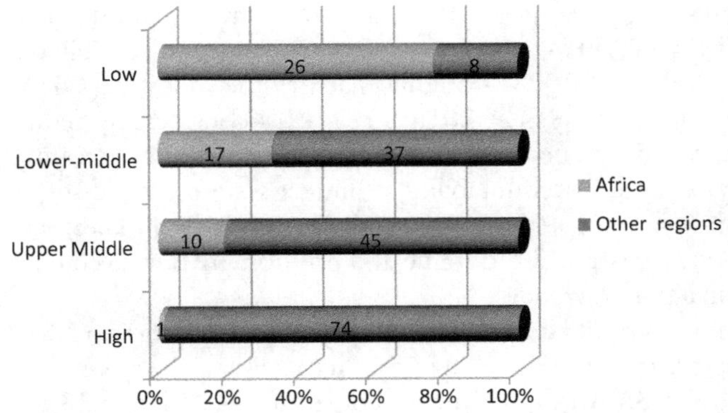

Fig. 4.1 Number and proportion of countries in Africa in each income grouping compared to countries in other regions (World Bank classification for 2015) (*Source*: Compiled from http://data.worldbank.org/about/country-and-lending-groups)

bunched in the low income per capita country groupings; their share falling at higher groupings (Fig. 4.1).[2]

Much of the economic growth is resource extraction-based. Since the Finance for Development Conference in Monterrey in 2002, gross private capital flows to Sub-Saharan Africa (SSA) have on average grown at 19.5% annually, overtaking Official Development Assistance (ODA), which is on a falling trend (Sy 2015). About three-quarters of the investment flowed to the resource-rich extractive industries, which tend to have weak links with domestic financial systems (Sy 2015: 25). ODA remains a main source of external finance for most less developed countries and a conduit for economic reform and PFM reform in aid-dependent low income and highly indebted countries. Even for emerging, rapidly liberalising middle income economies within Africa with very small shares of ODA in total budgetary resources, such as Morocco and Mauritius, compliance with "good" macroeconomic performance—delivered through the surveillance mechanisms of the International Financial Institutions (IFIs), and as used by international credit rating agencies—is critical to leverage private foreign investment and international capital flows.

Private financial flows add another layer of complexity as examined in the case of Mauritius and more diffusely in the case of other economies focusing on accelerating economic growth. Portfolio investment has grown massively but is less than half of the remittances from non-resident Africans over the last decade, at $21.8 billion. It is estimated that the amount lost in Illicit Financial Flows (IFFs) over the last 50 years—around $50 billion annually between 2000 and 2008—roughly matches the inflow of ODA over the same time frame (UNECA 2015a: 13). IFFs considerably reduce the fiscal space to finance development. They also put under scrutiny the state of transparency and accountability in budget systems, processes, regulatory and audit institutions (de Renzio and Simson 2013).[3] These trends have implications for strategies to frame and position GRB in overarching evolving national policy agendas.

The human rights deficits are compelling. There was no African country among the countries in the very high human development category in 2014, and 35 African countries constitute 81% of the 43 low human development countries.[4] While the average loss in human development index (HDI) value due to inequality has been falling globally, the highest percentage loss is in SSA (33.6%). It also has the second highest percentage loss in terms of the income inequality component, after Latin America and the Caribbean (UNDP 2014).

In 2012, SSA had the highest Gender Inequality Index value of 0.575,[5] the highest share of men and women in vulnerable employment (77%), as well as the highest proportion of working poor (40%). The majority of fragile and conflict-affected states (FCAS) are in the region. Despite the pace of trade in its natural resources, in 2008, Africa's total ecological footprint was 7.7% of total global footprint (World Wildlife Fund for Nature & African Development Bank 2012). However, African women and men are disproportionately vulnerable to cross-border implications of climate change, environmental degradation and erosion of natural resources, and to interlocking systemic crises, which have led wealthy food-insecure countries to engage in cross-border adaptation measures such as cross-border land grabs.

The current situation of gender equality and human rights in Africa is troubling. As underscored by FEMNET, violent fundamentalisms and retrogressive laws are clawing back the progress made to challenge violence against women and sexual aggression and put the rights, security and lives of women and girls in Africa at risk (FEMNET 2015). The erupting sites of conflict and humanitarian disaster can push into further invisibility the structural crisis of unpaid care work which falls disproportionately on women and girls in a continent with acute deficits in infrastructure and services.

The commitment and mobilisation of gender-equality advocates in and outside government remain firm. The Beijing +20 national reports indicate that 52 out of 54 nation states in Africa have ratified CEDAW; 36

member states have ratified and 18 have signed the (Maputo) Protocol to the African Charter on human and peoples' Rights on the rights of women in Africa. All 51 reporting member states have national gender machineries; have put in place legal, policy or strategic frameworks to promote gender equality and women's empowerment; and have legal frameworks to address the types of violence against women.

Mapping Gender-Responsive Budgeting Initiatives in Africa

Africa is a pioneering continent for GRB. South Africa became the first country globally and in Africa to join the pioneering Commonwealth Secretariat Pilot programme aimed at gender mainstreaming in finance ministries. GRB took root on the continent there, radiating first through Southern and Eastern Africa.

The five-yearly Beijing Platform for Action reporting mechanism shows a gathering momentum for GRB. It charts the progress from reporting on awareness to more practical operations for "making" budgets, and the strategies, tools and methodologies used.

In 2002, the following African countries were deemed to have been involved in GRBIs (Commonwealth Secretariat 2002):

- Botswana, Egypt, Kenya, Malawi, Mauritius, Mozambique, Namibia, Rwanda, South Africa, Swaziland, Tanzania, Uganda, Zambia and Zimbabwe.

Apart from Botswana, Swaziland and Namibia, the other countries have seen either continuous and progressive GRB experimentation or discontinuities and moments of rekindling GRB. UN Women, as at end of 2011, supported the following 15 countries at national and/or sub national levels.

- Burundi, Cameroon, Central African Republic, Democratic Republic of the Congo (DRC), Ethiopia, Egypt, Kenya, Mali, Morocco, Mozambique, Rwanda, Senegal, Sierra Leone, Tanzania and Uganda.

Twenty years after the Beijing Conference, the Addis Ababa Declaration of African Ministers responsible for Gender and Women's Affairs, places the adoption of gender-sensitive planning and budgeting schemes at the top of the list of its call to action (UNECA 2015b).

GRB's continued high profile and resonance in Africa raise questions of how it has fared in the intervening 20 years and particularly in Africa. The diverse GRB trajectories have been shaped by the successive instruments for fiscal policy and budgetary reform, such as the Poverty Reduction

Strategy Papers (PRSP) since the 2000s and the New Aid Modalities since the Paris Declaration on Aid Effectiveness in 2005 as well as since the global crises, the rise of new global economic players and different economic growth dynamics accompanying market-led globalisation.

Two broad dimensions are relevant to this scrutiny of GRBIs: What configuration makes for success and how it is measured? And how can the policy and practical institutional environment moulded by PFM reform, as underpinned by an economic liberalisation tenet, become more responsive to a transformative approach?

A Prism for Mapping the Trajectories of Gender-Responsive Budgeting Initiatives

The knowledge generated by GRB experimentation is a rich source to draw on. Rhonda Sharp, a leading GRB innovator of the pioneering Australian experience which galvanised interest in GRB at the Beijing Conference, has identified three goals of GRB: to raise awareness, to promote accountability and to make changes in policies and budgets, positing a *progressive hierarchy of these three goals of GRB* (Sharp 2002). Debbie Budlender, a lead researcher in the South African Women's Budget Initiative (WBI) distilled one of the key lessons learned of what makes for a successful GRB initiative: an interacting "*triangle of players*" : proactive and well-informed coalitions of civil society organisations, well-trained staff in government institutions and progressive elected representatives (Budlender 2002: 123; Elson 2004).

Certainly, if budgets were to change, governments, and crucially Ministries of Finance, would have to be involved, in a leadership or at least enabling and supportive role. The mainstream of public financial governance and management reform can be also cast in terms of two other trilogies. One is the formidable triumvirate of players made up of Ministries of Finance, the national joint public–private sector mechanisms overseeing economic and budgetary policy and the IFIs. The other is a game-defining triangle of goals or level of outcomes in the new economic management (World Bank 1998: 2). The outcomes are as follows:

Level 1: macroeconomic stability and aggregate fiscal discipline,
Level 2: effective allocation of resources according to strategic national policy priorities and
Level 3: efficient and effective use of budgeted resources in implementation.

In practice, as the individual case studies show, there is an *actual hierarchy of goals* with Level 1 firmly predominant, with Level 2 being prioritised equally highly or in fact turn out to be last, depending on how national policy priorities are defined (in particular in the case of Mauritius).

The course of GRB experimentation is shaped by the complex *rapports de force* and interplay among these diverse players and agendas.

The paradox and challenges of engendering state budgets at a time when state action and public finance were being squeezed by liberalisation and market-driven globalisation have been recognised, conceptualised and engaged with from the beginning of GRB experimentation (Elson 1996; Cagatay et al. 2000; Bakker 2002; Elson 2004). The feminist critique of the three biases of macroeconomic policy, as articulated by Elson and Cagatay (2000), the deflationary bias, commodification bias and the male breadwinner bias, plays out in the prioritisation and definition of the above levels of PFM outcomes. Diane Elson has incisively and consistently problematised the implication for GRB thus: Budgets are not governed to be compliant to human rights standards but by imperatives of market-driven liberalisation (Elson 2006). These tensions were behind the urgency for focusing on macroeconomic policy through budgets as entry points at the 1995 Beijing Conference. They gave rise to the first wave of support by the Commonwealth Secretariat, to pilot countries, including South Africa, to initiate GRB and which targeted central Ministries of Finance, Planning and Economic Development (MFPED).

Two tracks of work can be seen in the unfolding dominance of the neoliberal agenda: one which broadly challenged it, while the other also at the same time identified areas of common ground for critical engagement in the related PFM reform. There has been detailed crafting of bridges to find common, even "symbiotic" ground between GRB and shifts towards programme-based budgeting (PBB) (Budlender 2000: 14 and also Norton and Elson 2002; Sharp 2003; Holvoet 2006; OECD 2010), and identify entry points in the mainstream of PFM reform. It has been the ground on which the author has worked.

There is some fit between the standards for monitoring budgets for compliance with CEDAW, such as about whether budgets are adequate to finance gender equality and the results-based management principles of the Paris Declaration. Rhonda Sharp has expanded the performance and results-based orientation of PFM reform by adding a fourth E, equity, to indicators of efficiency, effectiveness and economy (Sharp 2003).

One of the principles of the Paris Declaration is to streamline development assistance with PFM reform through aligning with national systems. It is an obvious conduit for embedding financing for gender equality through GRB in national budgetary systems and processes. The principle of harmonisation among development partners carries the promise that there is harmonisation over gender equality, which can thus reinforce the potential for upscaling GRB interventions from small, fragmented discrete pilot projects of limited duration, and to make them more effective.

Sectoral budget support and sector-wide approaches—using both alignment and harmonisation principles—have been the platform to mainstream gender, using a twin-track strategy of specific gender-equality objectives as well as sectoral objectives which address gender disparities (Holvoet 2013). Holvoet has examined how far there has been application of the entry points for engendering new aid modality (NAM) instruments, and in particular sector and general budget support (GBS) in a sample of African countries.[6]

The political dimensions of economic liberalisation and the implications for GRB have also been flagged early on by a number of scholars (Norton and Elson 2002; Browne 2014).[7] However, the interplay among economic liberalisation, politics and political liberalisation and how it shapes GRBI prospects, in particular given the nature of financial flows and the economic growth stance, still remains largely undocumented. The political and institutional elements in GRBIs have tended to be elided for several reasons, including the crafting of donor-supported projects which focus on the politically "neutral" technical aspects of delivering concrete results and impacts in a very short time scale. However, these political and institutional elements are also highly contextual (Budlender 2002; 2005) and often behind the scenes, making it hazardous to gauge the complex interplay. This is particularly the case as institutional memory fades, in a context of institutional turnover. They are also not fully discernible in "real time" in specific settings, from a practitioner's hands-on perspective, to review and adjust the "theory of change". A lesson learned, as the case studies highlight, is that a *long view is needed in applying and assessing GRB*, to track when and whether GRBIs lose and then may regain momentum, as well as reflect on the shifting dynamics and learn from them to review pathways. Hence, a case study approach can generate useful insights for a reflexive approach.

Part II: Case Studies of African GRB Experiences

This section examines more closely and extensively the trajectories taken by GRB in the context of PFM reform. It picks out reasons why specific GRBIs have struggled so far to live up to their own or others' expectations and takes a measure of what they have achieved as well as the pathways they have been able to open up in environments underpinned by neoliberal, macroeconomic precepts.

A case study approach, however limited in view of the scope of the chapter, also enables to make sense of how different strategies and enabling factors have been deployed and put in context and perspective the weight to be given to different lessons learned regarding the prerequisites of GRB and the mix of strategies, which have been described and analysed in the other regional chapters (See Chapter 6, Barba and Coello and Chapter 7 Mishra and Sinha)

South Africa

The South African WBI grew out of the exploration of the ways and means to implement the South African Women's National Coalition's Charter for Effective equality in the space opened by the new post-Apartheid constitutional provisions[8] (Govender 2002; Budlender 2002; 2005).

Inspired by the Australian WBI, showcased at the Beijing Conference, it built on the local political configuration which led to the launch of a WBI, but from an outside government coalition of parliamentarians and civil society activists and researchers.

Developed under a progressive government, the trajectory of the Australian WBI was in fact later checked, in the context of economic crisis, by the coming to power of a neoliberal government, which adopted fiscal austerity policies. The checked trajectory of the Australian WBI has been seen in GRB circles in terms of the absence of civil society organisations, to constitute the third part of the virtuous triangle of players, so as to sustain the experience even with changes in governments.

Yet the South African Pilot Initiative was not able to be sustained beyond the two-year Pilot support. This is the case, despite being stimulated by the "local political dynamics" (Budlender 2000), of very strong civil society coalitions which generated the evidence base for making gender-sensitive budgets, supported the pilot sectoral initiative, contributed to the introduction of the child support grant to primary care givers in poor households and made the case for paraffin to be zero-rated for VAT to reduce the gender and poverty bias of state revenue mobilisation (Elson and Sharp 2010). The triangle of players had been well poised to progressively achieve the third GRB goal of making policies and budgets for tangible impacts on gender-based deprivation and intersecting inequalities.

The inspirational beacon for many initiatives across the African Continent, the South African Initiative in fact stumbled against the closing doors of the Ministry of Finance (now the Treasury). The latter now veered, through its Growth, Employment and Redistribution (GEAR) strategy, towards a path of fiscal austerity and economic liberalisation as modes of stimulating and accelerating economic growth (Elson 2004). It also ushered in PFM reform in the package, which did open up possibilities through medium-term expenditure frameworks (MTEF) and programme and results-based changes to budget structures, to plan and track long-term transformational shifts, but with GRB sidelined.

Tanzania[9]

The experiences of the early GRBI in Tanzania have been well documented (Mhina 2007). This case study highlights the tensions and ambiguities in the longstanding and enduring feminist critical engagement with policy and budget processes under economic liberalisation as well as the shifting political economy conditions prevailing in Tanzania. The Tanzania Gender Network Programme (TGNP) was formed in 1993 as a non-profit feminist activist organisation, collaborating with Feminist Activism (Fem Act), a coalition of more than 20 CSOs, itself a member of a broader coalition, the Policy Forum.

GRB has been initiated in the wake of a protracted and continuing period of turbulent relations between Tanzania and its development partners. The state budget was being restructured and more open to scrutiny at the same time that its overall size and share in the economy was reduced, as part of the macroeconomic agenda underpinning PFM reforms. This tension was seen by TGNP as an important reason to critically but constructively engage in the budget process, contest the marginalisation of women and most citizens in the processes to introduce and design reforms which have implications for them (Rusimbi 2002).

The TGNP/FEMAct has been influenced by the approach of the South African WBI to develop an evidence base on the impacts of economic liberalisation. The TGNP actively lobbied government to revision budgets and macroeconomic policy with a gender lens, upstream of the budget cycle, confronting policy to the evidence base in relation to poverty and gender-based forms of inequality. After organising training workshops in 2002 on gender and macroeconomic models for the Ministry of Finance and Economic Affairs (MOFEA) and the President's Office for Planning and Privatisation, MOFEA started a within-government GRB initiative. It commissioned TGNP as ongoing consultant for gender budgeting for six pilot ministries engaged in the MTEF process. This put pressure on TGNP to deliver the technical capacity to engage in supporting actual budget preparation, when such expertise is thin on the ground and has to be invested in.

With the move to align budgets to policy frameworks, a Gender Mainstreaming Working Group- Macro Policy (GMWG-MP) was formed to ensure that gender analysis was included in each component of the process of drawing up the national policy framework, the MKUKUTA (as the PRSP was called). These were the gender-sensitive diagnostic studies across the thematic clusters, the drawing out of policy outcomes for the clusters and the inclusion of key selected gender equality indicators to be monitored through a gender-disaggregated Monitoring and Indicator Information Framework.

One of TGNP's enduring achievements in this context has been the spearheading of the conduct of a Time Use Survey as part of a labour force survey by the National Bureau of Statistics, to contribute data for enlarging the macroeconomic framework, generate data on women's unpaid care work, in particular on water collection and distribution; then supporting the Ministry of Water to include gender and poverty issues in its budget guidelines, leading to an increase of the Ministry's budget, from 3% to 6% (Elson and Sharp 2010; Budlender 2011).

Making the case for gender equality and growth has a long but chequered track record in SSA, depending on the internal champions present in key organisations, which are by no means monolithic, at the time. The World Bank's Strategic Country Gender Assessment in 2004 for Tanzania underscored that gender was an economic issue, not just a social or equity issue, and reviewed existing gender-equality interventions (World Bank 2004). It recommended to undertake a Gender and Economic Growth Assessment reviewing the PRSP/MKUKUTA from these angles, to incorporate the analysis and data in the World Bank's Country Economic

Memorandum, to coordinate this work with the World Bank's support to the Public Expenditure Reform (PER) and the MTEF, and not least, to consolidate gender-focused GRB work more firmly in future Poverty Reduction Support Credit processes.

By 2008, a review of the Performance Assessment Frameworks (PAFs) attached to the joint assistance Memorandum of Understanding as well as other key tools and processes for implementation of GBS, such as Poverty Reduction Budget Support, and the annual GBS review cycle show that gender mainstreaming was not explicitly practised (Kytola 2008).

Some of the reasons put forward at the time are related to how Paris Declaration principles play out in practice: The move to GBS, the principle of ownership, mutual accountability and harmonisation can be working against each other as far as the gender-equality objective is concerned. The institutional dynamics can also conspire to the eclipse of the gender-equality agenda, for which no one stakeholder is able and willing to take responsibility for. There is reluctance on the part of some donors to be proactive on gender equality lest it is seen as being a donor's agenda and not nationally owned, while other donors take for granted that a gender-sensitive MKUKUTA is sufficient, and does not need to be tracked in Joint Assistance Strategy for Tanzania (JAST) processes. More importantly, the influential PFM thematic group was predominantly staffed by macroeconomists, who were considered to be not really open to including gender analysis at macro level, even when they may acknowledge its relevance at sectoral level. The 'distance' between gender analysts and budget officers was also invoked by Kovsted and Jacobsen (2008). The priorities for inter-cluster allocations were the need to balance long-term economic growth and development with basic needs but within the frame of fiscal discipline. Ministries of Finance for their part point out that it is up to sectoral ministries to mainstream gender, as under GBS, they have to contest for funds given the indicative budget ceilings allocated to them, in order to encourage prioritisation and sequencing: Gender equality and women's empowerment do not feature high among the priorities, unless embedded in individual programmes.

The institutional space for gender-informed macroeconomic policy dialogue within the World Bank particularly has not been sustained beyond the mid-2000s (as was also the case in Uganda). The engagement of TGNP in this process had already been considered stalled by the World Bank in 2004, when the latter explored entry points to reinvigorate it. The policy and institutional space for multi-stakeholder dialogue for gender equality in Tanzania were also difficult to sustain. While the Development

Partners' Group deplored the low participation of CSOs, parliament as well as sectoral MDAs, the CSO perspective was that the conditions for open, participatory dialogue over development priorities needed to be improved for meaningful participation. For the different triangle of players to interact, there was also the obstacle of insufficient human resources, time and thus financial resources as well as capacity to engage in all these processes in the policy cycle meaningfully. This is especially when there is an intensive schedule compressed over a short period of time, so that effective participation space becomes a mirage. As far as sectoral MDAs were concerned, the move towards GBS as opposed to sectoral budget support may have been seen as increasing the leverage of MOFEA over the budgeting process and discouraged participation and encouraged passive resistance (see also the case of Mauritius).

The CSO practitioners of GRB have tried to engage in all the entry points for GRB and have also focused on advocating for revisioning macroeconomic policy and development paradigms, which may have dispersed energies (Kovsted and Jacobsen 2008). The MKUKUTA and upstream processes such as the PER were highly gender-inclusive. But gender was not given much priority in the budget process further downstream.

TGNP has consistently considered the risks of being co-opted in the government project and of losing the autonomy to scrutinise, contest policy and hold government to account in the process of deepening democracy in the economic arena (Mhina 2007).

It seems for the moment to have resolved the inherent tensions of CSO engagement with government. It appears to have foregone direct involvement to preparing budgets on a ground shaped by Level 1 PFM outcomes of macroeconomic stabilisation and Level 2 outcomes framed in terms of economic growth, competitiveness and liberalisation, and to focus on interrogating these outcomes on the one hand as well as monitor issues of political economy as regards Level 3 outcomes.

In 2012, it registered itself as TGNP Mtandao Limited, which aims to build a "transformative feminist movement to challenge patriarchy and neoliberalism", recognising the intersections between gender, class, race/ethnic and national/global power relations.[10] It has a resource centre which acts as a hub for a variety of collaborative organisations and is recognised as a SADC-wide centre of learning on GRBI and continues to provide training for GRB to government actors.

TGNP continues to issue position papers on the Budget Guidelines. In the 2014–2015 Position Paper, it commended government for including more concrete gender-responsive guidelines for the fiscal year. But it also highlighted a range of issues including the corruption and financial management which have led to the suspension of GBS by donors, months before the 2015 General elections.

The case of Tanzania illustrates the potential of a GRB triangle of players which can aim towards a progression to transform budget allocations, but which dissipates because it is not underpinned by policy convergence about the objectives and conduct of macroeconomic policy, and is undermined by the inequalities of power and resources between the major players, and contested visions and practices of who should benefit from state resource allocations.

Uganda

The gender-responsive budget initiative was started in Uganda in 1999 in a highly favourable political conjuncture of sweeping political change and national rehabilitation measures after a long war. Initiated by a caucus of female parliamentarians from special interest groups, led by the Forum for Women in Democracy (FOWODE), it was the second country in Africa, and inspired by South Africa, to engage in GRB. The caucus was broadly supportive of the policy of the National Resistance Movement (NRM) which came to power in 1986, committed to institutionalising gender equality, representative and participatory democracy measures in legal and regulatory frameworks and mechanisms. It supported the GRB initiative (Budlender 2004). The caucus had been able to engender the new Ugandan Constitution, which enshrined affirmative action and under which women MPs and councillors are elected in special reserved seats which represent one third of available seats. The FOWODE-led caucus used the favourable political environment to go beyond ground-breaking female representation to influence policy and budgeting for women's empowerment and gender equality. The 2001 Budget Act had increased Parliament's role in the budgetary process, requiring the government to table before Parliament a Budget Framework Paper (BFP), which sets out how the government intends to achieve its policy objective through the budget. A Memorandum of Understanding was concluded with the Parliamentary Budget Office to provide technical support in gender analysis and the Parliamentary Budget Committee provided an entry point to lobby parliamentary oversight committees, both organs having been newly set up by the Budget Act.

The commissioning of gender analyses of the previous year's education, health and agriculture budgets, using gender-informed facts and figures, shifted parliamentarians' perception towards gender issues as development issues which would resonate with female constituents. It also forged links between members of parliament, government officials and civil society (Byanyima 2003). However, the lessons learned were that the issue briefs on previous years' budgets were not really able to influence the following year's budgets unless the MFPED was convinced of the policy and resource allocation implications of gender inequality and of addressing the institutional weaknesses in meeting commitments to gender inequality and women's empowerment.

The review of the Poverty Eradication Action Plan (PEAP) II and period of development of PEAP III provided the opportunity to shift gears for GRB. The PEAP set priorities for post-war economic rehabilitation based on economic reform measures of macro stabilisation and economic growth, through a broad-based national task force made up of stakeholders. It commissioned nation-wide poverty surveys focused on marginalised groups and those impacted by the war. The PEAP had served as a PRSP in 2000, whose approval qualified Uganda for Enhanced Highly Indebted Poor Countries (HIPC) debt relief. Its participatory revision process[11] became a model for PRSPs worldwide (Ssewakiryanga 2005). The monitoring and evaluation of the Poverty Action Fund—a mechanism for protecting and monitoring HIPC and donor funds to poverty programmes and which was integrated in the budget—was gathering evidence from bottom-up qualitative participatory poverty assessments of the regional disparities among the ten districts and the failure of the economic reform strategy to reduce poverty especially in war-torn areas. In an electoral context, poverty and regional disparities in poverty rates were the issues high on the political agenda (Ssewakiryanga 2005).

The gender-aware survey evidence base showed that addressing unequal household gender relations and gender-based economic insecurity could lead to as much as 2% annual increase in gross domestic product (GDP). A multi-stakeholder PEAP Gender Team used it to review the PEAP and showed the need to address gender-based obstacles to economic growth across sectors. The performance matrix of agreed targets and triggers of the Poverty Reduction Support Credit V linked to the implementation of PEAP III contained a number of specific gender-focused actions, across the cluster areas, including a pilot Gender and Equity Budgeting Initiative and a revision of the National Gender Policy. It committed development partners and government to mutual accountability for GEB's success.

The Policy Monitoring and Analysis Unit set up under the Ministry of Finance secured the support of the Budget Director for Gender and Equity Budgeting (GEB) preparation. The enlarged scope was designed to include social exclusion and broader equity issues, such as regional disparities as well as poverty and disability dimensions. The Budget Call Circular (BCC) for financial year 2003–2004 included a paragraph on gender and equity budgeting. It was accompanied by a number of official documents: customised guidelines to ensure sector compliance, to assess past performance and to justify future funding needs, as well by manuals to build capacity in gender analysis.

Six priority pilot sectors were identified for the Gender and Equity Budgeting Initiative—health, education, agriculture, roads and works, water and sanitation, and justice law and order. Sectoral policy briefs based on commissioned research to generate gender and equity disaggregated data were developed to support Sector Working Groups to review sectoral gender policy and develop gender-equality monitoring indicators. The review was conducted in the wake of the revision of the National Gender Policy in 2007, included as part of the PRSC actions, and to inform the design of National Development Plans.

Civil Society has been active in bolstering the demand and momentum for GRB and in keeping the issue on the agenda. FOWODE has been proactive in building gender budget advocacy coalitions and linking with other CSOs engaging in budget advocacy and applied budget work to make budget processes more gender-inclusive, open and accountable. The Gender Budget Coalition in Uganda led by FOWODE included university Gender teams, associations of professional women. It is part of the Uganda Debt Network and the East African Gender Budget Network. FOWODE also helped create the Civil Society Budget Advocacy Group (CSBAG) as a loose coalition at both national and local levels to advocate for pro-poor and gender-sensitive budgets through public dialogues on the budget and participation in Public Expenditure Review (PER) meetings. The coalition has become larger and its work more technical.

FOWODE to this day produces regular post hoc gender analyses of the annual budget, and CSBAG produces a Civil Society Position paper on the annual budgets, interrogating how pro-poor, socially inclusive and gender-sensitive it is. FOWODE's annual budget scrutiny has highlighted the declining trend in pro-poor expenditure, which also tends to encompass women's priorities. It points to the mismatch between budget estimates and appropriations and women's priorities, analysing concrete examples. It underscores the reasons for poor outcomes, which are traced to poor service delivery, corruption and inefficiency.

Nevertheless, CSOs face issues of legitimacy. Their comments can be ignored by Governments, even while they also engage in delivering technical assistance to the Government. Thus, working in closer partnership with parliamentarians has thus been identified as a key strategy to develop greater effectiveness and strengthen accountability. The Uganda Parliament has well-staffed Parliamentary Budget Offices to provide technical support. In 2010, FOWODE had obtained a grant from the UN Women-managed Fund for Gender Equality (FfGE) to build on its ongoing work with Parliamentary Budget Offices to support the incorporation of gender analysis and gender equality in parliamentary work.

Since 2009, there have been indications that current NAM processes were not carrying over the initial breakthrough made in the inclusion of GEB in the PRSC results and policy matrix. The reasons put forward have been the reported reluctance of macroeconomists to engage with GEB, which can be a crucial blockage, given that the development of the MTEF continues to be the preserve of the macroeconomists in the MFPED, with little input from other stakeholders such as Parliament, research and academic institutions and CSOs. They also play a dominant role in technical support to NAM instruments, such as Joint Assistance Strategies Teams and annual reviews of GBS and Sector Budget Support.

The lack of congruence between gender-equality policies and NAM approaches has also been pointed out. First, public sector restructuring has eroded the capacity for gender mainstreaming, with gender offices abolished and functions co-opted with others (Tiwambeda and Kabuchu 2008). Second, both the World Bank Group and the African Development Bank Group's governance strategies only selected aspects of governance such as transparency of PFM among the broader range of economic and political governance issues, such as those restricting access to service delivery which could have economic, financial implications and gender equity dimensions (ADB 2009). Third were the difficulties of harmonisation among development partners over the theme of gender equality and women's empowerment when both their sectoral and cross-cutting approaches can be quite different. Some donors fund MGLSD without taking into account its cross-cutting technical and monitoring role.

Since 2006, BCCs have been issued through advocacy efforts, but without much effectiveness. As from 2010, GRB work in Uganda has worked on two fronts: on the parliamentary front and on backing up policy commitments to and institutional directives regarding GEB with legislation. Technical work has been done to update and identify entry points for gaining ground in GRB in the budget process in Uganda.

With revenue from petroleum production about to come on stream, there has been intense policy focus and broad based discussion and negotiations on how to manage the revenue stream, what to invest it in, and to increase Parliament's monitoring and oversight on how it is used. After much advocacy from FOWODE, CSBAG and the women's caucus, a new Uganda Public Finance Management Act of March 2015 was finally passed which contains articles strengthening Parliament's powers over the budget process, to analyse policy issues and programmes that affect the economy and the annual budget and, where necessary, to make recommendations to ministries on alternative approaches to the policy or programme, and in respect of the report of the Auditor General. There have been extensive negotiations about whether it was the MOFED or the Equal Opportunities Commission (EOC)—a Constitutional body—who would issue the mandatory certificate, under the new Act, that the BFP and the annual Ministerial Policy Statements are gender and equity responsive. Enlarging parliament's role and oversight functions in the budgeting process in relation to the executive has opened space for gender budgeting.

But it is still a contested agenda. MOFED attempted in November 2015 to repeal the provisions of the Certificate of Gender and Equity responsiveness in the 2015 Public Finance Management Act, enacted in March 2015, on grounds that it is cumbersome to implement. At the same time, there had been delays in setting up and making operational the EOC, which is also underfunded. However, Parliament rejected the proposal to repeal the provisions of the Act. But non-compliance remains, so far as does the limited capacity as yet of the EOC to monitor compliance.

The trajectory of the Uganda GEB shows how a long view is needed to really understand the dynamics, and that a multi-pronged approach is needed to influence the policy cycle and embed GRB. Despite political economy risks with political patronage such as the cooptation of women parliamentarians (Goetz and Hassim 2003; Tanzarn 2008; Lakwo 2009), the dynamics can shift towards exerting influence which goes beyond representation to enlarging parliament's legislative and oversight role. Such a dynamic holds the potential to advance GRB work along a number of pathways in the policy cycle, and ensure that greater domestic resource mobilisation with petroleum revenue actually enlarges the fiscal space for financing gender equality and addressing intersectional discrimination and marginalisation. The current challenge is now to actually progress to preparing gender-responsive results-based budgets that are transformational.

Senegal

The Senegal case highlights facets of GRB experimentation when the specifics of the process of economic restructuring and its political implications are not visible in "real time" to those engaged in it. When the state downsizing erodes the capacity of ministries to engage in the newly introduced multi-year results-oriented budgeting, it is not clear whether and what other institutions take over the functions of dissolved state agricultural support agencies. It is also not evident what traction there is for financing for gender equality and women's empowerment and engaging with a set of players who may have different and divergent views over agricultural policy and strategy in responding to the triple financial, food and fuel crises starting in 2007.

Senegal was among the first 20 countries involved in the first phase of the Global GRB programme of the former UNIFEM, now UN Women, in 2003–2004. This case study deals with the second phase of the programme, with which the author was also involved as international consultant on short missions.

Following the capacity development sessions of the first phase, which also involved the General Budget Directorate of the Ministry of Finance, the latter issued a BCC in 2007 requesting sectoral ministries to improve on the inclusion of gender issues in the preparation and execution of their budgets. The Minister of Agriculture and Food Security (MOFS) requested support for a GRB pilot intervention: The champion was the gender focal point attached to the Minister's Cabinet who was particularly keen and committed. The Budget Director thought that it would be instructive to develop a concrete case to demonstrate how to engage in GRB for other ministries to learn from and adapt, as it was quite a novel and also far reaching exercise. Senegal was initiating results-based budgeting at the time: The MOFS still needed to finalise the decrees for implementation of the Law orienting forestry, agriculture and livestock rearing (LOASP); harmonise it with the National Agricultural Development Plan (NADP), with the PRSP as framed by the Millennium

Development Goals (MDGs), and also translate the agricultural sector priorities into MTEFs and then programme budgets. In principle, all these instruments should be aligned and harmonised. The results-oriented GRB sequence along the policy cycle is predicated on this articulation. The LOASP contained an Article 54, which states that the state should ensure equal rights for men and women in rural areas especially agricultural holdings, which provided a legislative framework and a clear entry point for GRB. The mission found out that all these aforementioned instruments had been developed by different ad hoc teams and in separate divisions through short term workshops. A separate thematic team was working on the decrees to apply the NADP.

In view of the urgency of developing the MTEF, engaging in hands-on preparation to embed GRB within it was seen as a strategic opportunity. The location was the Directorate of Analysis of Forecasts and Statistics (DAPS) which was tasked to develop the MTEF. However, the actual work fell to a small team of external consultants, as the downsizing of the ministry was accompanied by outsourcing of key planning and analytical competencies. At the time, the attention of senior decision makers and technical cadres was engaged in the President's response to the food crisis through the Plan REVA—plan to return to agriculture—and GOANA—a great agricultural campaign for food and abundance. In this context, the gender focal point of the MOFS was lobbying to obtain seed allocation quotas and access to other agricultural inputs for women farmers. It did not materialise, for reasons outlined below.

On working on the MTEF, it became evident that the extensive, detailed sex-disaggregated data at the level of agricultural small holdings and plots, from the Agricultural Census of 1998—as Senegal was a pilot country for FAO's support to produce such ground-breaking data-, was neither known nor had been used in the first draft of the MTEF. So, as part of the GRB work, the data was used in the narrative, descriptive and diagnostic part and to develop gender-equality indicators, such as regarding land rights, access to inputs, as well as in providing recommendations to incorporate them in regular statistical reporting. But it also became clearer why this existing spatially fine-grained Census data on women's critical role in farming systems was ignored. It was not considered relevant for policy purposes. Senior technicians and agricultural analysts in the ministry were not really focussed on small holder agriculture. The focus was on getting away from it and engaging in structural transformation towards large scale modern agriculture, and on increasing domestic production as well as the sector's export competitiveness. It resonated with the political ambitions to massively increase production.

The GRB Programme, in response, initiated the process of engaging the Ministry staff in producing a Gender report, which would be a rapid gender-aware policy evaluation and institutional analysis of the agricultural sector. One of the recommendations put forward was a PER for the sector to make sense of all the new PFM instruments and to set a baseline for MTEF interventions and for priority setting, and in its wake conduct a more thorough gender-aware policy evaluation, an institutional mapping of the sector and a review of the statistical database and instruments to facilitate gender-aware MTEFs. However, the GRB support programme ended the second phase in 2008. It was not able to sustain further progress in institutionalising gender responsiveness in agricultural sector policies, plans and budgets, swept aside by the mainstream policy responses to the triple food, financial and fuel crises of 2007–2008.

In 2012, several years past that particular GRB episode, a PER was in fact carried out and published. It illuminated the political economy dimensions of resource allocation choices over the relevant period (République du Sénégal 2012). As anticipated, it found that REVA and GOANA were disconnected from agricultural sectoral strategies and programmes; it dissected the misalignment among all the instruments; the disconnect when input-based budgeting was still practised in reality and the current Organic Budget Law (OBL) did not enable the preparation of medium-term economic frameworks.

The agricultural PER scrutinised the return to a system of producer subsidies and distribution of agricultural seeds and inputs, whose budget share was 30% of public expenditure in agriculture. As they were not included in the annual Budget Law, the MOF refused a supplementary budget, meaning that there had to be intrasectoral reallocations to finance the subsidies. The prices at which private operators, chosen without any transparency, sold to the state were up to three times current market prices. As well as providing the inputs, the private operators also distributed the seeds, leading to a conflict of interest. The seeds were distributed after the sowing period, which meant that the farmers used them for food. The operators were the biggest producers, including among them the "marabouts", religious leaders, who play an influential political role in Senegal. The PER which was not tasked to be gender-responsive considered that producer subsidies did not reach poor farmers, whether men and women, nor were targeting sectors which had more potential for increasing production. Agricultural liberalisation had left the field clear to other modes of resource allocation, which reinforced the local powerholders, including the political power of patronage of well-connected rural elites and notables not necessarily open to gender equitable redistribution of agricultural inputs and women's economic empowerment. A transformatory theory of change would need to be aware of the gender-based power relations of powerful triumvirates to engage with turning around allocations to finance gender equality from a broad-based and long-term agenda. But also, the Senegal case study shows the limits of short-term, pre-designed GRB projects in being able to engage in supporting transformational institutional change over time.

Mauritius

The case study does not focus on early GRB episodes in Mauritius since its uptake of the call to engage in GRB, following the Commonwealth Secretariat Finance Ministers' meeting in 2002. The study focuses on the latest episode of GRB since 2008. Throughout this period, the small Gender Unit of the Ministry of Gender Equality, Child Development and Family Welfare (MGECDFW) has remained consistently committed to GRB. It highlights the role that "femocrats" (Sawer 1996) can play within government to persevere in pushing the gender-equality agenda. One of the achievements of that period had been the conduct of a Time Use Survey in 2003, which generated data for later GRB work as from 2008. The valuation of unpaid care work was carried out which revealed the disproportionate total work burden faced by employed women, especially in the context of trade liberalisation.

A ten-year economic reform programme started in 2005 to respond to the implications of the erosion of trade preferences in clothing, textiles and sugar in the wake of the implementation of World Trade Organisation rules. The economic reform programme, 2005–2015, which the Ministry of Finance and Economic Development oversees, has four pillars, supported by a consortium of development partners—the European Union, the World Bank and the African Development Bank—through aid-for-trade instruments, development policy lending and GBS. They are as follows:

Pillar 1: Fiscal consolidation and improving public sector efficiency
Pillar 2: Sharpening competitiveness

Pillar 3: Improving the business and investment climate and
Pillar 4: Democratising the economy through participation, social inclusion and sustainability.

The first pillar corresponds to Level I outcome of PFM and illustrates the deflationary bias of macroeconomic policy. The next two pillars correspond to the commodification bias. In view of the dominant policy agenda of making Mauritius achieve high income country status by 2020 through profit-led globalisation, these pillars correspond to the Level 2 outcome of PFM. Their deployment in effect also reveals the male breadwinner bias, which is outside the scope of this chapter to examine thoroughly.

The programme ushered in the shift from input-based budgeting to programme-based budgeting (PBB). This was seen as a strategic entry point to embed gender-equality financing in the policy and budget cycle. To reenergise GRB, the author as consultant supported the development of an overarching National Gender Policy Framework (NGPF), which would enable each ministry, department or agency to develop its gender policy to be able to articulate/review their sector policies and provide specific guidelines to develop their programme-based budgets (PBB). Concomitantly, the PBB manual had been reviewed to embed GRB approaches. A BCC was issued in 2008–2009, but it did not continue in later fiscal years.

In spite of the strong political support of the then Finance Minister to GRB, the then Financial Secretary was reluctant to support the deployment of GRB, spelling out at the time that it was not a priority. Nevertheless, after some internal negotiations bolstered by the high-level political support and of some former staff of the defunct Ministry of Planning and Economic Development, 11 sub-programmes of different sectoral ministries were selected by MOFED for GRB experimentation. The process of engaging the sectoral ministries to review their programmes using gender analysis and the existing statistical database to develop gender-responsive performance indicators was started during the time frame of the UNDP-supported programme.

The Gender Unit has been proactive since then in mobilising resources to support the development of sector gender policies and their action plans for implementation, as well as in the setting up of an interministerial committee and MDA gender cells for its implementation, as stipulated by the NGPF adopted in 2008. Since 2012, ministries who have already developed their gender policies have started identification of some gender-responsive services in their Programme-Based Budgets: For instance, there are PBB outputs relating to the employment of women in mangrove re-afforestation for coastal restoration and climate change mitigation as well as women's economic empowerment, measures supporting alternative livelihoods to women octopus fishers and providing income transfers during the closed season.

To establish Level I outcomes, a Public Debt Management Act in 2008 mandated that public debt should remain to below 60% of GDP. As Mauritius became a low tax jurisdiction to attract foreign investment and high net worth residents as an offshore financial centre, government spending had to fall. The Government cut primary spending far in excess of the target envisaged as prior action in the Development Policy Lending programme (World Bank 2012). It also accelerated debt reduction, accumulating substantial international reserves prior to the 2008 crisis.

In 2003, the World Bank had advocated the merger between the Ministry of Economic Planning and Development and the Ministry of Finance. Planning was subsumed under finance. It was expected that the planning staff which formed the sector ministry sector teams would provide the planning framework for PBBs, which was the working assumption of the GRB Initiative. However, the Bank's Implementation Complementation Report regarding Development Policy lending stated that their essential purpose was to strengthen monitoring to ensure fiscal discipline (World Bank 2012). In effect, the approach over the past decade has been to first engage in reform at the budget phase without an upstream overarching policy framework to provide guidance for strategic planning and which cascades downstream to programme-based budgeting and monitoring. The sequencing approach of GRB has been the reverse, and there was a lack of fit with the actual course of PFM reform.

The impacts of the fiscal discipline stance and the liberalisation policy have been not only to increase real incomes and consumption but also to exacerbate income inequality and unemployment, particularly of women: The Gini coefficient which had fallen to 37% in 1991—as a result of previous investment in universal social welfare provision—rose to reach 0.38 in 2005–2006 and 0.41 in 2012. Income poverty is disproportionately borne by households with children and female-headed households, with indications of considerable working income poverty in Mauritius, exacerbated by time poverty (through the unpaid care work burden), again disproportionately affecting women.

An informal assessment of the impact of the economic reform programme on ministries' budgets has been gleaned through the author's support to the sectoral policy development process and in examining the narratives of the ministerial PBB statement under the rubric "Challenges": They are the chronic difficulties in negotiating with MOFED successfully to recruit staff, in particular adequate technical staff, for policy analysis, planning, monitoring enforcement, the ability to effectively fulfil mandates for coordination, regulation, oversight, monitoring and evaluation; to commission studies and research and have appropriate equipment: In the Ministry of External Affairs, because of the squeeze on recruitment, the workload has intensified putting work/life balance at risk. These conditions have tended to exacerbate the sidelining of gender concerns further and in general, contributed to weaken the capacity of staff to engage effectively in their mandates. These are for instance preparing effectively for key international and regional negotiations, including trade negotiations, in the face of limited substantive backup support. The Ministry of Social Security has also dwelt on its unsuccessful resistance to the introduction of narrow social protection targeting as required by the economic reform programme. Under these conditions of the erosion of state capabilities, it is difficult to effectively practise GRB and indeed work towards achieving Sustainable Development Goals.

By 2011, the World Bank had effectively reviewed its own policy advice in 2003 to merge planning with finance. It now considered that the merger led to a loss in strategic planning capacity, in particular the capacity to make the link between planning and national objectives (World Bank 2012).

In the aftermath of the elections of December 2014, which the incumbent government lost unexpectedly and comprehensively, there were a number of policy reversals. The PBB reform was abandoned on the declared basis that it was not transparent and to revert to input-based budgeting.[12] This context is not a favourable environment for GRB to take root. Currently, the advisory support for GRB is to continue with the pre-budget phase including drawing up an action plan for implementation of the sectoral gender policy and its costing which can be a basis for preparing input-based budgets.

However, there are complex undercurrents at play which influenced the electoral debacle. The competitive election process in Mauritius as well as economic governance has been seen as characterised more by the clientelist politics of political parties as a means of mobilising voters than by programmatic politics.[13] Using welfare benefits, rendering services to one's constituency are the main levers to obtain votes (Van de Walle 2007: 65).

These informal institutions and the nature of the political and institutional culture have not changed and have been exacerbated by economic liberalisation: The African Peer Review Mechanism Report for Mauritius observed that the governance system was to regulate tension and guarantee business, which can facilitate public–private partnership but at the risk of the privatisation of the state and at the cost of defending the public interest (APRM 2010: para. 8.2).

It is likely that the electorate voted to reject the then incumbent government also because of a number of scandals relating to the abuse of power and privilege in the allocation of resources, the undermining of institutions and the increasing social and economic inequalities, in a country with a strong history of political mobilisation, social development which had buttressed its economic development. The full scale of the abuse of power is becoming evident in the aftermath of the elections with revelations of the extent to which there may have been IFFs and the possible misuse and mismanagement of public funds including the bypassing of procedures for procurement in state-owned agencies and enterprises as a result of close business and powerful politicians' relationships, which have been widely commented in the media. Accountability institutions such as the Public Accounts Committee have lost their vitality. Many of the decisions to engage in large scale investment projects and the related awards of state contracts have been motivated more from personal gain than the social and economic return from investment. A major financial conglomerate, close to the previous government, has been virtually nationalised, and the pension fund holders, including many who had invested their redundancy payments through adaptation measures to mitigate the impacts of economic reform, have been bailed out through public funds.[14]

The absence of political incentives to achieve Level 3 outcomes of public expenditure, together with the rigid fiscal consolidation, had squeezed the Level 2 outcomes in regard to social and environmental goals, but also put at risk the financial sector itself, now representing about 10% of GDP.

The numerous strands of why the GRBIs have been sidelined under economic reform have become clearer, but only with hindsight, when evaluations are conducted and made public. PFM, which provided the framework for piloting GRB, had become inextricably associated with fiscal discipline and the preponderant role of the IFIs at the Ministry of Economy and Finance (MEF) and resisted by the sectoral Ministries, departments and Agencies (MDAs) as one downsizing and onerous package. It has been the political casualty of the democratic electoral process. The impact of the pursuit of accelerated economic growth on prospects for gender equality is acutely posed. On the other hand, there exist—albeit tenuous—opportunities in the current context if there is political commitment and much more substantial civil society engagement in a human rights-based approach (See chapter 3, Elson), as the principle of maximum available resources can be powerfully deployed to analyse current and past policy and bring out the scope for better gender-responsive PFM.

Morocco

Morocco's GRBI has been widely celebrated for its achievements as a result of which it became the first country to qualify for sectoral budget support from the European Union[15] to finance the Gender equality action plan 2012–2016 (now called the Governmental Programme for Gender Equality GPGE). The action plan is to implement the National Strategy for Gender Equality and Equity of 2006 (NSGEE). The implementation is to be through GRB embedded in results-oriented Programme Based Budgets under experimentation at the time. However, the real potential for making budgets from gender equality principles has not yet been able to be engaged in because of some striking similarities and patterns with the pace, sequencing and effectiveness of PFM reform in Mauritius. This short case study focuses on the role of the triangle of GRB players in the interplay between GRB and PFM; in shaping the progression of the three goals of GRB as well as the future course of GRB in Morocco.

The origins of GRB in 2002 at the same time that PFM was being introduced have been documented (Burn 2008). Indeed, it was a study of the gender dimensions of a PER to initiate PFM reform conducted with the support of the World Bank that triggered the GRB experience and shaped its strategy. Morocco is a particularly illuminating example of the GRB triangle of players: a progressive government in the wake of an important phase in the political democratic transition in Morocco, bent on reducing socio-spatial inequalities, and in the context of the recent accession to the throne of King Mohamed VI; strong, vibrant and active coalitions of women's rights organisations pushing for a number of women's status measures, regarding their civil and political rights (Htun and Weldon 2010) and the presence of a few women parliamentarians, who were champions of participatory budgeting and of GRB. They would drive the modernising process leading to the reform of the Family Code and a suite of legislative reforms to address what Htun and Weldon consider to be class-related measures covering social and economic substantive discrimination, as distinct from women's status measures. The reform of these codes set an agenda for their implementation through GRB.

GRB was initiated in a context of particularly tense polarisation between women's rights advocates and more conservative forces hostile to the gender-equality agenda. There had been a standoff. It led to the shelving of the National Plan of Action to Integrate Women in Development, as a joint document accompanying the Economic and Social Plan. The GRBI was seen as a soft, less visible way of introducing gender mainstreaming through the more "technical" budget process. The terrorist attacks in Morocco in 2003 gave the ascendancy to the progressive forces more friendly to gender equality and women's rights. The agenda followed two tracks which involved the gender focal points in MDAs: the renewal of the elaboration of a strategy for gender equality and equity, spearheaded by the national gender machinery, followed by the development of its action plan on the one hand as one dynamic and on the other hand, the production of an annual report to Parliament on the gender dimensions of their mandates, under the aegis of the MEF.

During that time, there has been consistent leadership of the women's rights organisations to find levers and entry points to embed gender equality in key institutions and policy processes. When the Arab Spring exposed the vulnerability of the country to a further wave of polarisation, a new Constitution in 2011 was advocated and adopted which gave Constitutional primacy to the gamut of universal human rights instruments over domestic legislation. Women's rights and gender-equality advocates worked hard to introduce women's rights and gender-equality provisions. The elections in late 2011 had seen the coming to power of conservative political formations. Yet the NSGEE was not shelved nor was the European Union's budget support for the implementation for the national gender-equality plan, with a set of gender-equality indicators to be able to monitor implementation through the budget. Its implementation however slowed down.

Women's rights organisations then actively lobbied for embedding GRB in the reform of the Organic Budget Law to be aligned to the new Constitution. The Directorate of Budget of MOFED had been ambivalent about whether the GRB experimentation was sufficiently mature to be included in the revised OBL, but open to its inclusion in lower level laws, such as application decrees. Following the political momentum and lobbying post 2011, and after 12 years of the initiation of GRB and PFM, they have been enshrined in the new OBL, which came into force in 2015.

From the beginning, the GRBI was located in the MEF, first in the Budget Directorate, then, as from the second phase of the UN Women supported programme, in the Directorate of Studies and Financial Forecasts. The move followed the appointment of a leading champion, who at the launch of the initiative was at the Cabinet Office, as Director of Studies and Financial Forecasts. It also shifted the focus to policy evaluation of the sectoral mandates, which was one of a number of strategic recommendations made to initiate GRB, along with Gender Statements integrated in programme-based budgets. The policy evaluation focus gave rise to the annual production of a Gender Report, an official budget information document accompanying the Finance Bill presented to Parliament for deliberation and approval, which was within the mandate of the Directorate of Studies and Financial Forecasts to produce. The first Gender Report was presented to Parliament in 2005, including reports of the four pilot ministries engaged in the PFM reform process. Since then the number of MDAs has risen to over 27 as at 2014–2015.

The successive reports reveal an increasing, albeit uneven culture of evaluation across MDAs. There is also a noticeable difference in the quality of the content of the Gender Report between those ministries that had benefited from hands-on capacity development up to 2008 and the new ministries, who have not been given the opportunity to internalise the template of the Gender Report. An examination of the Gender Reports shows that by and large, using the template and guidelines for producing the Gender Report, MDAs highlight the deficiencies in sectoral policies and strategies, their weak internalisation of a gender mainstreaming approach in mainstream expenditure, while they describe its pertinence through a gender-aware situation analysis. Many of the MDA Reports highlight the budget lines that are gender-specific and/or gender-equality targets and present the priority actions included in the Gender Equality Action Plan as such types of measures. The reports do highlight some of the gains made to turn around budget allocations towards accountability to women's rights. This is particularly the case for the Ministry of Justice's implementation of reforms of the Family Code, assessed using the human rights indicators of availability, access, quality adaptability and acceptability.

The MDAs filing a Gender Report question the pertinence of the large number of process and activity-related indicators of the mainstream budget submissions, as well as point out the weaknesses and gaps in terms of gender-responsive indicators in the budget document dedicated to performance indicators which accompany the finance bill as well as the detailed budget data based on economic and administrative classification.

But so far, their annual suggestions for improving the quality, relevance and coherence of mainstream indicators and their gender-responsiveness do not seem to have had any ostensible take-up by the relevant divisions and units of the MDAs in subsequent years. This is the case even though the Gender Report is developed iteratively by a team based in the sectoral ministry and the Gender Report Team of the Directorate of Studies and Financial Forecasts and also involves to some extent the Directorate of Budget at the MEF. It goes through an internal validation process at the level of the sectoral ministry, but there is not as yet a feedback mechanism to influence the review of the sectoral policies, strategies and budget allocations and the development of indicators.

The reasons for this limited response have to do a large extent to do with the iterative, experimental and pragmatic character of the PFM reforms. When they were introduced in the wake of accelerated economic liberalisation, the economic and social plan was not renewed, despite the then OBL enshrining it as the framework for budget allocation. The reform started at the input budgeting end and focused also on Level 3 types of reform to increase transparency, streamline the spending circuit, develop an integrated financial management system and to increase efficiency as measured by the time it takes to complete a transaction.

The World Bank's Implementation Completion and Results Report (ICRR) of the PARAP IV, the Public Administration Reform Programme supporting the PFM reform, covered all three levels of PFM outcomes (World Bank 2011). In its review, the ICR acknowledges that there had not been a strategic plan for the PFM reform. It had started at the level of inputs regrouped within a "paragraph" at the activity or sub-output level, which is not strategic for a results-based approach aligned to policy priorities and delineated in terms of the outputs needed to achieve them and the actions and measures to produce the outputs. This process was not started until 2009; but then, introduction of the Medium-Term Expenditure Framework (MTEF) was at the sectoral level without integration into a general MTEF which is linked to the real intersectoral prioritisation of allocation of resources. The report indicated that there were a number of public policies, which have not been developed in a strategic manner; the reform could have been carried out with broader participation to avoid building up resistance to it, the reform process showed signs of fatigue that could only be revitalised with the forthcoming new OBL which would enshrine results-based budgeting, and last but not least, the gender dimension had not been integrated in the reform process, but in the sectoral policies.

The ICRR goes a long way to help map out the disconnect and dissonance between the GRB approach and the PFM reform methodology. But there are even more ways in which it did not provide the right incentives for GRB and worked in opposite directions: The concept of performance does not make sense outside of a strategic results framework to measure it; the PARAP focused on results in terms of allocations, activities and outputs and not in terms of linking to development results and outcomes. In successive PARAPs, the MEF and sectoral ministries were locked into meeting the prior actions and trigger indicators of GBS for the reform, as in the case of Mauritius. The focus was on quantitative indicators, not the quality of their content: the numbers of sectoral MTEFs, percentage of credits globalised within a paragraph, production of a Guide for performance and for MTEF preparation but without indicators to track its effective use. The incentives worked against quality and development effectiveness (Level 2 outcomes of PFM) leaving little space and incentives for GRB.

The yearly Gender Reports have described and analysed in detail this situation and also proposed gender-responsive and more composite indicators. They displayed an understanding of the articulating and more precisely of the aligning of budgets to policy which has proved so intractable with mainstream expenditure.

The GRB in Morocco did not make sufficient headway because it was in fact far in advance of the mainstream, which is yet to be prepared for such a cross-cutting results-oriented innovative approach. Now that the new OBL of 2015 enshrines GRB in the preparation and monitoring of budgets, there is scope to deploy GRB using human rights standards as flagged since an international GRB conference in Marrakech in 2012. It will take a huge investment in capacities including the political will and leadership. The launch of a GRB Centre of Excellence could provide an integrative and innovative platform for such a long-term exercise.

Conclusions

GRB has been credited for uncovering the paltry and insufficient sums allocated to ministries with gender-equality mandates. But it also provides a rich, varied seam of knowledge about how fiscal consolidation together with the drive to prioritise state support to trade and economic liberalisation, promote competitiveness, business and investment facilitation, can work to weaken state institutions: It blunts the capacity of MDAs as duty bearers to fulfil their mandates effectively, and exercise their powers of regulation, policy and spending review, implementation, monitoring and enforcement, let alone be able to engage in ex ante and ex post impact assessment in support of gender equality and other sustainable development goals. Their effectiveness has been undermined and capacities eroded.

Were macroeconomic policy upstream to become more geared to target full employment, support sustainable development goals and promote human rights, they would place demands on the administration that it would be difficult be able to respond to and leverage the finance made available. The failed attempts up to now to engage in PFM effectively are a stark indicator of the state of affairs. Rights-holders—women rights and gender-equality advocates both within and outside government—have been in the forefront of keeping the chequered trajectories of GRB initiatives on course. They face increasingly organised forces hostile to their agenda, such as violent extremisms on the one hand, and bureaucratic inertia on the other, without adequate resources. The Level 2 PFM outcomes, which can translate global commitment and standards to advance women's rights and gender equality, have buckled. It is a serious challenge to being able to implement the Global 2030 Agenda. They have been squeezed under the rigid application of fiscal austerity and consolidation, in tandem with the orienting of budgetary resources to promote economic liberalisation on the one hand and the more nuanced and accommodating treatment of political economy considerations on the other hand in regard to reaching Level 3 outcomes.

Progressing along the three GRB goals will be shaped by the capacity to reconfigure the international and domestic financial architecture as well as prise open democratic, policy and fiscal space to do so. Of the three sets of actors, it is perhaps the role of Parliaments that need to be strengthened substantially, given their formal mandates and the leverage they can exert on the executive arm of Government, as the case of Uganda, for instance, shows. Such a process of democratic reform, again propelled by civil society advocacy and activism, is under way, albeit timidly. Understanding the context more deeply is a prerequisite for GRBIs. It will be yet another milestone to the quest for enduring pathways of GRB learning, innovation and achievements on the African continent in Africa and across the rest of the world.

Notes

1. Tanzania and Uganda were two of the countries in a multinational study of GRB for the African Development Bank during 2009–2010, which included Ghana and Mauritius, which the author conducted.
2. http://data.worldbank.org/about/country-and-lending-groups#Sub_Saharan_Africa, accessed 2 May 2015. The data set has been used as the groupings constructed are used by countries for benchmarking economic performance. Economic growth and reaching higher groupings often dominate the discourse in Ministries of Finance and the environment which GRB attempts to break into.
3. See de Renzio and Simson (2013), regarding the state of budget transparency in Africa based on 2012 data from the Open Budget Index : they are Angola, Botswana, Burkina Faso, Liberia, Mozambique, Namibia, Nigeria, Rwanda, Sierra Leone, South Africa and Uganda; the last two are the two top countries in Africa with user-friendly budget structures, presented by sector, agency and programme. The ODI, IBP and the Collaborative Africa Budget Reform Initiative (CABRI) have come together to improve access to clear, accessible and useful budget information in Africa.
4. http://hdr.undp.org/en/content/table-4-gender-inequality-index, Human Development Report, 2014.
5. The sub-components reflect achievements in reproductive health, empowerment and the labour market.
6. Benin, Botswana, Burkina Faso, Burundi, Cape Verde, Central African Republic, Chad, Djibouti, Eritrea, Gabon, Gambia, Ghana, Guinea Bissau, Ivory Coast, Kenya, Lesotho, Madagascar, Malawi, Mali, Mozambique, Namibia, Niger, Rwanda, Senegal, Sierra Leone, Sudan, Tanzania, Uganda and Zambia.
7. See Norton and Elson's analysis to inform GRB strategy, from a rights framework, and their detailed treatment of PFM and its entry points for gender budgeting. In the mainstream literature and practice, Political economy analysis (PEA) has gained traction in the mainstream since the seminal Drivers of Change Programme of the Department for International Development (DFID) in the UK, to attempt to analyse the disconnect between technical design and actual implementation processes, to uncover formal and informal institutions, such as in the budget process and PFM reform. Since the systemic global crises, it has been part of the analysis of IFFs, given the surge in interest in domestic resource mobilisation and global inequality patterns. PEA is relatively gender blind. See Browne (2014).
8. This Charter was drawn up through an extensive participatory process, by the Women National Coalition in 1994, composed of parliamentarians of the first democratically elected government of post-Apartheid South Africa

and women's groups and civil society organisations, based on a new Constitution affirming socio-economic rights and the role of Parliament in the legislative and budget authorisation process.

9. The material for this case study is based on the unpublished background paper of the author, commissioned by the African Development Bank in 2009.
10. http://www.tgnp.org/.
11. The Uganda Debt Network is a coalition of civil society groups, teams of researchers and community members, who originally came together to campaign for debt relief and which now coordinates the monitoring of the Poverty Action Fund, together with the Policy Monitoring and Analysis Unit (PMAU) of the Ministry of Finance.
12. See de Renzio and Simson (2013) about the notion of opaque transparency.
13. See also Wergin (2012).
14. The author as a Mauritian national and resident daily tracks newspaper reports that it would be fastidious to reference in this chapter.
15. The European Union estimates that the budget for the Gender equality Action Plan was about 0.05 % of the 2011 GDP and about 0.2 % of the general budget, excluding debt. The European Union contributes 17 %, the rest to be financed by the general budget.

References

African Development Bank (AfDB), 2009, *Uganda Country Assistance Evaluation, 2001-2007; Joint IEGWB/OPEV Country Assistance Evaluation* (Abidjan: African Development Bank).

African Peer Review Mechanism. (2010). *Republic of Mauritius*, Country review report No 13.

Bakker, Isabella. 2002. "Fiscal Policy, Accountability and Voice: The Example of Gender Responsive Budget Initiatives", Human Development Report Office Occasional Paper. New York: UNDP.

Browne, E. (2014). *Gender in political economy analysis.* Helpdesk research report 1071. Birmingham: GSDRC. http://www.gsdrc.org/go/display&type=Helpdesk&id=1071

Budlender, D. (2000, July). The political economy of women's budgets in the south. *World Development, 28*(7). Special Gender Issue.

Budlender, D. (2002). A global assessment of gender responsive budget initiatives. In *gender budgets make more cents: Country studies and good practice* (pp. 83–164). London: Commonwealth Secretariat.

Budlender, D. (2004). *Budgeting to fulfill international gender and human rights commitments, UNIFEM regional office for Southern Africa and Indian Ocean states.* Harare: UNIFEM.

Budlender, D. (2005). *Expectations versus realities in gender-responsive budget initiatives.* Cape Town: UNRISD. Available at: http://www.unrisd.org/80256B3C005BCCF9/(httpAuxPages)/0D98E65D9D993D4AC1257013005440D 1/$file/dbudlende.pdf

Budlender, D. (2011). *The care economy in Tanzania.* Tanzania Gender Networking Programme: Dar es Salaam.

Burn, N. (2008). *Integrating gender responsive budgeting into the aid effectiveness agenda: Morocco Country Report.* European Commission, UNIFEM and ILO International Training Centre. New York: UNIFEM.

Byanyima, W. (2003). *Politics, good governance and gender: Gender budgeting experiences in three African countries.* Paper presented at the Fifth global forum on re-inventing government: Innovation and quality in the government of the 21st century, Mexico City.

Cagatay, N., Keklik M., Lal, R., & Lang, J. (2000). *Budgets as if people mattered: Democratising macroeconomic policies.* SEPED conference paper Nr 4. http://www.in.undp.org/content/dam/india/docs/budgets_people_mattered_democratizing_macroeconomic_policies.pdf

Combaz, E. (2013). *Positive impact of gender-responsive budgeting* (GSDRC helpdesk research report 977). Birmingham: GSDRC, University of Birmingham.

Commonwealth Secretariat. (2002). *Gender-responsive budgets: A review of commonwealth experiences paper by Guy Hewitt, Gender Section, Social Transformation Programmes Division FMM(02)1.* London: Commonwealth Secretariat.

De Renzio, P., & Simson, R. (2013). *Transparency for what? The usefulness of publicly available budget information in African countries.* Report, Overseas Development Institute (ODI) and International Budget Partnership (IBP). London: ODI.

Elson, D. (1996, November). *Integrating gender issues into national budgetary policies and procedures within the context of economic reform: Some policy options.* Paper for fifth meeting of Commonwealth Ministers Responsible for Women's Affairs, Trinidad.

Elson, D. (2004). *Gender equality, public finance and globalization.* Paper for conference on egalitarian development in the era of globalization in honor of professor Keith Griffin, University of Massachusetts Amherst. http://www.peri.umass.edu/fileadmin/pdf/conference_papers/Elson_paper_Griffin_Conference.pdf. Accessed 26 Feb 2015

Elson, D. (2006). *Budgeting for women's rights: Monitoring government budgets for compliance with CEDAW.* New York: UNIFEM.

Elson, D., & Cagatay, N. (2000). The social content of macroeconomic policies. *World Development, 28*(7), 1347–1364.

Elson, D., & Sharp, R. (2010). Gender -responsive budgeting and women's poverty. In S. Chant (Ed.), *International handbook of gender and poverty: Concepts, research, policy.* Cheltenham: Edward Elgar Publishing Ltd.

FEMNET. (2015). *Africa civil society Beijing+ 20 shadow report.* African Women's Development and Communication Network, on behalf of CSO Taskforce on Beijing+20 and NGO/CSW Africa.

Goetz, A.-M., & Hassim, S. (2003). *No shortcuts to power, African women in politics and policy making.* London: ZED Books.

Govender, P. (2002). Lessons from practice: The role of parliament in South Africa's Women Budget. In United Nations Development Fund (UNIFEM) (Ed.), *Gender budget initiatives, strategies, concepts and experiences.* New York: UNIFEM.

Grown, C., Bahadur, C., Handbury, J., & Elson, D. (2006). *The financial requirements of achieving Gender equality and women's empowerment.* Paper prepared for the World Bank, Working paper No. 467, Levy Economics Institute.

Holvoet, N. (2006). *Gender Budgeting: Its usefulness in programme-based approaches to aid,* Briefing Note EC Gender Desk.

Holvoet, N. (2013). *Multiple pathways to gender-sensitive budget support in the education sector. Analysing the effectiveness of sex-disaggregated indicators in performance assessment frameworks and gender working groups in (education) budget support to Sub Saharan African countries,* WIDER working paper No 2013/105, UNU-WIDER.

Htun, M., & Weldon, S. L. (2010). When do governments promote women's rights? A framework for the comparative analysis of sex equality policy. *Perspectives in Politics, 8*(1), 207–216.

Kovsted, J., & Jacobsen H. J. (2008). *Gender-responsive budgeting in Tanzania.*

Kytola, L. (2008). *Integrating gender-responsive budgeting into the aid effectiveness agenda.* Tanzania Country Report UNIFEM and European Commission.

Lakwo, A. (2009). Making decentralization work for women in Uganda. *African studies collection* (Vol. 16). Leiden: African Studies Centre.

Mhina, E. H. (2007). *Financing for gender equality and the empowerment of women: Experiences from Tanzania.*

Norton, A., & Elson, D. (2002). *What's behind the budget? Politics, right and accountability in the budget process.* London: Overseas Development Institute.

OECD. (2010). Integrating gender equality dimensions into public financial management reforms. *Gender equality, women's empowerment, and the Paris declaration on aid effectiveness: Issues Brief 6, DAC Network on gender equality.* Organisation of Economic Cooperation and Development (OECD). http://www.oecd.org/dac/gender-development/46142807.pdf. Accessed 5 Dec 2010.

République du Sénégal. (2012). Revue Diagnostique des dépenses publiques de base dans le secteur agricole, Rapport Final. *strengthening national comprehensive public expenditure in Sub-Saharan Africa.* www.worldbank.org/afr/agper-program. Accessed 12 Dec 2013.

Rusimbi, M. (2002). Mainstreaming gender into policy, planning and budgeting in Tanzania. In K. Judd (Ed.), *Gender budget initiatives: Strategies, concepts and experiences* (pp. 119–125). New York: UNIFEM.

Sawer, M. (1996). *Femocrats and ecorats: Women's policy machinery in Australia, Canada and New Zealand.* Occasional paper 6, March 1996, United Nations Research Institute for Social Development, United Nations Development Programme.

Sharp, R. (2002). Moving forward: Multiple strategies and guiding goals in United Nations Fund for Women (UNIFEM). *Gender budget initiatives, strategies, concepts and experiences.* New York: UNIFEM.

Sharp, R. (2003). *Budgeting for equity: Gender budget initiatives within a framework of performance oriented budgeting.* New York: UNIFEM.

Ssewakiryanga, R., (2005), *The Politics of Revisiting the PEAP/PRSP in Uganda*, Presented at the International Conference on Political Dimensions of Poverty Reduction, Lusaka, Zambia.

Stotsky, J., Kolovich, L., & Kebhaj, S. (2016). Sub-Saharan Africa: A Survey of gender budgeting efforts. IMF Working Paper WP/16/152. https://www.imf.org/external/pubs/ft/wp/2016/wp16152.pdf

Sy, A. (2015). 2015: A crucial year for financing development in Africa. In *Foresight Africa: Top priorities for the continent in 2015.* The Brookings Institution, Africa growth Initiative Washington, DC: Brookings Institution. http://www.brookings.edu/~/media/Research/Files/Reports/2015/01/foresight%20africa/financing%20african%20development%20sy.pdf. Accessed 14 May 2015

Tanzarn, N. (2008). Integrating gender-responsive budgeting into the aid effectiveness agenda. Uganda Country Study. European Commission, UNIFEM and ILO International Training Centre New York: UNIFEM

Tiwambeda, A., & Kabuchu, H. (2008, March). *Gender mainstreaming performance measure for effective local government: Uganda case study.* Presented at workshop on strengthening the development results and impacts of the Paris declaration on aid effectiveness through work on gender equality, social exclusion and human rights. London.

UNDP. (2014). *Human development report 2014.*

UNECA. (2015a). *Illicit financial flows.* Report of the high level panel on illicit financial flows from Africa, commissioned by AU/ECA Conference of Ministers of Finance, Planning and Economic Development. http://www.uneca.org/iff Accessed 12 May 2015.

UNECA. (2015b). *Addis Ababa declaration on accelerating the implementation of the BFA for a transformational change for women and girls in Africa, Beijing +20.* Addis Ababa: United Nations Economic Commission for Africa.

Van de Walle, N. (2007). Meet the new boss, same as the old boss? The evolution of political clientelism in Africa. In H. Kitschelt & S. I. Wilkinson (Eds.), *Patrons, clients and policies. Patterns of democratic accountability and political competition*. Cambridge/New York: Cambridge University Press.

Wergin, C. (2012). Trumping the ethnic card: How tourism entrepreneurs on Rodrigues tackled the 2008 financial crisis. *Island Studies Journal*, *7*(1), 11–134.

World Bank. (1998). *Public expenditure management handbook*. Washington, DC: The International Bank for Reconstruction and Development/The World Bank. http://www1.worldbank.org/publicsector/pe/handbook/pem98.pdf

World Bank. (2004). *Strategic gender assessment for Tanzania*. Washington, DC: World Bank.

World Bank. (2011). *Implementation completion and results report*. Kingdom of Morocco, Second Series of Public Administration Reform Development Policy Loans (PARL III &IV), amount of €139.7 million, (USD 220 million); Social and Economic Development Group, Middle East and North Africa Region, World Bank

World Bank. (2012). *Implementation completion and results report on 4 credits in the amount of US$ 210 million equivalent to the Republic of Mauritius for a Programmatic DPL 1-2-3-4 Series Report No:1639*.

World Bank (2015) Country and lending groups 2015 http://data.worldbank.org/about/country-and-lending-groups#Sub_Saharan_Africa, accessed 2 May 2015.

World Wildlife Fund for Nature & African Development Bank (2012) Africa Ecological Footprint Report, Green Infrastructure for Africa's ecological capacity.

CHAPTER 5

GRB Initiative in Andalusia: Reconciling Gender Equality and Economic Growth Perspectives

Buenaventura Aguilera Díaz, Paula Cirujano Campano, and Alicia del Olmo Garrudo

Introduction

Gender equality is one of the cornerstones of any democratic society and is therefore one of the principles that should be taken into account to achieve social cohesion and facilitate the effective exercise of citizenship rights. While gender equality has been considered by some economic approaches as an added cost, the fact is that more and more gender equality is being seen as an investment that generates social welfare and that is favourable to economic development.

Gender equality policies have traditionally been considered a source of increasing government spending that could hinder growth and economic

B. Aguilera Díaz (✉)
Regional Government of Andalusia. Regional Ministry of Finance and Public Administration, Seville, Spain

P. Cirujano Campano (✉) • A. del Olmo Garrudo (✉)
Instituto de Estudios de la Hacienda Pública de Andalucía (ieHpa), Seville, Spain

© The Author(s) 2017

Z. Khan, N. Burn (eds.), *Financing for Gender Equality*,
DOI 10.1057/978-1-137-46101-8_5

development, and as interventions that can be postponed until "ideal" development conditions are achieved. In fact, this approach constitutes a limited vision of economic growth in the short term, framed exclusively within the consumption perspective.

However, more and more studies imply that gender equality can have a major productive role in advanced economies (Smith and Bettio 2008). This approach is built on the idea that the focus should not be solely on consumption but on investment, therefore attributing to equal opportunities policies a key role in economic growth (Nallari and Griffiths 2011). The consideration of gender equality as a productive factor is directly linked to the notion of social policies as beneficial for production and for a more efficient labour market (Pazos 2008).

In this sense, equality can be seen not as a cost but as a benefit, and can be considered a "public good", a key factor to protect and enhance. In the same way that competition is, to the market system, the essential element that explains its efficiency and promotes quality improvement and the increased productivity of all factors, gender equality is an element that brings sustainability and stimulates the system of economic relations.

Studies and research conducted by the World Economic Forum (WEF) and the International Monetary Fund (IMF) have established the positive relationship between gender equality and economic growth. When women can fully develop their potential in the labour market, significant macroeconomic benefits are obtained. On average, the European Union's GDP could be improved by nearly 30 % if women worked at the same level as men (Löfström 2009: 26). Other studies suggest that, in some regions, gender inequalities in the labour market generate losses that can be as high as 27 % of the GDP per capita (IMF 2013). Therefore, gender equality is a goal that is related to the objective of economic growth and greater welfare for citizens.

In addition to the effects that inequality produces on growth during periods of economic crisis like the one we have been experiencing since 2008, another important aspect to be analysed is the implication on public expenditure of implementing measures to reduce gender imbalances.

From a fiscal perspective, these policies have direct and indirect effects on revenues by enlarging the tax base through the increased volume of people and earned income, contributing actively to the long-term sustainability of public finances. With regard to public spending, these policies help to maintain pension programmes, and reduce others like the ones designed to compensate low incomes and supplements to pensions and the programmes designed to stimulate educational performance in the later stages of compulsory education. They also help to prevent the loss of public spending productivity due to over-education when people, and women in particular, abandon the labour market.

In this regard, it should be recalled that promoting the entry and participation of women in the labour market can have positive tax effects. This fact has been illustrated by a study conducted by the German Bundesbank and cited by Maier and Carl (2003), in which the productive efficiency of greater integration of women in the economy is proved. The study shows the positive tax effects of facilitating the return of women to the labour market after the maternity period by increasing and improving public care services for children.[1]

In conclusion, there are reasons based on empirical evidence to believe that gender equality is no longer a policy option and that it has become an essential requirement for increasing economic development, maintaining public services and generating wealth.

Gender Responsive Budgeting (GRB) as a Tool to Improve the Efficiency of Public Spending

Equality between women and men has made significant progress in the international arena over the past 30 years. The introduction of gender equality in the international political agenda and the impetus provided by governments and civil society commitments at Women's Summits have allowed the development of new strategies for equality (Sharp 2003). Among them, gender mainstreaming in political action stands out for its innovative and extensive projection in various contexts. Its immediate objective is to ensure that gender equality is a responsibility for all people and that it can be used as an indicator of the quality of public services.

GRB has been one of the first forms of gender mainstreaming, designed as a tool to analyse the different impact that the real distribution of public resources have on women and men, and to design a more equal redistribution. Since the first initiatives in Australia until now, methodologies of implementation and analytical elements have evolved greatly, although the aim of gender budgeting remains, through revenues and spending, removing the existing gender inequalities in contemporary societies.

Gender budgeting has occupied a space in the ideology of those who, in addition to seeking greater social justice, also pursue a more efficient economy that can recover and maximize the investment in people, transforming it into competitiveness and economic growth for the benefit of society as a whole.

At the same time, gender budgeting has aimed to achieve a sustainable economic development that integrates and makes the most of all the available human capital, meeting the needs and life aspirations of all citizens equally, men and women. The budget that is gendered not only integrates gender equality in the budget policy. Since all public policies are subject to a budget process, gender is placed at the heart of the planning, management and implementation of any public policy: education, health, agriculture, employment or infrastructure.

Hence, the strategic and cross-cutting character of budget and its transforming potential has made it one of the key instruments to mainstream gender in all public planning and governance that is geared towards economic growth. It has been proved that stereotyped gender roles and the gender inequalities that these cause, especially the discrimination of women in the labour market, are a burden and have a significant negative impact on economic growth and development (WB 2001; Seguino et al. 2010).

In this respect, GRB permits the prioritization and maintenance of those expenses that have a greater contribution towards a more equal society between women and men. Budgetary restraint does not have to lead to the destruction of equality policies, and indeed budgetary spending may be maintained in those programmes that have more gender impact, such as early childhood schools, protection against gender-based violence, research and equality in public universities and so on. Likewise, gender mainstreaming in statistical activities, dissemination and training activities, among others, would not necessarily mean an increase in public spending but a maximization of existing resources with a gender perspective.

Viewed in this way, gender equality is a budgetary decision criterion that promotes the efficiency of spending, directing the scarce resources towards programmes that produce better results and achievements from the point of view of social welfare and gender equality. However, it has also been observed that the degree of influence of gender equality on social spending depends on the type of expenditure and the policy to which it relates. For example, investment in providing services for the participation of women in the labour market tends to have more influence on spending than cash transfer benefits for women (Bolzendahl 2011).

At a time of limited public resources like the present, it is even more important to consider the efficiency of spending by analysing the impacts, wanted or not, of each measure. The analysis of budget actions based on gender equality criteria is fundamental to avoid externalities, which in addition to their own pernicious effect could increase inefficient spending. Gender equality should be placed increasingly at the centre of decision-making in the design of public policies, because inequalities between women and men are not only unfair but a huge waste (Morrison et al. 2007).

The implementation of gender budgeting provides greater transparency and leads to greater efficiency and effectiveness as the objectives of public policy are better defined and they are linked directly to the practical and strategic needs of men and women. Thus, the invested resources, albeit limited, contribute to reducing gender inequalities and to building a more egalitarian and fair society.

Gender Budgeting in Andalusia as a Tool for Advancing in Gender Equality

Progress towards equality between men and women has always been a constant in the objectives and policies of the Andalusian Regional government. Andalusia is undoubtedly a pioneer in the implementation of gender equality policies as it has continuously promoted them since the 1980s. In this respect, the Andalusian government has incorporated innovative work proposals echoing the developments and commitments on equality between men and women that have taken place in the international arena.

Specifically since 2008, the Andalusian government has developed gender mainstreaming in management, public policy and the regional budget, incorporated explicitly and as a priority among the fundamental political commitments expressed by their presidents.

The introduction of gender mainstreaming in Andalusia was facilitated by the horizontal nature of the public budget under the responsibility of the Regional Ministry of Finance. Through the creation of an effective and progressive legal framework and the design of a procedure carried out in specific phases of the budgetary cycle, the gender perspective has been systematically integrated into each public policy.

Gender mainstreaming in the budget responds not only to a search for advancing the rights of citizenship but also to a logic of effectiveness and economic efficiency. A gender responsible budget promotes the creation of a virtuous circle in which the policy itself facilitates the reduction of gender inequality (Budlender et al. 2002).

The public budget is the structure around which political priorities are set, and therefore it has sufficient capacity to steer public actions towards gender equality. In addition, the budget may decisively influence the adoption of a new organizational culture and changing procedures and work routines, which is essential to achieve the goal of equality.

In this regard, the enactment of various laws has been instrumental in laying the foundations for gender budgeting. On such is Law 18/2003, of 29 December, on the fiscal and administrative measures of the Autonomous Community of Andalusia. This law establishes a mandatory Gender Impact Report of all bills and regulations adopted by the Governing Council (Martinez Aguayo 2007). Also, in order to ensure that the budget of the Autonomous Community is an active element to this end, the law creates the Gender Budget Impact Commission, dependent of the ministry responsible for finance and with the participation of the Andalusian Institute for Women, which will issue the gender impact report on the draft budget law. This commission will promote the preparation of bills with a gender perspective in the various ministries and carry out gender audits in ministries, companies and agencies of the Government of Andalusia.

Another is Organic Law 2/2007, of 19 March, reforming Andalusia's Statute of Autonomy, which defines the effective equality between men and women as one of the basic goals of the autonomous community and, in terms of public spending, determines the equitable allocation of the available funds to meet the needs to be covered, bearing in mind the principles of economic stability, efficiency and economy governing budget planning and implementation.

For this purpose, a specific organizational structure, the aforementioned Gender Budget Impact Commission, is created, as a cornerstone of the structure of this model that provides the most accurate knowledge and ensures both the coordination and dissemination of the programme to all the bodies and departments involved.

This commission consists of two members (a woman and a man) from each regional ministry and two people from two autonomous entities, the Andalusian Women's Institute and the Institute of Statistics and Cartography of Andalusia, both strategic and technically essential to the gender budgeting process. The Women's Institute, which depends on the Ministry of Equality and Social Welfare, is the entity which sets the gender equality goals in the Andalusian policy (Aguilera and Cirujano 2011). The Statistics Institute is the body responsible for developing the statistical data required to analyse the reality with a gender perspective and to have disaggregated data by sex.

The chair and vice chair of this commission hold high-level positions within the Ministry for Finance. Within this commission, the annual gender impact report of the budget (which is detailed below) is approved and the steps to be taken to move forward in the process of implementing the GRB strategy are discussed and decided. In addition, the two members from each ministry disseminate the work in their centres as they all have budgetary and technical responsibility at the highest level.

The Gender Impact Report of the Budget is the synthesis document that discusses the impact that the investment of public resources will have on Andalusian men and women for the coming year. It is an *ex ante* evaluation of credits allocated to the policy measures that are designed to correct gender inequalities.

After ten editions,[2] the report has become an essential assessment document and it also serves a monitoring purpose in an environment of great public exposure due to the time in which budget preparation and publication occur. Currently, from an instrumental point of view, the report is a pedagogical tool for managing centres since systematizing the budget information provides a basis for measuring progress in gender mainstreaming in various policies and its translation into the budget. The progress made in the various ministries' diagnosis of the potential impact that decisions on resource use can have on gender citizenship is also reflected in the report. Thus, areas such as urban planning and the environment, which traditionally have been considered neutral from a gender point of view in light of the level of responsibility conferred on the Andalusian government, now show significant progress in this regard.

Regarding the structure of the report, it begins with an introductory chapter in which the major milestones of the implementation of the gender budget strategy in the previous year are described. Next, the information is structured around a scheme called the 3-R/3T model, inspired by a Swedish working methodology,[3] which serves as a general analytical framework for implementing gender mainstreaming in the annual budget. The logic underlying this report is, first, to provide the necessary information to the management bodies of public resources so that they can make informed decisions about a gendered reality. This helps to avoid the idea of the apparent neutrality of policies or use of stereotypes about the real and strategic needs of women and men. Second, based on facts and data, the report offers a preliminary analysis of the impact that these measures and their associated budgetary resources will have on citizenship (Martínez Aguayo 2008).

The three main elements around which the document is organized are Reality, Representation and Resources-Results, which, as mentioned above, are analysed in parallel with three temporal dimensions (3 T), past, present and future.

First, the report presents a gendered analysis of Reality on which budget decisions are made. This section is based on collaborative work between the ministries and the centre responsible for the collection and processing of statistical data, the Institute of Statistics and Cartography of Andalusia (IEA). The data are selected because of their relevance in the area of competence of each ministry but also seeking consistency with the indicators used internationally to measure gender inequalities, especially in the framework of the European Union and United Nations. Each year new indicators are added in order to provide information on areas of competence that have been less addressed, at least in Andalusia, from a gender point of view.

The second R, meaning Representation, is a chapter that describes the gender breakdown of the decision-making and management positions for each policy area of the Andalusian government, comprising more than 250,000 people. Intra-organizational analysis constitutes an important aspect of gender mainstreaming because it demonstrates the extent to which the institution is sensitive to gender equality in the recruitment, promotion and working conditions of its staff, and whether it is able to leverage improvements in productivity, effectiveness and efficiency associated with gender diversity throughout the years.

The information about staff is obtained from the exploitation of internal sources and refers to the current situation. In the 2015 Budget Report, all personnel groups are included in the analysis: general administration staff, teachers, health workers, law enforcement personnel and managers of public enterprises.

The third and last major section of the report is called Resources-Results and includes several key elements for analysing the budget potentialities for reducing gender inequalities in the future. The trends in the allocation of credits are analysed in light of the G+ classification of the budgetary programmes, as described below.

Next, each of the ministries offers a gender diagnosis (micro) in its field and analyses the impact that the measures contained in the budgetary programmes will have on its equality policy goals, using a set of budgetary gender indicators. In this respect, improving the quality of gender indicator beyond the mandatory disaggregation by sex is recommended. Despite these efforts, incidents still occur as a result of the deletion, substitution or rotation of budgetary indicators due to changing functional and organizational structures as well as their special political nature. Avoiding interruptions in the temporal series is a major challenge for any administration that wants to have consistent and reliable data on trends.

Lastly, the gender impact report of the budget has become an indispensable tool for the budget itself, not only because of the learning and analysis generated throughout the process but also because it serves as the reference document for managers for rest of the financial year.

Having established the rules of the commission and the Gender Impact Report, the application of G + Programme commenced in 2008. Its main aim is to facilitate the achievement of planning, management and budgetary assessment taking into account the needs and interests of both men and women and focusing efforts on those budgetary programmes with greater responsibility and ability to make progress in gender equality. It also aims to achieve the necessary cultural change in the organization and to provide the personnel with useful tools for both the analysis of the reality and the planning of actions.

Furthermore, the G+ Programme has a series of specific goals that have steered the successive phases and actions undertaken. The most notable ones are:

(1) To bring about a cultural change in the organization so that it has the capacity to introduce the gender dimension in all of its actions.
(2) To define tools and methodologies for analysing the reality affected by the budget programmes.
(3) To create simple strategies for determining the gender impact of budget programmes.
(4) To use an effective methodology that facilitates the introduction of the gender perspective in routine management activities.

The G+ Programme comprises three stages: identifying and classifying programmes according to the G+ Scale; creating the Strategic Orientation Documents (known as DOE G+, after their initials in Spanish) and fulfilling the commitments defined in them; and monitoring and evaluating the results. From the implementation point of view, the first stage focused on classifying the budget programmes according to their capacity to impact on the obstacles that prevent effective equality between women and men, ruling out the purely instrumental programmes. This led to the creation of the G+ Scale, which classifies each budget programme according to a range of four possible scores (G+, G, g1 and g0 in descending order). These scores are not definitive but are reviewed annually by the Gender Budgeting Impact Commission.

In general, the classification of budget programmes on the G+ Scale is governed by the criteria of pertinence and relevance. Gender pertinence divides budget programmes into those that have an effect on people and those with no effect on people. Additionally, programmes that are regarded as pertinent have a high, medium or low gender relevance, based on specific criteria. One, the programme's capacity of impact, defined according to the number of people affected by the actions undertaken; two, its functional relevance, which refers to whether the programme's sphere of action is regarded as a "lever of change" for gender equality; and three, the transformative capacity of the actions carried out and their relevance for gender equality. Once the programmes have been classified and rated according to the scale, they are linked to a series of steps and stages to be completed in order to gradually incorporate the gender perspective.

Having established the pertinence and relevance of each budget programme, the necessary foundations are laid to permit the introduction of the long-term G+ strategy in all the centres involved. This means linking the G+ score obtained by every budget programme to the contents and scope of the actions to be undertaken. In other words, depending on the score obtained, each managing centre defines the commitments it needs to undertake in order to ensure that the gender perspective is included in its budget programme.

Thanks to the classification methodology created in Andalusia, we are able to assess the allocation of budget items according to their effect on gender equality. Thus, of all the budget programmes for 2015, approximately 35.7% are classified as G+, 33.3% as G, 23.1% as g1 and 7.9% as g0. The priority accorded to the gender perspective within the Andalusian government is also reflected in the structure of the budget when measured with the G+ scale, because 73.3% of the budget is allocated to G+ programmes and 19.7% to G programmes, while g1 and g0 programmes receive 5.9% and 1.1% of the budget, respectively.

This task of adopting a series of commitments based on the score granted to each programme is performed by creating a Strategic Orientation

Document (DOE G+) for each managing centre. The DOE G+ is a methodological document whose purpose is to encourage the commitment of the staff directly involved in designing, managing and assessing budgetary policy in line with gender equality. The DOE is the basic gender strategy planning tool used within the framework of the G+ Programme and will continue to steer gender mainstreaming in the budget process during the next years. Because of this process, nearly every single budget programme now has a DOE G+ thanks to the efforts of the managing centres in creating it and their pledge to improve equality.

Once the managing centres designs the DOE G+, the next phase is to support capacities and provide advice on the gender mainstreaming process. This is also accompanied by the dissemination of the methodologies and materials for implementing the different applications required by each managing centre and sphere of action in order to incorporate the gender perspective. The training actions provided for public administration staff have played a crucial complementary role in supporting the strategy and turning it into a process. Between 2010 and 2014, 7444 people (59% women and 41% men) attended more than 90 courses on gender and the public budget, gender responsive budgeting in the Andalusian government and the methodologies designed to implement this practice and obtain results in the region's finances.

This same line of action also gave rise to the G+ Fund in 2010 as a tool to further encourage the practice of gender responsive budgeting in the Andalusian government. The G+ Fund offers financial incentives for the development of innovative projects to introduce the gender perspective in the budgets managed by the different regional ministries in Andalusia. Twenty-two projects were approved with an overall investment of 845,652 euros: 72% of the funds were allocated to 15 projects to carry out gender surveys and diagnoses, while the remaining 28% was used to promote training actions on gender equality in the sphere of action of each respective department.

The G+ Programme has therefore managed to introduce new routines and procedures for drawing up budgets that take into account gender equality by improving the budgetary tools and creating a method for evaluating how budget items are allocated according to their effect on gender equality. Furthermore, in the field of administrative activity and management, there have been significant advances in creating tools to manage spending on subsidies and public procurement, and in women's participation in areas of greater responsibility and decision-making. Different public policies in the fields of education, employment, actions overseas, trade, sport, innovation and culture have introduced gender equality criteria in their rules and regulations for awarding subsidies and tenders.

The Andalusian GRB initiative is also supported by research, dissemination and the creation of networks for sharing experiences and engaging in collaborative projects. One important example of this is the organization of the Economy and GRB Conferences, coordinated by the Regional Ministry of Finance, whose purpose is to further examine the importance of using the public budget to reinforce the commitment to equality between men and women, especially in times of economic crisis. With regard to research, sharing experiences and creating networking opportunities, the Andalusian strategy is a member of the European Gender Budgeting Network, which includes prestigious academic experts, consultancies and public administrations.

There has been significant interest in the technical advice on gender budgeting provided to the various regional ministries, training platforms and other educational modules on the same theme developed by the Regional Ministry of Finance. Meanwhile, the systematization of educational materials and the creation of a gender responsive budgeting space in the social media have helped to raise awareness about the process carried out in Andalusia among institutions and experts in other countries as well as international organizations. Furthermore, since the Andalusian experience has inspired numerous national and international experiences, the Andalusian government has received various requests for advice and invitations to participate in international events, forums and networks. For example, technical assistance to the government of Chile and Korea was given. In addition, in 2010 the United Nations Development Fund for Women (UNIFEM) and the Andalusian government collaborated in the GRB projects of several Balkan states (Macedonia, Bosnia-Herzegovina, Serbia), and in June 2014 a delegation of the Albanian government visited Seville. Lastly, the social media that the programme and strategy have created as a window for communicating with the reality on the ground and with specialists and others interested in this field are constantly updated and the number of followers has grown.

The usefulness of the Andalusian GRB strategy has not only been recognized nationally and internationally but is very highly rated by the staff of the Andalusian government. According to a 2011 survey conducted among senior staff with decision-making powers, 73.2 % believe that the GRB strategy is useful and 75.7% believe that the budget is an efficient tool for addressing gender inequalities from a comprehensive point of view. This is one of the most important indicators regarding the effectiveness of the change that is currently taking place across the entire Andalusian government in relation to the introduction of gender mainstreaming.

Gender Budget Audits

Evaluation has been planned from the outset in the Andalusian gender budgeting initiative, based on the firm belief that assessment is part of the cycle of public policy and is crucial to measuring its efficiency and effectiveness. Gender audits, contemplated in Law 18/2003 of 29 December (approving the fiscal and administrative measures of the Autonomous Community of Andalusia for 2004), are a tool for assessing the effectiveness and degree of gender budgeting institutionalization and mainstreaming.

Gender Budget Audits have four objectives. The first is to assess the fulfilment of objectives assigned to the budgetary programmes under the G+ classification. The second is to analyse and measure the integration of gender analysis in the design, implementation and accountability budget process. Third, they evaluate the strategies developed by managing centres to implement the methodology and achieve the desired results. Finally, they identify good practices and offer recommendations in order to give a new impetus to gender budgeting in Andalusia.

The process consists of three phases: planning and preparation, implementation and monitoring. The first phase, completed in 2013, comprised the programme selection and design of an agenda of audit programmes.

During the second phase of implementation, carried out during 2014, the personnel of budget programmes and the staff of the auditing department held workshops and produced reports based on criteria and a predefined structure, which after joint review were finally approved by the Gender Impact Commission (CIG). This commission is responsible for promoting gender audits in Andalusian regional ministries and government entities each year.

Therefore, in the monitoring and review phase, the managing centres in charge of the budgetary programmes receive audit reports with recommendations. Based on these documents, they are responsible for reviewing and developing a new Strategic Guidance Document (DOE G+) in gender budgeting. The DOE G + is the aforementioned strategic planning tool which will guide gender mainstreaming in the budget for the next four years.

During this same stage, the government's performance in the field of gender budgeting is presented outside the government. For this purpose, a public information period is established in order to promote the participation of citizens specialized in public finance and gender equality and to collect contributions for each budget programme. All this will contribute to more transparent governance, closer to citizens, as well as improving the quality of the public services offered by the Andalusian government.

A profound analysis of the audit results reveals that gender budgeting improved during the audit period 2009–2012. Both fulfilment of strategic commitments (DOEG +) and budget integration and the identification of best practices for integrating gender budgeting exceed half of the expected compliance (Fig. 5.1).

Within the fulfilment of the commitments made in the DOE.G+, certain elements have experienced more significant progress, since four of the five programmes have adapted the existing sources of information to

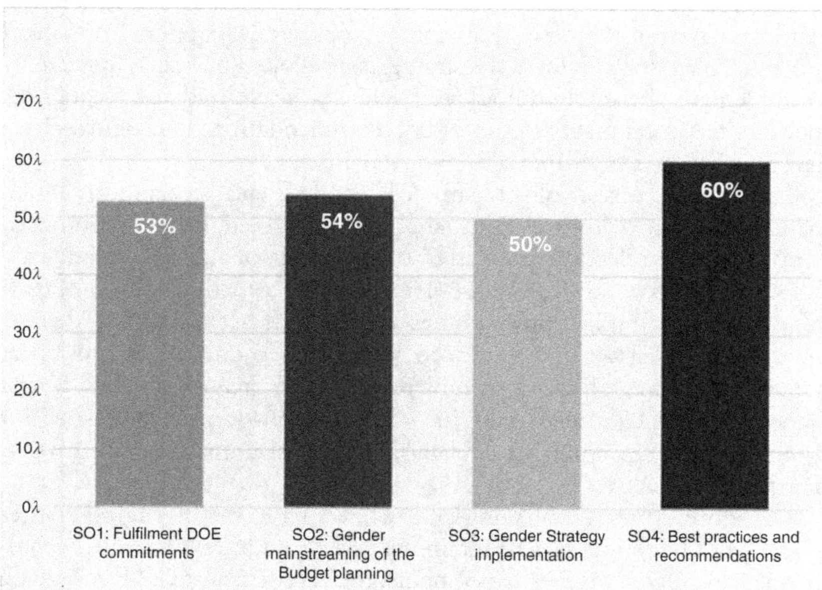

Fig. 5.1 Implementation of the GRB strategy, 2009–2012

create disaggregation by sex and provide data suitable for analysing equality. The same percentage of programmes have delivered training in gender to improve staff abilities to mainstream gender in public policy. However, only one of the programmes has performed a gender diagnosis, necessary to understand the reality of men and women in Andalusia, and there are three programmes that have obtained an average score in the indicators used to measure progress or setbacks in gender equality.

Another result revealed by the audits is related to the integration of gender in the draft budget documentation. It is clearly necessary to continue improving the integration of gender analysis in the draft documents and to ensure that this integration is consistent across all documentation during the budget process.

Finally, it can be stated that although the G+ methodology works and programmes that have fulfilled their commitments are those with greater integration of gender, it is also true that there is another factor with great influence on the success of gender mainstreaming in the budget. The results of the gender budgeting audits improve when gender is at the core of the budget programme in terms of its sectorial policy and its policy guidelines.

During 2015, the efforts to forge ahead with gender budgeting audits have continued in the Andalusian government. There are several criteria for selecting new programmes. First, budgeting programmes from the same regional ministries were grouped in order to generate synergies and inertia in gender budgeting and promote the coordination of common elements in the budgetary programmes with shared themes. This facilitated decision-making and helped the relevant technical personnel to participate in meetings. Second, policy actions with a markedly strategic character for the 2015 Budget were prioritized: employment and entrepreneurship, education, health and innovation and research. Third, the selection emphasized budget programmes classified as G+ or G since they are the highest in terms of their gender relevance. Last, there was a combination of ministries and instrumental entities, as determined by law.

Conclusions

For over a decade, the Andalusian government has made significant efforts, through the implementation of a comprehensive gender budgeting strategy, to advance in the achievement of public policies that contribute to both social justice and economic growth. The significant investment of resources in a context of budget restraint has allowed the public budget to be implemented more efficiently and transparently, to help maintain the welfare of citizens and to further progress towards the equality of women and men.

This effort, which involves both senior government staff and managers of budgetary programmes, is reflected both in the abilities of administration staff and in the quality of budget planning and the budgetary documents drafted annually, as it provides greater efficiency and effectiveness to each programme.

In this respect, the Andalusian experience stands out as one of the most successful initiatives in Europe and a pioneer experience in Spain due to its capacity to generate mechanisms and techniques that integrate the gender perspective in the annual budget in a sustained way. It is, in fact, an opportunity to plan and manage policy actions with greater sensitivity to the needs of men and women, but also to apply a concept of budgetary policy that better addresses the challenges imposed by fiscal responsibility and budget discipline.

The implementation and development of the Gender Budgeting Audits in 2015 confirms that the Andalusian government remains committed to gender equality implemented through an instrument that has proved to be useful and effective and that should be further strengthened and innovated. The Andalusian government's experience in implementing gender budgeting also serves to update and consolidate the existing theory and practice on gender mainstreaming in public policies and further improve the analysis of different practices in this regard.

Finally, it can be stated that although the G+ methodology works and programmes that have fulfilled their commitments are those with greater gender mainstreaming broadly in its budget programme, it is also true that another variable is detected with great influence in the success of gender mainstreaming in the budget. The results of the audit budget and gender improve when the budget programme has had a gender axis in its sectorial policy, the policy guidelines of its scope that are not within its competence as a programme.

Notes

1. In 1999, in Germany, the estimated childcare services expenditure was 7400 million euros but the additional employment of women, associated with the integration of all mothers with at least one child between 2 and 12, who wish to return to work, was estimated to generate nearly 9000 million euros in additional taxes and 15,600 million euros in additional contributions. The results were unaffected by spending on child care, as even with an

increase of 100 % on such spending, the fiscal impact would remain positive, while generating sufficient employment. In this potential scenario, both revenues could be increased, those addressed directly to the state and those aimed at sustaining social security.

2. The first Gender Impact Report published corresponds to the Budget for 2006.
3. The model of the 3-R is created in the 1990s within the Swedish Association of Local Authorities in order to implement gender mainstreaming in municipalities. Subsequently, it has become one of the methodologies used by administrations at different levels in the Nordic countries.

References

Aguilera, B., & Cirujano, P. (2011). Género, Presupuesto y Políticas Públicas: Una alianza estratégica para la igualdad. In O. Marcenado (Ed.), *La cambiante situación de la mujer en Andalucía*. Sevilla: Fundación Centro de Estudios Andaluces.

Aguilera, B., Del Olmo, A., & Escobar, A. I. (2011). La experiencia de presupuestación con perspectiva de género en la Junta de Andalucía: análisis de las diferentes fases del proceso. *Presupuesto y gasto público, 64*, 59–80.

Bolzendahl, C. (2011). Beyond the big picture: Gender influences on disaggregated and domain-specific measures of social spending, 1980–1999. *Politics and Gender, 7*, 35–70.

Budlender, D., Elson, D., Hewitt, G. & Mukhopadhyay, T. (eds.) (2002). *Gender budgets Make Cents: Understanding Gender Responsive Budgets*, Commonwealth Secretariat, London.

Löfström, A. (2009). *Gender equality, economic growth and employment.*

Lozano, A., Aguilera, B., & García de Bustos, F. (2008). Hacia un presupuesto orientado a resultados en Andalucía: la perspectiva de género como objetivo y oportunidad. *Presupuesto y gasto público, 51*, 361–382.

Maier and Carl (2003). *The Costs of Non-Equality: German report.* European Expert Group on Gender and Employment Report to the Equal Opportunities Unit, DG Employment.

Martínez Aguayo, C. (2007). Aplicación del enfoque de género en los presupuestos públicos de Andalucía. *Nuevas políticas públicas: anuario multidisciplinar para la modernización de las Administraciones Públicas, 3*, 19–35.

Martínez Aguayo, C. (2008). Presupuestos sensibles al género: la experiencia de la Comunidad Autónoma de Andalucía. In O. Alonso-Villar (dir.), *Economía e igualdad de género: retos de la Hacienda Pública en el siglo XXI.* Madrid: Instituto de Estudios Fiscales.

Morrison, A.; Raju, D. and Sinha, N. (2007). *Gender equality, poverty and economic growth.* Policy Research working paper; no. WPS 4349. Washington, DC: World Bank.

Nallari, R., & Griffith, B. (2011). *Gender and macroeconomic policy.* Washington, D.C.: The World Bank.
Pazos, M. (2008). Género, orientación del presupuesto público y eficiencia económica. In en Pazos (dir.), *Economía e igualdad de género: retos de la hacienda pública en el siglo XXI.* Madrid: Instituto de Estudios Fiscales.
Seguino, S., Berik, G., & Rodgers, Y. (2010). *An investment that pays off. Promoting gender equality as a means to finance development.* Berlin: Friedrich-Ebert-Stiftung-Department for Global Policy and Development.
Sharp, R. (2003). *Budgeting for equity. Gender budget initiatives within a framework of performance oriented budgeting.* New York: United Nations Development Fund for Women.
Smith, M. and Bettio, F. (2008). *Analysis Note: the Economic Case for Gender Equality.* European Commission's Network of Experts on Employment and Gender Equality issues. Fondazione Giacomo Brodolin.
World Bank. (2001). *Engendering development: Through gender equality in rights, resources, and voice.* New York: Oxford University Press and The World Bank.

CHAPTER 6

Gender-Responsive Budgeting in Latin America: Regional Learning to Advance Financing for Gender Equality

Lorena Barba and Raquel Coello

Introduction

Following international trends over the past 15 years, Latin America saw an emerging and increasing number of Gender-Responsive Budget Initiatives (GRBIs). These experiences were driven by a great diversity of actors ranging from governmental institutions, to civil society organizations or academic centres, as well as different partnerships among them, both at national and local levels. GRBIs are undertaken in diverse contexts. Each one has its own political configuration as well as its own history and lived reality. They differ in their strategic priorities that are operationalized within different planning and budgetary systems. However, as has happened in other parts of the world, it is possible to identify a learning process that spanned initial gender budget analysis carried out since the late 1990s to

L. Barba (✉)
Programme Specialist, UN Women Ecuador, Quito, Ecuador

R. Coello (✉)
Associate Researcher, Complutense Institute for International Studies (ICEI), Madrid, Spain

© The Author(s) 2017

Z. Khan, N. Burn (eds.), *Financing for Gender Equality*,
DOI 10.1057/978-1-137-46101-8_6

effective and real changes in budget processes in the pursuit of institutionalizing GRB. Institutionalizing GRB means the process by which modifications and improvements are introduced to existing planning and budgeting systems and organizational processes to promote a more gender-responsive content and outcomes of policies and public budgets (Alami 2008). Taking these achievements further poses the challenge to transform such changes into real budget allocations and moreover into improvement in terms of gender equality and women's empowerment (Coello and Wretblad 2012) (See Fig. 6.1). In this regard, GRB has proved to be a cumulative process, where it is important to ensure solid and sustainable bases in the first steps to generate the pre-conditions for further accomplishments.

In order to gain some insights about such learning processes in Latin America, the authors of this chapter undertook a study of a selected group of GRB experiences aiming at capturing common elements within the two intermediate elements of the chain: changes in the budget processes and in the funds allocated for gender equality. The study was grounded on the hypothesis that, despite the great diversity that characterizes GRBIs, it was possible to identify certain patterns followed in the process of institutionalization that finally lead to improvements in terms of financing for gender equality. In this regard, the study sought to respond to two main questions: What were the key common elements that allowed to move a GRBI from an "experimental" experience to an institutional regular practice? How has such progress in terms of institutionalization finally led to improvements in financing for gender equality?

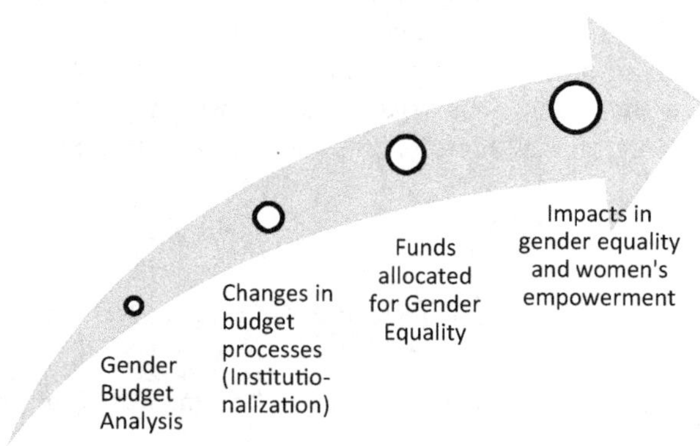

Fig. 6.1 GRB learning process (*Source*: Adapted from Coello and Wretblad (2012))

To present its main findings, the content of this chapter is organized as follows: After this introduction, the next section explains the methodology and scope of the study. The following section introduces some of the main elements of the regional context that surround the implementation of the GRBIs. Section "Selected GRBIs in Latin America: Some Features and Characteristics" describes the main features that characterized the GRB experiences included in the study while section "Highlighting Some Common Strategies" focuses on the analysis of the common strategies used by them. Section "Synthesis of Main Achievements" is then dedicated to present the synthesis of their main achievements: both in terms of GRB institutionalization and in how this resulted in effective changes in improved mechanisms for financing for gender equality. The chapter ends with a section of final conclusions.

Methodology and Scope of the Study

Rather than using an "all inclusive approach", the study opted for a selected group of experiences, focusing on those supported by UN Women from 2000 to 2013 mainly through its GRB regional programme in Latin America.[1] The reason for this was because this programme placed a particular emphasis on promoting knowledge sharing and exchange among the different experiences across the region. The study thus focused on those GRBIs that were interconnected, to be able to distil some conclusions drawn from this enabling regional learning opportunity.

However, it is important to mention that GRBIs in the region are far more numerous: a mapping exercise carried out in 2009 identified 52 different experiences present in 17 of its 18 countries (Coello 2009, p. 109). At that time, more than half of them (35 in total) were oriented to gender budget analysis, setting the bases for the learning chain. Taking this background into account is fundamental, as probably most of the results shown by the study will not be able to be explained without the bases of knowledge and engagement previously generated in the region.

The delimitation of the GRBIs included in the study was based according to its leading actor and its specific level of intervention (central, subnational or local). The study used secondary data based on an extensive desk review research of the documents produced by UN Women and the different GRB partners (UN Women 2007–2009; UN Women 2008; UN Women 2010; UN Women 2012 and UN Women 2013). Table 6.1 shows the list of the 21 GRBIs included in the study identified according to their country, location, and leading actor.

Table 6.1 GRBIs included in the study

Country	*Location*	*Leading actor*
Argentina	National	Ministry of Economy Public Finance
Argentina	Local	Municipality of Rosario and *Colectivo de Mujeres por un PSG* (Women's network for GRB)
Bolivia	National	National Roundtable on Gender Responsive Budgeting (Network of civil society organizations for GRB)
Bolivia	National	Ministry of Production
Bolivia	Subnational and Local	National Service for Autonomy (Ministry of Decentralization)
Bolivia	Subnational and Local	*Instituto Femenino de Formacion Integral*, IFFI and *Colectivo Cabildeo* (Women's NGOs)
Brazil	National	*Centro Feminista de Estudos e Assessoria,* CFEMEA (Feminist organization and research centre)
Brazil	Subnational	*Foro Estadual da Reforma Urbana de Pernambuco (FER U-PE)* (Network of Civil society organizations)
Brazil	Local	*Colectivo Leila Diniz* (Feminist organization) of the City of Natal
Brazil	Local	Special Secretariat for Public Policies for women of the Municipality of Recife (Local women's machinery)
Colombia	National	High Counselor for Women's Equality (National women's machinery)
Ecuador	National	Ministry of Finance
Ecuador	National	*Foro Permanente de la Mujer Ecuatoriana* (Women's NGOs)
Ecuador	Local	*Centro Ecuatoriano de Desarrollo y Estudios Alternativo,* CEDEAL (Women's NGO)
Honduras	National	National Institute for Women (National women's machinery)
Honduras	Local	Municipality of Santa Rosa de Copan
Nicaragua	National	Ministry of Finance and Public Credit
Peru	National	Ministry of Finance
Peru	Local	Municipality of Villa El Salvador
Uruguay	Local	Secretariat for Women of the Municipality of Montevideo (Local women's machinery)
Venezuela	National	National Institute for Women (National women's machinery)—Women's Bank, BANMUJER

Following a similar approach used in a global study (Coello and Wretblad 2012),[2] the information collected for each one of the initiatives was organized in four different types of variables:

- **Contextual variables**, describing the context in which the GRBIs took place, characterizing it by its gender-responsive normative and policy frameworks and the existence of institutional mechanisms oriented to promote gender equality.

- **Descriptive variables**, including location, maturity according to the years of implementation, key stakeholders—looking both at the leading actor and other partnerships—and budget coverage, whether income or expenditure, complete or partial budget, and number of phases covered within the budget cycle.
- **Strategy variables,** mapping the different strategies used in the GRBIs.
- **Results variables,** characterizing the results achieved by the GRBIs at two levels, following the learning process chain:

    (a) Achievements in terms of institutionalization. That is, how GRB practices were internalized in the mainstream planning and budgeting frameworks. In this regard, the study looked at five different types of institutional elements: (1) normative and legal framework; (2) programming and budgeting formats, manuals and guidelines; (3) accounting and financial systems; (4) budgetary reports; and (5) institutional areas or mechanisms.

    (b) Results achieved to improve financing for gender equality. That is, how GRB practices resulted in: (1) a reorientation of policies and programmes to better address gender gaps; (2) an increase in the amount of resources allocated for gender equality and the realization of women's rights; and/or (3) better mechanisms for transparency and accountability to know and track budgetary resources allocated for gender equality.

As the study was looking for common elements between the GRBIs, the approach was basically quantitative. That is, it focused on the number of initiatives that succeeded in achieving certain types of results, rather than on the way these results were achieved. Certainly, this entails some limitations in the kind of conclusions one can draw from the study, while at the same time leaves the field open for further research in the area.

The Latin American Context for GRBIs

The Latin American context has been particularly successful in stimulating GRB. Since the 2000s, an important number of these exercises emerged within the framework of increased legitimacy of the agenda of women's rights together with a renewed interest for the relevance of public budgets. On the one hand, economic crisis and structural adjustment policies applied in the previous decades had struck women harder, especially among the poor, notably because of the cutbacks in social spending and in the delivery of public services (Raes 2006). On the other hand, most of the countries of the region were undergoing widespread processes of state reform and decentralization, which opened up spaces for citizen's more active and direct engagement in public affairs. Laws on access to public information and the creation of civil society oversight mechanisms brought new opportunities for greater monitoring and accountability of elected officials. Local governments in particular provided a space where citizens could get more directly involved in influencing decision-making and demand transparency and accountability. Therefore, as part of the study, it was important to look at some of the main common elements of the contextual background in which the GRBIs analyzed took place.

The first variable to describe the context relates to the **international women's rights international legal framework**. In this regard, all ten countries had ratified the Convention on the Elimination of All Forms of Discrimination Against Women (CEDAW), nine of them in the 1980s and only one (Bolivia) in the 1990s (See Fig. 6.2).

The CEDAW Committee's Concluding Observations to national reports recommend all countries included in the study to increase resources allocations to national women's machineries and to guarantee the implementation of laws or plans on gender equality, eradicating gender-based violence, and to improve women's health.

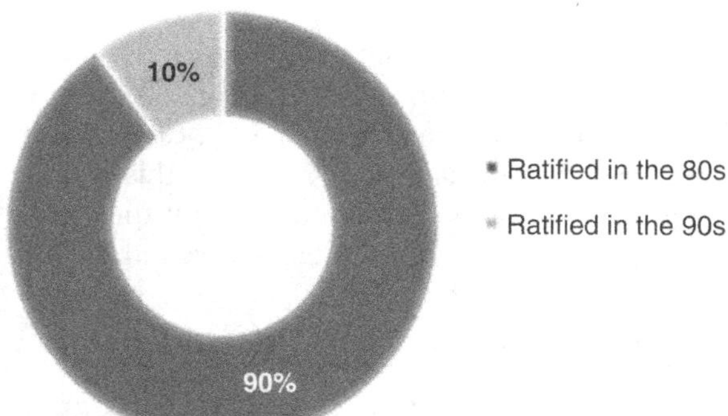

Fig. 6.2 CEDAW ratification date

Another variable related to the context refers to the **national legal framework**. In this regard, the study analyzed the way gender equality is addressed in National Constitutions dividing them in three levels: general recognition, implicit but indirect recognition and specific address to gender equality (Bohrt 2005). As shown in Fig. 6.3, six countries have Constitutions which make an explicit and specific recognition of gender equality and three of them do it implicitly. Only one barely makes a general recognition. In the case of Bolivia and Venezuela, one of the enabling factors for GRB within the Constitution is that it requires civil society participation to define national priorities, and in the case of Ecuador, the Constitution goes as far as including a specific article that requires the State to incorporate the gender perspective in plans and programmes[3]

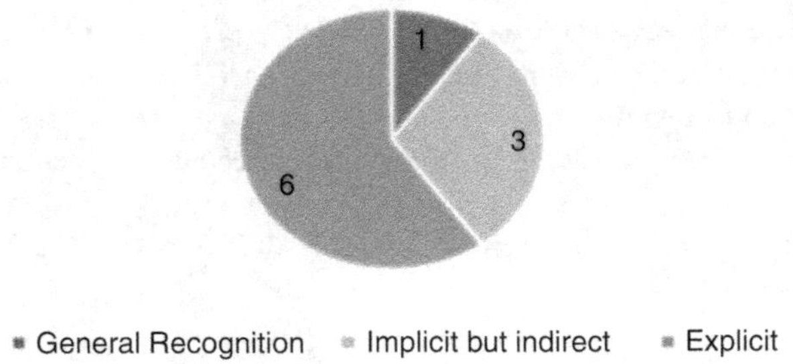

Fig. 6.3 Gender equality in national constitutions

Regarding the existence of other legislations that promote gender equality and women's rights, all ten countries have specific legislation on key issues for gender equality and women's rights (such as laws to combat violence against women or laws to promote women's political participation). Additionally, four of countries have also general laws in place to promote gender equality,[4] three of them (in Honduras, Nicaragua, and Peru) explicitly state the need to allocate resources for their implementation, calling upon the governments to advance GRB. The example of Nicaragua is described in Box 6.1.

A third contextual variable refers to the **national policy framework.** All countries included in the study have in place national policies for gender equality or specific action plans to promote women's rights.[5] All of them already include GRB as one of their components: In the case of Ecuador, Honduras, Nicaragua, Peru, Uruguay, and Venezuela, GRB is

Box 6.1: Gender Equality Laws Promoting Gender-Responsive Budgeting: The Case of Nicaragua

The "Law of Equality in rights and opportunities" (2008) of Nicaragua goes beyond principle declarations by specifying the need of investment to guarantee laws implementation.

In **Nicaragua**, the Law ***requests resource allocation to implement gender responsive public policies to all State Powers at all governmental levels*** (Art. 7) and establishes that the Executive must ***ensure to the Nicaraguan Institute for Women sufficient resources*** to accomplish its responsibilities (Art 33). The Article 15 specifies that National, Regional, and Local Budgets will ***include the gender perspective at the stages of formulation, approval, execution and evaluation***, will disaggregate resources allocated to each institution with specific activities related to the Law. The Law ***demand the Ministry of Finance and Public Credit to formulate budgetary policies*** to guarantee Law implementation and adequate resources allocation (Art. 37) and stress the ***National Assembly to approve the National Budget analysing if from the gender perspective*** guaranteeing clear identification of institutional budget items to implement the Law (Art. 44).

Source: *Law of Equality in rights and opportunities*, Nicaragua, 2008

defined as a tool to mainstream the gender perspective in the public policy cycle.

In Brazil and Colombia, GRB appears as a mechanism to improve the management of the Plan. In Bolivia, the Plan establishes specific responsibilities to the Ministry of Finance to allocate resources to guarantee its implementation, as well as to sectoral institutions to plan and budget their specific actions.

Finally, another key element of the context that appears as an enabling factor for the implementation of GRBIs is the existence of a **specific mechanism in charge of gender equality and women's human rights**, often called National Women's Machinery (NWM). As shown in Table 6.2, all countries covered by the study have a NWM within their national governmental structure. Five of them were Ministries, three institutions directly depending on the Presidency and two are departments under a Ministry. As we will see in the following sections, Women's Machineries led five of the GRB experiences: in Brazil at local level, Colombia, Honduras, Uruguay and Venezuela and in many others, they have had a direct involvement as

Table 6.2 Hierarchical level of National Women's Machineries by country

Ministry	*Directly Depending to the Presidency*	*Under a Ministry*
Brazil	Argentina	Bolivia
Honduras	Colombia	Uruguay
Nicaragua	Ecuador	
Peru		
Venezuela		

Source: Authors' elaboration based on institutional information published on the internet

partners of the leading actor; thus, their existence appears to be an important GRB enabling factor of contextual elements.

In summary, notwithstanding their differences and specificities, all countries included in the study shared certain contextual conditions in terms of legislation, policy, and institutional frameworks that facilitated a more enabling environment to promote GRB.

Selected GRBIs in Latin America: Some Features and Characteristics

The study looked at some of the main characteristics and features of the selected GRBIs focusing on specific information about their location, their maturity (according to the years of implementation), their main key stakeholders—looking both at the leading actor and other partnerships—and their budget coverage.

(a) **Location of the GRBIs**

Out of the 21 initiatives analyzed, 11 of them (52 per cent) were undertaken at a national level, while the other 10 (48 per cent) were carried out at a local level (this including both municipal and other intermediate decentralized levels).

(b) **Maturity of the GRBIs, according to the years of implementation.**

Previous to 2005, the date when UN Women's regional GRB programme started, there were already four initiatives in place.[6] The majority of the GRBIs assessed through the study (14 out of the 21) were initiated between 2005 and 2011, showing the important contribution of the programme in increasing the number of initiatives. After this programme ended in 2011, three other initiatives emerged, with the support of UN Women global programmes.

It is important to notice that, out of the 21 experiences, almost two thirds of them (13) were still ongoing with different degrees of intensity. As shown in Fig. 6.4, this has resulted in a set of experiences in which more than half of them have completed a period of at least five years duration (ten of them, 48 per cent, between six to ten years, and three of them, 14 per cent with more than eleven years). Given the importance of cumulative learning effects, long-term sustained initiatives are fundamental to enabling GRB progressing from analysis to budget transformation and institutionalization and from them on to appropriate and adequate budgetary allocations.

Fig. 6.4 Years of duration

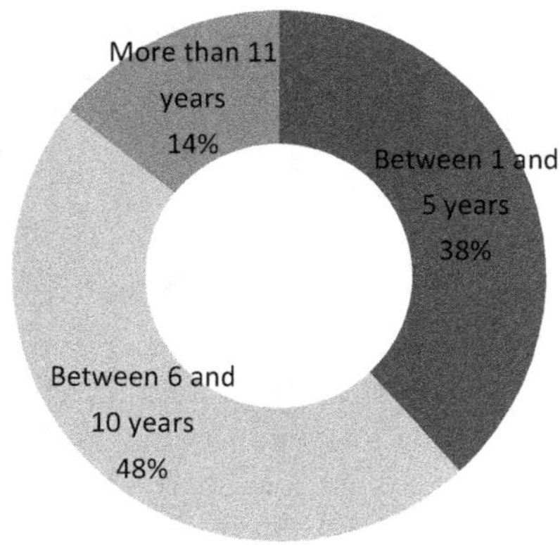

(c) **Key stakeholders**

Regarding the leading institution, two thirds of the initiatives (14 out of the 21) were driven by a state institution and the other third (7 in total) by a civil society organization. As observed in Fig. 6.5, an important number of initiatives (eight of them) were led by the gender equality mechanism or NWM, followed closely by women's and feminist organizations (six of them). At local level, gender equality advocates—whether from the State or from civil society—have had a particularly important role in the promotion of the ten GRBIs as they led all of them. Half of the local initiatives were driven by women's and feminist organizations and half by the gender unit of the local government. Gender equality advocates also participated as key partners in a significant number of experiences (six in the case of the Gender Equality mechanism and nine in the case of feminist organizations). This means that women's organizations and gender advocates' active leadership and engagement was a vital part of promoting GRBIs in the region and a fundamental element in understanding their success and their sustainability.

At national level, the Ministries of Finance (MFs) have gained an increasing role being now the leaders in four of the initiatives (Argentina, Ecuador, Nicaragua, and Peru) and participating in two of them as partners (Colombia and Honduras). Sectoral ministries also appear as leaders in two of the cases (the Bolivian initiatives led by the National Service for Autonomy and the Ministry of Production). Ministries of Planning and the National Assembly (or their equivalents at local level) also emerge as partners in four of the initiatives, but their participation is still limited. As regards planning, the annual budget calendar and deadlines as well as the traditionally short-term rationality of the budgetary cycle are not always easily reconciled with the wider and longer-term vision of the planning process and cycle. The two different temporalities constitute an important challenge for planning institutions to get more involved in GRBIs. Gender advocates and women parliamentarians are still underrepresented in the legislature and are caught up in the internal dynamics of political parties, their majority groups, and political alliances. Such a situation undermines their engagement in GRBIs.

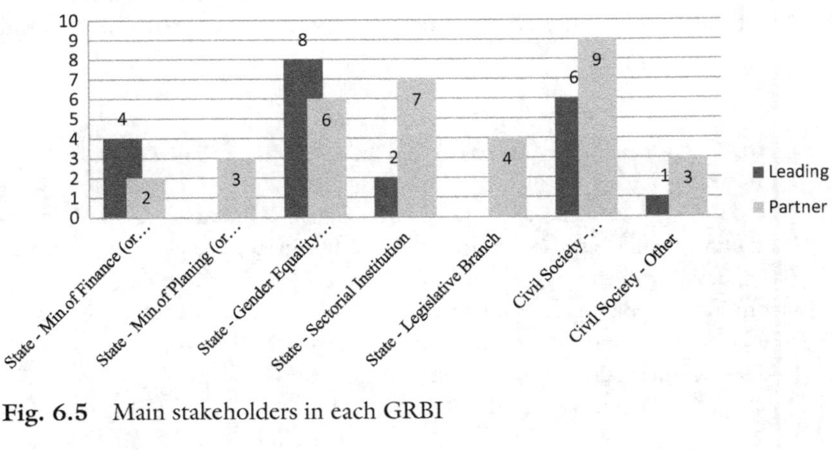

Fig. 6.5 Main stakeholders in each GRBI

(d) **Budget coverage**

All the GRB initiatives analyzed through the study were focused on the expenditure side, while only two of them also addressed the revenue side (Bolivia and Honduras as described in Box 6.2). This also reflects the trend followed at global level, where the revenue side of the budget has received limited attention from GRB experiences worldwide despite the fact that it is an important element of the budget that also affects women and men differently (Coello and Wretblad 2012) and has direct implications in terms of redistribution and gender equality. Some of the reasons behind the lack of initiatives focusing on the revenue side are fewer instruments and tools for assessing the revenue side, inadequate solid sex-disaggregated data regarding the taxation system and a need for stronger revenue and safety net systems (Holvoet 2006). Nevertheless, analysing expenditure and revenues simultaneously is essential to fully understand the gender impact of government's fiscal policy. Thus, bringing more attention to revenue side of the budget is one of the main challenges to be addressed in the region.

Regarding the proportion of the budget addressed, 13 of the initiatives (62 per cent) addressed the whole budget, while 12 of them (57 per cent) selected a part of the budget to work on. In the four experiences addressing participatory budgets,[7] the GRBIs progressively moved to also address the entire budget.

As for the phase of the budget cycle in which the GRBI intervened, the great majority of them (18 out of the 21) have been targeting the formulation phase. A big proportion also focused on the implementation phase (13 in total), while only six of them addressed the approval phase and

Box 6.2: Addressing the Revenue Side of the Budget: The Case of Honduras

In the local government of Santa Rosa de Copán, Honduras, a GRBI has been implemented since 2006. In 2011, the Financial Management System was updated by the local government's department for Taxation Control to incorporate sex-disaggregated information. For the Fiscal year 2011–12, an adjustment in the taxation system was undertaken, benefitting women who paid less for the stalls they occupy in farmers' markets.

Source: Coello and Wretblad (2012).

barely one of them reached the evaluation and audit phase (see Fig. 6.6). This situation is, in a sense, a reflection of the profile of the actors participating in the experiences and their role in the budgetary cycle. The more the institutions of the executive branch get involved (MFs, gender machineries, and sectoral ministries), the more GRBIs are engaged in formulation. The focus on implementation also had to do with the participation of women's organizations and their role as "watch-dogs" through civic engagement. The scant involvement of Parliaments limited their intervention during the approval phase.

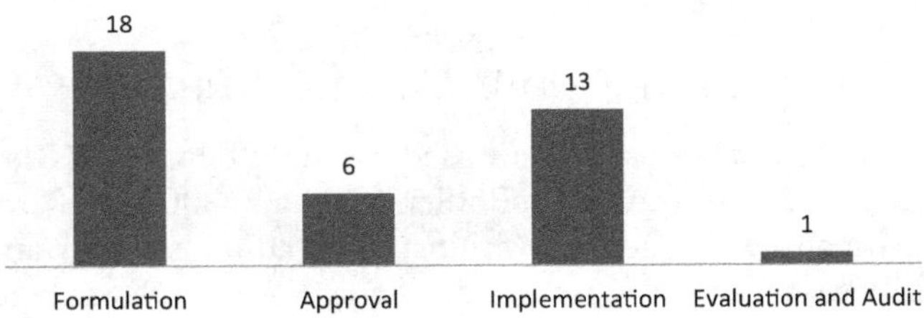

Fig. 6.6 Phases of the budget cycle covered within the GRBI

As a matter of course, ten of the initiatives (48 per cent) focused on just one phase while four (19 per cent) covered two phases and six (28 per cent) intervened in three phases—formulation, approval, and implementation (Fig. 6.7). Only one initiative, in Bolivia, addressed all the four phases (including evaluation).

Fig. 6.7 Amount of phases of the budget cycle covered

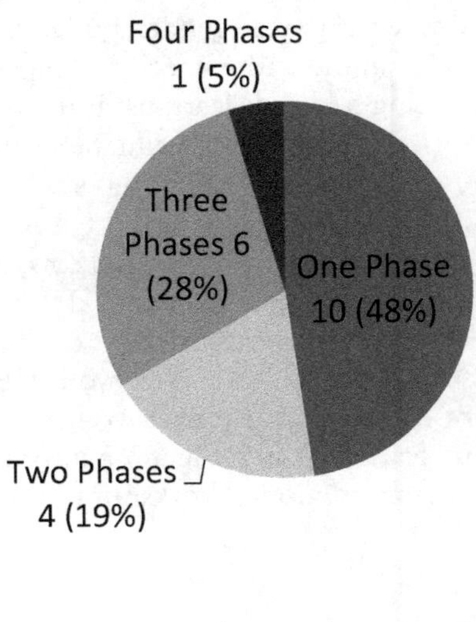

This pattern is similar to the one followed at global level, where most initiatives apply the gender perspective when it comes to identifying the objectives for the coming fiscal year and in monitoring its implementation while there is a long way to go in terms of getting a more active engagement in influencing the budget approval and also at the time to evaluate it (Coello and Wretblad 2012). In this regard, deepening and broadening GRB engagement throughout the whole budget cycle poses a challenge for leading actors to expand their alliances as well as for other actors—such as parliaments or budget accountability and monitoring bodies—to take the lead in their own mandates and sphere of competence.

Highlighting Some Common Strategies

This section looks at the strategies used by the different GRBIs assessed through the study. As argued by Budlender et al. (2002), GRB is itself a strategy to mainstream gender within public administration and public finance and to achieve a more gender equal society. Nevertheless, each GRBI develops their specific sub-strategies on how to start and continue the path towards that objective.

While it has been widely recognized that there is no single recipe or no "one size fits all" approach for Gender Budgeting, the study looked at the strategies used in the initiatives. It grouped them into the following different categories as indicated in Fig. 6.7.

As Fig. 6.8 shows, all the GRBIs used **exchange of experiences** as a strategy for achieving their goals. This can be attributed to the fact that many of the initiatives analyzed through the study were part of the UN women regional gender budgeting programme for Latin America. This programme had a specific component dedicated to promote knowledge sharing and peer learning at national and regional level. It supported several mechanisms to facilitate exchange between and within 18 of the 21 experiences included in this study. For example, in seven countries, several national workshops were held with the participation of local partners to share knowledge, unify concepts, criteria, and methodologies and to coordinate advocacy strategies. There were also bilateral meetings between countries to share specific expertise on one domain, such as the working session organized between the MFs of Ecuador and Peru or the exchange of experiences between women's organizations of Argentina and Bolivia to learn about budget monitoring tools. Moreover, specialized multi-country regional workshops and seminars were organized to discuss a

Fig. 6.8 Strategies used in the GRB initiatives

common issue from the perspective of different experiences (see various examples in Box 6.3). Latin American GRBIs also participated in global seminars and events where they had the opportunity to share and learn from other regions' experiences. An example of this was the *High level Forum on Gender and aid effectiveness* organized by UN Women in Kigali in 2001 with the participation of the Ministry of Finance of Ecuador (UN Women 2012) or the *Global Seminar on Costing Experience and Methodologies for Gender Equality* organized by UN Women in alliance with the Ministry of Autonomies and the Ministry of Justice of Bolivia the European Commission and the UNDP in Santa Cruz de la Sierra in September of 2013 (Coello 2013a).

The second most commonly used strategies identified in the study were the provision of technical assistance, training, and development of manuals and methodologies. The three strategies were used by 19 of the initiatives showing the relevance to build and permanently improve capacities on GRB. To this end, different partnerships were established with academia making available specialized postgraduate programmes on GRB,[8] which became, in some cases, part of the regular academic offer of these institutions.

Advocacy and studies are the third most frequent group of interlinked strategies: In an important number of cases, studies, and research generated

Box 6.3: Gender-Responsive Budgeting Regional Workshops
Regional workshops created value-added spaces for sharing experiences and adapt knowledge to the GRBIs analyzed in this research. They met similar partners from different countries to discuss and present advances about similar issues to develop regional lessons learned.

The ***International Seminar "Improving effectiveness of public resources to gender Equality: Exchange of experiences and discussion about tools to promote Gender Responsive Budgets in Latin America"***, organized by the Ministry of Economy and Finance of Peru and UN Women in 2010, convened for the first-time *ministries of economy, finance and planning of 11 Latin American countries* to share good practices and enhance the use of methodologies and tools to promote GRB. As result of the Seminar, a set of proposals to include the gender perspective in budget guidelines, templates, and reports was elaborated. Participants committed to maintain a communication mechanism to exchange information and continue contact.

Regarding women's organizations share of experiences, the ***International Seminar "Public Policies and Budgets for Good Living: Advances and challenges Latin American women perspective"***, organized by the Bolivian organization Colectivo Cabildeo and UN Women in 2011 in Bolivia, joined together more than 200 women from Bolivia and 40 representatives of women's organizations from Argentina, Colombia, Brazil, Ecuador, Honduras, Mexico, Peru, Uruguay, and Venezuela. In this workshop, *participants presented about 16 experiences on advocacy, monitoring, development of proposals on social accountability and GRB led by women's organizations.* The most important result was the network created by women's organizations from nine Latin American countries working on advocacy and social control on GRB.

Source: UN Women (2012), pp. 35–36.

2

the evidence and data about gender gaps and about the underfunding of gender equality commitments used advocacy interventions, while advocacy strategies also called for research to find adequate responses to the issues raised.

Costing exercises appear to have been carried out in only two of the GRBIs, first in Bolivia in 2010, followed by Honduras in 2012. This low number of reported cases reflects the fact that costing of gender equality action plans and interventions is a recent development.

Synthesis of Main Achievements

The Road Towards Institutionalization

GRBIs act upon budgetary processes, which are institutional processes. Therefore, one of the main challenges for these initiatives to succeed is to become embedded within the process and in the systems and structures themselves in such a way that they can be carried out in a more gender-responsive manner. As it was mentioned in section "Selected GRBIs in Latin America: Some Features and Characteristics", after more than a decade of implementation, the study showed an important amount of initiatives with more than five years of maturity. The study therefore aimed to look at the key elements that allowed a GRBI to move from an "experimental" to a regular institutional practice. In this regard, it is important to take into account that not all initiatives have real possibilities to reach a certain degree of institutionalization. As a matter of fact, this depends to a great extent in the leading actors and the partnerships they are able to establish. For instance, it is quite difficult to change programming and budgeting formats or financial and accounting systems if the responsible institution for its regulation, usually the Ministry of Finance, is not involved. Nevertheless, the study showed that in many of the initiatives, the driving force that pushed for such changes came from other key actors, such as women parliamentarians, women's machinery or women's organizations that finally were successful in advocating and partnering with MFs to buy the idea and implement it technically and institutionally (see Box 6.4).

Moreover, the study identified certain patterns in the road to institutionalization and grouped them in five institutional categories:

(1) *Regulatory and legal framework,* regulating different elements linked to public budgets such as: the law governing the process as a whole as well as the guidelines issued by the MFs to orient it annually (the Budget Call Circulars),[9] norms linked to the fiscal and tax system, as well as those regulating transparency and accountability, including access to budgetary information, citizenship participation in the formulation, and monitoring of public planning and budgeting, among others.

(2) *Programming and Budgeting formats, manuals and guidelines,* referring to the standard templates, forms, and documents that staff responsible for the budget process in each institution need to

Box 6.4: Gender Advocates as the Driving Force for GRB: The Case of Peru

In Peru, initial advocacy for GRB was led by congresswoman Rosario Sasieta, who in December 2007 proposed a law that was supported by the Budget Commission of the Congress. The Law, no. 29083, amends the general law on the national system of budgeting to incorporate gender analysis and evaluation of the execution of the public budget. The law underscores, in particular, the importance of using gender indicators to track budget outcomes. The Ministry of Women and Social Development was given the task of elaborating how gender would be coded or tracked within the annual budget. A working group was established under the Budget Commission of the Congress including representatives of the Ministry of Women and Social Development, Ministry of Economy and Finance, representatives of civil society, and Development partners.

In compliance with the law and the agreed tasks of the working group, the Ministry of Finance carried out the analysis of 26 institutional budgetary programmes selecting 5 of them with the higher potential to contribute to gender equality. In the context of the shift towards performance budgeting, these programmes were reformulated from the gender perspective and three of them were integrated into 2013 budget

Source: M. Roeder, C. Takayama, P. Fuertes and I. Hurtado (2008)

complete, as well as the manuals and guidelines orienting this process.

(3) *Accounting and financial systems*, including the systems in which the budgetary information is registered—regularly through an Information and Technology (IT) application—as well as the way in which the budgetary items are codified (budget classification codes).[10]

(4) *Budgetary reports*, which are documents containing detailed information about the budget being presented. They might be attached to the official budget document but also can be produced as a separate report.

(5) *Institutional structures or mechanisms* created or re-profiled in order to have a specific mandate to promote Gender Budgeting. They could be, for instance, Gender Units within the Ministries of Planning or Finance (or their equivalent at local level), working

groups or sub-commissions within a legislative commission, inter-institutional committees with the participation of representatives from different departments, sectors or ministries.

Table 6.3 summarizes the way in which the 21 selected initiatives achieved changes in the different institutional categories.

(1) **Changes introduced in regulatory and legal framework regulating different elements linked to public budgets**

As Table 6.3 shows, the study registers that up to two thirds of the initiatives (14 in total) were able to modify the *regulatory and legal frameworks.* In eight cases, this was possible through changes in call circulars or annual budgetary guidelines. In some cases (Ecuador, Peru, and Venezuela), the MFs led the initiative, while in others, the norms were changed as a result of advocacy from civil society organizations (as in Bolivia and Brazil).

In one third of the initiatives (seven in total), changes in the legal framework were achieved by altering the norms to promote citizenship participation. These GRBIs were led by women's machineries in four cases (Rosario-Argentina, Villa El Salvador-Peru, Recife-Brazil, and Montevideo-Uruguay), women's organizations in two cases (Brazil at national level and Bolivia at local level) and in one case by the Ministry of Finance (Ecuador). In six of these seven cases, alterations were introduced to promote participation at local level initiatives and only in Brazil did civil society involvement extend to the national planning process.

Ecuador and Peru were two initiatives that were able to modify the law that regulates the budgetary process as a whole. In both cases, the initiatives were led by the Ministry of Finance but had the legislative power as one of the main partners.

Another five GRBIs introduced changes in other types of norms as, for instance, in the laws regulating the decentralization process (*Ley de Autonomias* in Bolivia) or in equal opportunity laws (Nicaragua and Peru) in which specific articles were introduced to institute gender budgeting. On the other side of the balance, no changes have been achieved within the laws linked to the fiscal and tax system, given that few of the initiatives focused on the income side of the budget.

Table 6.3 Types of institutional changes produced by GRBIs

Type of change		*Number of initiatives*	*Countries*
1. Regulatory and legal framework		**14**	
1.1	Laws regulating the process as a whole	2	Ecuador (national), Peru (national)
1.2	Budgetary guidelines issued by the ministries of finance (or equivalent) orienting its formulation annually (Call circulars)	8	Bolivia (national and local), Brazil (1 sub-national, 2 local), Ecuador (national), Peru (national), Venezuela (national)
1.3	Laws linked to the fiscal and tax system	0	
1.4	Norms relating to transparency accountability and access to budgetary information	3	Bolivia (national and local), Ecuador (national)
1.5	Norms promoting citizenship participation in the formulation and monitoring of public planning and budgeting	7	Argentina (local), Bolivia (local), Brazil (national and local), Ecuador (local), Peru (local), Uruguay (local)
1.6	Others	5	Bolivia (sub-national), Nicaragua (national), Peru (national), Uruguay (local), Venezuela (national)
2. Formats and manuals used to elaborate and implement programmes and budgets		**9**	
2.1	Manuals, Guidelines for programming and budgeting	4	Bolivia (national, local), Ecuador (national), Nicaragua (national)
2.2	Formats and forms used for programming and budgeting	5	Bolivia (national, nat/sectoral, local), Ecuador (national), Venezuela (national)
2.3	Others	3	Bolivia (sub-national, local), Honduras (local), Uruguay (local)
3. Accounting and financial systems		7	
3.1	Financial System	6	Bolivia (national), Brazil (local), Ecuador (national), Honduras (local), Nicaragua (national), Venezuela (national)

(*continued*)

Table 6.3 (continued)

Type of change		*Number of initiatives*	*Countries*
3.2	Budget classifiers	4	Bolivia (national), Brazil (local), Ecuador (national), Honduras (local)
4. Budget Reports		**5**	
4.1	Budgetary reports attached to the budget main document	1	Ecuador (national)
4.2	Other reports containing budgetary information	4	Bolivia (national), Brazil (national), Honduras (local), Uruguay (local)
5. Institutional Structures/Mechanisms with a specific mandate for Gender Budgeting		**9**	
5.1	Gender Units within the Ministry of Planning, Finance (or equivalent)	5	Colombia (national), Ecuador (national), Honduras (national and local), Nicaragua (national)
5.2	Gender working groups/sub-commissions on GRB within legislative commissions	1	Argentina (local)
5.3	Inter-institutional Committees (delegates from different departments, sectors, etc.)	3	Brazil/Recife (local), Ecuador (local), Uruguay (local)

Source: Authors' compilation based on the study

(2) **Changes achieved in programming and budgeting formats and manuals**

As indicated in Table 6.3, up to nine initiatives introduced specific changes in these budgetary tools, four of them through manuals and guidelines that orient the process and five of them by modifying the forms used for programming and budgeting.

When analyzing the type of change introduced (see Fig. 6.9), five of the initiatives (Bolivia, Ecuador, Nicaragua, and Venezuela at national level and Uruguay at local level) required to formulate specific activities and results oriented to promote gender equality, and indicators to measure their progress. Also five of them (Nicaragua and the four Bolivian GRBIs) require to define specific budget allocations to such activities, results, and indicators. In four of the initiatives analyzed (Bolivia at

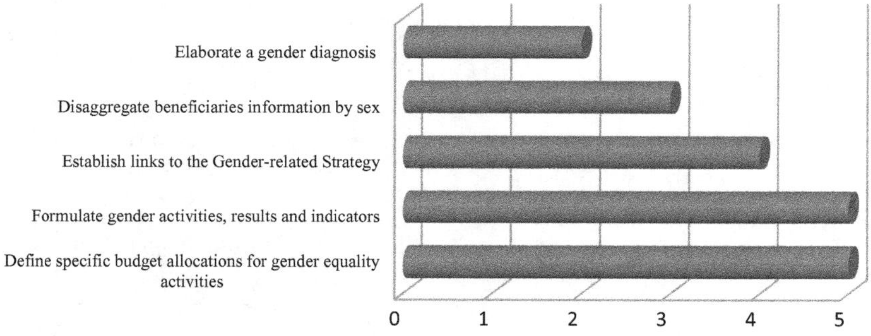

Fig. 6.9 Types of changes introduced in formats and manuals used to elaborate and implement programmes and budgets

national and local levels, Ecuador and Nicaragua), the changes were introduced to request the identification of the link between the programmes or their activities and the national (or local) gender equality strategy. In three cases (Ecuador and Venezuela at national level and Uruguay at local), the strategy was to demand the disaggregation by sex of the information about the beneficiaries. In two initiatives (the local ones of Santa Rosa de Copan-Honduras and Montevideo-Uruguay), it was requested to introduce information on gender equality or to elaborate a gender diagnosis as part of the context described in the programme.

(3) **Changes introduced in the accounting and financial systems.** Seven GRBIs institutionalized gender-responsiveness in accounting and financial systems. As mentioned in Table 6.3, in six cases, the changes were introduced within the systems in which the budgetary information is registered (normally consisting of IT applications where users are able to introduce and obtain information on-line), while in another four cases, the budget classification codes were altered to include specific categories to identify gender equality allocations. In the case of Ecuador, the Ministry of Finance created a specific budget classifier (see description in Box 6.5).

(4) **Changes introduced in Budget Reports**
Five GRBIs achieved institutionalization through the elaboration of *Gender Budget reports*, in four cases produced as separate documents,

Box 6.5: Gender Budget Classification Codes: The Case of Ecuador

The development of specific accounting instruments to register the resources directed to gender equality has been one of the most internationally well-recognized practice of the Ecuadorian GRB initiative led by the Ministry of Finance. Initially, the Ministry created a specific category (named the "K" function for "Gender Equality") within the functional catalogue of expenditure. The K Function put *gender equality* at the same level as the rest of the functions of the State such as: health, education or defense. However, after two years of implementation, the evaluation made by its own users (the sectoral institutions) identified as its principal weakness, the impossibility to register simultaneously one activity into two functions. This means that, even if an activity was to contribute to several functions, it could only be registered under one category, forcing to choose the most relevant function. For example, in the case of a sexual and reproductive health programme, it could be registered in the functional catalogue of health or gender; the institutions must register it in one catalogue, and in general, they preferred to register it in health. Consequently, the resources directed to the close of gaps of gender were not totally visible.

Consequently, the Ministry of Finance developed a specific *Classification Code of Expenditure Orientation in Gender Equality Policies*. This code is applicable to all budgetary lines, therefore allowing to quantify the total amount dedicated to gender equality regardless of the economic, administrative or functional classifiers used in the different budgetary items. The code includes a set of categories and sub-categories corresponding to the prioritized areas of work of the National Gender Strategy (Currently the National Agenda for Women and Gender Equality 2014–2017), which also makes it possible not only to know the total amount but also the strategic area to which it contributes. The content of the *Classification of Expenditure Orientation in Gender Equality Policies* is available at: http://www.finanzas.gob.ec/reportes-de-equidad/

Source: Barba (2013) and Coello (2013c).

while in one initiative (the Ecuadorian "Gender Equality Report"), it is attached to the budget pro-forma presented for approval.

As for the information contained in the report, in the five initiatives, the reports contained information about the amount allocated to programmes that contribute to gender equality, but in the case of Santa Rosa de Copan-Honduras, it also included information about the content of the programmes funded by such allocations.

Regarding the actors in charge of producing the report, in the case of Ecuador, the Ministry of Finance led its elaboration, while in Montevideo-Uruguay and Santa Rosa de Copan, it was produced by a municipal multi-department gender commission. In the case of Bolivia and Brazil, the reports were developed by civil society organizations, in this latest case, using official information available in the internet site of the Senate (SIGA-Brazil).

(5) **Institutional areas or mechanisms to promote GRB**

Within the 21 initiatives analyzed, 9 of them succeeded to achieve GRB institutionalization through the creation or re-profiling of institutional structures or mechanisms with a specific mandate to promote Gender Budgeting. In five of the cases, Gender Units were created or re-activated within the Ministries of Planning or Finance or their equivalent at local level. Three initiatives opted for the creation of inter-institutional committees in which representatives of different departments or ministries participated. These are the cases of the *Foro de gestores* (Managers fora) of Recife-Brazil, the Budgetary group of the Gender Equality Commission of Montevideo-Uruguay and the inter-institutional committees to promote gender equality created at the municipalities of Portoviejo and Eloy Alfaro in Ecuador. In the case of Rosario-Argentina, a specific sub-commission to monitor the implementation of GRB was created within the local legislative commission of budget and finance, allowing also women's organizations to participate in it.

Two thirds of these institutional mechanisms (six out of the nine) count on their own staff as well as their own budget: four have a staff of three people, one has two people and another one has one person. The three mechanisms conformed by a delegates from different departments function without specific staff and budget designated.

Achievements to Improve Financing for Gender Equality

Institutionalization of GRB elements was clearly an important result achieved in all the cases analysed in many diverse ways. Nevertheless, as mentioned in the introduction to this chapter, taking these achievements further poses the challenge to translate such changes into actual budget allocations. Therefore, the study analyzed how results in terms of institutionalization finally turned into improvements in financing for gender equality, considering three different types of achievements: (1) if there was any reorientation of policies and programmes to better address gender gaps, (2) if there was an increase in the amount of resources allocated for gender equality and the realization of women's rights, and (3) if there has been an improvement in accountability mechanisms or an increased in transparency that allow to better track resources allocated and implemented for gender equality.

Eleven out of the twenty-one initiatives analyzed (52 per cent) achieved a reorientation of policies and programmes to better address gender gaps, 16 of them (76 per cent) resulted in an increase in the amount of resources allocated for gender equality and 19 of them (90 per cent) improved transparency and accountability mechanisms that allowed a better tracking of resources allocated and implemented for gender equality (See Fig. 6.10).

Within the eleven initiatives that succeeded in reorienting policies and programmes, the great majority (ten of them) did it over the expenditure side of the budget, but there was one (the previously mentioned case of Santa Rosa de Copán, Honduras) that achieved to reorient the income side of the budget, through changes in the design of some local tax policies.

As for the 16 initiatives that obtained an increase in the amount of resources allocated for gender equality, Table 6.4 shows the different ways in which this result was achieved. In six of them, there was an improved allocation in previously existing programmes that were explicitly oriented to promote gender equality (namely, increasing the resources allocated for the implementation of the equal opportunity plan or the implementation of the law and the plans to combat violence against women). Nine initiatives also succeeded to allocate resources for new programmes explicitly designed to promote gender equality. This was the case, for example, for new local projects approved in the participatory budget that explicitly addressed women's priorities or new programmes oriented to address gender inequality formulated, approved, and funded within the general budget. In six of the GRBIs, the result was achieved by including within

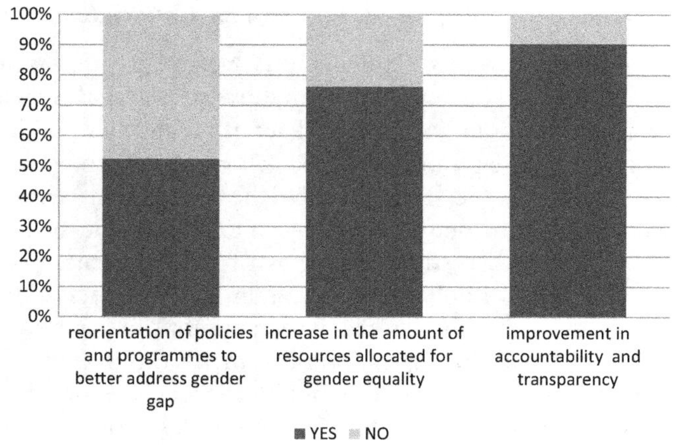

Fig. 6.10 Achievements in improved mechanisms for financing for gender equality

Table 6.4 Ways in which the increases in the amount of resources allocated for gender equality occurred

Type of increase	*Number of initiatives*	*Countries*
Increase in the amount of existing programmes explicitly oriented to promote gender equality	6	Argentina (local), Bolivia (sub-national), Brazil (national, local), Peru (local)
Increase in the amount of new programmes explicitly oriented to promote gender equality	9	Argentina (local), Bolivia (national, sub-national and local), Colombia (national), Ecuador (local), Honduras (local), Peru (local), Venezuela (national)
Allocations in existing "general" programmes to include activities and interventions to turn them more gender responsive	6	Bolivia (national-sectorial), Colombia (national), Ecuador (local), Honduras (national), Nicaragua (national), Uruguay (local)
General increase of resources distributed throughout the budget (e.g. a percentage of an income source)	2	Bolivia (sub-national), Ecuador (local)

Source: Authors' elaboration based on the study

general programmes—that is the programmes not explicitly oriented to address gender inequalities—specific interventions that turned them more gender responsive. Finally, in two of the experiences, a general increase of funds for gender equality purposes was achieved through the allocation of a percentage of funds (for example, in one municipality of Ecuador, a 0.5 per cent of the local budget was guarantee by decree to be allocated for gender equality).

Last, but not least, a big portion of the gains in financing for gender equality can be attributed to the fact that almost all of them (19 out of the 21) improved their accountability mechanisms and increased their transparency, allowing to count with more information on gender equality investment and a better tracking on how such resources were implemented. As Table 6.5 shows, in 19 of the initiatives, the information was available on the resources allocated initially in the approved budget, but 11 of them also achieved in obtaining information on how the initial allocations were finally implemented. A challenging element of this result is that in barely a quarter of the initiatives, the information is public and/or available through the internet, so in many cases, the information was internally managed by the government or had to be requested by civil society.

In 10 of the 21 initiatives, permanent tracking systems to monitor financing for gender equality were created, and in 6 of them, there were periodic accountability mechanisms, where governmental institutions

Table 6.5 Number of initiatives that resulted in an increase in the information on resources allocated and/or implemented for gender equality

	YES		*NO*
Increased information of resources ***allocated*** for gender equality	19		2
	YES	**NO**	
The information is public	6	13	
The information is available through the internet	5	14	
Increased information of resources ***implemented*** for gender equality	11		10
	YES	**NO**	
The information is public	5	6	
The information is available through the internet	4	7	

Source: Authors' compilation based on the study

needed to report on resources allocated for gender equality. Figure 6.11 shows the institutions responsible for such mechanisms.

Women's and feminist organizations have been in the forefront of developing tracking systems. An example is given in Box 6.6.

There were also initiatives that have a State institution taking the lead (sometimes two of them responsible to co-lead). As for the accountability mechanisms, the MFs have taken responsibility in three of the initiatives while the gender equality mechanism and the sectoral institutions have taken the lead in two GRBIs and the ministry of planning in one.

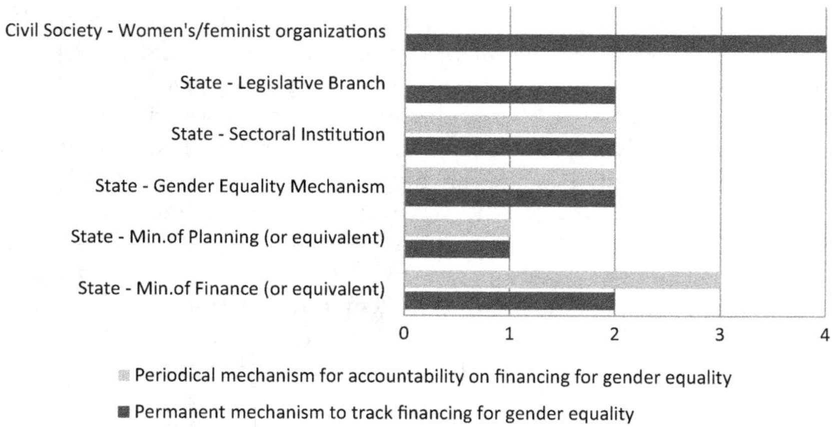

Fig. 6.11 Institutions responsible for accountability and tracking mechanisms

Conclusions: Lessons Learned, Success Factors and Challenges of the GRBI in Latin America

The Latin American region provides a positive environment for GRBIs to be implemented. All countries included in the study present normative, political, and institutional contextual elements that are enabling factors for the initiatives and/or sought to improve the enabling factors. Hence, in these countries, GRB is positioned as an important mechanism that allows the implementation of international and national commitments on gender equality by translating them into specific public interventions and resources.

Box 6.6: Gender Investment Categories in Bolivia: A Methodological Approach for Women's Groups to Influence and Track Budget Allocations

Since 2005, the Annual Guidelines for the elaboration of municipal plans and budgets in Bolivia incorporate an article that makes it mandatory to assign resources to promote gender equality at municipal level. To monitor its implementation and also influence the type of projects to be funded for an effective contribution to gender equality and women's rights, women's organizations, through the coordination mechanism for GRB advocacy (the *Mesa Nacional de Presupuestos Sensibles al Género*), formulated the "gender investment categories".

(a) **Direct investment**, consistent of three different types of categories.

- *Investment focused on women (FM),* exclusively oriented to women in the different phases of the cycle of life, oriented to close inequality between men and women and to promote women's and the exercise of their rights. This investment is constituted by measures of affirmative action or special promotion.
- *Investment in the social and public co-responsibility for care and sustainability of life* (CSV), among the State, society, community, and all the members within the household, in the work of social reproduction, generating conditions for a better distribution of domestic work and care responsibilities. This investment is targeted to diminish the burden of domestic and unpaid care work within the households, mostly carried out by women and to leave them time to expand their opportunities in the exercise of human rights and enhance their wellbeing.
- *Investment for a culture of equality (CI*), promoting structural changes in the patriarchal system, public management and the power relations between men and women. It contains actions directed to generate changes in the institutionalization and public management (regulations, policies, planning, and structure) and the way of thinking and acting of the society and its institutions to reach social, ethnic and gender equality, the modification of

the social and cultural representations and the power relationships between men and women, crosscut also by ethnic and intergenerational discriminations.

(b) **Indirect investment,** *Investment in re-distribution for social and gender equality*: Includes investments that will improve the living conditions of women and men, their ability to exercise their human rights and the access to well-being of people in necessity, and with few economic resources. This is a category that indirectly supports positive changes in women's lives.

With these categories, a set of indicators have been developed and used by local women's groups, supported by the feminist Non Governmental Organizations (NGOs) IFFI and Colectivo Cabildeo to monitor the compliance of the article included in the annual budgetary guideless. For instance, in the Department of Cochabamba, a scoreboard ranking the amounts allocated by each of its 47 municipalities was developed. This information was published in reports that were used by women organizations as a monitoring tool and to exert political pressure to increase policies and budgets orientated towards gender equality and women rights.

Source: Authors' elaboration based on Colectivo Cabildeo (2012), Coello (2013b), IFFI (2011) and Zabalaga (2013).

Following the global trend, Latin America GRBIs are also diverse. Their nature varies from country to country and from place to place. Some of them are coordinated and led by governments and others by civil society organizations. Often, different institutions interact in informal ways or define formal partnerships. There are experiences addressing national, sub-national, and local budgets, some of them covering the whole budget while others concentrate in selected areas or programmes. They focus on different phases of the budget cycle, mainly in the formulation and implementation phases, while little attention is paid to the approval and the evaluation phase. In a sense, this shows the strengths of having involved key relevant actors such as the MFs, women's machineries, and civil society organizations, but also points out the need to enhance GRB work by involving other stakeholders, particularly parliaments and audit and evaluation institutions within public management systems.

Within this diversity, the initiatives also used a wide range of strategies, but the regional programmes, such as the one supported by UN Women LAC, have provided a unique opportunity to promote knowledge sharing and the exchange of experiences, a strategy present in all the GRBIs analyzed. This has proved to be a crucial element to advance GRB in the region, particularly when we look at GRBIs as the result of a learning process where knowledge is built by doing and evolves by means of experimentation. Moreover, this has had a direct impact in the development of common tools and mechanisms that pave the road for the institutionalization of the processes.

Through the analyzed initiatives, it was possible to identify certain patterns followed in order to influence the existing normative and legal frameworks, the programmatic and budgeting formats, and accounting and financial systems. There were also commonalities in the creation of ad-hoc mechanisms, such as budgetary reports and institutional areas explicitly in charge of promoting GRB. Looking at the actors behind the scene, alliances between MFs and gender specialists—NWM or women's organizations—have proved to be factors of success for such institutionalization to happen. On the one side, MFs opened the door to intervene at the core of the process, and on the other side, gender specialists enhanced the quality of the gender contents of such interventions.

Beyond GRB institutionalization, the great majority of the initiatives also succeeded in achieving enhanced mechanisms for financing, as well as increased finance for gender equality, whether it was through an increase in the amount of resources allocated for gender equality, a reorientation of policies and programmes or an improvement in transparency and accountability that allowed more information on gender equality investment and better tracking on how such resources were implemented.

Despite these important advances, the study also found that GRB is still an ongoing process with a long way to run to be fully integrated into public management systems. There are also important challenges in terms of addressing the income side of the budget as well as in assessing the real impact that the achieved investments have had on women's life and gender equality. Therefore, external support from development partners and South–South cooperation still appear as crucial levers to consolidate the experiences in the region and to continue upgrading their leverage and depth.

Having used a mainly descriptive quantitative approach, the study leaves the field open for future research in the area. By exploring the links among the different components of the study—contextual elements, GRBIs characteristics, strategies, and results—further analysis will certainly allow to complement and deepen the findings, contributing to refine guidance for potential interventions. Going deeper into the learning process chain will also require to assess and make visible how achievements in terms of institutionalization and changes in budget allocations have effectively contributed to gender equality and women's empowerment.

In the present context characterized by the definition of a new global development agenda, the need to allocate adequate funding for gender equality remains a crucial issue to be resolved. GRBIs can definitively contribute to providing strategic evidence to mobilize high-level commitments in the allocation of domestic and international resources to reduce gender gaps and promote women's empowerment. Moreover, they can indeed contribute to improve accountability mechanisms that allow a better assessment of the impact that such allocations have on gender equality and the improvement of women's lives.

Notes

1. The UN Women GRB regional programme "Gender Budgeting: A contribution to Democratic Governance and Gender Equality in Latin America" was funded by the Spanish Agency for International Cooperation, the United Nations Volunteers Programme and Basque Government. It was implemented from 2005 to 2011 in 9 countries (Argentina, Bolivia, Brazil, Colombia, Ecuador, Honduras, Peru, Venezuela and Uruguay) supporting 19 of the 21 initiatives analyzed through the study. Additionally, several UN Women GRB Global Programmes funded by the Belgium Government and the European Commission also contributed to some of the initiatives of Bolivia, Ecuador, Honduras, Nicaragua and Peru.
2. This study, based on 18 GRBIs profiles located in different countries and regions, was commissioned by UN Women in preparation for the high-level international conference on Gender-Responsive Budgeting: *Sharing knowledge and shaping policies and budgets to achieve gender equality*, organized in Marrakech in November 2012 by the Ministry of Finance of Morocco and UN Women.

3. Article 70. National Constitution of the Republic of Ecuador.
4. The four laws referred are: "Law of Equal Opportunities for Women" in Honduras (2000), "Law of Equality in rights and opportunities" in Nicaragua (2008), "Law of Equal Opportunities between Women and Men" in Peru (2007) and "Law of Equality in rights and opportunities between Wen and Men" in Uruguay (2007).
5. In the case of Argentina, the plan refers to gender equality only in the labour sector.
6. These experiences were also supported by UN Women (at that time UNIFEM) through country initiatives.
7. The Participatory Budget experiences consist on an innovative experiment in policy-making and budgeting, in which citizens are incorporated in the decision-making process about how resources are allocated within public budgets. It also involves them in tracking fulfilment of commitments through citizen oversight mechanisms. Although participatory budget processes have different legal frameworks, they all emphasize citizen participation in defining projects and budgets to be directly implemented by their governments or co-implemented with the communities. Usually, the decision process affects only a portion of the budget (that varies but that is lower than 10 per cent in most of the cases) and is mainly implemented at local level. The projects are usually planned for a fiscal year period.
8. The academic institutions which offered courses on GRB and Feminist Economics are: the Latin American Faculty of Social Sciences (FLACSO) in Argentina, Ecuador and Mexico; the Faculty of Economics of the National University of Rosario, the office of the National Pedagogic University of Honduras in Santa Rosa de Copan and the Post Grade Programme on Social Sciences of the University of San Andres in Bolivia.
9. Call circulars or annual budgetary guidelines are the official notices that are issued by the Ministry of Finance, Planning Commission or similar agencies near the beginning of each budget cycle with the purpose of instructing government agencies on how they must submit their demands for budgets for the coming year.
10. The budget classification codes, also known as budget classifiers, are accounting codes that provide information about the different elements of the budgetary item according to various types of criteria, such as: its "economic classification" (types of revenues—tax, fee, etc.—or expenditures—salaries, goods and services, etc.), its "administrative classification" (public sector organizations that incur expenditures or receive revenues) or its "functional classification" (which organizes revenue or expenditure according to their broad objectives or purposes).

References

Alami, N. (2008). *Institutionalizing gender responsive budgeting: Lessons learned from UNIFEM's programmes.* Paper for The Korean Women's Development Institute Symposium 'Institutionalizing Gender Budgeting: Achievements and Challenges" Seoul, 22–23 October 2008. http://www.gender-budgets.org/joomdocuments/other-grb-programmes/Institutionalizing%20GRB%20_%20paper%20by%20Alami.pdf. Accessed 8 Mar 2015.

Barba, L. (2013). *Evaluación cualitativa del uso del Catálogo de Orientación del Gasto en Políticas de Igualdad para hacer visible la inversión para la igualdad de género en Ecuador. Años 2012 y 2013.* Buenos Aires: FLACSO Argentina.

Bohrt, C. (2005). *El enfoque de Género en el Derecho Constitucional Comparado. Document prepared to the 'International Seminar Constitutional Reforms and Gender Equality' Santa Cruz de la Sierra, 21–23 February 2005.* Santiago de Chile: ECLAC.

Budlender, D., Elson, D., Hewitt, G., & Mukhopadhyay, T. (2002). *Gender budget make cents: Understanding gender responsive budgets.* London: Commonwealth Secretariat.

Cabildeo, C. (2012). *Deliberación para la Incorporación de la Igualdad de Género en las Políticas Públicas Sistematización de la Experiencia 2009–2011.* La Paz: Colectivo Cabildeo.

Coello, R. (2009). Experiencias de Presupuestos con Enfoque de Género en América Latina. In *Feminismo ante la Crisis. XIX Taller de Política Feminista* (pp. 107–115). Madrid: Forum de Política Feminista.

Coello, R. (2013a). *Costing of interventions and policies for gender equality. Concepts, methodologies and practical experiences.* La Paz: UN Women & UNDP.

Coello, R. (2013b). *Incidiendo en la Política Fiscal y los Presupuestos Públicos en Bolivia: El Largo Camino Recorrido por las Organizaciones de Mujeres en el Ejercicio de su Derecho a la Participación y al Control Social* (Estudio de caso sobre la Experiencia de Presupuestos Sensibles al Género de Bolivia). ONU MUJERES, Oficina Regional para las Américas, Panamá.

Coello, R. (2013c). *Incorporando el Enfoque de Género en el Presupuesto General del Estado Ecuatoriano: Aprendiendo del Vuelo de los Gansos.* (Estudio de caso sobre la Experiencia de Presupuestos Sensibles al Género de Ecuador). ONU MUJERES, Oficina Regional para las Américas, Panamá.

Coello, R., & Wretblad, E. (2012). *GRB world tour.* Report prepared for the International high-level conference on Gender-Responsive Budgeting, 'Sharing knowledge and designing policies and budgets to achieve gender equality', Marrakech, November 9–10th, 2012. Ministry of Economy and Finance of Morocco & UN Women.

Holvoet, N. (2006). *Briefing note, gender budgeting: Its usefulness in programme-based approaches to aid*. Antwerp: Institute of Development Policy and Management University of Antwerp.

IFFI. (2011). *Sistematización del proceso de Acceso a la Información Ciudadana y Rendición de Cuentas a Autoridades Municipales del Municipio de Cercado-Cochabamba (2003–2010)*. Cochabamba: IFFI.

Raes, F. (2006). *What can we expect from gender sensitive budgets? Strategies in Brazil and in Chile in a comparative perspective*. New York: UNIFEM.

Roeder, M., Takayama, C., Fuertes, P., & Hurtado, I. (2008). *Integrating gender responsive budgeting into the aid effectiveness agenda. Perú country report*. New York: UNIFEM.

UN Women. (2007–2009). *Fortaleciendo la gobernabilidad democrática a nivel local: Iniciativas de presupuestos sensibles al género en América Latina*. Informes de avance para la Agencia Española de Cooperación Internacional (AECI).

UN Women. (2008). Engendering budgets: Valuing women's voluntary contributions to national development in Latin America. Final Narrative Report UNV-UNIFEM.

UN Women. (2010, January–December). *Gender budgeting and volunteering through civic engagement: A contribution to democratic governance and gender equality in Latin America*. Annual Progress report to the United Nations Volunteers.

UN Women. (2012). *Final report of the regional programme strengthening democratic governance: Gender responsive budgeting initiatives in Latin America – fase II*. Quito: UN Women.

UN Women. (2013). *Increasing accountability in financing for gender equality revised updated first progress report to the European commission. October 2011-March 2013*. New York: UN Women.

Zabalaga, C. (2013). *Inversión Pública para la equidad de género en Bolivia: Sistematización de la Experiencia "Categorías para el Análisis y la Orientación de la Inversión Pública en Igualdad de Género en Bolivia"* (Cuaderno de Trabajo n°12, Serie En la Economía Contamos Todos y Todas). La Paz: UN Women.

CHAPTER 7

Gender Incursions in the Domain of Budgets: The Practice of GRB in Asia Pacific

Yamini Mishra and Navanita Sinha

Introduction

Rising inequalities have been the predominant leitmotif for the world community as it works towards establishing a more robust framework for sustainable development, and draws for itself a new social contract.[1] Voices from the global north and south have highlighted the need to address structural issues and multiple forms of discrimination that generate inequalities, including gender inequality (UN Women 2014a, UNESCAP 2014a, United Nations 2013). In the same vein, they have also reiterated the need for a stronger focus on the ways in which the SDGs will be implemented through a corresponding commitment to adequate financing for sustainable development, in particular, for gender equality and women's

Y. Mishra (✉)
GRB Specialist (Asia-Pacific), UN Women, New Delhi, India

N. Sinha (✉)
Programme Specialist (Governance), UN Women Multi Country Office for India, Bhutan, Maldives and Sri Lanka, New Delhi, India

© The Author(s) 2017

Z. Khan, N. Burn (eds.), *Financing for Gender Equality*,
DOI 10.1057/978-1-137-46101-8_7

rights. This is seen as critical for realizing the transformative potential of the new 2030 Agenda for Sustainable Development.

Gender-responsive budgeting (GRB) has achieved recognition globally as a key strategy to translate policy commitments on gender equality and women's empowerment into effective implementation. It has a long history in the Asia-Pacific (AP) region with Australia being the first country to prepare a Women's Budget Statement in 1983. Akin to other regions, there is no single GRB narrative in AP. This diversity, as reflected in the multiple and variegated practices of GRB that have evolved over the years, offers important learning to harness the potential of GRB as we move forward.

The 2030 Agenda for Sustainable Development agenda provides opportunities to re-examine and shift GRB into directions that are slowly being drawn and position it firmly as a lever of public action and finance for realizing women's rights in SDG implementation. But in order to do so, we need to first understand how GRB has been applied in different contexts and policy environments, teasing out what has been achieved and learned. This chapter makes an attempt to answer this question in the specific context of the AP.

The chapter is divided into three main sections. Section "Analysing the Development Context in the Asia-Pacific Region" focuses on understanding the development context and the major gains and gaps in promoting gender equality in the AP region. The second section maps out GRB work in the region and attempts to draw the common threads across the different experiences in terms of the nature and scope of GRB initiatives, the key actors and strategies. The final section "Analysing the GRB Journey" traces some of the critical debates and questions that have emerged over the years. We would like to mention at the outset that the analysis in this chapter is constrained by lack of a comprehensive assessment/evaluation of GRB in the region. It relies largely on country-specific reports/experiences, to draw the common threads of the regional story together.

Analysing the Development Context in the AP Region

With the onset of the global economic crisis in 2007–2008, cross-border financial flows slowed down considerably including in the AP where exports felt an immediate decline in their trade volumes (UN 2013).

Despite this, AP remained the fastest-growing economic region in the world even during the crises, indicating that it will serve as the world's economic growth engine in this "Asian Century". Several countries[2] in the region will be part of what is termed as a "permanent shift in the global political and economic landscape".[3]

However, the counter-narrative to this suggests that despite astonishing rates of growth, there remain deep seated vulnerabilities and fissures in the region. A report by the Asian Development Bank (2012) emphasized that the very same drivers of economic growth in the region have contributed to rising inequality within it. The recent crisis provides important evidence of the ways in which structural inequalities (by class, ethnicity, race and gender) have developed in tandem with crisis tendencies within financial markets and reinforced each other.

The region is thus marked by persisting and intersecting inequalities which further undermine the achievement of women's empowerment and gender equality. It has the second highest gender gap, globally ranking fifth out of six regions across a range of indicators from economic participation and opportunity, educational attainment, access to health and survival and political empowerment (UNDP n.d).

The recent Beijing plus 20 Survey by UNESCAP and UN Women provides an instructive summary of key achievements and challenges to gender equality in the AP region (UNESCAP 2014b).[4] It highlights three categories of achievement as reported by member states: (a) strengthening gender equality in national governments and governance; (b) addressing violence against women and girls (primarily through legislation and policy measures) and (c) promoting the leadership and political participation of women.[5]

These "successes" notwithstanding, countries across the region report severe challenges to greater gender equality ranging from low political participation, high incidence of violence against women to low workforce participation.[6] Existing gender inequalities seem to have been exacerbated by the recent global crisis. Several studies show that women have been disproportionately impacted by job losses due to their concentration in small-scale manufacturing.[7] Moreover, the number of women in vulnerable employment has also escalated. To illustrate, the proportion of workers in vulnerable employment among women workers ranged from 41% in West and Central Asia to over 80% in South Asia.[8] There is also evidence to suggest that women home-based workers have been disproportionately affected by the crisis (Sugarda and Tambunan 2009 and Wijaya 2010, cited in Floro and Pichetpongsa 2010: 39).

From a gender lens, other worrisome trends in the region pertain to: (a) increasing migration with significant increases in the number of women migrant workers[9]; (b) promotion of extractive industries (mining, logging and fishing), resulting from the emphasis on export production or trade-led growth which have had deleterious social and environmental impacts that are disproportionately borne by women and girls[10]; and (c) persistently low budgetary priority for social sectors (refer Tables 7.1 and 7.2). The region comes second from last in the share of social protection expenditure in GDP (World Social Protection Report 2014/15, share of health and education in public expenditure (Human Development Report 2013)).

In most countries of the region, the dwindling priority for social sector spending is apparent, and so is the intensification of the unpaid care burden, with "women as provisioners of the last resort" (Elson and Cagatay 1999). According to Marina Durrano and Josefa Francisco, "while the crisis appears to have furthered the shift in economic power to Asia, it has done so without a critical analysis of the burden of economic growth on the region's women" (UN Women forthcoming).

The global economic and financial crisis has had profound implications on the gender equality agenda, and in a sense has also altered the landscape for mainstreaming efforts including GRB.[11] In its aftermath, there have been strong calls, notably from women's rights coalitions, to use GRB to mitigate the impacts and build resilience among poor and marginalized women (UNIFEM 2010). However, in order to reinvigorate and shift GRB into directions that are slowly being drawn, we need to reflect on the emerging trends, draw the common threads across the different contexts, highlight the gaps in knowledge and experience and apply lessons learnt, more vigorously and comprehensively.

Mapping GRB in the AP Region

GRB has emerged as a practical strategy used by national governments in the region to advance implementation of gender equality commitments. By 2007, of the 90 countries that engaged in GRB worldwide, a quarter was found in the AP region. These include Afghanistan, Bangladesh, Bhutan,

Cambodia, China, Fiji, Indonesia, India, Marshall Islands, Maldives, Mongolia, Nepal, Pakistan, Papua New Guinea, Philippines, Samoa, Sri Lanka, South Korea, Thailand, Tunisia, Vietnam, China, Japan, Malaysia, Timor-Leste and South Korea.

Key Actors in the Region[12]

An important hallmark of GRB in the AP region is the range of actors engaged in this process. There are three possible ways of mapping this diversity.

The first classification pertains to initiatives led by the *government versus those led by civil society*. In the AP, a majority of initiatives have been spearheaded by the government, which includes countries like India, Cambodia, Indonesia, Sri Lanka, Bhutan, Nepal, Bangladesh and Pakistan. The experience of GRB in these countries clearly demonstrates the advantage of government-led initiatives, primary among which is greater national ownership. However, there have been concerns with regard to the limited institutionalization of GRB in most countries, despite national governments being at the forefront. As compared to government-led initiatives, the number of initiatives spearheaded by the civil society is much less. Philippines and Indonesia present interesting examples of countries where CSOs have taken the lead in promoting GRB especially at the local level. These initiatives have also drawn significantly from strategic partnerships with departments of local government, for instance.

The second classification pertains to *donor-led initiatives versus domestic initiatives*. Barring a few, in most countries, the initial impetus for GRB was provided by donor agencies, especially in the context of governance and public sector management reform programmes including in countries like Mongolia, Pakistan and Malaysia. The prominent donors in the region include World Bank, United Nations Development Programme (UNDP), UN-Women (previously UNIFEM), Commonwealth Initiative, Asian Development Bank, the Asia Foundation and bilateral partners, namely United Kingdom Department for International Development (DFID), Deutsche Gesellschaft für Internationale Zusammenarbeit (GIZ), Canadian International Development Agency (CIDA) and Australian Agency for International Development (AusAID).

The third pertains to the involvement of *traditional and non-traditional actors* on GRB. Again, the AP region provides an interesting template for this. While in most countries, GRB work has benefited from the engagement of traditional actors (apropos of the gender agenda) such as women's rights organizations and national women's machineries (NWM), there are several initiatives which have built synergies across tradition and non-traditional actors to engage Ministries of Finance (MoF) , Ministries of Planning, policy research organizations, CSO networks including those working on technical issues such as taxation and macroeconomic policy including the International Budget Partnership (IBP) which has partner budget groups in several countries like Bangladesh, Egypt, India, Indonesia, Nepal and the Philippines.

Given the diversity of actors involved, it would not be incorrect to state that GRB in the AP has emerged as a multi-stakeholder project drawing on the energies of a range of stakeholders—both government and non-government.

Identifying the Entry Points for GRB in the Budget Making Process

GRB initiatives in the AP region vary in scope, objective, strategy, entry points to the budget, tools of analysis, participants and the politics of engagement. What is even more striking is that this diversity cannot simply be attributed to the fact that GRB has emerged in very different country contexts, but as much to the persistent efforts of practitioners to experiment with new methodologies and tools to steer GRB in directions rather unique.

Given this diversity, it becomes difficult to capture GRB work in a single framework. However in this section, we make a preliminary attempt to do so, by using the budget making process as the framework to plot GRB interventions and entry points. However, there are two important caveats. Firstly, governments and CSOs have different roles to play in each of these phases, which could be either complementary or adversarial, depending on the political context as the latter holds the government to account by tracking and monitoring budgets. Therefore, it is important to note that while entry points for CSOs and government agencies may be similar or dissimilar, their approaches will may not necessarily be same. For instance, while producing a Gender

Budget Statement (GBS), which provides sector ministries with GRB instructions, falls within the mandate of the government, lobbying for its production, tracking and monitoring is the domain of civil society. In this section however, given the limitations of space, such distinctions have not been made. It is also important to remember that the engagement of non-government actors in the budget making process is itself contingent on how open and transparent these processes are.[13] Secondly, while entry points could be pegged to specific phases of the budget making cycle, formulation, legislation, implementation and auditing,[14] these are not water-tight compartments. Thus, it is important to note that the groundwork for one phase may be initiated in the previous phases, and likewise tracking and monitoring may take place in subsequent phases.

While details differ from country-to-country, the budget making cycle typically can be encapsulated in four stages: (a) formulation; (b) legislative (c) execution and (d) auditing.[15] Drawing on the country-specific experiences, we present here the key entry points that GRB initiatives have used.

At the Formulation Stage[16]

(a) **Budget Call Circulars**

Budget Call Circulars (BCCs)[17] have been used by many countries in the region—Afghanistan, Bangladesh, Bhutan and Timor Leste—to propel (in a way compel) ministries to start reflecting on gender in their budget submissions to the MoF. While the details of how gender has been integrated in a circular differ from country to country, the fact remains that once gender is mentioned in the CBC with some guidance on "how to" report, line ministries have no option but to include gender in their budget submissions, even though they may not otherwise be committed to addressing gender inequalities.[18] Therefore, while it may appear to be an "arm twisting strategy" of sorts in the initial years, the advantages gradually become palpable. The process of mechanically filling out formats or ticking checklists may eventually trigger off a more substantive engagement with gender issues, in other words develop a "gender consciousness" amongst policy makers and officials (Mishra and Sinha 2012).

In the table below, we provide a snapshot of the ways in which circulars in the region have included gender.

Table 7.1 Examples of "engendering" BCCs [This section is taken from Debbie Budlender's review of BCCs and GBS commissioned by UN Women (Budlender 2015)]

Country	*Description*
Bangladesh	The first BCC issued for each year requires that all ministries and all divisions within the ministry consider poverty reduction- and "women's advancement"-related impacts in respect of their strategic objectives and associated projects and programmes; sex-disaggregate key performance indicators where data are available
Bhutan	The first page of the 6-page BCC of January 2014 includes: *In formulating the budget proposal, budgetary agencies are required to ensure that budget proposals are gender responsive and incorporate ECP (Environment, Climate Change and Poverty) initiatives*
Pakistan	The gender-budget initiative proposed simple refinements to the budget circulars and the Medium term expenditure framework (MTEF) to increase their gender sensitivity and better align budgets with policies (See Mahbub and Budlender 2007).
South Korea	For 2006–2007, the Ministry of Planning and Budget required that every ministry report on budget allocations that aimed to promote gender equality: monitor the impact of mainstream programmes on gender equality; provided a format for the statements based on the existing national financial database, which records information on budget allocation, execution, performance evaluation and management. The GBS was to be included as part of this database (See Ichii and Sharp 2013; Elson et al. 2009).
Timor Leste	The 2014 budget circular, in respect of the 2015 budget year, includes the following sentence, but without further instruction as to how this should be done: *The programme of the fifth government commits that gender equality and nutrition for children are MDG objectives which need to be given attention from all.*

(b) **Gender Budget Statements**

In several countries, revision of the budget guidelines/call budget circulars has been followed by the production of GBS.[19] A GBS is a statement/document produced by the government which reports what a particular year's budget contains for gender equality/women's empowerment. The AP region provides an interesting mélange of GBS in terms of methodology, scope and format. Some of the most cited examples are provided in Table 7.2.

Table 7.2 GBS formats used in the Asia Pacific region

Country	*Description*
Australia	One of the first methodologies to track expenditures in relation to women was developed in the 1980s by Rhonda Sharp. It identified three categories for expenditures: (UNIFEM/UNFPA 2006) 1. Women-specific expenditures allocations to programmes specifically targeted at groups of women and girls. 2. Equal opportunities in public service allocations that promote the equal representation of women in management and decision-making, equitable pay and conditions of service of existing and prospective civil servants. 3. General or mainstream expenditures—the rest of the allocations.
India	Starting 2005, sectoral ministries in India have been following a methodology that identifies two categories of programmes: 1. Part A captures allocations that were 100% targeted at women and girls. 2. Part B captures allocations where at least 30% of the funds were targeted at women and girls. These data are compiled in the gender budget statement (Statement 20) that accompanies the Union budget.
Indonesia	The gender budget statement (also known as the gender-responsive budget sheet) includes the following components: 1. Programme, activity, performance indicator and output (as in "mainstream" budget document). 2. Objective of activity: How to achieve the output. 3. Situation analysis: Gender issues (in terms of access, participation, control and benefit) to be addressed by the activity. 4. Action plan: Sub-output/component inputs relevant for gender. 5. Amount of funds allocated. 6. Impact/result of activity output. 7. Signatories: those responsible for the activity.
Japan	Since 2004, appendices to the White Paper on Gender Equality have included allocations for programmes relevant to promoting gender equality: the Bureau requests each ministry to list the previous year's expenditure and planned expenditure in the twelve priority areas of the Plan. In 2009, the total allocated for the priority areas was estimated at 4% of the general account budget. Since 2009, the Bureau has published information on sub-categories of the budget for gender equality priorities. This information adds detail to what is in the appendices of the White Paper.
Malaysia	A GBS-type format was piloted, and a Manual on Gender Budgeting in Malaysia produced. The format of the GBS closely followed the performance-based approach used by the Malaysian Government for internal planning of development programmes in the country. The documents were not, however, made public, and the GBS thus did not serve as an accountability instrument.

(*continued*)

Table 7.2 (continued)

Country	*Description*
Nepal	The MoF formally introduced a GRB system developed by the GRB Committee in the financial year 2007–2008. In compliance with this system, 13 sectoral ministries were required to categorize their programme budgets according to three prescribed categories: 1. directly responsive where more than 50% of the allocation directly benefits women. 2. indirectly responsive where 20–50% of the allocation directly benefits women. 3. neutral, where less than 20% of the allocation benefits women. Nepal's approach to gender classification and rating of agency expenditures has been refined over the years in which it has been implemented The current system is based on five criteria, namely: (a) women's participation in programme formulation and implementation; (b) benefit accruing to women; (c) capacity building of women; (d) contribution to women's employment or income generation and (e) reduction in women's work load and qualitative improvement in time use. Each programme is given a score between 0 and 20 for each criterion. If the sum of the five scores is 50 or more, the associated programme is classified as directly gender-responsive; if the sum is in the range 20–49, the programme is regarded as indirectly gender-responsive; and the remaining programmes are classified as gender neutral

A review of the different GBSs developed in the AP offers interesting insights. Essentially, GBSs in the region can be categorized into two types: (a) those that have purely quantitative information (for instance India and Nepal), and (b) those that have a mix of quantitative and qualitative information (for instance Pakistan and Indonesia). The advantage of using a purely quantitative methodology is that these are easy to read documents and provide a single figure to demonstrate the quantity of funds flowing towards women or towards promoting gender equality. They also limit the space for ministries to hide behind verbose and text-heavy narratives, as seen early on in Australia (Budlender n.d.). On the flip side, however they are often too simplistic and end up reducing complex gender relations into a simplistic metric. The Indian experience of a purely quantitative GBS, for instance, draws attention to such problems. While the allocation reflected in the GBS is meant for women, the question that escapes scrutiny is whether these allocations in any way seek to redress gender imbalances. Furthermore, by reducing GBS to a number crunching exercise, it neither serves as a tool that informs policymaking nor does it enable policy makers to assess the additional steps needed to make policies/schemes more gender responsive. Therefore, while it helps answer the question as to how much is supposedly being allocated and spent on women, it does not directly facilitate nor demonstrate a gender-responsive planning and budgeting approach. We have argued earlier that those which use a mixed format are more analytical and provide a space for purposive gender planning (Mishra and Sinha 2012).

The other way of categorizing GBSs is to differentiate between: (a) those that disaggregate budgets by the sex of the beneficiary (India, Bangladesh, for instance); and (b) those that disaggregate budgets by the objective of the expenditure (Pakistan, Indonesia, for instance). An objective-based bifurcation is a much more useful way of disaggregating public expenditure. It is clearly more informative about the direction public policy ought to take to be more gender responsive. A further consideration is that classifying allocations and expenditure by sex can be relevant only for specific ministries where beneficiaries can be counted. For other ministries, one is bound to get stuck in a hair splitting exercise of how to arrive at the proportion flowing to women (ibid.). Allocations for "Ocean Science & Services" under the Ministry of Earth Sciences and "University Grants Commission" under the Department of Higher Education of the Indian GBS are cases in point.

(c) **Pre-Budget Consultation**

Distinct from the tools/processes discussed above, which largely capture work within the government, some interesting strategies have been used globally to enhance citizen participation in the budget formulation phase. There are hardly any examples from the region where finance ministries have arranged and institutionalized regular pre-budget consultations to ascertain key gender priorities with the notable exception of Nepal. This was discontinued in 2011 due to the volatile political situation. India too has experimented with this, although in an extremely limited and sporadic manner.

(d) **Participatory Budgeting**

Participatory Budgeting (PB), which was first developed in Brazil in 1989, inspired over 1500 such initiatives around the world, mostly at the municipal level .[20] Akin to other regions, there are very few examples in the AP in which PB has been used to foreground gender concerns/issues. An example is the 2012 GRB Pilot Project, a flagship project under the Penang Women's Development Corporation (PWDC) of Malaysia. Famously referred to as the Penang Model, it dovetails GRB with PB: the GRPB-Gender Responsive Participatory Budgeting was started with the premise that GRB is not by default participatory nor is PB by default gender responsive. The Penang model made a conscious attempt to dovetail GRB and PB to ensure that the process of deciding policy and budget allocations is as inclusive as possible so that priority needs within communities were identified and addressed.[21]

At the Legislative Stage[22]

(a) **Demystifying Budgets from a Gender Lens**
More often than not budget documents tend to be difficult to read, run into thousands of pages that unleash a barrage of numbers. However, in countries where budgets are available in the public domain, budget analysts step in and try to make sense of the budget. In a similar vein, GRB advocates in the region have provided critical analysis of the budgets from a gender perspective to inform public debates on the budget in the country. In India for instance, the Centre for Budget and Governance Accountability (one of the leading budget-work organizations) has a dedicated section on "women", as part of its overall Response to the Union Budget that is put out every year following the presentation of the government's budget to the Parliament.

(b) **Informing Budgetary Debates, Parliamentary Questions and Submissions to Relevant Parliamentary Committees**
Another interesting strategy that CSOs have employed is lobbying and advocating with parliamentarians to raise questions pertaining to GRB in parliament. In the recent past, several important questions have been raised by Indian Members of Parliament ranging from the extent to which GRB has been adopted, as a tool for gender mainstreaming at all levels and stages of budgetary process, to more specific questions about the proportion of funds reported in the GBS.

(c) **Modifying Parliamentary Rules of Procedure**

> The Parliament of Fiji Rules of Procedure provides that the standard committee "shall ensure that full consideration be given to the principle of gender equality so as to ensure all matters are considered with regard to the impact and benefit on both men and women equally". The clause is relevant to the extent that the Public Accounts Committee deals with budget-related documents and also is relevant at legislative, budget appropriation, execution and oversight phases.

At the Implementation Stage[23]

This is the stage when the executive produces important data through In-Year, Mid-Year and Year-End Reports. From a GRB perspective, an important parameter to assess these documents would be the extent to which the government provides data that is sex disaggregated, i.e. a prerequisite for conducting any gender analysis.

During this phase of the budget making cycle, CSOs can play an extremely significant role. It is only "by tracking budgets throughout their implementation, [that] civil society ensure that public resources were spent as they were supposed to. Also the impact of the budget can be assessed only once it has been implemented" (Ramakumar 2008: 3). Several tools including expenditure tracking and community monitoring tools, such as citizen's report cards, community score cards and social audits, have been developed and used by CSOs (ibid). From a GRB lens, this remains a rather unexplored area of work, as very few women's rights organizations have actively engaged with these tools.

There are only a handful of examples where these tools have been used to advance the gender agenda in the region. In Bangladesh, data was collected from over 125,000 people, mostly women, in 250 communities to assess their use and perceptions of health and family planning services as part of the evaluation of the country's Health and Population Sector Programme. In Pakistan, an audit of the gender gap in primary education revealed that teachers were demanding unofficial charges from students. A social audit on this issue of abuse against women sought to identify ways in which local action could improve the situation of women.

UN Women supported organizations working with *Dalit*,[24] *Muslim* women as well as transgender persons to track and monitor selected schemes meant for advancing gender equality (UN Women 2014b). Field data gathered as part of this exercise highlighted several gaps in implementation including the poor utilization of budgets and extremely low unit costs of services provided. These studies also brought out the heightened marginalization of women/persons belonging to the socially excluded groups. In Table 7.3 below, we provide a comparison of unit costs of two education schemes—one meant for girls from disadvantaged groups namely the *Kasturba Gandhi Balika Vidyalaya* (KGBV) and another for rural children, *Navodaya Vidyalayas* (NV) (Table 7.3).

However, such examples are few and far between. Although these tools have not been used much by gender advocates, they hold tremendous potential to strengthen GRB as an accountability tool. Adapting these tools for GRB would entail their application in a gender-sensitive manner or designing them in a way that will help raise and address critical gender questions.[25]

At the Audit Stage[26]

An important entry point is the audit stage. Typically, a gender audit (GA) exercise is carried out by experts at the organizational level to assess the "personal and institutional biases" in the culture of organizations that

Table 7.3 Differences in key budgetary heads between KGBVs and NVs

S.No	*Item*	*Kasturba Gandhi Balika Vidyalaya*	*Navodaya Vidyalaya*
1.	**Construction**	INR 3,875,000 for main building, boundary wall, boring/hand pump, and electricity	INR 120,000,000 in two phases for 14 classrooms, library, staff room, principal and vice principal's rooms, labs, three dorms, 23 teachers' quarters, kitchen and dining hall, playfield, water, sewerage, electricity, internal road
2.	**Equipment for furniture, kitchen provisions, etc.**	INR 300,000	INR 675,000
3.	**Bedding (Unit cost)**	INR 400	INR 750
4.	**School Uniform**	No provision	Summer—unit cost : INR 1,250 Winter—unit cost: INR 1,550
5.	**Medical care/ contingencies (Unit cost)**	INR 750	INR. 1,117

Source: Kumar and Gupta (2008)

prevent gender equality objectives being taken forward. However, the scope of GAs is now being broadened to include initiatives such as working with Supreme Audit Institutions to identify gender parameters and gender markers which should be part of the mainstream audit process.

GA as a tool could be useful in drawing the link from allocations to implementation, outputs and outcomes. In a way, integrating GA in GRB ensures that the interrogation is not purely at the level of allocations. Some work on this has been initiated in the region, for example, the annual report accompanying the Indian performance and outcome budgets tabled in Parliament forms one of the bases on which the Parliamentary Standing Committees that are constituted department wise[27] examine the department's Demand for Grants for the next financial year. Since 2007, the guidelines on outcome budget require each ministry/department highlight sub-targets for coverage of women and castes and tribes under various departmental schemes, disaggregated by sex and other relevant factors, put in place data collection systems to develop indicators of performance and impact relating to individuals as part of a suite of specifications regarding unit cost norms and quality standards, quantification/ factoring in of environment, community and empowerment outcomes of social capital formation. Moreover, the Ministry of Women and Child Development (MWCD) spearheaded an effort to develop GA guidelines which, at the time of writing, are awaiting approval by MoF. The Ministry of Rural Development has also developed and adopted GA guidelines.[28]

Entry Points Across the Budget Making Cycle

In addition to these entry points that are specific to certain stages in the budget making cycle, there are some other strategies which have been used significantly in the region but are not necessarily aligned to a particular stage in the budget making cycle. Some of these are discussed below.

Sectoral Application of GRB

Global experiences show that application of GRB at the sectoral level is an essential step in mainstreaming gender throughout the planning and budgeting cycle. Some countries in the region have identified this as an effective strategy to apply GRB tools at the central and decentralized levels of government. In Pakistan, for instance Gender Aware Policy Appraisals were conducted for the Education, Health and Population Welfare Sectors which became part of the gender-related inputs for the sector review reports of the government. Gender-Aware Beneficiary Assessment surveys were also undertaken in the two districts of Punjab province (Mahbub and Budlender 2007; Government of Pakistan and UNDP 2008). Countries like Bhutan which have recently started GRB are also focusing on sectoral application as a key strategy. Other examples range from gender budget analysis (India), to preparation of results-based GRB sectoral budgets, with gender-sensitive indicators (Indonesia, Nepal, Bangladesh)[29] and movement towards performance-based budgeting (Sharp 2003). These will be discussed further in section "Analysing the GRB Journey".

Creation of GB Focal Points/Cells/Committees/Task Forces

Another important strategy that has been used in several countries has been the creation of dedicated cells on GRB. Different countries have experimented with different structures—some have set up committees and task forces, others have set up cells within line ministries and/or a secretariat to coordinate, among others. An important task of these is to scrutinize Annual Work Plans (AWPs) and budgets of line ministries from a gender perspective. In some countries, this has provided a useful entry point for GRB. For instance in Cambodia, the Gender Mainstreaming Action Groups (GMAGs) are responsible for formulating a Gender Mainstreaming Action Programme (GMAPs)—a document in which the line ministry tries to identify the key gender gaps within the sector and delineate priority action points to address them (NGO CEDAW and CAMBO 2011). GMAPs thus offer an opportunity to integrate gender concerns in the line ministries plans and budget (Wong and Lay 2010).

Similarly in Indonesia, efforts have been made to screen for gender content in the context of shifting towards programme-based budgets,[30] which included developing sex-disaggregated indicators at the output level in its performance budgets, as well as performance targets to distinguish benefits by sex of the beneficiary. It built on previous methodological work undertaken on gender analysis, the Gender Analysis Pathway (GAP) to engender specific Sectoral ministry programmes at output/activity level (UNIFEM APAS strategy 2009–11- Background Papers, n.d.)

Capacity Building of Key Stakeholders

Capacity development has arguably been the most common strategy across the region, with significant investment made to develop GRB capacity at the organizational and functional levels. This is significant from a human rights-based perspective, since the success of GRB, to a large extent, is contingent on institutional mechanisms with the appropriate technical capacity (of duty bearers), as well as capacity of rights holders to review policies/plans/budgets and hold the government accountable on its commitments to implement GRB. However in most countries of the region, capacity development has been ad-hoc fashion and not underpinned with a proper strategy.

Emerging Trends and New Directions of GRB

Gender-Responsive Taxation

As the discussion in the previous section shows, most of the GRB work in the AP region has focussed on the expenditure side of the budget. As compared to other regions where work on the taxation has a much longer history (UK, Egypt and Tanzania), some countries in the AP, with more established GRB initiatives, have recently initiated this line of work, such as India and Nepal. Pakistan has already done some work in gender-aware revenue incidence analysis and has undertaken reforms in its tax regimes and tax laws to reduce discriminatory treatment of women.

Costing of Laws/Policies

The AP region has developed a compelling body of work on costing gender-based violence aimed to draw the attention of and trigger action from policy makers on this issue. The early studies conducted in Australia, Philippines and Fiji focused on computing the direct and indirect, tangible and intangible socio-economic costs of violence to women, their families, the community and society at large (see Laing 2001; Day et al. 2005; Artez et al. 1999). In recent years, in addition to socio-economic impact studies (in countries like Vietnam), a new body of work focusing on costing of legislation (Palau, Marshall Islands and Cook Islands) National Action Plans (Timor Leste, Nepal) and delivery of multi-sectoral package of services (Cambodia and Indonesia) has emerged (see UN Women 2013).

Application of GRB to Other Sectors/Domains

The region has also contributed to applied GRB work, in areas such as social protection, HIV and AIDS. This body of applied work has not just proved to be valuable to the sector in which GRB has been applied but has also deepened GRB itself, sometimes prompting practitioners to move beyond the first-generation questions such as how much is being allocated and spent on women or on gender equality to how particular expenditure addresses the causes and consequences on gender inequality. In the context of HIV and AIDS, given that much of the disease burden falls on women both in terms of prevention and care, it would follow that more resources would be allocated to programmes supporting women. The application of GRB to HIV and AIDS has therefore raised concerns not just about the adequacy of budget allocations for programmes that deliver quality services to women, but equally towards financing initiatives that contribute to the "transformation" of the unequal gender dynamics in the AIDS context. Similarly in applying GRB to social protection, it has become obvious that to be effective, existing GRB tools would have to be sharpened and would have to engage with the more fundamental debates around universal approach *versus* a targeted approach, direct cash transfers *versus* addressing supply side bottlenecks and so on.

Analysing the GRB Journey

The previous section has gleaned common threads from the diverse range of experiences of GRB. Given this diversity, in this section, we do not attempt to evaluate how successful GRB has been in the region but rather capture some of the key debates that have emerged and analyse in very broad terms the gains/gaps of implementing GRB. The discussion in the following section rarely offers any prescriptions of the "dos'" and "don'ts", but simply highlights the pros and cons of different choices.

The Key Debates

Some of the difficult and central questions that the GRB work in the region has struggled with are as follows:

(a) ***Where should GRB be located?***
Given the nature of GRB work, its effectiveness depends on the institutional mechanism responsible for implementing it. While the specificities differ from country to country, this discussion has mainly revolved around the role of the MoF and the Ministry of Women/NWM as the key drivers of GRB.

The oft-repeated argument for one side is that GRB is fundamentally about gender relations, it should find its logical placement in the NWMs/Ministry of Women, while the counter-argument for the other side is that since GRB entails engaging with budgets, the MoF should play the lead. The Beijing Platform for Action (1995) stipulates that the NWMs (albeit the Ministries of Women Affairs) have the critical mandate to mainstream gender which entails an advocacy as well as oversight to monitor policy action on gender equality commitments. On the other hand, an initiative led by the MoF facilitates greater institutionalization of GRB, given the strategic role it plays in defining and setting economic directions for a country's long-term growth (Sen 2000).

The AP provides an interesting mix of the two models and useful insights about the limitation of placing GRB squarely in either of these agencies. For instance, while in India, the MWCD is the nodal ministry for GRB, the MoF is the key driver of GRB in Bangladesh. The MoF in India played an important role in the initial years of GRB, but subsequently withdrew. Several commentators have cited this as possibly the weakest link in the GRB story in India (Chakraborty 2014, Mishra and Sinha *op. cit.*). In Bangladesh, while both the Ministry of Women and Children's Affairs and MoF were active in the formative years, the MoF has gradually emerged as the key driver of GRB, and under its stewardship, the process has become centralized, leading to some confusion among sectoral officials about reporting mechanisms, such as the RCGP (Recurrent, Capital, Gender and Poverty) database which serves as the primary source for computing gender allocations across specific sectors and is primarily managed by the MoF (UN Women-ADB evaluation of GRB forthcoming).

An important learning that the region offers is that models where MoF, MoW and other important ministries have come together tend to work better. In Indonesia, four ministries have come together as drivers of GRB—MoF, Ministry of Women's Empowerment and Child Protection, Ministry of National Planning and Ministry of Home Affairs (Government of Indonesia 2013). In Nepal, for instance, a GRB Committee was established in 2005 under the leadership of the Chief Budget and Programme Division, MoF, with representations from National Planning

Commission, Ministry of Women, Children and Social Welfare, Ministry of Federal Affairs and Local Development, Financial Comptrollers General Office and UN Women. [31]

What these examples demonstrate is the importance of having certain ministries *act as key drivers* for GRB, and given the nature of work, the Finance Ministry, Women's Ministry and the Planning Agency are critical to this equation. Moreover, they also in a sense reiterate that identification of leading actors should not forestall efforts to build synergies and seek active alliances with other key stakeholders including civil society.

(b) ***Should we set a minimum floor as a benchmark for what needs to be allocated under GRB or should we satisfy ourselves only with analysing the gender differential impact of budgets?***

Another important debate in the region pertains to the strategies of "appropriating/apportioning" budgets. On the one hand, there are models like Philippines where every government-related agency is required to allocate at least 5% of its budget for Gender and Development Budget (Budlender 2006), and the state of Kerala in India where 10% of devolved funds were earmarked for women (Eapen 2004). On the other, there are models such as Nepal, Bangladesh, India and Indonesia, where the emphasis is on interrogating allocations from a gender perspective and disaggregating them, mostly *via* GBSs.

Examining the practice of earmarking a certain percentage of funds for women, some GRB purists would argue that this approach is antithetical to what GRB stands for, i.e. not advocating a separate budget for women. More importantly, the focus on small proportions such as 5% and 10% takes the scrutiny off the rest of the budget where larger sums of money go. For other GRB practitioners, besides the more fundamental critique, there may be challenges in operationalizing this approach, especially in countries where the political class is uncomfortable with the idea of providing any kind of quotas for women.

However, we argue that this approach still holds merit since it establishes at least a floor minimum for implementing gender equality commitments. The most famous example is the GAD budget of Philippines. While there have been several challenges at the implementation level (including cases where GAD budgets have been used to fund events such as aerobics classes, cooking lessons, ballroom dancing and office outings (Jimeno 1999)), there is evidence to suggest that it has acted as an enabling mechanism for broadening the democratic and participatory governance process (Valdeavilla and Manapat 2001), or as Josefa Francisco (2001) describes, "a springboard to seek from government the basics of good governance for poverty eradication and gender-fair social development".

The experience of using the second model too has been mixed. As mentioned, the tool that most governments have used is the GBS. The foremost advantage of using the GBS is that it helps gender advocates answer the most basic question of estimating how much the government spends on women or gender equality targeted interventions. However, the main limitation of this approach is that efforts often stop at a mere "interrogation of allocations". It is important to remember that the ultimate objective should be to make budgets and policies an instrument to advance gender equality; merely the interrogation of the incidence of public expenditure (to assess whether it falls on men or women) does not suffice. For GRB to be effective, it is critical therefore to move beyond a mere review of allocation to actively track how financial investments are contributing towards the advancement of gender equality.

(c) ***Should GRB be a whole-of-government approach or should it be applied to select ministries?***

The third critical question that many countries have asked revolves around the appropriate scope of GRBIs—should GRB be applicable to the government in its entirety or should it be selectively applied to ministries.

The obvious pitfall of the latter approach is that there is a proclivity to focus on those ministries/sectors that are traditionally considered "women related" or "soft sectors", i.e. the social sectors, mainly health, nutrition and education. This could be for many reasons including the fact that it is easier to analyse expenditure targeted to individuals and generate sex-disaggregated data for these sectors. As a result, mainstream sectors such as infrastructure, trade and industry remain untouched, despite the larger political call of gender advocates that no sector is gender neutral (See UN Women 2014b). Experiences from the region show that this approach tends to work better as an initial strategy for introducing

GRB at the national level. By focusing on a few ministries, GRB practitioners are able to streamline their efforts to demonstrate the value added of this approach thereby creating a strong evidence base for further advocacy on GRB. Moreover, review of GRB work in the region suggests that even the so-called whole-of-government approaches often remain policy prescriptions. For instance in India, despite MoF guidelines since 2005–2006, the number of demand for grants has stagnated at 33 (out of total of 106) over the last few years.

The AP region provides some useful models to demonstrate that it may be prudent for governments to focus on a select few ministries in the initial years, but with a clear roadmap on how these efforts would be upscaled and sustained. However, this will be contingent on a range of factors including political and bureaucratic will and presence of champions. In Indonesia, for example, as per the National Strategy, the GBS was initiated with 10 Ministries in 2012, with the plan to include another 10 in 2013, and expand to all 34 Ministries by 2014. A slightly different entry point was used in Timor Leste where initially, with UN Women's support, the focus was on Ministries and State Secretaries responsible for the implementation of the Law against Domestic Violence and/or National Action Plans on Gender Based Violence such as Ministry of Justice, Ministry of Social Solidarity, Ministry of Education, Ministry of Health, Secretary of State for Security and the Ombudsmen for Human Rights and Justice. This was later extended to all ministries/sectors.

(d) ***Do we need to legislate on GRB or would a policy commitment suffice?***

In the AP region, there are no examples, such as in Austria or Ecuador, where GRB is mandated by the Constitution as a result of strong advocacy and lobbying by women's rights organizations. What exists is a broader, in principle commitment to gender equality in the Constitution. GRB is positioned at the level of policies in most countries, and laws in some others, again through the agency of women's rights organizations and commissions. In Korea, the 2006 National Finance Act dictated that starting the fiscal year of 2010, the submission of gender budgets will be mandatory. In Philippines, the 1996 and 1997 General Appropriations Act mandated agencies to set aside a minimum of 5 % of their 1998 budgets for projects addressing gender concerns. In Timor Leste, a Formulating Gender Budgeting Resolution was passed by Parliament in 2009–2010. Japan's Basic Act for Gender Equality of 1999 provided for a five-yearly Basic Plan for Gender Equality, in which Article 11 reads: "The Government shall take legislative, financial and other measures required to implement the policies related to promotion of formation of a gender-equal society".

As mentioned earlier, GRB in most countries is located in the domain of policies. Examples include India, the MWCD adopted "Budgeting for Gender Equity" as a mission statement in 2004–2005; and Bangladesh, where adoption of GRB by the government was triggered by the process of public finance management reforms.

There is no doubt that commitment from the highest levels is a must to take GRB forward for any country. While some practitioners argue that it is critical to push for legislation, since GRB would then become justiciable and to a large extent irreversible,[32] others argue that once enacted it is cast in stone which would thwart the potential of GRB to adapt and respond to the changing dynamics of the development context. The jury is therefore still out on this one.

A Critical Reflection on the Gains and Gaps

In this section, we analyse in very broad terms the key gains and gaps of GRB initiatives in the region, by setting out three fundamental questions that help assess the expected results of GRBIs in the short, medium and long term.[33]

(a) ***Has GRB resulted in more budgetary allocations for the gender agenda?***

Answering this question is difficult, even in countries with relatively long-standing initiatives on GRB. This can primarily be attributed to the lack of a proper mechanism/system to track that part of the overall budget meant for the advancement of gender equality. In the few countries that have such mechanisms, a rather mixed picture emerges. On the one hand, there are countries where the amount of budgets made available for gender equality has increased both in absolute terms and a proportion of the overall budget.

This includes Indonesia where the first evaluation of Gender-Responsive Budgeting and Planning (GRBP) in 2011 indicated an increase of budget allocation in some of the seven participating Ministries in Indonesia (Ministry of National Planning, Indonesia, 2011). In the previous years too, there is evidence to suggest that efforts by civil society since 2005 produced concrete results in project districts including a reallocation of total budgets to Indonesian Rupiah, Rp 10 billion, which resulted from savings of wasteful expenditure and reallocations (Asia Foundation 2008). In Nepal, the government's "directly gender responsive budget" allocation increased to 21.93% in 2014–2015 from 11.30% in 2007–2008.[34] While it is difficult to get the aggregate picture at the national level, budgets of certain local government units and sectors in Philippines have shown improvements (see Honculada 2009; Budlender 2006 *op.cit.*). For instance, in Sorsogon City, the increase in the health budget from 25 million pesos in 2005 to 37 million pesos in 2006 allowed for a much bigger allocation for reproductive health programmes.

On the other hand, there are countries like India that have shown a more stagnating trend with allocations in the GBS hovering in the range of 5.7 % to 5.8 % for the past several years now (Jhamb et al 2013). However, the recent Union Budget 2015–2016 shows a decline in the magnitude of the gender budget, not just in relative terms (as a percentage of Total Allocations, the magnitude reported under the GBS has declined from 5.5 % to 4.5 %) but also in absolute numbers from 980300 million to 792580 million. Similarly in Bangladesh, the gender allocation as percentage of total budget has not shown significant increase over years, and the figure has hovered around 26% since 2009–2010.

This differential and contradictory picture notwithstanding, the important point to underline here is that even if in a limited way, GRB has made it possible for this question to be asked and answered.

(b) ***Has GRB resulted in changing budgets and policies?***

This question can be answered at two levels—first at the level of assessing changes in sectoral policies and budgets and second at the level of changes in budgetary practices and processes, which in most countries is led by MoF.

There is much evidence to show that applied GRB work in sectors has demonstrable results. In India, Ministry of Overseas Indian Affairs initiated several gender-responsive policy measures including pre-departure orientation training for women migrant workers as well as review of the existing scheme for providing legal/financial assistance to Indian women deserted by overseas spouses.[35] Similarly, the Department of Telecommunications (DoT) launched an innovative scheme "*Sanchar Shakti*"[36] to provide mobile value-added services and information and communication technologies (ICT) related livelihood skills for Women's Self Help Groups.

With regard to changes in institutional practice, GRB has made budgetary processes and policies more gender responsive through instruments like the BCC and the production of GBSs. In Nepal, the MOF revised its Budget Management Information System (BMIS) and Line Ministry Budget Information System (LMBIS) of sectoral ministries to integrate the GRB classification criteria in the budgeting system. The Financial Management Information System (FMIS) operated by Financial Comptroller General Office (FCGO) also integrated GRB classification criteria to track the budget expenditure regularly against GRB criteria. The Office of Auditor General has made provision of the GRB criteria in their audit checklist.

In India, there has been a revision in the Expenditure Finance Committee[37] format to include gender questions in order to assess the extent to which gender concerns have been integrated in new programmes and schemes. In Bangladesh, the adoption of GRB as part of the larger Public Financial Management System (PFMS) has facilitated the inclusion of gender concerns and impact in the medium term budgetary framework process—the centrepiece of budgetary reform process in the country (UN Women-ADB forthcoming).

(c) ***Has GRB resulted in better outcomes for women?***

Where increased allocations are recorded, they can be attributed to a GRBI; however, outcomes are not easy to establish or attribute. Even in cases where this link can be established, these remain at best micro models and do not capture the big picture. In Barugo in Lyte province of Philippines, GRB has resulted in a women's desk being set up in the police station allowing privacy to rape survivors (2007), or separate toilets for women have been built in the municipality. Similarly, the GRB initiative in the Indian state of Kerala resulted in concrete changes to support gender equality investments in sectors which typically tend to neglect gender issues, such as infrastructure and transport. These include: the allocation of funds for a housing scheme that provides low-cost accommodation for low paid workers, particularly women (in Poojapura, Trivandrum Corporation and Kakkanad, Cochin Corporation); the creation of gender friendly infrastructure in transport depots, such as separate rest rooms and drinking facilities; allocation of funding to provide counselling facilities for women who experience violence; and to ensure the safety and welfare of women workers in minor ports, two buses for conveyance of women workers in Beypore and Vizhinjam (Ports) and night shelter for fisherwomen in two fish landing centres (Mishra 2011).

Some Challenges and the "Over Flogged Horses"

The review of GRB initiatives clearly demonstrates that it has a chequered history in the region. While there have been several significant gains, the potential of GRB remains untapped in the region—owing to a plethora of factors ranging from the regional fixation on a few tools (with the GBS being the most popular), lack of sex-disaggregated data, weak or non-existent monitoring and evaluation of GRBIs, to more broad based gaps in policy commitments and actions, as reflected in the absence of clear roadmaps on GRB. The recent regional Beijing plus 20 survey notes "countries in Asia and the Pacific have, however, yet to universally adopt gender-responsive budgeting as one means of advancing gender equality and of enabling implementation of the Platform for Action" (UNESCAP 2014b). The reluctance to embrace GRB was noted by, for example, Papua New Guinea.

> "To date there have been no significant initiatives to ensure any degree of gender responsive budgeting. The common assumption or expression of concern is that there is little political will to do so and that there is a lack of capacity to plan and monitor and report on budgeting per se without the addition of gender related planning and budgeting. Calls by various

> individuals to promote gender responsive budgeting from both in and out of Government have not been followed up."
>
> (Papua New Guinea, 2014 Beijing+20 national review report, p. 9)

Within the policy circuits however, no conversation on challenges faced by GRB seems to end without discussing the severe limitations that this line of work faces on account of the limited capacities of NWMs. This has in a sense become the "over flogged horse" in the GRB story. While we recognize this as an extremely critical gap, the reference to the "low capacity of NWMs" perhaps points to a much deeper malaise. The experience of GRB in the region demonstrates that more often than not, NWMs are made responsible for conducting capacity building workshops and producing training manuals, while other ministries go on with the more "serious" issues at hand. This is but a small illustration of how the gender agenda remains under-prioritized. It also remains extremely under-funded as captured in the Beijing Plus 20 review which shows in 15 of the 17 countries of the region, national budget allocation for the institutional mechanisms for the advancement of women is less than 1 %. This clearly demonstrates that despite policy announcements to promote gender equality, these remain empty promises. The gaps between rhetoric and reality will persist, unless and until concerted efforts are made to mainstream gender in the planning and budget making cycle, including to ensure that the GRB architecture finds legitimate space in the budget making cycle of the country and strengthen the application of GRB as an accountability tool by a cross section of civil society actors and women's rights activists.

Conclusion

As we move towards the implementation of the SDGs, it is imperative to reclaim the early understanding of GRB that the budget is as much a political as it is a technical process, and that essentially means examining the ways in which the distribution of power within that process affects the subsequent distribution of public resources (Norton and Elson 2002). GRB can be a strategic lever for transformational change, only if we reposition it within the emerging debates over policy and fiscal space for mitigating and building resilience to multiple crises (financial, food, fuel, climate), and employ it to support action and investment that will place gender equality at the heart of our development goals and macroeconomic frameworks.

Notes

1. The Post-2015 Development Agenda consisted of two processes coming out of the 2010 MDG Summit and the 2012 Rio+20 outcome documents. The MDG Summit requested the Secretary-General to initiate thinking on the global development agenda beyond 2015, while the Rio+20 Conference on Sustainable Development initiated an inclusive process to develop a set of sustainable development goals through the Open Working Group (OWG) on Sustainable Development Goals (SDGs). Member states adopted the Post-2015 Development Agenda at the UN Summit on 25 September 2015 *"Transforming Our World: The 2030 Agenda for Sustainable Development"*.
2. For instance, China is expected to grow at under 8%, while India and five key south-east Asian countries—Indonesia, Malaysia, the Philippines, Thailand and Vietnam—are all projected around a robust 6%. Other countries include the highly developed Singapore to countries with huge risks but electrifying potential, such as Bangladesh, Cambodia and Myanmar.
3. Statement by Asia Pacific Foundation of Canada President Yuen Pao Woo, Available at http://www.vancouversun.com/business/emerging-markets/Asia+Pacific+forefront+permanent+shift+global/8969148/story.html#ixzz3P9fFkMYG.
4. UNESCAP conducted a survey of Asia-Pacific member states that specifically focused on the 12 "critical areas concern" of the Platform for Action. ESCAP received 40 regional survey submissions and 32 national review reports. The analytical review encompassed ESCAP member States geographically located in the Asia and Pacific region. The analytical review also benefitted from inputs from civil society.
5. Successes in the area of education include increased female literacy levels; improved school performance amongst girls; greater numbers of women continuing to tertiary education and gender parity in primary school enrolments. Several countries have also recorded achievements in relation to women's and girls' health, particularly maternal health as evidenced by the reduction in maternal mortality rates and the construction of maternity facilities in hospitals.
6. In the area of women's political participation despite some advances in women's democratic representation (especially in countries where quota laws have been introduced such as Nepal and Timor Leste), there has been little overall increase in women's representation. The Pacific Islands remain the world's worst region for women's political representation. Moreover, despite the introduction of significant legislations/policy measures, violence against women remains pervasive as large numbers of women/girls across the Asia Pacific suffer from physical and/or sexual violence, usually at the

hands of their intimate partners. In the area of employment, inequalities prevail between women and men, such as are demonstrated by lower rates of female, than of male, labour force participation, the gender pay gap and both vertical and horizontal occupational segregation.

7. In the Philippines, 40,000 jobs were lost in export processing zones where women make up 80% of the workforce. In India, the textile industry lost over 700,000 jobs. In Cambodia, 63,000 women or 18% of the total workforce of the garment industry lost their jobs. In Yogyakarta, Indonesia, for example, as manufacturers replaced traditional handmade cloths with cheaper factory-made ones, the number of home-based workers dropped to 60% of their pre-crisis levels. For details see, Emmett, B. 2009; ADB and ILO 2013, 2014.
8. Within South Asia, these gender-based gaps are particularly large in India, Nepal and Pakistan. Some 1.08 billion workers in the region are classified in vulnerable employment—defined as own account and unpaid family workers—not benefiting from social protection. See Sen forthcoming; PWESCR 2011.
9. The policy prescriptions out of the previous Asian Crisis of 1997–1998 were trade and investment liberalization for export led growth and building of foreign reserves were prescribed; deregulation of financial markets; deregulation of labour markets; procyclical fiscal policy and social policies based on minimizing the state's role in employment protection and generation and in social protection, except for targeted and limited safety nets. For details, see UNIFEM APAS Strategy 2009–11. n.d.
10. The Future Asia Pacific women want Outcome Statement from women's and civil society networks and organizations present at the Regional Dialogue on Sustainable Development and the Post-2015 Development Agenda, Convened by Development Alternatives with Women for a New Era (DAWN) and Asia Pacific Gender and Macroeconomic Network (APGEM) in collaboration with United Nations Entity for Gender Equality and the Empowerment of Women Regional Office for Asia and the Pacific, 3–5 November 2012, Bangkok. http://www.dawnnet.org/advocacy-cso.php?id=268.
11. For a discussion on the Global Economic and Financial Crisis and its impacts on women, see Sirimanne 2009.
12. For details, see UNIFEM APAS Strategy 2009–2011 (n.d.).
13. For more details see http://internationalbudget.org/what-we-do/major-ibp-initiatives/open-budget-initiative/.
14. For more details, see Steps in Budget Cycle, http://internationalbudget.org/getting-started/why-are-budgets-important/steps-budget-cycle
15. For more details see Steps in Budget Cycle, http://internationalbudget.org/getting-started/why-are-budgets-important/steps-budget-cycle/

16. In the Formulation stage, the executive formulates the annual budget proposal. This is the most closed stage of the budget making cycle, and a stage that is dominated by the executive with the legislature and civil society having little direct access to this stage.
17. A Call Budget Circular (CBC) is a circular which serves as an instructional tool to guide all government spending ministries/entities as they begin the preparation for a new fiscal year budget. Although the format of BCCs differs widely across countries, typically BCCs instruct government agencies on how they must submit their bids (i.e. the format), in some countries they mention budget ceilings and in some countries they also underline budgetary priorities of the government.
18. For a more detailed account, see Debbie Budlender's report on BCCs and GBS (UN Women 2015).
19. According to Budlender (UN Women 2015) unlike call circulars, a gender budget statement is a tool specific to GRB. Where a gender budget statement is part of the budget planning and prioritisation process, the call circular or an associated document will almost certainly refer to it, and usually also describe the approach to be used, format, and the like. Where a gender budget statement is an accountability document, the call circular will not necessarily refer to it.
20. http://www.participatorybudgeting.org/.
21. For more details, see Asian Regional Conference, Gender Responsive Budgeting Narratives: Transforming Institutions, Empowering Communities, Gender Responsive Participatory Budgeting in Penang: The People Oriented Model, by Shariza Kamarudin, 24–25 February 2014, Bayview Hotel.
22. In the Legislative stage, the executive's budget proposal is presented to the legislature for approval. This is the stage in which people, the legislature and in fact many agencies of the government as well get the first comprehensive sighting of the budget. This stage is a high point in the budget making cycle with budgets getting a lot of attention from various quarters including the media.
23. The Execution of Implementation stage is the stage in which budgets are implemented, an executive function, however, but CSOs can develop effective oversight mechanisms.
24. The word "Dalit" comes from the Sanskrit root dal- and means "broken, ground-down, downtrodden, or oppressed". Those previously known as Untouchables, Depressed Classes are today increasingly adopting the term "Dalit" as a name for themselves.
25. See Concept Note—Asia Pacific Consultation on "Making Budgets Accountable to Women", 30 Sep–1 Oct, 2014, Bali, Indonesia organized by UN Women.
26. The last stage is the Auditing stage in which the audit reports of the Supreme Audit Initiation are tabled for legislative scrutiny.

27. In India, Departmentally Related Standing Committees (DRSCs) were introduced in 1993 to ensure oversight over each ministry. These Committees also hear expert witnesses and representatives of special interest groups. For details, see www.prsindia.org/.../1370586468_ Strengthening%20Parliamentary%20 Committees.pdf.
28. MoRD Gender Audit Guidelines. Available at http://drd.nic.in/drd/downloads/programmes-schemes/Gender_Audit.pdf.
29. These are mostly components of broader donor supported Public Financial Management Programmes.
30. This was introduced as pilot projects in six ministries which include National Planning Board, Ministries of Finance, Agriculture, Health, Education and Public Works.
31. The GRBC was established as a permanent body within the MOF with the mandate to design a GRB system that can be applied both at macroeconomic and sectoral levels, to scrutinize budget allocation and public expenditure from a gender perspective and finally to assess the impact of development policies on women and men.
32. In most countries, laws can only be changed/altered through Amendments which tend to be long drawn, unless they change laws, which is not an easy process.
33. In the short term, GRB work would become aligned to the national budget cycle, changes to national budget processes would be introduced, budget tracking mechanisms would be improved and documented, and linkages between gender advocates and budget decision makers would be strengthened. In the medium term, policy and budget processes would become more gender aware, budget allocations would reflect the priorities of poor and excluded women and good practices and lessons learned would be replicated through networks and knowledge sharing. In the long term, feminized poverty and exclusion would be reduced. See UN Women 2012.
34. Available at http://mof.gov.np/en/gender-responsive-budget-76.html.
35. Available at www.wcd.nic.in/gb/material/Training/2012-2013/12.pdf. *MWCD-IIPA Workshop on Gender Budgeting for State.*
36. Available at http://indiagovernance.gov.in/news.php?id=708.
37. One of the main committees which undertakes appraisal of public funded plan projects and schemes.

References

ADB, & ILO. (2013). *Gender equality in the labour market in Cambodia.* Mandaluyong City: Asian Development Bank.

ADB, & ILO. (2014). *ASEAN Community 2015: Managing integration for better jobs and shared prosperity.* Bangkok: ILO and ADB.

Artz, L., Saban, G., & Johns, L. (1999). *Gender and crime*. Institute of Criminology Annual Report, Captetown. web.uct.ac.za/depts/criminology/annrpts/anrep99.htm. Accessed 4 Feb 2015.

Asia Foundation. (2008). *Towards gender responsive budgets in Indonesia: The Asia Foundation's experience in Indonesia*. Jakarta: Asia Foundation.

Asian Development Bank. (2012). *Asian Development Outlook 2012: Confronting rising inequality in Asia*. Mandaluyong City: Asian Development Bank.

Budlender, D. (2006, June). *GRB work in Philippines*. Compiled by Debbie Budlender based on presentation by Florencia Casanova-Dorotan,Programme Manager WAND Philippines during UNIFEM/UNFPA GRB Workshop in Bangkok.

Budlender, D. (n.d.). *Review of gender responsive budget initiatives*, Commonwealth Secretariat. http://www.internationalbudget.org/wp-content/uploads/Review-of-Gender-Budget-Initiatives.pdf. Accessed 20 Jan 2015.

Chakraborty, L. (2014). *Gender responsive budgeting, as fiscal innovation: Evidence from India on "Processes"*. Working Papers 14/128, National Institute of Public Finance and Policy.

Day, T., McKenna, K., & Bowlus, A. (2005). The economic costs of violence against women: An evaluation of the literature, United Nations.

Eapen, M. (2004, November). *Report on gender analysis of select gram (village) panchayat*. Plan-Budgets in Trivandrum District, Kerala.

Elson, D., & Cagatay, N. (1999). *Engendering macroeconomic policy and budgets for sustainable development*. http://www.google.co.in/url?sa=t&rct=j&q=&esrc=s&source=web&cd=6&ved=0CDYQFjAF&url=http%3A%2F%2Fciteseerx.ist.psu.edu%2Fviewdoc%2Fdownload%3Fdoi%3D10.1.1.377.6464%26rep%3Drep1%26type%3Dpdf&ei=NO3BVMGeMMzN8gXF_YGIDw&usg=AFQjCNEyZUj1LVYIzzziyd4_XfKblb6a7Q&sig2=_hwtZBoCZkphZDqW1a6NXw&bvm=bv.84349003,d.dGc. Accessed 25 Jan.

Emmett, B. (2009). *Paying the price for the economic crisis*. Oxfam International: Oxfam International Discussion Paper.

Floro, M., & Pichetpongsa, A. (2010). Gender, work intensity, and well-being of Thai home-based workers. *Feminist Economics, 16*(3), 5–44.

Francisco, J. (2001). *The GAD budget examining public financing with a gender and poverty lens*. http://www.google.co.in/url?sa=t&rct=j&q=&esrc=s&source=web&cd=1&ved=0CB4QFjAA&url=http%3A%2F%2Fwww.aer.ph%2Fpdf%2Fsw2001%2Farticlec2001_phi.pdf&ei=un1AVZ6MLseWuATevIE4&v6u=https%3A%2F%2Fs-v6exp1-v4.metric.gstatic.com%2Fgen_204%3Fip%3D182.73.237.187%26ts%3D1430289851729912%26auth%3Dlre6q43w5dl2qrt5grjtakiwmknikvw6%26rndm%3D0.48925077913865045&v6s=2&v6t=3604&usg=AFQjCNFmg3wBS_4qHoK-SWd7OvKFR3w3gw&sig2=AAcy-vm_GCRVCSZsB3HVkQ&bvm=bv.91665533,d.c2E. Accessed 20 Jan 2015.

Government of Indonesia. (2013). *National strategy on accelerating gender mainstreaming through gender responsive planning and budgeting*, Govt. of Indonesia. http://www.google.co.in/url?sa=t&rct=j&q=&esrc=s&source=web&cd=3&v

ed=0CCgQFjAC&url=http%3A%2F%2Fpattiro.org%2F%3Fp%3D2522%26lang%3Den&ei=_ntAVaD0GJK1uQT6jYDQCw&usg=AFQjCNG0AuBc2Prz2ebiN16Xf3Q45VnuKw&sig2=u_out3qLr7OjPTvhmSIC3g&bvm=bv.91665533,d.c2E. Accessed on 10 Feb 2015

Government of Pakistan & UNDP. (2008). *Gender aware policy appraisal: Education sector*, Sindh by Saba Gul Khattak. Strengthening PRS Monitoring Project. Finance Division. http://www.grbi.gov.pk/grbidoc.asp. Accessed 18 Feb 2015.

Honculada, J. A. (2009). *Gender and good governance, examples of local innovations in gender responsive and results oriented budgeting*. Bangkok: UNIFEM.

Human Development Report. (2013). *The rise of the South: Human progress in a diverse world*. http://hdr.undp.org/en/2013-report. Accessed 10 Feb 2015.

Ichii, R., & Sharp, R. (2013). *Government budgets and the promotion of gender equality in Japan and South Korea*. Paper presented to the IAFFE panel of the Society of Heterodox Economics Conference University of New South Wales, Sydney, 2–3 Dec 2013.

Jhamb, B., Mishra, Y., & Sinha, N. (2013). The paradox of gender responsive budgeting. *Economic and Political Weekly, 48*, 35–38.

Jimeno, J. F. (1999, March 8–9). *Government women's budget goes to frivolous projects*. Business World.

Kumar, K., & Gupta, L. (2008). What is missing in girls' empowerment? *Economic and Political Weekly, 43*(26/27), 19–24.

Laing, L. (2001). *Australian studies of the economic costs of domestic violence*, Australian domestic and family violence clearing house, 2001; Henderson, Monika, impacts and costs of domestic violence on the Australian Business/Corporate Sector, Brisbane: Lord Mayor's Women's Advisory Committee, Brisbane City Council.

Mahbub, N., & Budlender, D. (2007, November). *Gender responsive budgeting in Pakistan: Experience and lessons learned*. http://www.gender-budgets.org/index.php?option=com_joomdoc&view=documents&path=resources/by-region-country/asia-documents/gender-responsive-budgeting-in-pakistan-experience-and-lessons-learned&Itemid=543. Accessed on 28 Jan 2015.

Ministry of National Planning, Indonesia. (2011). *Evaluation of gender responsive planning and budgeting implementation*, Ministry of National Planning, Republic of Indonesia.

Mishra, Y. (2011). *Breaking new frontiers of gender responsive budgeting: The Kerala model*. http://www.gender-budgets.org/index.php?option=com_joomdoc&view=documents&path=suggested-readings/breaking-new-frontiers-for-gender-responsive-budgeting-the-kerala-model&Itemid=587. Accessed 15 Feb 2015.

Mishra, Y., & Sinha, N. (2012). Gender responsive budgeting in India: What has gone wrong? *Economic and Political Weekly, 47*, 50–57.

Norton, A., & Elson, D. (2002). *What's behind the budget? Politics, rights and accountability in the budget process.* London: Overseas Development Institute.

PWESCR. (2011). *Global financial and economic crisis and its impact on women: A human rights perspective* (South Asia regional workshop report). New Delhi: PWESCR.

Ramakumar, V. (2008). *Our money, our responsibility: A citizen's guide to monitoring public expenditure.* Washington, DC: International Budget Partnership.

Sen, G. (2000). Gender mainstreaming in finance ministries. *World Development, 28*(7), 1379–1390.

Sen, G. (forthcoming). *Addressing risks, vulnerabilities and the need for social protection in the post 2015 development agenda: Challenges and pointers*, 2013.

Sharp, R. (2003). *Budgeting for equity: Gender budget initiatives within a framework of performance oriented budgeting.* New York: UNIFEM.

Sirimanne, S. (2009). *Emerging issue: The gender perspectives of the financial Crisis, Written statement, INTERACTIVE EXPERT PANEL, Fifty-third session of Commission on the Status of Women*, 2–13 March 2009, New York. http://www.un.org/womenwatch/daw/csw/csw53/panels/financial_crisis/Sirimanne.formatted.pdf

UN Women. (2012). *Evaluation of UN Women's work on gender responsive budgeting in India.* Conducted by FSG.

UN Women. (2013). *The costs of violence, understanding the costs of violence against, women and girls and its response: Selected findings and lessons learned from Asia and the Pacific*, UN women. http://www.google.co.in/url?sa=t&rct=j&q=&esrc=s&source=web&cd=3&ved=0CCgQFjAC&url=http%3A%2F%2Fasiapacific.unwomen.org%2F~%2Fmedia%2FField%2520Office%2520ESEAsia%2FDocs%2FPublications%2F2014%2F1%2FUNW_The_Costs_of_Violence_FINAL%2520pdf.pdf&ei=f3lAVbqxCYzguQTVxYHwBw&usg=AFQjCNHIDwSITVhj6J6TRPP4bTQH3h84Dg&sig2=0BZwo9LrveyNYjpuoE7JnA&bvm=bv.91665533,d.c2E. Accessed 30 Jan 2015

UN Women. (2014a). *World survey on the role of women in development 2014: Gender equality and sustainable development.* http://www.google.co.in/url?sa=t&rct=j&q=&esrc=s&source=web&cd=1&ved=0CB4QFjAA&url=http%3A%2F%2Fwww.unwomen.org%2F~%2Fmedia%2Fheadquarters%2Fattachments%2Fsections%2Flibrary%2Fpublications%2F2014%2Funwomen_surveyreport_advance_16oct.pdf&ei=aVZAVfenDdKdugSH14D4AQ&usg=AFQjCNHYsc8MaHYNt0QfQmUddmcAXRD0Wg&sig2=rv9nTb-IsoQoy2ys5FnaEQ&bvm=bv.91665533,d.c2E. Accessed 10 Feb 2015.

UN Women. (2014b). *Policy pack on 'People at the margins: Whose budgets? Whose rights?'* New Delhi, India.

UN Women-ADB. (forthcoming). *Assessing the effectiveness of gender responsive budgeting in Bangladesh.* Unpublished report.

UN Women. (2015). Budget Call Circulars and Gender Budget Statements in the Asia Pacific. A Review, New Delhi: UN Women.

UNDP. (n.d) *Challenges in Asia and the Pacific.* http://www.asia-pacific.undp.org/content/rbap/en/home/ourwork/womenempowerment/in_depth.html. Accessed 5 Feb 2015.

UNESCAP. (2014a). *Working paper on confronting inequalities in Asia and the Pacific: The role of social protection.* http://www.unescap.org/resources/working-paper-confronting-inequalities-asia-and-pacific-role-social-protection. Accessed 28 Feb 2015.

UNESCAP. (2014b). *Review of the progress and remaining challenges in implementation of the Beijing Declaration and Platform for Action in Asia and the Pacific.* http://www.unescap.org/resources/review-progress-and-remaining-challenges-implementation-beijing-declaration-and-platform. Accessed 20 Feb 2015.

UNFPA/UNIFEM. (2006). *Gender responsive budgeting and women's reproductive rights: A resource pack.* New York: UNIFEM.

UNIFEM. (n.d.). *Regional gender responsive budgeting strategy for Asia Pacific and Arab States [APAS] 2009–2011.*

United Nations. (2013). *World economic and social surveys 2013: Sustainable development challenges.* New York: United Nations Department of Economic and Social Affairs.

Valdeavilla, V. E., & Manapat, F. C. (Eds.). (2001). *Breaking new grounds for women's empowerment and gender equality: Experiences and insights in implementing the GAD budget policy.* Manila: NCRFW.

Wong, F. F., & Samkol, L. (2010, March). *Mid-term review of the partnership for gender equality (Phase 2 Extensions)*, Phnom Penh, Cambodia.

CHAPTER 8

Politics, Policies and Money: Delivering the Sustainable Development Goals for Women

Zohra Khan

It is clear that we have not invested sufficiently in gender equality. We know that persisting gaps in gender equality and women's empowerment in the world have been a barrier to the full achievement of the Millennium Development Goals. This has been explicitly confronted in the course of negotiating the Addis Ababa Action Agenda and in Goal 5 of the new [2030 Agenda for Sustainable Development]. It is also reflected in the multiple targets across the new agenda relevant to gender equality and women's empowerment.

Ban Ki-moon, United Nations Secretary General, July 14, 2015, UN-Women/World Bank high level side event at the third International Conference on Financing for Development, Addis Ababa, Ethiopia.

The views expressed in this chapter are those of the author and do not reflect the official position of the UN-Women.

Z. Khan (✉)
Policy Advisor, Governance and National Planning UN-Women, New York, USA

© The Author(s) 2017

Z. Khan, N. Burn (eds.), *Financing for Gender Equality*,
DOI 10.1057/978-1-137-46101-8_8

Introduction

The United Nations (UN) Secretary General's Report on the 20-year review and appraisal of the Beijing Declaration and Platform for Action (BPfA) paints a worrying picture. It found that while gains have been made in normative commitments on gender equality and women's rights since the adoption of the Platform for Action, persistent gaps remain across all 12 critical areas of concern.[1] The report cites several reasons for this including, amongst others, discriminatory social norms and practices, volatile economic contexts resulting from financial crisis and austerity, and the rise of extremism(s) and armed conflict. It further notes the "chronic" and "persistent" underinvestment in gender equality as a major contributing factor to slow progress globally.

This is not a new observation but comes at an important time as UN Member States have adopted a comprehensive set of agreements to achieve sustainable development by 2030.[2] Together, these agreements aspire to deliver decisively on poverty eradication, the protection and sustainability of the planet and the realization of human rights for all. Gender equality and the empowerment of women and girls is central to this vision and is firmly embedded in all three agreements. Specifically the 2030 Agenda for Sustainable Development, which provides the overarching framework for implementation, consists of 17 universal Sustainable Development Goals (SDGs) including a goal on gender equality and gender-related targets across a further 11 goals.[3]

The universality of these goals and its grounding in human rights represents a significant advance over the Millennium Development Goals (MDGs). The stand-alone goal to "achieve gender equality and empower all women and girls" includes targets on ending violence and harmful practices against women, recognizing care work and the right to social protection, addressing women's sexual and reproductive health and rights[4] and ensuring equal access to economic resources including land, property, inheritance and natural resources. The full implementation of the SDGs would substantially reduce gender inequality but only if they are buttressed with the right policies and adequate financing. The financing framework for implementing the SDGs is set out in the Addis Ababa Accord and Action Agenda, the agreed outcome of the third international Conference on Financing for Development, which proposes over 100 policy options for financing many of which include financing for gender equality and women's rights.

This chapter addresses financing for gender equality in the context of the 2030 Agenda for Sustainable Development and the Addis Ababa Action Agenda (AAAA). It argues that while gender equality, women's rights and empowerment is firmly embedded in these new frameworks, governments have historically failed to adequately invest in programmes that eliminate discrimination and promote women's human rights. This lack of investment is a major obstacle to implementing normative standards and agreements and therefore poses particular challenges to the implementation of the SDGs. The chapter draws on the AAAA to tease out the gender policy dimensions and explores a number of strategic policy options, including gender-responsive planning and budgeting, to support increased financing for gender equality and women's rights.

Financing for Gender Equality: What Is the Evidence?

The normative basis for financing gender equality and women's rights is set out in a number of international agreements, policies and treaties. Elson's chapter in this volume deals with two of these, namely the Convention on the Elimination of all Forms of Discrimination Against Women (CEDAW) and the International Covenant on Economic, Social and Cultural Rights (ICESCR). The BPfA further sets out the financing arrangements required to achieve the strategic objectives and actions of the Platform across all 12 critical areas of concern. It emphasizes that all sources of financing should be mobilized to meet gender equality goals and provides a clear framework for mobilizing resources at national, regional and international levels, including through regional development banks and international organizations. It further calls on states to resource institutional mechanisms to advance gender equality, or national machineries, as well as civil society organizations.

Additionally, many UN summits, conferences and meetings, including the 23rd Special Session of the General Assembly, the International Conferences on Financing for Development and various sessions of the Commission on the Status of Women,[5] have called on governments to increase investments in gender equality. Moreover, the Secretary General's report for the 52nd Session of the Commission on the Status of Women in 2008 went further to define *financing for gender equality* as the process of "ensuring adequate resource allocations to translate commitments on gender equality and women's empowerment into action, including financing of critical stakeholders within national women's mechanisms and women's organizations". [6] It called on government actors to:

> Ensure an enabling policy environment for financing for gender equality through macroeconomic policies that are conducive to increased financing

for gender equality; address systemic issues to ensure coherence between economic policies and financing for gender equality requirements; strengthen capacity for gender responsive planning and budgeting and implementation in the public sector; ensure gender responsive public finance reform to enable gender responsive accountability in public finance management; strengthen parliamentary oversight and citizen engagement in monitoring financing for gender equality; and strengthen systems for measuring financing for gender equality.[7]

Quantifying financing gaps is challenging due to lack of sex-disaggregated data and comprehensive, standardized methodologies on costing gender equality. In 2006, the United Nations Millennium Project Task Force attempted to estimate the financing gap for MDG 3 on promoting gender equality and empowering women. Using data from five low-income countries,[8] the study found that the financing required to meet the targets of this goal ranged from US$ 8.6 billion in 2006 to US$ 23.8 billion in 2015 in these countries.[9]

More recently, a number of countries have undertaken costing exercises to estimate the financing requirements for implementing national gender equality action plans and strategies. These have highlighted significant funding gaps. For example, the 2nd National Action Plan for Gender Equity and Equality (2010–22) in Honduras was estimated at US$ 13.3 million per annum however, only US$ 2.8 million per annum had been allocated to the Plan, resulting in a 78 % financing gap. Similarly in Jordan, the 2013–17 National Strategy for Women was estimated at US$ 5.8 million per annum, but only US$ 254,237 per annum was allocated, resulting in a 79 % gap. While in Kyrgyzstan, the National Action Plan for Gender Equality (2012–14) was estimated at US$ 10 million. UN-Women's costing analysis found that only 10 % of activities were covered by the State budget resulting in a 90 % financing gap.[10]

Inadequate financing hinders the implementation of laws and policies with dire consequences for women. To illustrate, despite the 45 % decrease in the maternal mortality ratio between 1990 and 2013, approximately 300,000 women died from *preventable* causes related to pregnancy and childbirth in 2013.[11] Data on the number and distribution of midwives from 47 countries reveal an average of only four midwives per 1000 live births to respond to the expected rate of obstetric and newborn complications of 337 per day.[12] Investment gaps that contribute to the high rate of maternal mortality and morbidity include under-resourced health systems, limited coverage of quality services, and the lack of skilled attendants at birth.[13]

Similarly in the area of girl's education, while gender disparities have narrowed since the introduction of the MDGs, significant differences remain across regions due in large part to underinvestment. In 2012, 64% of countries in the developing regions achieved gender parity at the primary level, 36% of countries in developing regions reached parity at the secondary level, while only 4% of countries in this category reached parity at the tertiary level.[14] Considering that education is the third largest funded sector, preceded by economic infrastructure and health, with expenditures ranging from 7% to 30% of total government spending,[15] it is concerning that countries have not done better on these MDG targets. UNESCO[16] highlights a number of structural barriers, including early marriage and the sexual division of household labour, that prevent girls from staying in school. The report also cites the lack of water and sanitation and long travel distances as key factors leading to uneven progress in this area. It recommends that greater investment, in the form of cash transfers and feeding schemes, is made to improve girls' retention rates and calls for gender-responsive budgeting to ensure that sufficient funds are allocated to these policy actions.

Programmes to eliminate violence against women, while high on the global policy agenda, remain largely underfinanced with governments allocating only a fraction of national budgets to violence prevention and the provision of essential services. The Belém do Pará Convention,[17] signed by 35 member states from North, Central, South America and the Caribbean in 1994, found budget allocations to address violence against women ranged from 0.1% to 1% of national budgets. The review body therefore recommended that signatories to the Convention "approve budget appropriations for the execution of public policies, plans, and programs that guarantee equality in preventing, responding to, punishing, and progressively eradicating violence against women in the public and private spheres, and that the budget appropriations approved match the severity of the problem in each country".[18]

Financing for Institutional Mechanisms in Support of Gender Equality

A key indicator of government commitment to gender equality is financing institutional mechanisms for the advancement of women or "national women's machineries". The BPfA underscores the importance of strengthening national machineries through the provision of adequate resources and technical expertise to accelerate delivery on the strategic objectives and actions of the Platform. Women's machineries play a critical role in promoting gender equality and women's rights especially in supporting the design and implementation of gender-responsive national development strategies and action plans. However, they often lack resources required to meet this mandate, limiting the potential of these agencies to influence mainstream policy development, planning and budgeting. Government Spending Watch[19] (2013) found that in 13 countries with available data, government spending on national women's machineries was less than 0.4% of GDP, and spending levels had either remained flat or fallen as a percentage of GDP since the financial crisis.[20] Similarly, the UN Secretary General's report cites several studies that have analyzed the nature, scope and effectiveness of national women's machineries and found that resource constraints were a recurring pattern across countries and regions.[21]

At the global level, international organizations tasked with promoting and protecting gender equality and women's rights face similar constraints. UN Women was established in 2010 through General Assembly Resolution 64/289 in response to calls for system-wide coherence on gender equality and women's empowerment. UN-Women has a comprehensive and wide-ranging mandate that includes support to intergovernmental bodies in their formulation of policies, global standards and norms; support to Member States to implement these standards and support to the UN system's work on gender equality. In announcing the establishment of UN-Women, Secretary General Ban Ki-moon estimated that approximately US$ 500 million was needed for the full operationalisation of the Entity in its first year. In 2013–14, the UN-Women funding target was estimated at US$ 610 million, but contributions from Member States were a mere US$ 275.4 million, the highest level of voluntary contributions received since the Entity was established.[22] The universal, comprehensive and ambitious mandate of UN-Women has not been matched with requisite resources, which has limited the potential of the Entity to fulfil its mandate. Even preceding the establishment of UN-Women, the BPfA explicitly called for increased funding to the UN system to fulfil its gender equality mandate, in particular to UNIFEM and INSTRAW, which were severely under-resourced.[23]

Bilateral and Multilateral Financing

Similar trends of underinvestment are prevalent in both bilateral and multilateral funding. While the MDGs have galvanized donor support for gender equality and women's empowerment in the areas of health and education, funding gaps remain in the economic sectors and in peace and security.[24] To illustrate, despite relatively high levels of funding in the health sector overall, the OECD's own analysis found that funding for family planning has declined substantially from 71% (1995) to 36% in 2012. Overall aid in support of family planning remained critically low at US$ 678 million on average per year in 2011 and 2012. The low levels of investment are of particular concern considering the unmet need for family planning estimated at 222 million women of reproductive age and the recognition that investment in family planning is a strategic investment that contributes both to women's health and improved status and realization of their rights.[25]

Donor aid flows that target gender equality in peace and security have remained stagnant despite the increasing and disproportionate impact of conflict on women and girls and the commitments under the various UN Security Council Resolutions. In 2008, UN-Women[26] assessed 3000 activities, indicators and budget lines of planning frameworks including Post Conflict Need Assessments (PCNAs), Poverty Reduction Strategy Papers (PRSPs) and UN Development Assistance Frameworks (UNDAFs) in 12 countries to determine if women's priorities were included in peacebuilding projects.[27] The review revealed a persistent gender bias. It found that on average only 5.7% of total resources were allocated to activities directly related to addressing women's needs in postconflict situations. The study also revealed that only 2.9% of the budget in the PCNAs was allocated to gender-specific priorities and only 2.6% of the budget allocated in PRSPs addressed gender equality. This despite the UN Secretary General committing the UN system to allocate at least 15% of UN-managed funds in support of peacebuilding to projects that *"address women's specific needs, advance gender equality or empower women"* as their principle objective. Douglas and Mazzacurati's chapter in this volume unpack some of the more structural reasons for peacebuilding funding targets remaining elusive. These include women's lack of access to decision-making processes and low implementation capacity at the country level, amongst others.

Scant attention is paid to women's needs in humanitarian contexts too. In 2012, Gender Action and Haiti Grassroots Watch conducted a gender analysis of the World Bank and the Inter-American Development Bank's (IADB) post-earthquake financing in Haiti. From January 2012 to August 2013, the World Bank and the IADB invested US$ 667.34 million and US$ 1.087 billion, respectively, in post-earthquake reconstruction. Using a gender checklist,[28] they found that only US$ 2.4 million out of US$ 1.75 billion, or 0.14 %, was allocated to gender-specific priorities and that only 4 out of 24 projects conducted consultations with women during the planning and implementation of these projects, while only 7 collected sex-disaggregated data.[29]

Similarly, a 2013 Care International study assessed donor funding for emergency appeals and humanitarian assistance in 17 conflict-affected countries. Using the Gender Marker,[30] the study measured the percentage of total emergency appeal funding allocated to projects that were gender focused/sensitive or specifically addressed gender equality. The findings revealed that the top 10 donors[31] contributed 0–5 % of the total projects to gender-specific interventions. In addition, up to 14 % of the total interventions were gender blind. In countries like the Democratic Republic of Congo and Afghanistan, where women are severely affected by ongoing conflict, a large proportion, 54 % and 22 %, respectively, failed to address women's specific needs.[32]

The financing deficits highlighted above, at all levels and across all sectors, for both bilateral and multilateral funding as well as national and international machineries, point to a broader trend of underinvestment in gender equality and women's rights. Inadequate financing coupled with underinvestment in public services presents a major challenge to achieving gender equality commitments. Public investment is particularly important to eliminate structural bias and reverse widespread discrimination against women and girls.

The Political Declaration adopted during the 59th Session of the CSW (2015) called on governments to "take concrete actions to ensure the full, effective and accelerated implementation of the Platform for Action through significantly increased investments to close the resource gaps which hinder the achievement of gender equality".[33] This requires robust and predictable financing from all sources and at all levels including enhanced domestic resources, increased and better focused official development assistance (ODA), private financing that is fully aligned with national gender plans and the efficient leveraging of non-traditional types of financing including innovative and blended financing.

The *Addis Ababa Action Plan on Transformative Financing for Gender Equality and Women's Empowerment,* launched by member states, women's organizations and UN-Women on the margins of the third international Conference on Financing for Development, aims to galvanize political support and action to increase financing for gender equality and foster greater accountability to meet gender commitments. It maps the policy and financing actions needed at national level to mobilize the resources for implementation of the SDGs and other existing gender commitments as set out in the BPfA (see Annexure 1). Framed around the actions areas of the AAAA, it proposes concrete policy measures to increase domestic and international, public and private sources of financing for gender equality.

Policy Options for Financing Gender Equality and Women's Rights From the AAAA

Enhancing Domestic Resource Mobilization

In most countries, domestic public resources are the largest and most stable source of financing for development. To illustrate, according to the OECD, in 2012, total tax revenue in Africa was ten times the volume of ODA received.[34] Governments are responsible for ensuring that domestic resources are raised and spent in ways that advance national development objectives including the provision of basic public services (water and sanitation, energy, health, education) and enhancing human development through decent work and social protection. The 2014 report of the UN Intergovernmental Committee of Experts on Sustainable Development Financing (ICESDF) recommended that governments use fiscal policy to address inequalities and tackle poverty.[35] It follows that fiscal policy instruments should be used to redress systemic discrimination and support the goal of greater equality.

The growing body of feminist research and analysis (See Stotsky 1996; Grown and Valodia 2010) on tax policy shows that tax measures often fail to take into account gender differentials in the household and economy. In most countries, tax policy is based on the nuclear family model of a male breadwinner and female caregiver. Women's unequal position in the economy as workers, employers, consumers and care givers is ignored and policies fail to recognize the role of the care economy in contributing both to the commodity and the public services economy through the provision of human and social capital (Elson 1997). As a result, tax policies are based on incorrect assumptions about women and men's time, work patterns and income.

The categorization of gender biases in tax systems as "implicit" and "explicit" was developed by Stotsky (1996) who identified such biases in both direct and indirect taxes. She argued that explicit gender biases are usually "specific provisions of the law or regulations that treat men and women differently" while implicit biases "depend on [prevailing attitudes] and value judgements as to desirable social and economic behavior of men and women".[36] For example, explicit gender bias in personal income tax (PIT), a form of direct tax, may involve inequity in the allocation of tax deductions and exemptions where primary earners (usually men) receive favourable tax breaks not afforded to secondary earners (usually women). On the other hand, an implicit bias may involve a higher tax rate for secondary earners (usually women) as their income is seen as supplementing the primary earner (usually men) when taxes are filed jointly.

Another form of implicit bias vis-à-vis indirect taxes that has asymmetric and negative impacts on women is tax on consumption. While these indirect taxes, such as sales tax, are uniformly applied, they may have unintended discriminatory impacts if commodities consumed mostly by women, such as menstrual hygiene products, are taxed at higher rates than those consumed mostly by men. In Canada, a petition to remove general sales tax on menstrual products was successful after it was established that in 2014 alone, the government of Canada received $36,398,387.00, or 6.9%, of the $519,976,963.00 spent on menstrual products while general sales tax went down from 7% to 5%.[37] Some taxes can even have the effect of increasing women's care work. For example, in Kenya, taxes levied on kerosene had a disproportionate negative impact on poor families since they could not afford to use kerosene and so switched to cheaper sources of energy such as wood and coal. From the perspective of labour and time, this required much more input from women, as compared to men, as they were responsible for collecting firewood.[38] In general, women are subject to greater indirect tax because they spend a larger proportion of their incomes on goods and services subject to these taxes. As a result, they bear a higher tax burden than men often without the commensurate increase in public services that would reduce and support the redistribution of care work between the household and State and enable greater economic participation.

Since tax policy can and does influence women's economic choices and impacts gender outcomes in several ways, it is important that principles of equity are built into tax measures. Grown (2005) notes however that "equity" or "fairness" is a normative or value-based principle and as such differs across countries and contexts. In outlining the various definitions and principles of fairness, she argues that the most commonly accepted idea of fairness is that taxes should be "progressive", i.e. those with lower incomes should have a lower tax burden and vice versa.[39] Given the potential of tax policy to reverse discrimination in this regard, it is imperative that governments implement fair and progressive tax policies that eliminate both implicit and explicit gender biases and shift the tax burden to groups, including corporations, with higher incomes.

Corporate tax is an important source of domestic revenue, but tax avoidance and evasion continues to rob countries of vital resources. Christian Aid estimates that developing countries lose approximately US$ 160 billion each year to tax evasion of which 80% may be attributed to the "deliberate minimization of the tax share of multinational corporations and wealthy individuals".[40] Additionally, many countries reduce corporate tax rates in order to attract foreign direct investment (FDI). Globally, average corporate tax rates have declined from 38% in 1993 to 24.9% in 2010.[41] Profit shifting too is a major problem as multinational corporations move corporate income to tax haven subsidiaries with low tax liability. A recent report by Citizens for Tax Justice found that 500 US companies have US$ 2.1 trillion in offshore tax havens.[42] This substantial loss of domestic revenue deprives countries of investing in essential public services including education, health, water and sanitation that are particularly important for women.

Despite the herculean effort of developing countries and civil society organizations during the FfD negotiations, agreement to establish an intergovernmental body on tax cooperation was not reached. Such a body would have allowed, amongst other things, stronger cooperation on tax matters across countries including curbing tax evasion, avoidance and illicit financial flows. Nonetheless, the AAAA emphasizes the importance of "inclusive cooperation and dialogue among national tax authorities on international tax matters"[43] and commits to strengthening the work of the UN Committee of Experts on International Cooperation in Tax Matters.

It is vital that this tax committee is resourced with gender expertise and has stronger representation from developing countries.

In addition to raising revenue in ways that are gender responsive, it is equally important to allocate resources in a similar fashion. Gender-responsive budgeting (GRB) is a strategic policy approach that explicitly seeks to address inequality and discrimination in fiscal policy. It seeks to integrate gender equality concerns into government planning and budgeting in order to align policy commitments with resources. By introducing principles of equity and equality into government budgets, GRB strengthens systems of planning and budgeting and democratizes the budget process. Globally, over 100 countries implement GRB at national and local levels. The AAAA explicitly calls for governments to "increase transparency and equal participation in the budgeting process, and promote gender responsive budgeting and tracking". [44] This provides an important entry point to systematically capture data on government spending and monitor investments against new and existing commitments.[45]

In countries where tracking systems have been developed, promising results have emerged. In Ecuador, budget allocations for gender equality doubled in 2012 reaching 4.77% of the total budget, while Nepal reported increased allocations from US$ 0.877 billion in 2012–13 to US$ 1.36 billion in 2014–15 accounting for 22% of the total budget.[46] Several countries in Latin America and the Caribbean have introduced GRB laws mandating sector ministries to address gender gaps in planning and budgeting decisions. In 2006, Bolivia added an article to Ministry of Finance regulations requiring that municipal governments allocate public resources to support gender equality. Over a 4-year period, gender-responsive allocations in 36 municipalities increased from US$ 384,885 to US$ 23,879,989.[47] Similarly, Mexico City mandated the earmarking of public funds for 40 institutional activities that aimed to improve gender equality. As a result, funds allocated to gender in the period 2008 to 2010 have increased from US$ 95 million to US$ 104 million.[48]

Many GRB experiences have been effective in strengthening women's voice and participation in the budget increasing citizen/state accountability. In Libokemkem district in Northern Ethiopia, women community members began analysing the local government plan from a gender perspective. They felt strongly about walking long distances to fetch water and therefore demanded representation on the 11 water committees in the district. They successfully secured three out of seven seats in each committee and ensured that water collection sites were placed closer to their homes reducing time and labour spent collecting water.[49] Investments in public infrastructure and quality public services are absolutely vital for women as they support women's increased incomes and labour productivity as well as generate tax revenues.

If domestic resource mobilization is central to the new development agenda, then fair and progressive tax systems that tackle discrimination and bias must be in place. Governments must cost and adequately resource national policies, strategies and plans on gender equality across all sectors of public expenditure, and ensure they are integrated into national development financing strategies. Investments in accessible, affordable and quality social infrastructure and essential public services that reduce and redistribute care and domestic work and enable women's full participation in economic and political life must be prioritized. It is the duty of the State to provide the enabling policy, regulatory and institutional environment for gender equality by enacting and enforcing non-discriminatory laws, policies and institutional practices. Realigning fiscal policy to prioritize investment in gender equality and women's rights can stimulate inclusive economic growth and achieve the objectives of inclusion and non-discrimination.

More and Better International Public Resources

ODA is critical for financing sustainable development especially in countries with low capacity to mobilize resources domestically. Between 2002 and 2013, Development Assistance Committee (DAC) members' aid commitments to gender equality and women's empowerment rose from US$ 8 billion to US$ 28 billion[50] and increased at a faster rate than overall aid, growing by 4% annually compared to 1% in overall aid flows.[51] Much of this gender-focused aid was closely aligned to the MDGs 3 and 5 on eliminating gender disparity in education and reducing maternal mortality ratios. As a result, significant funding gaps in women's economic empowerment; sexual and reproductive health and rights; and the women, peace and security agenda remain.[52]

The OECD-DAC uses a statistical instrument called the *gender equality policy marker* to capture the extent to which aid targets gender equality as a policy objective. The marker is used by 28 of the 29 DAC members screening 92% of all bilateral "sector allocable" aid and provides a good indication of how donors prioritize gender equality in their development cooperation. While the gender marker does not measure gender equality outcomes or the impact of gender programmes, it does provide data on the proportion of ODA focused on achieving gender equality, sectors prioritized for such aid, investment within the individual sectors and the recipient countries prioritized.[53] As such, it is an important indicator of donor priorities. The systematic collection of this data over time has been important in identifying gaps between donor political commitments and the resources allocated to gender equality.

Despite the gender equality marker showing increases in bilateral aid targeting gender equality and women's empowerment, the failure of most donors to achieve the UN target of 0.7% of GNI and 0.15% to 0.2% of GNI to least developed countries negatively affects the overall volume of ODA available. Only 5 DAC members have reached the 0.7% of GNI target, and the OECD average is around 0.4%. Coupled with the re-direction of aid to address humanitarian crises, such as that unfolding is Syria, it is likely that resources will be further constrained. On the other hand, given the low level of investment in women, peace and security, gender-focused aid should constitute a higher portion of overall redirected aid to reverse the underinvestment in the humanitarian response and support the women, peace and security agenda.

Given the catalytic role of ODA in many countries, and to enhance and maximize the quality of gender-focused ODA in the context of SDG implementation, ODA should be targeted to a wider range of sectors. For example, increased investment in key sectors impacting women's employment and care work such as agriculture, water and sanitation, transport and energy should be prioritized as these are essential for reducing and redistributing care and domestic work and for facilitating women's greater economic and political participation. Moreover, and in accordance with the principles of the Paris Declaration, gender equality-focused ODA must align with national action plans on gender equality, including those on ending violence against women and women, peace and security in conflict-affected countries, as well as support gender equality objectives in broader national and sectoral development strategies.

In order to increase gender-focused ODA overall, donors must strive to meet the UN targets, including that of the UN Secretary General's 15% of peacebuilding and recovery funds, and commit to clear allocations for gender equality and women's empowerment within these. ODA was a critical point of contention in the FfD negotiations particularly as it related to meeting targets, timetables and its convergence with vertical financing streams like climate adaptation and mitigation funds. Efforts over the last 18 years to strengthen the methodology and implementation of the gender equality policy marker have enabled us to now identify donor funding gaps across countries, sectors and between sectors. This data has contributed to increasing transparency of information and contributed to greater accountability and financing for gender equality. The *Transformative Financing Action Plan* calls on donors to systematically track and prioritize ODA allocations in support of gender equality and take specific actions to close financing gaps, and implement the UN target of 15% of peacebuilding funds targeting gender equality as a principal objective. These steps will go a long way to ensuring that aid responds to women's needs.

Promote a Socially-Responsible and Accountable Private Sector for Gender Equality and Women's Empowerment

It is estimated that the cost of SDG implementation will be in the region of US$ 3.5 to 5 trillion a year in developing countries.[54] Much of this investment is expected to be mobilized through domestic resources and ODA, but a large portion will be sourced from the private sector. Foreign Direct Investment (FDI) accounts for more than 40% of external development finance, and while global inflows fell to $1.23 trillion in 2014, it is projected to rise to $1.7 trillion by 2017.[55] As a long-term source of development finance, FDI can be an important driver of economic growth; however from a gender equality perspective, it has a mixed record.

While there has been a growth in jobs for women in export processing zones, feminist analysis shows that governments often relax labour and health regulations with negative repercussions for women. Businesses might also employ practices that further entrench gender inequality, for example, through occupational segregation where women are concentrated in particular types of jobs characterized by low pay and low skills. Further, Braunstein (2006) argues that while FDI has had a positive impact on women's employment in semi industrialized countries, there is increasing evidence that women either lose jobs to men as industries upgrade, or are pushed down the production chain into subcontracted, insecure work as competition forces firms to continually lower costs.[56]

The AAAA highlights the role of private business in development finance and encourages business to align with national sustainable development objectives and adopt models that consider the social and environmental impacts of their investments. The emphasis on women's economic empowerment and the role of business in supporting this objective is well articulated in the AAAA which encourages the private sector to "contribute to advancing gender equality through striving to ensure women's full and productive employment and decent work, equal pay for equal work or work of equal value, and equal opportunities, as well as protection against discrimination and abuse".[57] It also calls on governments to undertake legislative reforms to ensure women's equal access to land, property, credit and inheritance, amongst others, to support women's economic empowerment. It stresses the importance of financial inclusion as a central policy objective and urges commercial banks to support this noting that the vast majority of those who lack financial services and financial literacy are women.[58] It encourages the use of innovative tools such as mobile banking to address this problem.[59] There are many positive examples in this regard. Some companies like Safaricom in Kenya have introduced M-Pesa which is an e-wallet system that provides women with access to financial services in countries where banking systems remain exclusionary.

Another important area for private investment that is critical for gender equality is infrastructure. According to UNCTAD, the infrastructure investment gap in developing countries is estimated at US$ 2.5 trillion a year.[60] Poor and inefficient infrastructure has an enormous social and economic cost to households, communities and societies and is a key barrier to sustainable development. Infrastructure investments are *public goods* as they produce benefits to society as a whole by bringing public service to households, promoting economic growth and opportunities for people. Investment in sustainable and resilient infrastructure is especially important for reducing women's time poverty and care work. Unlike in developed countries where infrastructure funding is mostly sourced locally, developing countries turn to the private sector for such investment.[61] Blended finance, where public finance is used to leverage private capital in order to increase the volume of development finance, has been touted as a useful instrument for infrastructure development. Public–private partnerships (PPPs), a subset of blended finance, are often the main vehicles used to mobilize financing for infrastructure projects. However, PPPs can also increase public debt burdens and shift risks to the public sector. Debt burdens divert funds away from public expenditures for health care, education and other social services and can sometimes undermine human rights commitments. The AAAA acknowledges the potential and limits of using blended finance mechanisms and states that PPPs "should not replace or compromise state responsibilities, and should include clear accountability mechanisms".[62]

The private sector is an important actor for the provision of capital, job creation and infrastructure development, but State regulation is essential if private finance is to support implementation of the SDGs. While private financing flows might dwarf public flows, governments are responsible for delivering on the SDGs and for regulating the private sector. Governments should encourage long-term investments that create an enabling environment for the full realization of gender equality and human rights by contributing to the creation of decent jobs for women, ensuring equal pay for equal work or work of equal value, and providing support to women to balance paid and unpaid care work. Support to women entrepreneurs and women-owned businesses, including improving women's access to finance and expanding trade opportunities for women producers is vital for inclusive economic growth.

Private actors should also assess the gender and human rights implications of its investments as well as its own internal operations using legal and voluntary frameworks. This entails compliance with human rights and environmental standards as set out in legally binding as well as voluntary frameworks including the ILO Core Conventions,[63] the UN Guiding Principles on Human Rights and Business and the UN Global Compact's Women Empowerment Principles.

Conclusion

This chapter discusses financing for gender equality and women's rights in the context of the 2030 Agenda for Sustainable Development and the Financing for Development outcome. It has argued that despite the centrality of gender equality and women's rights in the new agenda, the "chronic and persistent" pattern of underinvestment threatens to hold and even roll back progress. Yet there is unprecedented political will to reverse this trend. The 2030 Agenda explicitly commits to working towards "a significant increase in investments to close the gender gap and strengthen support for institutions in relation to gender equality and the empowerment of women at the global, regional and national levels".[64] To achieve this objective, governments must adopt policy measures aimed at mobilizing all sources of financing in support of their national and international gender commitments. This will not be an easy task but one that is essential if the objective of "leaving no-one behind", so central to the vision of the new agenda, is to be achieved.

In this chapter, I have presented some strategic policy options for consideration. At the national level gender-responsive tax measures, costing and gender-responsive budgeting can support the mobilization of greater resources for gender equality programing. At the international level, gender targeted ODA used strategically and across a wider range of sectors, including agriculture, water and sanitation, transport and energy, will make a significant difference. Private, blended and innovative financing streams offer new opportunities for gender-responsive investment, but private actors must fully align with national gender equality objectives, set out in actions plans and strategies, and be held to the same accountability standards as public actors.

None of these financing sources alone will close the gender financing gap. All actors, whether governments, donors, international financial institutions, regional development banks, intergovernmental organizations, civil society or the private sector, must use all available financing sources and instruments to secure the requisite investment to meet their gender obligations. Multi-stakeholder partnerships for gender equality and women's rights at country, regional and international levels are vital to take this agenda forward. They must include civil society actors whose role it is to ensure that governments, donors and private actors are fully accountable for ensuring that the requisite capital (human and financial) is readily available. The transformative financing and policy actions needed require all actors to singularly focus on one goal—the achievement of gender equality and the fulfilment of women's human rights.

For both developed and developing countries alike, the task of implementing a universal, transformative agenda that covers all three dimensions of sustainable development, (economic, political and environmental) poses unique challenges. Moreover, this challenge is set against a backdrop of profound geopolitical shifts, an alarming rise in violent conflict and extremism(s), economic and financial volatility, war, climate change and the displacement of people. Agenda 2030, if understood in an interconnected and comprehensive manner, provides a framework for action on all these fronts. Yet, however well-defined and well-intentioned the SDGs are, achieving them will require fundamental shifts in fiscal policy, financial regulation and economic cooperation at national and global levels. Greater economic cooperation, deepened multilateralism buttressed with an international financial system that places human development as its top priority, is the lynchpin for success.

Notes

1. UN. 2014. Review and appraisal of the implementation of the Beijing Declaration and Platform for Action and the outcomes of the twenty-third special session of the General Assembly—Report of the Secretary-General.
2. The three agreements are the Addis Ababa Action Agenda adopted at the third International Conference on Financing for Development in July 2015; Transforming Our World: the 2030 Agenda for Sustainable Development adopted at the Special Summit on Sustainable Development in New York in September 2015 and the Climate Treaty adopted at the 21st session of the Conference of the Parties to the United Nations Framework Convention on Climate Change (UNFCCC COP 21) in Paris in December 2015.
3. Gender targets are included in the SDGs on poverty, hunger, health, education, water and sanitation, employment, inequality, cities, climate change, peace and the global partnerships.
4. The SDGs do not make reference to sexual rights.
5. Including the 52nd, 58th and 59th sessions of the Commission on the Status of Women.
6. UN, 2008. Commission on the Status of Women Report on the fifty-second session (25 February-7 and 13 March 2008) Economic and Social Council Official Records, 2008 Supplement No. 7.
7. Ibid.
8. Bangladesh, Cambodia, Ghana, Tanzania and Uganda.
9. Grown, Bahadur et al. (2006) "Financial requirements of achieving gender equality and women's empowerment". Paper prepared for the World Bank, Levy Economics Institute of Bard College.
10. UN Women, 2015. "Handbook on Costing Gender Equality". New York, USA.
11. United Nations. "The Millennium Development Goals Report 2014."
12. UNFPA (2011). *The State of the World's Midwifery (SoWMy).*
13. The Partnership for Maternal, Newborn and Child Health (2013). *New Global Investment Framework for Women's and Children's Health.*
14. UN. The Millennium Development Goals Report 2015, p. 29.
15. UNESCO, 2015. Education for All: Global Monitoring Report 2000–2015.
16. Ibid.
17. The Inter-American Convention on the Prevention, Punishment, and Eradication of Violence against Women was adopted in Belém do Pará, Brazil, in 1994. It states that violence against women constitutes a violation

of human rights and fundamental freedoms. The Convention established for the first time mechanisms for the protection of women's rights to eliminate violence against their physical, sexual and psychological integrity, in both the public and private spheres. The effective implementation of the Convention requires a continuous and independent evaluation process, which in 2004 led to the creation of the Follow-up Mechanism to the Belém do Pará Convention (MESECVI). MESECVI is a systematic and permanent multilateral evaluation methodology that is based on exchange and technical cooperation between the States Party to the Convention and a Committee of Experts. MESECVI analyzes progress in the implementation of the Convention by the States Party, as well as persistent challenges to an effective State response to violence against women.

18. Inter-American Commission of Women. Follow-up Mechanism to the Belem do Para Convention (MESECVI). *Second Hemispheric Report on the implementation of the Belem do Para Convention* (2012).
19. Government Spending Watch (2013). *Putting Progress as Risk, MDG Spending in Developing Countries.*
20. It is important to note that government spending through national women's machinery covers only a small portion of total gender-responsive spending.
21. United Nations Economic and Social Council, Report E/CN.6/2015/3. "Review and appraisal of the implementation of the Beijing Declaration and Platform for Action and the outcomes of the twenty-third special session of the General Assembly., Report of the Secretary General."
22. UN Women (2014). "Annual Report 2013–2014." New York.
23. United Nations (1995). "Beijing Declaration and Platform for Action."
24. OECD-DAC Network on Gender Equality (2014). *Financing the unfinished business of gender equality and women's rights: priorities for the post-2015 framework.*
25. Guttmacher Institute and UNFPA (2012). *Adding it Up: Costs and Benefits of Contraceptive Services – Estimates for 2012.*
26. UN Women (2008). *What women want: planning and financing for gender-responsive peacebuilding.*
27. Additionally, over 394 project documents were analyzed from Multi-donor Trust Funds (MDTFs) and Joint Programmes across six countries.
28. http://www.genderaction.org/publications/11/checklist.pdf.
29. Gender Action (2013). Building Back by Half? Gender Issues in IFI Investments in Post Earthquake Haiti. USA.
30. The UN Gender Marker is an important tool to address differing vulnerabilities of men and women in the design and implementation of the humanitarian responses. However, this is a relatively new system, with varying levels of consistent usage by donors, UN agencies and aid agencies delivering projects on the ground.

31. United States, EC, Japan, United Kingdom, Germany, Canada, Sweden, Norway, Switzerland and Kuwait.
32. Care International UK (2013). *Donor Spending on Gender in Emergencies 2013.* London, UK.
33. United Nations Economic and Social Council. Report E/CN.6/2015/L.1. "Political declaration on the occasion of the twentieth anniversary of the Fourth World Conference on Women".
34. OECD- DAC. 'Development Co-operation Report 2014: Mobilizing Resources for Sustainable Development'.
35. UN. 2014. Report of the Intergovernmental Committee of Experts on Sustainable Development Financing.
36. Stotsky, J. Gender Bias in Tax Systems (September 1996). IMF Working Paper, Vol., pp. 1–22, 1996.
37. https://www.change.org/p/no-tax-on-tampons-a-campaign-to-remove-the-gst-charged-on-menstruation-products-sign-the-petition.
38. Khan Z. 2006. The Likely Impact of Economic Partnership Agreements on Women's Rights and Gender Equality in Mozambique, Namibia and Zambia. One World Action. UK.
39. Grown, C. 2005 "What Gender Equality Advocates Should Know about Taxation" Paper for the Gender Equality and Economy Program Levy Economics Institute Bard College September 28, 2005.
40. Christian Aid. 2014. "Taxing Men and Women: Why gender is crucial for a fair tax system".
41. Ibid.
42. McIntyre, R. et al. 2015. Offshore Shell Games 2015—the Use of Offshore Tax Havens by Fortune 500 Companies.
43. UN, 2015 Addis Ababa Action Agenda of the third International Conference on Financing for Development. p14.
44. Ibid- p15.
45. Under SDG 5, indicator 5c will "*measures the number of countries which have set up systems to track gender equality allocations and to make those allocations [available to the] public*". The proposed indicator will allow the collection of comparable data over time to ascertain exactly how much financing goes towards gender equality.
46. UN Women. Increasing Accountability in Financing for Gender Equality: Programme Brief. 2015.
47. Coello, R., & Wretblad, E. (2012). *GRB world tour.* Unpublised Conference Paper. Report prepared for the International high-level conference on Gender-Responsive Budgeting, 'Sharing knowledge and designing policies and budgets to achieve gender equality', Marrakech, November 9–10th, 2012. Ministry of Economy and Finance of Morocco & UN Women.

48. Data from Mexico Ministry of Finance, 2013.
49. UN Women. 2015. Gender Responsive budgeting in Ethiopia: Fact Sheet.
50. "From Commitment to Action: Financing for Gender Equality and Women's Rights in the implementation of the Sustainable Development Goals" OECD DAC Network on Gender Equality, March 2015.
51. In 2013, ODA reached US$ 134.8 billion.
52. "Financing the unfinished business of gender equality and women's rights: priorities for the post-2015 framework." OECD-DAC, 2014.
53. Ibid.
54. While there are no agreed estimates on financing needs for the SDG, the Report of the Intergovernmental Committee of Experts on Financing Sustainable Development provides various estimates such as "$US 66 billion annually which is a rough estimate of the cost of a global safety net to eradicate extreme poverty in all countries (measured as increasing incomes of the poorest to the $1.25-a-day standard); $US5 trillion to $7 trillion globally annual investment requirements in infrastructure—water, agriculture, telecoms, power, transport, buildings, industrial and forestry sectors"—that will support employment generation. The Report also warns that quantifying financing needs is "complex and imprecise". P8.
55. World Investment Report 2014. UN Conference on Trade and Development (UNCTAD).
56. Ibid, p. 14.
57. AAAA, Para 41.
58. The World Bank estimates that about 2 billion women lack access to financial services.
59. Ibid, Para 39.
60. World Investments Report 2014. UN Conference on Trade and Development (UNCTAD).
61. Hruby, A and Jawara, D. 2015 "Closing the infrastructure investment gap in Africa" in Financial Times March 6, 2015.
62. The Addis Ababa Accord of the Third International Conference on Financing for Development. Revised Outcome Document (7 May 2015), paragraph 48, p. 11.
63. See ILO Conventions at: http://www.ilo.org/global/standards/lang--en/index.htm; UN Principles on Human Rights and Business: http://www.ohchr.org/Documents/Publications/GuidingPrinciplesBusinessHR_EN.pdf and UN Global Compact's Women Empowerment Principles: https://www.unglobalcompact.org/take-action/action/womens-principles.
64. UN. 2015. Transforming our World: the 2030 Agenda for Sustainable Development. Resolution adopted by the General Assembly on 25 September 2015, P6.

Annexure 1

Addis Ababa Action Plan on Transformative Financing for Gender Equality and Women's Empowerment

We, advocates of gender equality and women's empowerment, pledge to significantly increase investments, in both scale and scope, to close the financing gaps that hinder progress towards gender equality and women's empowerment. Our intent is to identify and agree on transformative policy and financing actions to accelerate implementation of existing commitments in the Beijing Declaration and Platform for Action and to meet new commitments in the context of the post-2015 development agenda.

We laud the strong gender focus in the negotiated outcome document and invite all stakeholders—governments, international financial institutions, regional development banks, intergovernmental organizations, civil society, the private sector and others—to translate these commitments into action through the endorsement and implementation of this Action Plan (Table 8.A).

Table 8.A Addis Ababa Action Plan, areas of commitment, policy and financing actions

Areas of commitment	*Policy and financing actions*
1. Domestic policy actions and public resources for gender equality and women's rights	Ensure fair and progressive tax systems by addressing explicit and implicit gender biases in tax policies Provide tax incentives to support ownership of assets/property by women Cost and adequately resource national policies, strategies and plans on gender equality across all sectors of public expenditure, and ensure they are integrated or closely linked to national sustainable development financing strategies Prioritize investments in accessible, affordable, and quality social infrastructure and essential services that reduce and redistribute women's unpaid care and domestic work and that enable their full participation in the economy
2. International policy actions and resources for gender equality and women's rights	Systematically track and prioritize allocation of ODA in support of gender equality and take specific actions to close financing gaps in order to meet new and existing targets on gender equality and women's empowerment Adopt the UN target of a minimum of 15% of all peacebuilding funds targeting gender equality as a principal objective Ensure that global trade, financial and investment agreements are conducive to the promotion of gender equality, women's empowerment and the human rights of women and girls through ex-ante and ex-post gender impact assessments as well as targeted incentives and investments, including Aid for Trade, capacity building and participation of women in global supply chains
3. Enabling environment for women's economic empowerment and sustainable development	Promote and enact legislative and administrative reforms to ensure women's equal rights to economic and productive resources, including to inheritance and access to, control over and/or ownership of land and other property, credit and other financial services, information and communication technologies and other forms of technology and capacity building to utilize and maximize the potential of these services/assets Develop strategies to support women entrepreneurs and women-owned businesses, including by improving women's equal access to finance and expanding trade opportunities for women producers Enforce core labour standards and anti-discrimination laws for decent work, including ensuring minimum wage legislation and equal pay for work of equal value Ensure women's equal rights, access and opportunities for leadership and decision-making in all sectors

(*continued*)

Table 8.A (continued)

Areas of commitment	*Policy and financing actions*
4. Multi-stakeholder partnerships for gender equality and women's rights at country, regional and international levels	Use all available opportunities and processes to build political commitment—from governments, international organisations, civil society organisations, academia, and the private sector—in support of transformative financing for gender equality and women's rights Adequately resource local, national, regional and global women's rights institutions and organisations to advance gender equality, women's empowerment, and the human rights of women and girls
5. Data, monitoring and follow-up	Track and publish allocations to and public spending on gender equality Close data gaps by investing in national statistical capacity to systematically collect, analyse, and use data disaggregated by sex and age through appropriate financial and technical support and capacity-building Develop and enhance national standards and methodologies to close data gaps

References

Braunstein, E. (2006). Foreign direct investment, development and gender equity: A review of research and policy (Occasional Paper 12). UNRISD.

CARE International UK. (2013). *Donor spending on gender in emergencies 2013: An investigation by CARE international UK into the UN data on donor aid to emergency appeals for 17 countries in crisis.* London: CARE International UK.

Christian Aid. (2014). *Taxing men and women: Why gender is crucial for a fair tax system.* Christian Aid UK.

Development Finance International (DFI) & Oxfam International. (2013). *Putting Progress at Risk? MDG Spending In Developing Countries.* General: Oxfam GB for Oxfam International under ISBN 978-1-78077-331-5. Web. 19 Nov 2015. Government Spending Watch Report.

Elson, Diane. (1997). *Gender-Neutral, Gender-Blind or Gender-Sensitive Budgets?: Changing the Conceptual Framework to Include Women's Empowerment and the Economy of Care.* Commonwealth Secretariat.

Gender Action. (2013). *Building back by half? Gender issues in IFI investments in post-earthquake Haiti.* Washington, DC.

Gender Action. (2015). *Gender action's essential gender analysis checklist.* General: Gender Action.

Grown, C. (2005). *What gender equality advocates should know about Taxation.* Paper for the Gender Equality and Economy Program Levy Economics Institute Bard College September 28, 2005.

Grown, C., & Valodia, I. (2010). *Taxation and gender equity*. London: Routledge. Print.

Grown, C. et al. (2006). *Financial requirements of achieving gender equality and women's empowerment*. Annandale-on-Hudson: The Levy Economics Institute. Web. 19 Nov 2015. Papers Prepared For The World Bank.

Hruby, A., & Jawara, D. (2015, March 6). Closing the infrastructure investment gap in Africa. Financial Times.

Inter-American Commission of Women. (2015). *Follow-up mechanism to the Belém Do Pará convention (MESECVI)*. General: Organization of American States. Web. 19 Nov 2015. Second Hemispheric Report On The Implementation Of The Belém Do Pará Convention.

Khan, Z. (2006). *The likely impact of economic partnership agreements on women's rights and gender equality in Mozambique, Namibia and Zambia*. One World Action, UK.

McIntyre, R. et al. (2015). Offshore shell games 2015 – the use of offshore tax havens by fortune 500 companies.

OECD DAC Network on Gender Equality (GENDERNET). (2015). *From commitment to action: Financing gender equality and women's rights in the implementation of the sustainable development goals.* OECD The Development Assistance Committee: Enabling Effective Development. Web. 19 Nov 2015.

OECD Development Assistance Committee (DAC) Network on Gender Equality. (2014). *Financing the unfinished business of gender equality and women's rights: Priorities for the post-2015 framework.* General: OECD. Web. 19 Nov 2015. Policy Brief.

Organization of American States. (1994). *Inter-American convention on the prevention, punishment, and eradication of violence against women.* General: Department of International Law - Organization of American States. Print.

Secretariat, United Nations. (2015). United Nations Secretary-General Ban Ki-Moon's statements.

——— (2012). *Adding it up: Costs and benefits of contraceptive services estimates for 2012.* Guttmacher Institute & UNFPA. Web. 19 Nov 2015.

Stotsky, J. G. (1996, September). *Gender bias in tax systems* (IMF Working Paper). pp. 1-22.

The Partnership for Maternal, Newborn & Child Health. (2013). *Global investment framework for women's and children's health.* General: World Health Organization WHO.

UN Conference on Trade and Development (UNCTAD). (2014). World Investments Report.

UNESCO. (2015). *Teaching and learning: Achieving quality for all.* General: UNESCO. Education for All Global Monitoring Report.

United Nations. (2014). *The millennium development goals report 2014.* General: United Nations.

United Nations. (2015a). *Addis Abba action agenda*. United Nations. Web. 19 Nov 2015. Third International Conference on Financing for Development.

United Nations. (2015b). *The millennium development goals report 2015*. General: United Nations. MDG Reports.

United Nations Economic and Social Council. (2008). *Commission on the status of women - Report on the fifty-second session*. General: United Nations. Web. 19 Nov 2015. Commission on the Status of Women.

United Nations Economic and Social Council. (2014). *Review and appraisal of the implementation of the Beijing declaration and platform for action and the outcomes of the twenty-third special session of the general assembly*. General: United Nations. Web. 19 Nov 2015. Report of the Secretary-General.

United Nations Economic and Social Council. (2015). *Political declaration on the occasion of the twentieth anniversary of the fourth world conference on women*. General: United Nations Economic and Social Council. Web. 19 Nov 2015. Commission on the Status of Women.

UN Women (2008). *What women want: Planning and financing for gender-responsive peacebuilding*. UN Women. Web. 19 Nov 2015.

UN Women (2014). *Annual report 2013-2014*. General: UN Women.

UN Women (2015a). *Handbook on costing gender equality*. General: United Nations Entity for Gender Equality and the Empowerment of Women, European Commission, International Training Centre ILO.

UN Women (2015b). Gender responsive budgeting in Ethiopia: Fact Sheet.

United Nations General Assembly. (2010). *Resolution adopted by the general assembly 64/289. system-wide coherence*. General: United Nations. General Assembly Sixty-Fourth Session.

United Nations Population Fund UNFPA. (2014). *The state of the world's midwifery 2014 A universal pathway. A woman's right to health*. General: UNFPA.

UN Women, European Commission & International Training Centre ILO. (2015). *Increasing accountability in financing for gender equality: Programme brief*. UN Women.

CHAPTER 9

From Commitment to Action: Aid in Support of Gender Equality and Women's Rights in the Implementation of the Sustainable Development Goals

Emily Esplen and Patti O'Neill

Introduction

Governments from all regions of the world have placed a high priority on achieving gender equality and empowering all women and girls as a central ambition of the 2030 Agenda for Sustainable Development.[1] Agenda 2030 tackles the structural drivers of gender inequality which were left largely untouched by the Millennium Development Goals (MDGs), committing, inter alia, to eliminate violence against women and girls, early

This brief draws on the analysis contained in OECD (2014b) Financing the unfinished business of gender equality and women's rights: priorities for the post-2015 framework OEDC: Paris, France; and a forthcoming briefing by the OECD on Financing for women, peace and security.

E. Esplen (✉) • P. O'Neill
OECD, Paris, France

© The Author(s) 2017
Z. Khan, N. Burn (eds.), *Financing for Gender Equality*,
DOI 10.1057/978-1-137-46101-8_9

marriage and female genital mutilation, and ensure women's equal rights to economic resources and opportunities for leadership. In addition to Goal 5—*Achieve gender equality and empower all women and girls*—11 other of the 17 goals contain targets on gender equality. Ambitious financing will be needed to turn bold political aspirations into a reality.

It is well established that there can be no sustainable development without achieving gender equality[2] and that gender is a key dimension of vulnerability to poverty.[3] For financing to be effective in reducing poverty and achieving sustainable development, it needs to benefit women and men equally and contribute to achieving gender equality and building equitable societies. This needs to be specifically addressed by placing a high priority on gender equality in official development assistance (ODA), and ensuring that national budgets allocate sufficient resources towards the achievement of gender equality and women's rights.

The financing deal that was struck at the Third International Conference on Financing for Development in Addis Ababa in July 2015 provides a strong foundation, calling for gender equality to be integrated into all aspects of financial decision-making.[4] The 2030 Agenda also includes a breakthrough commitment to a "significant increase in investments to close the gender gap and strengthen support for institutions in relation to gender equality and the empowerment of women at the global, regional and national levels" (para. 22). Translating these commitments into concrete actions and resources will be critical in order to deliver on both long-established and newly won commitments on women's rights. The Addis Ababa Action Plan on Transformative Financing for Gender Equality, launched by UN Women and Member States at the Financing for Development Conference, is a key tool for turning around the historical underinvestment in gender equality and moving from commitments to action.

This chapter is a contribution to these debates on transformative financing for gender equality and women's rights. It provides an overview of OECD Development Assistance Committee (DAC) members' aid to gender equality since the MDGs and identifies priorities for financing gender equality in the implementation of the SDGs.[5] The figures are based on DAC members' aid that has been screened using the DAC gender equality policy marker—a statistical tool to measure whether aid activities target gender equality as a policy objective. Aid activities can be classified as targeting gender equality as a "principal" or "significant" objective, or as "not targeted." "Principal" means that gender equality was an explicit objective of the activity. "Significant" means that gender equality was an important but secondary objective. "Not targeted" means that the activity was screened using the gender equality policy marker but was found not to be targeting gender equality.

Data based on the marker is not an exact quantification but provides a "best estimate" of the aid that DAC members allocate in support of achieving gender equality. It is a measure of donors' commitment to gender equality and women's rights. By identifying gaps between policy commitments and financial commitments, the marker is also an important tool for strengthening transparency and accountability in donor financing for gender equality and women's rights. At present, 92 % of bilateral "sector-allocable" aid is screened against the gender equality marker.[6]

Part 1: Taking Stock of Trends in DAC Donor Financing for Gender Equality and Women's Rights Since the MDGs

Aid in Support of Gender Equality has Increased Rapidly to Reach an All-Time High

Official Development Assistance (ODA) remains a critical source of finance for achieving sustainable development. In 2014, ODA reached USD 135.2 billion. Aid will only be part of what is needed to deliver the SDGs but it remains a crucial part, especially for least developed countries (LDCs) and fragile states, which have a low capacity to attract other forms of external finance.[7] For LDCs, aid represents over 70 % of available external finance.[8]

ODA in support of gender equality and women's rights is at an all-time high. MDG3—*Promote gender equality and empower women*—galvanised new resources for gender equality and women's rights. DAC members' aid to gender equality has more than *tripled* since the MDGs, from USD 8 billion in 2002 to USD 28 billion in 2013. In fragile states, aid to gender equality has quadrupled over the lifetime of the MDGs to reach USD 10.3 billion.

Aid to gender equality has grown at a faster rate than aid overall. While total aid grew at around 1 % per year since 2008, aid to gender equality grew by 4 % annually. In fragile states, the rate of growth in gender equality focused aid has been even faster at 10 % per year over the same period, making up an increasing share of aid to fragile states. This suggests that the rise in aid to gender equality cannot be explained only in terms of an increase in overall aid but represents a particular priority being placed on gender equality and even more so in fragile states.

Aid to fragile states and economies also has a stronger focus on gender equality than aid to other developing countries. In 2012–2013, 35 % of DAC members' aid to fragile states targeted gender equality as a primary or secondary objective, compared with 27 % in other developing countries.[9] This may reflect the severity of gender disparities in fragile states, and the reality that fragile states are disproportionately lagging behind on the gender equality-related MDG targets.[10] It may also reflect improved implementation of UN Security Council Resolution 1325 and its associated resolutions.

These positive trends are supported by the findings of a survey of gender advisors in development cooperation agencies by the OECD–DAC Network on Gender Equality (GENDERNET)[11] in 2013. Eleven DAC agencies reported an increase in the budget for gender equality since 2006. Just four reported a decrease, mostly in the last few years due to a fall in volumes of ODA in their countries. In several agencies, the budget for gender equality increased in spite of a decline in the aid budget, reflecting the higher policy priority being given to gender equality. In the context of fiscal restraint in many countries it can be considered a success that aid to gender equality and women's rights is being maintained overall.

Several factors have coalesced to increase donor support for gender equality and women's rights. Gender equality is being championed at the highest levels, as evidenced by Sweden's recent commitment to pursue a feminist foreign policy. Gender equality is prominent in donor agencies' policy and results frameworks, with 24 of 29 DAC agencies reporting increased policy focus on gender equality since 2006.[12] In the UK, gender equality is one of just three thematic priorities for the development cooperation, while in Australia three of the ten objectives for development cooperation explicitly address gender equality.[13] This spotlight on women and girls has acted as an impetus to scale up resources for gender equality and women's empowerment. Increasing emphasis on achieving results has also helped to anchor gender equality within DAC agencies and strengthen accountability for implementing commitments on gender equality and women's rights. Some donor agencies have gone to great lengths to strengthen institution-wide accountability mechanisms for gender equality in recent years.[14]

Perhaps most significant is the catalytic role of MDG3 in galvanising resources for gender equality. Most of the aid for gender equality since the MDGs has focused on education and health, in line with MDG priorities.[15] By 2012–2013, around 54 % of aid to education had a principal or significant focus on gender equality, although the focus is weaker at the secondary and tertiary levels. Similarly, while progress on MDG 5—*improving maternal health*—has been disappointing, the goal nonetheless inspired an increase in bilateral aid to reproductive health care, which reached 1.6 billion USD on average in 2012–2013.

Investments Are Vastly Insufficient to Achieve Gender Equality and Only a Small Proportion of Aid Addresses Women's Specific Needs and Interests

Achieving gender equality requires a "twin-track" approach that combines targeted interventions with gender mainstreaming. Yet, financing for standalone projects on gender equality is far below that of programmes in which gender equality is mainstreamed. In 2012–2013, a meagre USD 4 billion on average per year targeted gender equality as a principal objective, representing 5 % of the aid screened against the DAC gender equality marker. Just 25 % (USD 22 billion) targeted gender equality as a secondary objective. Taken together, this means that only a small proportion of total aid (30 %) is responsive to women's needs and interests.

A sectoral breakdown of aid in support of gender equality also reveals a number of financing gaps which need to close. While the MDGs directed welcome attention to improving women's health and education, women's roles in and contributions to the economy and society were often overlooked. As a result, there is significant underinvestment in gender equality in areas that were omitted from the MDGs, particularly in "hard sectors" such as security and the economy. Achieving gender equality will require adequate and effective resources across *all* sectors.

Economic and Productive Sectors

Even though the case for investing in women's economic empowerment is well established,[16] aid in support of gender equality in the economic and productive sectors remains low. Gender equality focused aid as a share of total aid to the economic and productive sectors remained flat from 2008–2013. Despite a rise in 2013, only 2 % of aid to the economic

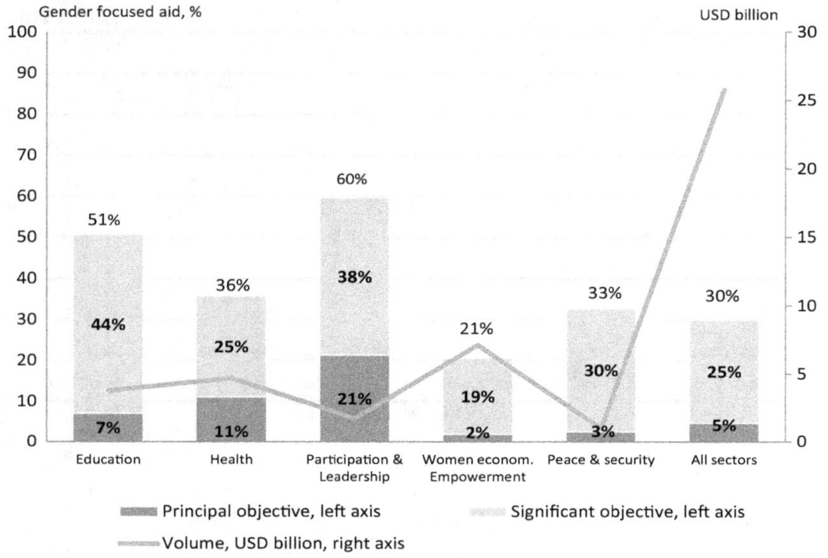

Fig. 9.1 Gender equality focused aid by sector, 2012–2013 (annual average commitments, USD billion, constant 2012 prices)

and productive sectors in 2012 and 2013 targeted gender equality as a *principal* objective (Fig. 9.1). The gender equality focus of aid to the energy sector, and to banking and financial services, is particularly low. The only exception is agriculture, which has consistently dominated the other productive sectors.[17]

Given the underinvestment in gender equality in the economic and productive sectors, it is not surprising that progress has been disappointing. Improvements in girls' education have not translated into reduced gender gaps in the labour market or in women's equal ownership and control over economic resources. Financing the implementation of the SDGs will require more attention to gender equality in the economic sectors, going beyond microcredit and enterprise to support comprehensive strategies that improve labour standards and conditions of work, and support equal access to the full range of credit, banking and financial services essential for business development, and equal ownership and control over economic resources such as land and property.

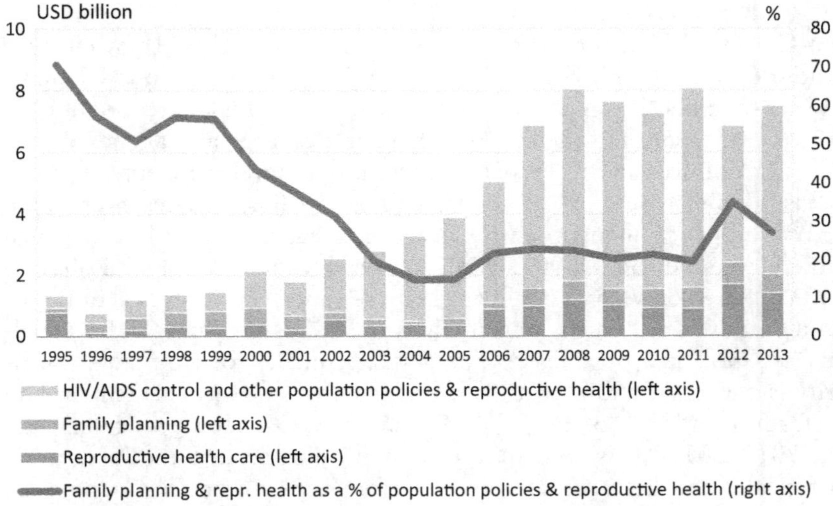

Fig. 9.2 Bilateral ODA to population policies/programmes and reproductive health, 1995–2013 (Commitments, USD billion, constant 2012 prices)

Sexual and Reproductive Health and Rights

Investment in sexual and reproductive health and rights is falling short. Bilateral funding to family planning remains low and makes up a small share of gender equality focused aid to the health sector. Aid to family planning has significantly declined as a proportion of total aid to population policies, programmes and reproductive health from 71 % in 1995 to plateau at around 20 % between 2007 and 2011 (Fig. 9.2). This may reflect the ideological swings towards family planning assistance in the USA, which is by far the largest bilateral donor of family planning assistance.[18] Research suggests that the Mexico City Policy, which restricts US aid to international NGOs that provide abortion-related services, has had a casual influence on keeping US assistance for family planning low.[19] Encouragingly, the last few years have seen a sharp rise in funding to family planning as a proportion of aid to population and reproductive health—up to 36 % in 2012 and 31 % in 2013. This may signal the start of a newly upward trend, which will be critical to reverse the global unmet need for family planning and achieve SDG targets 3.7 and 5.6 on sexual and reproductive health and reproductive rights.

Peace and Security

In October 2015, the international community marked 15 years since the adoption of United Nations Security Council Resolution (UNSCR) 1325—the first landmark decision to place women's interests and concerns at the centre of the international peace and security agenda. While greater political attention at the international level has contributed to a rise in aid in support of gender equality in fragile states overall, aid targeting gender equality in the peace and security sector has remained low at around USD 500 million on average per year since 2002. In 2012–2013, only 28 % of aid to the peace and security sector in fragile states addressed gender equality, and only 2 % targeted gender equality as a principal objective.[20] The gender equality focus of aid to security is particularly low. In the area of security system management and reform, only 27 % of aid (USD 96 million) addressed gender equality in 2012–2013. This is in spite of ample evidence that the integration of gender equality in security sector reform leads to better outcomes by enhancing local ownership, improving public confidence and helping to ensure that justice and security services are responsive to the needs of all citizens.[21] The high-level review of UNSCR 1325 is a critical reminder of the need to step up financial resources for the implementation of this agenda, for example, through adopting the UN target of 15 % of all peacebuilding funds targeting gender equality.

Violence Against Women and Girls

Violence against women and girls has become highly visible on international and policy agendas, and donors are attaching increasing importance to their work in this area. Almost half of DAC donors describe ending violence against women as a priority for their development cooperation, with particular emphasis on sexual violence in conflict, female genital mutilation and trafficking.[22] Ending violence against women and girls has also emerged as a priority for the SDGs, which is explicitly reflected in target 5.2.[23] In 2015, a new code was introduced in the DAC statistical system which will track and analyse—for the first time ever—ODA in support of ending violence against women and girls, including female genital mutilation and early and forced marriage. Improved tracking of aid targeting violence against women and girls will be essential to monitor donors' efforts in support of the elimination of violence against women and to hold governments accountable for delivering on SDG 5.2.

Governance and Democracy

DAC member aid in support of women's participation and leadership is difficult to track through the DAC statistical system. The best indication of DAC members' support for these priorities relies on a proxy measure based on an assessment of aid to democratic participation and civil society, elections and women's equality organisations and institutions. This reveals that even though donors have a strong gender equality focus in their aid to these sectors, the *amounts* of aid are low—just over USD 1.5 billion on average for the years 2002–2012.

The Environment and Climate Change

DAC members' aid in support of gender equality in climate change interventions has increased rapidly in recent years, from USD 4.4 billion in 2010 to USD 6.9 billion in 2013.[24] In 2013, 29 % of DAC members' bilateral aid to climate change was reported as gender-responsive. Attention to gender equality is much stronger in climate change adaptation than in mitigation. In 2013, 46 % of aid to climate change adaptation targeted gender equality compared with 19 % of aid to climate change mitigation. Similarly, while gender equality is quite well integrated in climate-related aid to agriculture and water, it is poorly addressed in "hard" economic infrastructure sectors. In 2012–2013, only 11 % of bilateral climate-related aid to transport and 12 % of bilateral climate-related aid to energy targeted gender equality. Almost no climate aid to these sectors targeted gender equality as a principal objective. Gender-responsive approaches are needed across all climate-related sectors; failure to do so constitutes a major missed opportunity, not least of all given the large amounts of climate finance being invested in sectors such as energy and transport.

There are positive efforts underway to integrate gender equality into climate finance. These include the UNFCCC's Green Climate Fund (GCF), which is expected to make a significant contribution towards the goals set by the international community to combat climate change. The Fund has been designed to integrate gender equality in its adaptation and mitigation-funding activities, including striving for gender balance in its governance bodies and engaging women as key stakeholders in the design, development, and implementation of the activities it finances.[25]

Part 2: Forging Effective Partnerships for Financing Gender Equality and Women's Rights in the Implementation of the SDGs

National Governments

The financing needs for achieving gender equality cannot be met through aid alone. Countries' own domestic resources, such as taxes, are the most important source of revenue for achieving gender equality, even in the poorest countries. In 2012, total tax revenue collected in Africa was ten times the volume of the development assistance provided.[26]

Progressive budgeting and tax policies have enormous scope to reduce gender inequalities. With increasing focus on "smart ODA"—including using ODA to support developing countries in mobilising their own domestic revenue—supporting the establishment of national gender equality priorities and gender-responsive public financial management systems will be critical to ensure that gender equality is prioritised in how domestic resources are mobilised and spent. Donors can play an important role in supporting national governments to institutionalise gender responsive planning and budgeting, and ensure that domestic resource mobilisation is pro-poor and gender-sensitive.

Box 9.1: The Global Partnership Gender Equality Indicator:
"Proportion of Developing Countries With Systems to Track and Make Public Allocations for Gender Equality and Women's Empowerment."
One entry point for ensuring that domestic resource mobilisation and allocation is gender-responsive is the Global Partnership indicator on gender equality, developed by UN Women and the OECD. This is one of just 10 indicators to monitor progress in the implementation of the Busan Partnership for Effective Development Cooperation (2011). The indicator provides data on whether governments track allocations for gender equality and make this information public.

There has been strong take-up and interest in the global indicator—even from countries without a system in place to track and make public resource allocations. The first progress report of the Global Partnership for Effective Development Co-operation on the implementation of the Busan commitments (2014) found that out of 35 countries that reported on the indicator, 12 have systems to track and make public allocations in support of gender equality.[27] Four additional countries have a tracking system but allocations are not made public. Many countries without a system in place reported dedicated efforts to develop one. The strong take-up of the indicator is a clear sign of the strength of government commitment to financing gender equality. Continuing to expand the number of countries engaged in monitoring the Global Partnership gender equality indicator will strengthen accountability in domestic financing for gender equality and encourage improvements in national systems for tracking gender equality allocations in the context of the post-2015 framework.

Multilateral Organisations

With substantial development finance being channelled through multilateral organisations, DAC members have an important role to play in influencing multilateral partners to place a high priority on gender equality and women's rights in their financial assistance. Since 2006, DAC donors have intensified their engagement with multilateral institutions on gender equality. A good example is the prominent role played by DAC members in the dialogue with the World Bank that resulted in gender equality being prioritised for the first time as a special theme in the 16th replenishment period of the International Development Association (IDA 16) (2011–2014). A range of strategies were effective, including active engagement at multilateral executive board meetings and coordination bodies, sitting on special committees and task forces, inputting into annual meetings and replenishment negotiations, and consistently raising gender equality in senior-level meetings with multilateral institutions.[28]

Newer Actors in the Field of Financing for Gender Equality

The Private Sector

DAC members are increasingly emphasising the role of the private sector as partners in development cooperation.[29] Recent years have witnessed the growth of private sector actors in financing, managing and implementing development programmes, including those relating to women and girls.[30] Corporate sector initiatives have focused on women's economic empowerment and entrepreneurship, such as Coca-Cola's 5x20 Programme and Wal-Mart's Women's Economic Empowerment Programme.[31] Public–private partnerships targeting women and girls are also prominent in the health sector.[32]

Private sector involvement in development finance could help to catalyse the serious money needed to accelerate progress towards gender equality, but these partnerships are not without challenges. Civil society has raised concerns about the focus on individual beneficiaries, for example through scholarships for girls or business training for women, rather than addressing issues that are more structural in nature.[33] Others are calling for mandatory regulatory frameworks to ensure that public–private partnerships are aligned with national gender equality priorities, and are transparent and accountable to development objectives and human rights principles. Agreed standards, such as the ILO standards and the Women's Empowerment Principles developed by UN Women and the UN Global Compact, could help to foster common values and standards as the basis for effective public–private partnerships. Donors can play a role in bringing "unusual suspects" together from business and civil society and acting as bridge-builders. Further work to rigorously monitor and evaluate private sector interventions that are investing in women and girls will be important for assessing the quality of these partnerships and their impact on women and girls.

Emerging Donors

An increasing number of non-DAC member countries are providing development finance, including the "BRICS" (Brazil, the Russian Federation, India, China and South Africa), Arab donors, and OECD countries that are not members of the DAC, such as Mexico and Turkey.[34] These countries' development cooperation programmes have varied objectives, often placing less emphasis on aid and more on trade, loans, technology sharing and direct investments,[35] although all aim to reduce poverty and foster sustainable development. Data on concessional development finance from non-DAC countries is rough and incomplete, and little is known about support for gender equality and women's rights. However, the increasing engagement of these emerging economies in development cooperation presents an opportunity for mobilising new resources for women's rights in the post-2015 period. Partnerships between DAC donors and non-DAC donors could help to ensure effective and coordinated support for gender equality from the entire donor community, yet to date there are few specific examples of such collaboration.[36]

Women's Equality Organisations and Institutions[37]

The essential role and impact of civil society, especially women's organisations, in driving change in support of gender equality is well documented.[38] Since 2006, aid to women's civil society organisations has increased as several important bilateral funds targeting women's organisations have been scaled up and renewed. The most substantial investments have been made by the Netherlands through the MDG3 and Funding Leadership and Opportunities for Women (FLOW) funds. Others have channelled resources through multilateral funds for gender equality, notably the UN Trust Fund to End Violence against Women and UN Women's Fund for Gender Equality.

Box 9.2: Innovative Funding for Women's Organisations: The Dutch MDG3 Fund

The MDG3 Fund created in 2008 was the largest-ever governmental fund for gender equality directed at women's rights and other civil society organisations. It awarded 82 million Euros in grants to 45 projects, of which 34 were led by women's rights organisations or women's funds. Analysis of the Fund has highlighted several characteristics that make it a particularly effective funding model.[39] The Fund:

- Targets women's organisations, including grassroots organisations.
- Supports intermediaries (women's funds and larger NGOs) with close links to women's organisations and movements. This enables funding for a wide range and scope of women's organisations.

- Supports a mix of well-known women's organisations in addition to lesser-known and newer organisations.
- Supports organisations to scale up the organising and rights work that they specialise in.
- Supports core funding, which is critical for women's organisations to make deeper and more sustainable impacts.
- Outsources the administration of the fund, making it a realistic model of bilateral funding.

By funding organisations with strong links to women's movements and grassroots women's activism, the grants had an amplifying effect. An impact study[40] found that grants succeeded in strengthening capacity in 105,304 women's organisations, increasing financial resources for 3662 women's organisations and raising awareness about women's rights for over 224 million people, including 65 million grassroots women. These efforts helped influence gender equality programmes and policies of 46 national governments, and 14 international policies and instruments. The Fund was also found to be critical in supporting women's organisations to survive and work in challenging contexts and to "hold the line" in the face of push back from conservative groups. These achievements were due to the flexible, core nature of the grants.

OECD (2014c), *From Ambition to Results: Delivering on Gender Equality in Donor Institutions*. OEDC: Paris, France

Despite pockets of good practice, funding for women's civil society organisations and institutions constitutes a very small percentage of total aid to gender equality. While aid in support of gender equality reached USD 28 billion in 2012–2013, funding for women's civil society organisations and institutions was less than USD 400 million on average per year. In fragile states, women's equality organisations and institutions received just 1 % of the total aid targeting gender equality. Investing in women's organisations as critical partners will be key to successful implementation of commitments on gender equality and women's rights. Effective funding for women's rights organisations requires multi-year and core funding, sizeable grants, and accessible and flexible resources to allow organisations to adapt activities in response to shifting opportunities and threats.[41]

Donor agencies are adopting varied approaches in their partnerships with civil society and agreed good practice is thin on the ground. There has been little evaluation of embassy or country office support to national NGOs, making it difficult to draw conclusions about the quality of the support provided. Research by the Pathways of Women's Empowerment Programme identified a number of lessons for donors committed to strengthening the quality of their support to women's organisations (Box 9.3).

Box 9.3: Improving the Quality of Support to Women's Rights Organisations

Head office gender specialists interviewed in the Pathways of Women's Empowerment research project about the effect of external financing on women's rights organisations wanted their donor agencies to improve the quality of their support by:

- Letting women's rights organisations own the agenda.
- Providing medium- to long-term financing, including institutional support.
- Being sufficiently in touch with the women's rights organisations to ensure that those they are supporting are well anchored and representative.
- Understanding the political context of the organisations' work.
- Investing time in managing the relationship with women's rights organisations because that is what matters most.
- Being better at articulating women's rights as a theory of change.
- Using women's rights organisations as a source of knowledge for policy dialogue.

Eyben, R. (2011) Supporting Pathways of Women's Empowerment: A brief guide for international development organisations. Brighton: Pathways of Women's Empowerment.

From Commitment to Action: Some Final Reflections

MDG3 galvanised new resources for gender equality but the agenda was a narrow one. The SDGs have laid the foundations for a comprehensive global agenda for advancing gender equality and women's rights, which could provide a stimulus to close financing gaps in donor funding.

However, it is no coincidence that the rise in aid in support of gender equality occurred during a relatively benign era for gender equality, characterised by unprecedented policy interest from donors in investing in women and girls. Sustaining this level of commitment over the longer-term is a challenge for the post-2015 era. Taking advantage of current political will to embed gender equality within the core business of development agencies could prove critical in maintaining the current upward trajectory in aid in support of gender equality during the years ahead.

Yet, achieving gender equality cannot be funded through aid alone. More important are domestic budgets that are responsive to women's specific needs and interests, supported by aid and other forms of finance that is aligned with national efforts to advance gender equality. Civil society especially women's organisations are critical partners in ensuring that money is spent in the right way on the right things at the right time.

There has been extraordinary support for gender equality and women's rights from governments across the world in negotiations on the post-2015 sustainable development agenda. Now is the time to ensure that political promises are backed up with the resources required to get the job done. Four key actions will be critical:

- All countries, including OECD countries, should establish robust systems to track allocations for gender equality and take action to address areas of underinvestment.
- The underinvestment in gender equality in the economic and productive sectors must be turned around. The strong focus of the SDGs on economic development is an important opportunity to accelerate efforts to empower women economically and shape an economy that works for women.
- Countries' own domestic resources, such as taxes, are the most important source of finance for achieving gender equality and must be responsive to women's needs and priorities. Donors, the UN and other partners can be effective in supporting these country-led efforts.[42]

- Women's organisations play a unique role in advancing women's rights. Governments and donors should invest in women's organisations at all levels and support their effective participation in national planning and budgetary processes.

Notes

1. *Transforming Our World: The 2030 Agenda for Sustainable Development*, https://sustainabledevelopment.un.org/post2015/transformingourworld.
2. OECD (2013) Gender equality and women's rights in the post-2015 agenda—a foundation for sustainable development, OEDC: Paris, France.
3. Kabeer, N. (2008) Mainstreaming gender in social protection for the informal economy, New Gender Mainstreaming Series on Development Issues, London: Commonwealth Secretariat; Woodroffe, J. and Esplen, E. (2012) Gender Equality and the Post-2015 Framework, Gender and Development Network.
4. United Nations, The Addis Ababa Action Agenda of the Third International Conference on Financing for Development, outcome document, Addis-Ababa-Action-Agenda-Draft-Outcome-Document-7-July-2015.
5. This brief builds on: OECD (2014) *Financing the unfinished business of gender equality and women's rights: priorities for the post-2015 framework*, OEDC: Paris, France.
6. The USA, which did not report against the gender equality policy marker from 2010 to 2012, has implemented a new data collection methodology for the gender equality marker and is included in the data for 2013. The screening for 2011 and 2012—which is being conducted retrospectively by the USA—had not yet been completed as of the time of this publication, but data for these years will be provided in the coming months.
7. Ibid.
8. OECD (2014) *Development Co-operation Report 2014: Mobilising Resources for Sustainable Development*, OEDC: Paris, France.
9. In 2012–2013, 29 % of aid to fragile states targeted gender equality as a secondary objective and 6 % targeted gender equality as a primary objective. In other developing countries, 23 % of aid targeted gender equality as a secondary objective and 4 % targeted gender equality as a primary objective.
10. OECD (2015), *States of Fragility 2015: Meeting post-2015 Ambitions*, OECD: Paris, France.
11. GENDERNET (2014). From ambition to results: delivering in gender equality in donor institutions. OEDC: Paris, France: http://www.oecd.org/dac/gender-development/fromambitiontoresultsdeliveringongenderequalityindonorinstitutions.htm
12. Ibid.

13. As of the time of the survey.
14. GENDERNET (2014). From ambition to results: delivering in gender equality in donor institutions. OEDC: Paris, France.
15. OECD (2014) Financing the unfinished business of gender equality and women's rights: priorities for the post-2015 framework OEDC: Paris, France.
16. See, for example, World Bank (2011) *World Development Report 2012—Gender Equality and Development.* Washington DC.
17. Grown, C. (2014) Aid and gender equality: position paper. UNU World Institute for Development Economics Research.
18. Grown, C. (2014) Aid and gender equality: position paper. UNU World Institute for Development Economics Research.
19. Ibid.
20. USD 1.9 billion was pledged to peace and security programming in fragile states by DAC donors in 2012 and 2013. USD 559 million of this targeted gender equality, and just USD 40 million targeted gender equality as the principal objective.
21. Kristin Valasek (2008), *Security Sector Reform and Gender. Gender and Security Sector Reform Toolkit.*
22. OECD (2014), *From Ambition to Results: Delivering on Gender Equality in Donor Institutions.* OEDC: Paris, France.
23. *Transforming Our World: The 2030 Agenda for Sustainable Development,* https://sustainabledevelopment.un.org/post2015/transformingourworld.
24. OECD (forthcoming) *Making Climate Action Work for* Women, COP 21 briefing.
25. Schalatek, L. (2014), *Of Promise, Progress, Perils and Prioritization: Gender in the Green Climate Fund, An Update on Efforts to Operationalize a Fund-wide Gender-Sensitive Approach after the 7th GCF Board Meeting,* Washington: Heinrich Boell Foundation North America.
26. OECD (2014) *Development Co-operation Report 2014: Mobilising Resources for Sustainable Development,* OECD: Paris, France.
27. UNDP-OECD. 2014. Making Development Co-operation More Effective: 2014 Progress Report, OECD Publishing, Paris.
28. OECD (2014), *From Ambition to Results: Delivering on Gender Equality in Donor Institutions.* OEDC: Paris, France.
29. OECD (2014) Development Cooperation Report 2014: Mobilising Resources for Sustainable Development. OEDC: Paris, France.
30. Miller, J. Arutyunova, A. and Clark, C. (2013) New Actors, New Money, New Conversations, Association for Women's Rights in Development.
31. Ibid.

32. Grown, C. (2014) Aid and gender equality: position paper. UNU World Institute for Development Economics Research.
33. Miller, J. Arutyunova, A. and Clark, C. (2013) New Actors, New Money, New Conversations, Association for Women's Rights in Development.
34. OECD (2014) Development Cooperation Report 2014: Mobilising Resources for Sustainable Development. OEDC: Paris, France.
35. Arutyunova, A. and Clark, C. (2013) Watering the leaves, starving the roots: The status of financing for women's rights organising and gender equality, Association for Women's Rights in Development.
36. OECD (2014), *From Ambition to Results: Delivering on Gender Equality in Donor Institutions.* OEDC: Paris, France.
37. The OECD DAC purpose code on *Women's equality organisations and institutions* is used to track trends in donors' support to women's civil society organisations and women's ministries. By definition, activities recorded under this purpose code get the score "principal" against the gender equality marker.
38. Cornwall, A (2014) *Strategies and pathways to make states more accountable for women's* rights. Background paper for UN Women's Expert Group Meeting on 'Envisioning women's rights in the post-2015 context', New York, 3–5 November 2014; Batliwala, S. et al. (2013). *Women Moving Mountains: The Collective Impact of the Dutch MDG3 Fund.* AWID: Toronto, Canada; Mexico City, Mexico and Cape Town, South Africa: http://www.awid.org/Library/Women-Moving-Mountains3; O'Connell, H. (2012) What added value do organisations that are led and managed by women bring to work addressing the rights, needs and priorities of women and girls? Comic Relief Review.
39. Pittman, A. (2011) The power of investing in women's rights and empowerment: a mid-term summary. Toronto: AWID.
40. Batliwala et al. (2013) *Women Moving Mountains: The Collective Impact of the Dutch MDG3 Fund.* AWID: Toronto, Canada; Mexico City, Mexico and Cape Town, South Africa.
41. Arutyunova, A. and Clark, C. (2013) Watering the leaves, starving the roots: The status of financing for women's rights organising and gender equality, Association for Women's Rights in Development; O'Connell, H. (2012) What added value do organisations that are led and managed by women bring to work addressing the rights, needs and priorities of women and girls? Comic Relief Review; Esplen, E. (2013) Leaders for change: Why support women's rights organisations? Womankind Worldwide.
42. See for example UN Women's ground-breaking work over the past decade to support gender responsive planning and budgeting in 75 countries: http://www.gender-budgets.org/http://gender-financing.unwomen.org/en.

References

Batliwala, S., et al. (2013). *Women moving mountains: The collective impact of the Dutch MDG3 fund.* Toronto/Mexico City/Cape Town: AWID.

Cornwall, A. (2014). *Strategies and pathways to make states more accountable for women's* rights. Background paper for UN Women's Expert Group Meeting on 'Envisioning women's rights in the post-2015 context', New York, 3–5 November 2014.

Esplen, E. (2013). Leaders for change: Why support women's rights organisations? Womankind Worldwide.

Eyben, R. (2011). *Supporting Pathways of Women's Empowerment: A brief guide for international development organisations.* Brighton: Pathways of Women's Empowerment.

Grown, C. (2014). Aid and gender equality: Position paper. UNU World Institute for Development Economics Research.

Kabeer, N. (2008). *Mainstreaming gender in social protection for the informal economy* (New gender mainstreaming series on development issues). London: Commonwealth Secretariat.

Miller, J., Arutyunova, A., & Clark, C. (2013). New actors, new money, new conversations, association for women's rights in development.

O'Connell, H. (2012). *What added value do organisations that are led and managed by women bring to work addressing the rights, needs and priorities of women and girls?* (Comic relief review). London: Comic Relief.

OECD. (2013). *Gender equality and women's rights in the post-2015 agenda – a foundation for sustainable development.* Paris: OEDC.

OECD. (2014a). *Development co-operation report 2014: Mobilising resources for sustainable development.* Paris: OEDC.

OECD. (2014b). *Financing the unfinished business of gender equality and women's rights: Priorities for the post-2015 framework.* Paris: OEDC.

OECD. (2014c). *From ambition to results: Delivering in gender equality in donor institutions.* Paris: OEDC.

OECD. (2015). *States of fragility 2015: Meeting post-2015 ambitions.* Paris: OECD.

Open Working Group proposal for Sustainable Development Goals. (2014).

Schalatek, L. (2014). *Of promise, progress, perils and prioritization: Gender in the green climate fund, an update on efforts to operationalize a fund-wide gender-sensitive approach after the 7th GCF board meeting.* Washington, DC: Heinrich Boell Foundation North America.

OECD DAC Statistics. (2014, September). *For further information on OECD DAC climate-related statistics.* Available at http://www.oecd.org/dac/stats/rioconventions.htm.

UN Women's website on gender responsive budgeting: http://www.gender-budgets.org/http://gender-financing.unwomen.org/en.

UNDP-OECD. (2014). *Making development co-operation more effective: 2014 progress report*. Paris: OECD Publishing.

United Nations, Transforming Our World: The 2030 Agenda for Sustainable Development. https://sustainabledevelopment.un.org/post2015/transformingourworld.

Valasek, K. (2008). *Security sector reform and gender. Gender and security sector reform toolkit*. Geneva: DCAF.

Woodroffe, J., & Esplen, E. (2012). Gender equality and the post-2015 framework, gender and development network.

World Bank. (2011). *World development report 2012 – Gender equality and development*. Washington, DC: The World Bank.

CHAPTER 10

Financing for Gender-Responsive Peacebuilding: Setting Financial Targets as a Tool for Increasing Women's Participation in Post-Conflict Recovery

Sarah Douglas and Cécile Mazzacurati

Introduction

Lack of financial resources coupled with insufficient prioritization and political commitment by decision-makers—from national governments or the UN alike—are commonly named the key factors for the disappointing implementation of the women, peace and security agenda.[1] Although women's participation in peacemaking, peacekeeping and peacebuilding is widely acknowledged at the policy level to improve the sustainability and inclusivity of peace, mechanisms for ensuring effective participation are still poorly developed. In addition, funding to provide the resources,

The authors thank Anne-Marie Goetz and Henk-Jan Brinkman for their extensive inputs on an early version of this chapter. This chapter reflects solely the views of its authors, not of their organizations.

S. Douglas (✉) • C. Mazzacurati (✉)
PBSO UN Peacebuilding Support Office, New York, USA

© The Author(s) 2017

Z. Khan, N. Burn (eds.), *Financing for Gender Equality*,
DOI 10.1057/978-1-137-46101-8_10

security, and opportunities for women to build collective and individual capacities for participation in political, economic and social recovery is low and inconsistent. Addressing this issue is complicated by a significant lack of clarity on actual amounts dedicated to and spent on promoting gender equality. This chapter will explore the relationship between increasing funding and improving peacebuilding outcomes for women and girls and analyze the relevance of gender-responsive budgeting approaches to peacebuilding interventions in the aftermath of conflict.

In 2010, the tenth anniversary of Security Council resolution 1325 (2000), policy-makers and practitioners developed and adopted an accountability regime on women, peace and security that heavily featured financial targets, signalling a recognition that financing had been a central constraint for implementation. The chapter will unpack some of the practical and structural reasons that the achievement of funding targets has remained elusive, including lack of prioritization at country level, weak design and implementation capacity and a failure to invest in infrastructure for gender-responsive delivery.

The chapter will then develop an argument for the importance of increasing allocations to women's empowerment within large-scale "mainstream" initiatives to promote gender-responsiveness in all areas of peacebuilding, rather than a primary focus on funding women-centred initiatives that could lead to ghettoization. The chapter will conclude by examining some promising practices and lessons learned that can inform the debates around financing for gender-responsive peacebuilding in the context of the Sustainable Development Goals and the implementation of the women, peace and security agenda.

Context

As the world prepared for a convergence of major policy debates on development and security priorities in 2015, analysis and advocacy focused on the considerable challenges faced by fragile and post-conflict states. In fact, the establishment of the International Network on Conflict and Fragility (INCAF) Forum in 2009, and the New Deal for Engagement in Fragile States at the 2011 Busan conference, were direct responses to the recognition that the Millennium Development Goals (MDGs) had failed to address the obstacles to sustainable development that are presented by post-conflict realities. Similarly, efforts to promote gender-responsive budgeting and financing for gender equality encounter unique challenges in post-conflict and peacebuilding contexts. Many post-conflict contexts simultaneously achieve low marks on gender equality indices and underperformed on their MDG targets.[2] Although certainly not the case in all contexts, several of the same features that make a country prone to conflict, such as endemic poverty, poor governance and weak rule of law, pose specific challenges to achieving gender equality as well. Therefore, a special focus on the intersection between women, peace and security, sustainable development and financing is warranted.

The tenth anniversary of Security Council resolution 1325 (2000) sparked calls for increased action on women, peace and security commitments. As part of an effort to build accountability for implementation, 26 global indicators were presented to the Security Council in April 2010 to track the UN's and Member States' performance on SCR 1325, including several focused on the proportion of programmatic and project spending in post-conflict situations allocated to gender equality (for instance budget allocations in strategic planning frameworks, funding disbursed to civil society organizations, total spending of the UN system to support gender equality issues, etc.[3]). In September 2010, the Secretary-General presented a report on *Women's Participation in Peacebuilding*, defining a Seven-Point Action Plan, which includes specific measures to meet commitments to increase women's participation in the areas of conflict resolution, post-conflict planning and financing, civilian capacities, post-conflict governance, rule of law and economic recovery. Most importantly, the Secretary-General committed the UN to allocate a minimum of 15 % of all peacebuilding and recovery funds to gender equality and women's empowerment.[4] A year later, the UN Strategic Results Framework on Women, Peace and Security applied this 15 % target specifically to the fields of security sector reform, disarmament, demobilization and reintegration, rule of law, economic recovery and other components of post-conflict peacebuilding and recovery.[5]

The establishment of these financial targets was based on the assumption that increased funding for women's participation and gender equality was the condition for peacebuilding and recovery to address women's security, social and livelihood needs better. An additional assumption was that while addressing women's needs, peacebuilding investments would also be more effective and sustainable for the entire community. In effect, increasing gender-equality-focused spending would, it was assumed, have a transformative effect on both peacebuilding and women's rights in post-conflict environments.

Indeed, UN Women-commissioned research has demonstrated that women invest more of their economic recovery dividends than men on family and community well-being, thereby making a higher relative investment in peacebuilding.[6] Peace processes that include women's organizations at the negotiating table dramatically increase their sustainability.[7] A number of declarations, policies and resolutions by international and regional institutions now assert the causal link between women's participation and more effective peacebuilding. In September 2013, the UN Peacebuilding Commission adopted a Declaration on Women's Economic Empowerment for Peacebuilding that underscored the centrality of women's participation to effective economic recovery.[8] In sum, we have an increasing body of evidence proving that investing in women yields high returns and demonstrates great value for money as compared to more expensive peacebuilding interventions.[9]

Box 10.1 PBF Gender Marker Coding

Score 3 for projects that have gender equality as a principal objective.

Score 2 for projects that have gender equality as a significant objective.

Score 1 for projects that will contribute in some way to gender equality, but not significantly.

Score 0 for projects that are not expected to contribute noticeably to gender equality.

And yet, increases of allocations to gender equality both as percentages and in absolute terms have been slow to occur. Data collected for the past three annual Secretary-General's Reports to the Security Council on Women and Peace and Security reveal almost complete stagnation when it comes to allocations to gender equality in post-conflict contexts. As Table 10.1 shows, the proportion of UNDP funds targeting activities with gender components showed virtually no change between 2011 and 2012.

A gender marker has also been used in the humanitarian arena since 2009 to track allocations to gender equality within humanitarian projects. In 2013, just like in 2012, only 4 % of projects had gender equality as a primary objective. Allocations to projects that included gender equality as a significant objective decreased from 48 % in 2012 to 35 % the following year (Fig. 10.1).

Table 10.1 UNDP project contribution to gender equality (%) 2011–12

Rating	*2011*	*2012*
GEN0: No noticeable contribution to gender equality	24%	21%
GEN1: Some contributions to gender equality	47%	49%
GEN2: Significant contributions to gender equality	23%	24%
GEN3: Gender equality is a principal objective	6%	6%

Implementation of UNDP Gender Equality Strategy 2008–13: Background Paper for the Annual Report to the Executive Board. January 2013, p. 22. This table includes all countries where UNDP has programmes, not uniquely conflict and post-conflict countries. The table excludes projects that have not been rated. Figures subject to rounding errors. *Source:* UNDP Atlas Financial System, January 2013

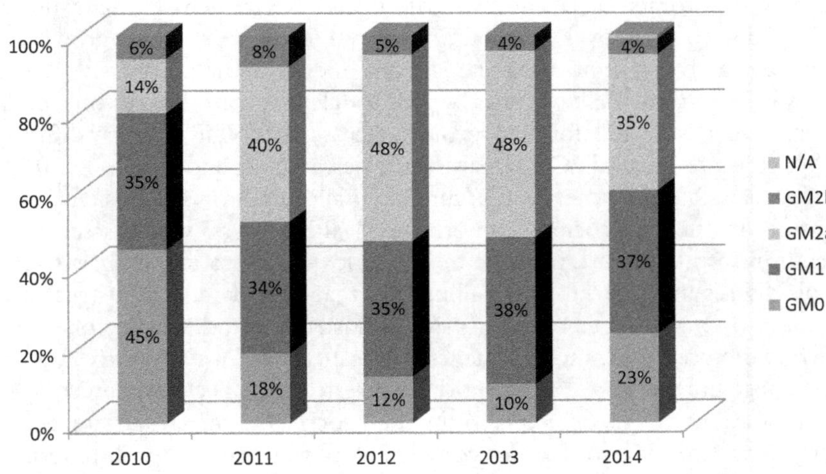

Fig. 10.1 Inter-Agency Standing Committee (The Inter-Agency Standing Committee (IASC) is the primary mechanism for inter-agency coordination of humanitarian assistance, involving the key UN and non-UN humanitarian partners) gender marker notation proportions, 2010–14 (IASC GenderStandby Capacity Project. Gender marker Report 2013–14. p. 2 (http://www.humanitarianresponse.info/system/files/documents/files/Gender%20Marker%20Report%202013-2014.pdf). Gender marker 2a signals a "potential to contribute significantly to gender equality" (equivalent to GM2 for UNICEF or UNDP) while Gender Marker 2b is for projects whose "principal purpose is to advance gender equality" (equivalent to GM3 for UNICEF or UNDP))

On the other hand, for this same period, UNICEF demonstrated an increase in gender equality-focused programming. Twenty-three per cent of UNICEF's 2013 funding for conflict and post-conflict countries to projects had gender equality as a principal objective; 46 % had gender as a significant objective. This represented an advance on 2012, when only 13 % of post-conflict funding was allocated to projects that had gender as a principal objective.[10]

Beyond the UN, the challenge of both effective tracking of funding that is targeted to gender equality, and of increasing the proportion of this funding out of the total allocated to peacebuilding, is shared by other institutions. The Organization for Economic Cooperation and Development (OECD) produced an issue brief in 2010 that argued for gender-responsive budgeting as a tool for promoting gender equality and better public sector management.[11] However, despite the dramatic evolution of the women, peace and security normative framework, allocations to gender equality by DAC countries in fragile contexts have grown at approximately the same rate as allocations in developing contexts.[12]

Breaking down allocations by sector also reveals interesting patterns. Data collected for 334 projects across 6 UNDP country offices (Afghanistan, Burundi, Guatemala, Iraq, Sierra Leone and Sudan) in 2012 show that a higher proportion of funding is allocated to women's empowerment in the civil society support and health sectors, whereas security sector reform and infrastructure boast the lowest allocations (Chart C).[13] This discrepancy reflects a prevailing bias that security and infrastructure are the domain of men. Security and infrastructure are the sectors that attract the preponderance of financial allocations and are often treated as the most urgent post-conflict priority investments. The low percentage of allocations to gender equality in the "social" sectors results in derisory allocation of resources to women's empowerment in absolute terms (Fig. 10.2).

The UN has made several attempts at increasing funding allocations to gender-responsive peacebuilding, although efforts have yet to infiltrate decision-making related to the largest pots of development and humanitarian funding. As noted, the formulation and adoption of the 15 % target was intended to stimulate increased financing by creating an obligation with which UN entities would need to comply. The UN Peacebuilding Fund (PBF)—established in 2006 to support post-conflict peacebuilding initiatives—has proactively sought out proposals focused on gender and peacebuilding. In 2011, it launched a Gender Promotion Initiative (GPI),

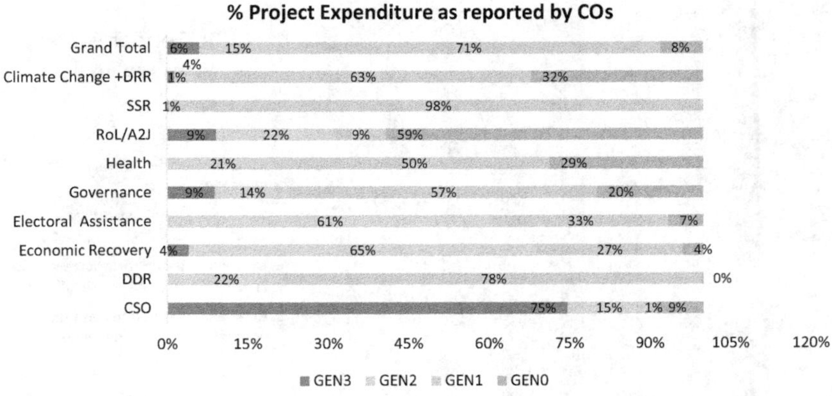

Fig. 10.2 Percentage of project expenditures as reported by country offices

a call for gender-specific proposals in countries eligible to receive PBF funding. As a result of the GPI, allocations to Gender Marker 3 category projects increased to over 10.3 % in 2012, but then dropped off again in 2013 to 7 %. In 2014, a second GPI was launched to provide further impetus to countries to design peacebuilding proposals with gender equality as principal objective. This helped PBF reach 9.3 % for GM3 projects in 2014, but still fell short of the 15 % target.

It is interesting to note that without the GPI, the allocation to gender equality in 2013 would have dropped to 5.4 %. Despite funds being available within PBF and the notable senior-level commitment within the PBSO to the funding target of 15 %, the PBF is not able to meet the target due, apparently, to lack of demand from UN Country Teams, who are the recipients of PBF funding. In other words, one explanation for the low levels of funding for gender equality post-conflict is an undersupply of fundable proposals from UN Country Teams.

Indeed, the challenge owes partly to a relative paucity of technical support for creative programming to support gender equality and to respond to women's needs. According to an evaluation recently carried out by UN Women, insufficient human resources at the country level is one of the key impediments to creating the demand for peacebuilding funds. UN Women offices are extremely small as compared to other UN Country Team entities and gender experts in the bigger entities are generally few and under resourced, if they exist at all (Fig. 10.3).

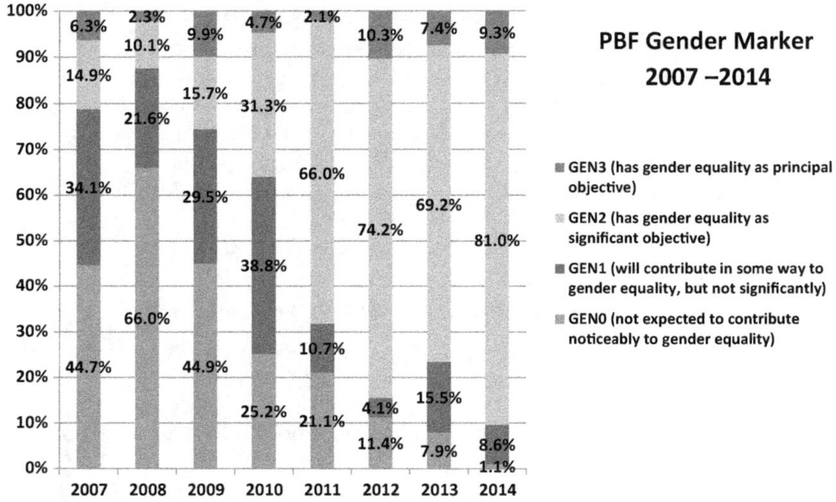

Fig. 10.3 PBF gender marker notation shares, 2007–14

As a result, gender equality advocates within the UNCT often lack the time or the staff power to avail themselves of funding opportunities, thus creating a vicious cycle where lack of resources allocated to gender equality results in lack of capacity to secure more resources. Innovative and successful interventions are, therefore, rarely brought to scale and fragile gains often face sustainability challenges. In fact, in some cases where interventions have been brought to scale like Nepal, the UN Country Teams have made a concerted effort to ensure adequate staffing and resourcing of gender advisory capacity. In Nepal, strong advocacy from the national government and civil society helped to galvanize the commitment on the UN side.

But the lack of technical expertise is far from being the only challenge. When such expertise exists, its political leverage is often limited. According to the Overseas Development Institute (ODI), "donors show a lack of understanding about gender issues across the different sectors [of peacebuilding]. The issues are left to the 'gender experts' with the result that gender-responsive approaches often remain peripheral to mainstream donor engagement in peacebuilding and statebuilding efforts."[14] More broadly, the lack of fundable proposals on gender and peacebuilding shows that in spite of the high-level policy agreements on women as key stakeholders for building sustainable peace, when it is time to decide where the money goes, activities that are considered to be more urgent or more important or more strategic activities are prioritized over gender equality. Women and their immediate recovery needs, as well as the need for investment in their capacities to engage in decision-making, are still an afterthought.

What About the 85%? Mainstreaming Gender in All Peacebuilding Versus Targeted Allocations to Gender Equality

The focus on projects dedicated to gender equality has in part overshadowed the progress that has been made in mainstreaming gender in broader peacebuilding portfolios. The PBF has seen an exponential increase of the proportion of its funding going to projects where gender is in theory mainstreamed (Gender Marker 2): from 10 % in 2008 to 81 % in 2014. In the meantime, projects that are "not expected to contribute significantly to gender equality" (gender marker 0) have decreased from 66 % of total allocations in 2008 to 1 % in 2014. These numbers—and the subjective assessments that go into gender marker scoring—need to be carefully unpacked. The gender marker score is assigned by the same UN agency—indeed the same individual—that develops the proposal. This self-monitoring system has been demonstrated to fuel a tendency to assign higher gender marker scores than what the project may deserve.[15] But this nevertheless signals a remarkable trend: it has become the norm to at least adopt a narrative about gender in most, if not all, peacebuilding interventions. While the discourse around gender is often simplistic (e.g. focusing on "women" as one group, often seen as victims rather than active agents), the fact that thinking about how the issues to be addressed and the interventions to be designed might play out differently for women and men has become standard nevertheless indicates that a gender approach has slowly but surely infused the peacebuilding agenda. And if gender-responsive budgeting is applied to large-scale peacebuilding programmes, such as the SSR and DDR processes that tend to capture large amounts of funding, a small percentage of funding earmarked for women's participation could imply large budget allocations, on a much bigger scale than the traditionally limited funding, in absolute amounts, allocated to interventions targeting women's empowerment specifically. While funding interventions fully focused on women's issues and gender equality remains indispensable, mainstreaming gender within larger peacebuilding programmes in ways that are not token gestures is also crucial for the transition from ghettoized project efforts to substantial system change. Not stressing the vital importance of fully mainstreaming gender to the core peacebuilding activities would send the message inadvertently that 85 % of peacebuilding funding did not have to tackle gender issues. Major processes like elections, infrastructure development and SSR have significant implications for women and girls and must all be approached with a view to ensuring that women and girls benefit equally with men and boys. While dedicated funding to women and gender mainstreaming are often pitted as binaries, both strategies must be aggressively pursued in order to make a real impact.

Improving the quality and impact of gender mainstreaming within large peacebuilding programmes remains particularly challenging. An analysis of OECD spending on GBV projects found that 40 % of projects targeting GBV in emergencies did so in a "gender-blind" way meaning that the social relations between men, women, boys and girls, or obstacles that women and girls face due to cultural, religious, social or political inequalities were not addressed in the project design or implementation.[16] In lieu of proper gender analysis, most projects limit themselves to mentioning women's acute vulnerability to the conflict and the importance of including them among beneficiaries. Clear definitions of what "gender mainstreaming" entails through the programme cycle are essential to streamline what the cross-cutting integration of gender implies. Developing gender-responsive budgets that clearly show how much will be allocated to activities specifically aimed at gender equality is essential to track funding allocations to gender within broader peacebuilding portfolios. So far, gender-responsive budgeting has not been the norm within post-conflict financing, and project designers have difficulty indicating approaches and impacts that will benefit women. In fact, UN Women, UNDP and PBSO's review of 2012 funding to peacebuilding programmes in six countries found it was impossible to distinguish the specific budget allocations for women and men in Gender Marker 2 projects.[17] In some cases, such as DDR and temporary employment programmes, the number of female participants is taken as a proxy indicator for gender responsiveness. The Secretary-General has reported on these indicators in his last three reports to the Security Council on Women, Peace and Security, showing the trends of female participation in these programmes. However, simply tracking female participants does not show that the programmes are using gender analysis, gender-responsive budgeting, or gender-responsive programme tools to ensure that women and girls who do participate receive adequate or appropriate services. For example, a joint UN project on women and young people's economic recovery in Guinea (2012–14) included a majority of women among its beneficiaries, but "*the activities were managed by men supervising groups of women undertaking the tasks, which they communicated were poorly paid and not leading to a sense of long-term skills and security.*"[18] More rigorous thinking and planning, involving the women themselves and their communities more broadly, is indispensable for gender mainstreaming to become transformative of unequal power relations and address—or attempt to—the roots of inequalities and exclusion.

Moving from Commitments to Cash: Why Are the Funding Targets so Hard to Achieve?

- Lack of resources—resources beget resources

The lack of resources—or, in the case of PBF discussed previously, the lack of demand—is limiting the number and the scale of projects dedicated to the implementation of the women, peace and security agenda, which is limiting the availability of evidence—good practice, case studies—needed to inspire and drive sound design in applications to secure more resources to further work in this field. The operational learning in this field therefore tends to remain constricted to pilot and small-scale initiatives, which are not upscaled into larger, more ambitious programmes. In addition, the front-line work at the field level is often carried out by women's civil society organizations. Although these are the engines of efforts to advance women's rights locally, women's organizations are often severely weakened by conflict. Often they are not equipped to meet the demands of international donors—in terms of accounting, reporting, results-based programming, monitoring and evaluation—simply because they may lack basic accounting systems, financial management capability, and even a computer or bank account.

For example, UN Women has supported the innovative Peace Huts mechanism in Liberia since 2007. In the Peace Huts, local women leaders *inter alia* mediate interpersonal disputes before they escalate into violence, alongside other peacebuilding and violence prevention activities. According to local police and community leaders, the Peace Huts are reducing incidents of violence against women and girls both because of the direct mediation that the women provide and the comprehensive approach that brings in awareness raising, engages men and boys, enhances economic empowerment for vulnerable women and girls, improves reproductive health services, and so on. The Peace Huts have proven successful because they are locally led and build on an indigenous and culturally relevant justice practices. However, UN Women and partners have struggled to replicate the Peace Hut model due in part to lack of human and financial resources to focus on capacity building and sustainability. While the Peace Hut model has been very successful, UN Women and partners struggled to expand from 1 village to only 17 over the course of seven years. The financial and human resources, as well as the time required to ensure the model was replicated effectively and sustainably, were the main impediments to scaling up this very successful model. According to UN Women's recent evaluation, more "value for money" could have been achieved by providing additional resources to partners to building their skills in areas such as monitoring and evaluation, reporting and accounting. Results could have been exponentially increased if more resources were allocated to the organizational infrastructure around the Peace Huts, which is provided by local NGOs who often had weak capacities in the aforementioned areas.[19]

- Lack of capacity, especially amongst partners and lack of investment in building capacity.

Programme evaluations commissioned by UN Women have repeatedly highlighted the challenges of scaling up good practices from the local to national level.[20] While participatory and locally led interventions are repeatedly shown to be effective and sustainable, extrapolating models and bringing them to scale rarely happens and is a slow and labour-intensive process. Comparing UN Women-supported peacebuilding initiatives in four countries, the evaluators found that in only one country (Uganda) did UN Women have the resources from elsewhere to hire a dedicated monitoring and evaluation specialist to support the peacebuilding workstream. The presence of this specialist made a measureable difference as local implementing partners in conflict affected Northern Uganda were supported to develop the tools to make their work more impactful and sustainable.[21]

Improving knowledge management and operational learning is one of the necessary conditions for a substantial increase in funding for gender-responsive peacebuilding. As demonstrated by O'Gorman, documentation of good practices must focus on analysing what works and could be replicated or upscaled; cross-learning across organizations also needs to be enhanced for the entire field to progress.[22] Strengthening monitoring and evaluation capacities of actors on the ground is indispensable to achieve this, and for the success of the programmes. The dedicated M&E capacity mentioned above in Uganda was assessed to have made a significant contribution to knowledge management as the work of implementing partners, their successes and challenges, was well documented from the outset.

- Ability of Gender Equality advocates to leverage and raise their voices in the UN Country Team (i.e. within UN Development Assistance Frameworks, Post-Conflict Needs Assessments or Joint Assessment Missions).

The creation of UN Women in 2011 was intended to address *inter alia* the low-level representation of gender issues within most UN Country Teams. Prior to the creation of UN Women, the former UN Development Fund for Women (UNIFEM) often lacked a permanent seat at the UNCT table and because it was a "fund" not a full-rank agency, it was represented at a much lower level than other entities.[23] Although the creation of UN Women has gone some way to address this issue, UN Women Country Offices are by and large much smaller and headed by staff not as senior as in UN entities.[24] In addition, teams working on gender within other UN entities, like UNDP and UNFPA, may also struggle to get traction within their respective decision-making structures.[25] In many situations, UN Women and gender staff in other entities are national staff. Although national staff possess invaluable cultural and political understanding that they bring to their work, they often lack the same access to decision-making as do international staff. As a result, decisions on peacebuilding programming and priorities often get taken without any gender analysis, without any representation of women' perspectives on national peace and recovery priorities, leading to cascading negative implications for planning and financing. Gender advocates with UNCTs may struggle with capacity constraints, echoing and compounding the challenges faced by partners, and may be challenged to influence decision-making in the Country Team, especially when perceived or real states of emergency lead to a culture of crisis management, in which investment in gender equality is regarded as a secondary matter to be postponed to a moment of greater stability.

- Women's voices, political leadership and the failure to develop the "infrastructure for delivery"

All of the technical constraints—resources, capacity—identified above have deeper political roots. A primary reason for slow progress in meeting funding targets on gender is the limited voice of women's rights activists in national decision-making and post-conflict planning processes, which remain dominated by voices from the Government, the UN and international donors—in spite of the involvement of civil society. The window of opportunity that post-conflict contexts open for women's participation is often cited, but it should not be missed: when women are not heard early on, they are not recognized as viable national actors and interlocutors. The longer they are left out, the harder it becomes to include them because they are not accepted as authoritative voices in national planning.

The institutional weakness of the national gender machinery—typically, in most countries, among the least funded and staffed Ministries—further limits the outreach of voices advocating for gender equality and means that there is no robust and trustworthy national implementation partner on the ground. This stems from a still largely prevalent lack of political will to invest in and prioritize women's participation and gender equality, both from national decision-makers and from UN leadership. UN Women, the entity that should speak for women within the UN, is not yet audible enough to trigger a shift in actual on the ground support for gender equality in UN peacebuilding operations.

All this contributes to an overall failure to develop the infrastructure required to deliver on women, peace and security commitments. Whereas lack of capacity can often be perceived as an individual or organizational weakness, it is essential to analyze and unpack the structural elements of these shortcomings. The lack of political will to act on international commitments remains the first culprit of this failure: too many national decision-makers do not feel compelled to translate into practice the international commitments that their countries willingly endorsed. This lack of political impetus is at the root of the low funding allocations, the lack of expertise, the poor prioritization of gender equality within peacebuilding interventions.

The case of Nepal is one of the best illustrations of how results can quickly be achieved with political will and impetus: Nepal has been at the forefront of innovative approaches to mainstream gender into peacebuilding interventions. For the 2012 round of funding, the UN Peace Fund (UNPFN) team made the integration of gender equality (either as the principal or as a significant objective) a condition for the funding eligibility of any project. They accompanied projects' team in the application process to help them integrate gender throughout the entire design (and later, implementation, monitoring and evaluation) process. The team also used gender-budgeting methodology to capture more precisely allocations to gender equality, including in programmes where gender equality is addressed but not the main objective. As a result of these efforts, the budget allocated to gender reached 30 % of the total UNPFN funding for 2012. The conjunction of strong awareness and leadership by the UN Resident Coordinator in Nepal, committed national authorities (the National Action Plan on SCR1325 had just been adopted the previous year by the Parliament) and supportive donors, and extensive technical capacities in the UNPFN led to a creative and bold approach to the integration of gender equality within the peacebuilding mechanisms in-country.[26]

Conclusions: Reaching International Funding Targets for Gender-Responsive Peacebuilding

Given that many fragile states and peacebuilding contexts are heavily aid dependent,[27]the UN and donors at large have an opportunity and a crucial role to play to ensure increased financing for gender-responsive peacebuilding. Many of the main bilateral donors to peacebuilding themselves have National Action Plans on Security Council resolution 1325 (2000) and are international champions of the women, peace and security agenda.[28] But rhetoric and policy commitments are failing to translate into the funding that is required to make a tangible impact. Renewed commitments were made to increasing financing at the 15th anniversary of resolution 1325 (2000), including in the adoption of Security Council resolution 2242 (2015) that recognized various efforts to attract resources and better coordinate WPS action. The independent Global Study requested by the Security Council in resolution 2122 (2013) also featured the issue of increased financing centrally.[29] All donors should adopt the UN principle that peacebuilding interventions dedicate a minimum of 15% to women's empowerment and gender equality. The UN should also encourage donors and national partners much more proactively to base all peacebuilding projects on an in-depth gender-responsive conflict analysis and that interventions mainstream gender issues. This should be done by going beyond numeric targets for beneficiaries and promoting a more refined understanding of the gender dynamics in any peacebuilding programme, for instance by taking opportunity of a restructuring of the security sector to work with armed combatants on conceptions of masculinity, power and gender relations or by making sure a National Dialogue process will substantively focus on discussing gender relations and power sharing, in addition to including a fair number of women. Investing in the infrastructure for delivery on gender-peacebuilding is the condition for this substantive shift to happen. It is essential to invest in gender expertise at country level, both through the national gender machinery (Ministry of Women/Gender Affairs, national women civil society organizations) and the institutionalization of gender expert posts within UN peacekeeping and political missions as well as within UN country teams. Further, projects and programmes focused on gender equality must be supplemented by institutional expertise in result-based management, monitoring and evaluation, communications and knowledge management. For this infrastructure to be able to significantly influence peacebuilding processes and funding allocations, another priority is to engage national and international leadership at country level and hold leaders accountable to international commitments on gender-responsive peacebuilding. Adequate and reliable funding will be a key milestone towards realizing the ambitious gender, security and development goals that must be met if the international community is to address this century's challenges.

Notes

1. The "Women, Peace and Security agenda" refers to a series of Resolutions adopted by the Security Council, starting by the seminal resolution 1325 (2000) and followed by resolutions 1820 (2008), 1888 (2009), 1889 (2009), 1960 (2010), 2106 (2013), 2122 (2013) and 2242 (2015). The Secretary-General of the United Nations also issued in 2010 a report on *Women's Participation in Peacebuilding* (A/65/354–S/2010/466), which defined a Seven-Point Action Plan on Gender-Responsive Peacebuilding. For the purpose of this chapter, we will use the terminology "women, peace and security" and "gender-responsive peacebuilding" interchangeably: while these two agendas have been kept as somewhat separate on the policy level, they do overlap significantly (gender-responsive peacebuilding being recognized as part of the women, peace and security agenda) and share the same objective of promoting both women's direct participation in building peace and founding all peace and security/peacebuilding interventions on an analysis of gender dynamics.
2. Organization for Economic Cooperation and Development. "Fragile States 2014: Domestique Revenue Mobilisation in Fragile States." 2014 http://www.oecd.org/dac/incaf/FSR-2014.pdf. Accessed 7 November 2014.

3. Report of the Secretary-General to the Security Council on Women and Peace and Security. 28 September 2010. (S/2010/498).
4. See The Secretary-General's Seven-Point Action Plan on Gender-Responsive Peacebuilding. Report of the Secretary-General to the Security Council on Women's Participation in Peacebuilding. 7 September 2010. (S/2010/466).
5. Report of the Secretary-General to the Security Council on Women and Peace and Security. 29 September 2011 (S/2011/598).
6. Justino, Patricia. "Women Working for Recovery: The impact of Female Employment on Family and Community Welfare after Conflict." UN Women Peace and Security Sourcebook. October 2012. http://www.unwomen.org/ru/digital-library/publications/2012/10/un-women-sourcebook-on-women-peace-and-security
7. Castillo Diaz, Pablo et al. "Women's Participation in Peace Negotiations: Connections between Presence and Influence." UN Women Peace and Security Sourcebook. October 2012. http://www.unwomen.org/~/media/headquarters/media/publications/en/03awomenpeaceneg.pdf
8. Peacebuilding Commission. Declaration: Women's economic empowerment for peacebuilding. 26 September 2013. (PBC/7/OC/3).
9. International Solutions Group, "Evaluation of "From Communities to Global Security Institutions" programme." September 2014.
10. Data from Secretary-General to the Security Council on Women and Peace and Security. 20 September 2014 (SC/2014/693).
11. DAC Network on Gender Equality. Gender Equality, Women's Empowerment and the Paris Declaration on Aid Effectiveness: Issues Brief 6. October 2010 (http://www.oecd.org/dac/gender-development/46142807.pdf).
12. OECD-DAC. "Fragile States Report 2014: Domestic Revenue Mobilization in Fragile States." Accessed 2 February 2015 http://www.oecd.org/dac/governanceandpeace/conflictandfragility/docs/FSR-2014.pdf
13. Douglas, Sarah. "What Gets Measured Gets Done: Translating Accountability Frameworks into Better Responses for Women and Girls in Peacebuilding Contexts." Journal of Peacebuilding and Development. 2015 10:1 pp. 90–96. Cueva, Hanny, Kuonqui, Chris, et al. "What Women Want: Planning and Financing for Gender-Responsive Peacebuilding." UN Women Sourcebook on Women, Peace and Security. October 2012. http://www.unwomen.org/ru/digital-library/publications/2012/10/un-women-sourcebook-on-women-peace-and-security
14. Overseas Development Institute (ODI). "Assessment of the Evidence of Links Between Gender Equality, Peacebuilding and Statebuilding: Literature Review." December 2013.
15. UNDG, Gender Equality Marker Guidance Note, 2013. http://www.undg.org/docs/13191/Item%206%20-%20Draft%20UNDG%20Gender%20Equality%20Guidance%20Note.pdf

16. Development Initiatives. "Trends in Donor Spending on Sexual and Gender-Based Violence." June 2014. http://devinit.org/wp-content/uploads/2014/06/SGBV-Briefing-June-2014-FINAL1.pdf. Accessed 14 November 2014.
17. Kundu, Sudarsana, Ibid.
18. Eleanor O'Gorman, op. cit., p.43.
19. International Solutions Group. "Evaluation of From Communities to Global Security Institutions (FC2GSI) Programme." Washington, DC. 2014.
20. Overseas Development Institute. "Thematic Evaluation on the Contribution of UN-Women to Increasing Women's Leadership and Participation in Peace and Security and in Humanitarian Response." Presented to UN Women's Executive Board 14 January 2014. http://www.unwomen.org/~/media/Headquarters/Attachments/Sections/Executive%20Board/2014/s1/EB-2014-S1-UNW-2014-CRP2-ThematicEvaluationReportOnWPS-en.pd
21. ISG Evaluation IBID.
22. O'Gorman, 2014.
23. ODI Thematic Evaluation IBID.
24. Report to UN Women Report to the Executive Board on Regional Architecture. 18 September 2012 http://www.unwomen.org/~/media/headquarters/attachments/sections/executive%20board/eb-2012-s2-unw-2012-10-regionalarchitecture-en.pdf. Accessed 2 February 2015.
25. Doucet, Carole. "UN Gender Architecture in Post-Conflict Countries." 20 September 2012.
26. Eleanor O'Gorman, p. 42, 63.
27. OECD DAC, IBID.
28. The list of donor countries that have developed their own National Action Plan on Women, Peace and Security includes: Denmark, Norway, Sweden, the UK, the Netherlands, Spain, Switzerland, Finland, Belgium, France, the USA, Australia, and Germany (see www.peacewomen.org/naps).
29. Coomaraswamy, Radhika. Preventing Conflict, Transforming Justice, Security Peace." New York. October 2015 http://wps.unwomen.org/~/media/files/un%20women/wps/highlights/unw-global-study-1325-2015.pdf. Accessed 10 December 2015.

Bibliography

Castillo Diaz, P., et al. (2012, October). *Women's participation in peace negotiations: Connections between presence and influence*. UN Women Peace and Security Sourcebook. http://www.unwomen.org/~/media/headquarters/media/publications/en/03awomenpeaceneg.pdf.

Coomaraswamy, R. (2015, October). *Preventing conflict, transforming justice, security peace.* New York. http://wps.unwomen.org/~/media/files/un%20women/wps/highlights/unw-global-study-1325-2015.pdf. Accessed 10 Dec 2015.

Cueva, H., Kuonqui, C., et al. (2012, October). *What women want: Planning and financing for gender-responsive peacebuilding.* UN Women Sourcebook on Women, Peace and Security. http://www.unwomen.org/ru/digital-library/publications/2012/10/un-women-sourcebook-on-women-peace-and-security.

Development Initiatives. (2014, June). *Trends in donor spending on sexual and gender-based violence.* http://devinit.org/wp-content/uploads/2014/06/SGBV-Briefing-June-2014-FINAL1.pdf. Accessed 14 Nov 2014

Doucet, C. (2012, September 20). A review of UN gender architecture in peacebuilding contexts.

Douglas, S. (2015). What gets measured gets done: Translating accountability frameworks into better responses for women and girls in peacebuilding contexts. *Journal of Peacebuilding and Development, 10*:1, 90–96.

Inter-Agency Standing Committee on Humanitarian Action. IASC gender standby capacity project. Gender marker Report 2013–2014. http://www.humanitarianresponse.info/system/files/documents/files/Gender%20Marker%20Report%202013-2014.pdf.

International Solutions Group. (2014, September). Evaluation of "From Communities to Global Security Institutions" programme.

Justino, P. (2012, October). *Women working for recovery: The impact of female employment on family and community welfare after conflict.* UN Women Peace and Security Sourcebook. http://www.unwomen.org/ru/digital-library/publications/2012/10/un-women-sourcebook-on-women-peace-and-security.

O'Gorman, E. (2014, March). Independent thematic review on gender for the peacebuilding support office.

OECD-DAC Network on Gender Equality. (2010, October). Gender equality, women's empowerment and the Paris declaration on aid effectiveness: Issues brief 6. http://www.oecd.org/dac/gender-development/46142807.pdf.

Organization for Economic Cooperation and Development. (2014). *Fragile States 2014: Domestic revenue mobilisation in Fragile States.* http://www.oecd.org/dac/incaf/FSR-2014.pdf. Accessed 7 Nov 2014.

Overseas Development Institute. (2014). *Thematic evaluation on the contribution of UN-women to increasing women's leadership and participation in peace and security and in humanitarian response.* Presented to UN Women's Executive Board 14 January 2014. http://www.unwomen.org/~/media/Headquarters/Attachments/Sections/Executive%20Board/2014/s1/EB-2014-S1-UNW-2014-CRP2-ThematicEvaluationReportOnWPS-en.pd.

Overseas Development Institute (ODI). (2013, December). Assessment of the evidence of links between gender equality, peacebuilding and statebuilding: Literature review.

Peacebuilding Commission. Declaration: Women's economic empowerment for peacebuilding. (2013, September 26). (PBC/7/OC/3).

Report of the Secretary-General to the Security Council on Women and Peace and Security. (2010, September 28). (S/2010/498).

Report of the Secretary-General to the Security Council on Women and Peace and Security. (2011, September 29). (S/2011/598).

Report of the Secretary-General to the Security Council on Women and Peace and Security. (2014, September 20). (S/2014/693).

Report of the Secretary-General to the Security Council on Women's Participation in Peacebuilding. (2010, September 7). (S/2010/466).

UN Women. (2012, September 18). Report to the executive board on regional architecture. http://www.unwomen.org/~/media/headquarters/attachments/sections/executive%20board/eb-2012-s2-unw-2012-10-regionalarchitecture-en.pdf.

United Nations Development Group.Gender Equality Marker Guidance Note. (2013). http://www.undg.org/docs/13191/Item%206%20-%20Draft%20UNDG%20Gender%20Equality%20Guidance%20Note.pdf.

United Nations Development Programme. (2013, January). Implementation of UNDP gender equality strategy 2008–2013: Background paper for the annual report to the executive board.

CHAPTER 11

Beyond Investing in Women and Girls: Why Sustainable Long-Term Support to Women's Rights Organizations and Movements is Key to Achieving Women's Rights and Gender Equality

Angelika Arutyunova

Introduction

As discussions on financing the new development goals unfold, it is crucial to recognize the role that feminist and women's rights organizations and movements have played and continue to play in achieving progress on key issues affecting women and girls globally. From women's political participation to access to education to changing discriminatory laws and practices, feminist and women's rights organizations and movements, in all their diversity, have employed diverse strategies to tackle these complex

This chapter is written with key contributions by AWID staff members: Nerea Craviotto, Amina Doherty and Kamardip Singh.

A. Arutyunova (✉)
Association for Women's Rights in Development (AWID), Toronto, Canada and Mexico City, Mexico

© The Author(s) 2017

Z. Khan, N. Burn (eds.), *Financing for Gender Equality*,
DOI 10.1057/978-1-137-46101-8_11

issues within their specific contexts.[1] Feminist and women's rights organizations have decades of experience with grassroots networks working for sustainable change. They have learned that achieving long-lasting change in the lives of women and girls take long-term integrated strategies. The efforts of feminist and women's rights organizations and movements have been critical for women in many countries to obtain, among others: voting rights, the right to education, to own and inherit property and to equal pay for work of equal value. Moreover, feminist and women's rights organizations have also driven changes in areas that were previously seen as 'private' or 'cultural' matters, including the right to a live free from violence; the punishment of rape as a war crime; sexual and reproductive health and rights. These organizations have vital expertise and knowledge to share about what works in often complex political, social and cultural settings.

Given the role of feminists and women's rights organizations in driving these changes, it is noteworthy that these organizations are grossly underfunded in comparison to other types of civil society organizations (CSOs). Since 2006, the Association for Women's Rights in Development (AWID) has been tracking the financial situation of feminist and women's rights organizations globally through action-research entitled 'Where Is the Money for Women's Rights?' Since then, AWID has conducted four surveys of feminist and women's rights organizations around the world to generate data on the funding situation, including amounts and sources, of feminist and women's rights organizations while simultaneously raising questions about their sustainability. The results have consistently shown very limited funding available to feminist and women's rights organizations with the latest survey results bringing in an unprecedented response rate from 1119 feminist and women's rights organizations from 140 countries. The median income of women's groups in 2010 globally was a mere USD 20,000.

Throughout the years of analyzing funding trends, AWID maintains that funding trends go beyond counting the money. AWID, and feminist and women's rights organizations globally, approach questions access to money and resources from a political standpoint. The question of 'what' is being funded and 'how' funding is distributed form part of this broader political understanding.

As this chapter explores, there are streams of funding available for women and girls that are not reaching feminist and women's rights groups who focus on embracing complex, integrated approaches to ensure long-term sustainable changes for women and girls on the ground. The financing landscape, as well as development approaches, has shifted tremendously with the emergence of new actors and financing streams. When AWID began its research in 2006, the role of the private sector in development was minimal compared to almost a decade later where the private sector, especially the corporate sector, has a strong and powerful presence in development agendas.[2] With the upsurge of corporate presence in development and philanthropy, there is a considerable and concerning shift in development frameworks from aid to investment.[3] The blend of international development assistance with trade and investment interests of rich countries is visible in a merge of development and trade missions and ministries in key donor countries like Canada, the Netherlands, the UK and Australia.[4] Development assistance has historically been connected to colonial and economic interests of the industrialized West, and this move is not necessarily a tremendous shift from the existing approaches, all of which perpetuate dependency and impose particular development frameworks on countries. However, this shift is even more concerning as it aligns development frameworks with primarily private interests and investments rather than public interests and investments.

As the next set of development goals are launched, it is essential to reflect on the lessons learned from funding of gender equality and women's rights over the past 15 years. One of the lessons is a detailed aggregate analysis of the Millennium Development Goal (MDG) 3 Fund, which was the only specific fund aimed at achieving MDG3. This fund brought unprecedented funding to feminist and women's rights organizations in the amount of 82 million euro. The experience of the MDG3 Fund offers strong evidence that when feminist and women's rights organizations are funded in strategic and flexible ways over a long period of time, they bring lasting changes to feminist and women's rights organizing.

Status of Financing for Feminist and Women's Rights Organizations

The 2011 AWID global survey was completed by 1119 feminist and women's rights organizations from over 140 countries.[5] The significant sample size represented geographic and sectoral diversity, including non-governmental, non-profit organizations or non-registered groups of women, and collectives or initiatives with a mission or work that primarily or significantly focused on promoting women's rights, gender equality and/or women's empowerment. Nevertheless, the sample is not the entirety of the feminist and women's rights organizing and movements globally. Eighty-five per cent of respondents to AWID's survey were legally registered organizations, which is important to note as questions asked in the survey around financial situation are harder to tackle for individual activists or unregistered collectives and groups. Over half of survey respondents worked at the national (55 %) and local (52 %) levels, about a fifth worked regionally (19 %) or internationally (12 %).

When combined, **the 2010 incomes of 740 feminist and women's organizations totalled just USD 106 million**—a fraction of the budget for the same year for many individual, large international NGOs, including $309 million for Greenpeace Worldwide, $1.4 billion for Save the Children International and $2.6 billion for World Vision International. While we know that this USD 106 million does not represent the complete 'pie' of resources for feminist and women's rights organizations, the large size of this sample means that these findings are broadly relevant for the diversity of feminist and women's rights organizations, the majority of whom are not being reached by large pots of resources available, for example, from bilateral and multilateral agencies.

More than a third of sampled organizations listed their primary sources of support as individual giving, membership fees and income generation activities.[6] Further, 17 % indicated they had never received external funding from donors but had relied on combinations of income generating activities, membership fees and other 'self-generated' resources. Respondents noted that 'self-generated' resources provide a basic level of financial security or can be used as a stop-gap measure in times of funding constraints. These resources provide freedom and flexibility in resource allocation and also demonstrate that organizations often look inwards, in their own communities, for raising resources. While self-generated resources generally do not account for a very substantial amount of overall income, it engages communities in work related to advancements in women's rights and gender equality.

Women's funds were the next most frequent source of income reported by over one quarter of survey respondents.[7] One sixth of feminist and women's rights organizations reported funding from multilateral agencies and private and public foundations. In contrast, only about one tenth of feminist and women's rights organizations in the sample, reported receiving finding from bilaterals, national governments and international non-governmental organizations (INGOs).

When analyzing funding by source, the results show bilateral and multilateral agencies at 27 % and private foundations at 15 %, with significant increases in funding from local and national governments, increasing from 11 % in 2005 to 20 % in 2010. In contrast, the share of income reported from INGOs appeared to decrease from 14 % in 2005 to 7 % in 2010. The share of income women's funds remained constant at 5%.

Organization size and sources of funding seem to be closely related. Bilaterals and multilaterals were each mentioned as funding sources by 49 % of organizations with budgets over USD 50,000. Foundations and women's funds are the donors reaching smaller organizations (with budgets under USD 25,000). Organizations with budgets under USD 25,000 also seem to be dependent on individual donations (53 %) and income-generating activities (56 %). Individual donations account for 25 % for organizations with budgets between USD 25,000–100,000 and 18 % for organizations with budgets over USD 100,000. Income-generating activities equalled 23 % for organizations between USD 25,000–100,000 and 19 % for those with budgets over USD 500,000.

In order to analyse what is being funded, AWID research attempted to unpack the concerns around 'donor-driven' agendas. The survey asked respondents to identify their priority issues, populations and strategies compared to those for which they receive dedicated funding.[8]

There was considerable alignment between the top ten priorities identified by women's organizations and the top ten issues to which donor funding was directed. These included gender-based violence/violence against women; women's leadership and empowerment and women's economic empowerment; reproductive health and rights; sexual health (including HIV and AIDS); peacebuilding and violence against women in contexts of conflict/post-conflict; and access to education. The three issues for which women's organizations reported not receiving external support were economic, social, and cultural rights (ESCRs), political participation and sexual rights.

When it comes to strategies, however, there appears to be slightly less convergence between feminist and women's rights organizations and their funders. The majority of feminist and women's rights organizations in the sample employed strategies of capacity building and women's empowerment programmes to achieve their goals. Over two-thirds prioritized awareness raising, advocacy and campaigning, and leadership development as key strategies. Around one quarter prioritized networking and alliance building, organizing meetings, convenings and dialogues, movement building and feminist/women's rights organizing, microfinance and income-generation and communications. In contrast, the preferred strategy of donors appears to be direct service provision. This was the most frequently reported activity for which survey respondents received funding while respondents themselves did not list service provision in the top ten priority strategies of feminist and women's rights organizations.

Other priority strategies of feminist and women's rights organizations but not within the top ten priority strategies for which they receive donor support include networking/alliance building, organizing meetings/dialogues to analyze and strategize, movement building and feminist/women's rights organizing, and communications and information. This aligns with what many feminist and women's rights activists have said over the years: that it is becoming increasingly difficult to convince donors to support crucial mobilization and movement-building work such as networking, meetings and communications, which are strategies that are difficult to quantify and/or link to direct impacts 'on the ground.'

In terms of the quality and flexibility of funding for feminist and women's rights organizations, multi-year and core funding[912] remain the exception rather than the norm. Fifty-two per cent had never received multi-year funding and nearly half (48 %) have never received core, flexible funding for their work. Some organizations reported receiving core and multi-year support in the past (13 % and 42 %, respectively) but few had received these types of funding in 2010 (28 % and 21 %, respectively).

Both multi-year and core funding—and flexible funding in general—are important both to foster financial resilience and to support initiatives that work to transform gender inequalities in more sustained ways. Paradoxically, it seems that the more donors become concerned with results, the more inclined they are to support narrowly focused and time—bound activities to see a 'return on investment'. It is precisely this approach to funding that makes it difficult to secure meaningful results on women's empowerment and gender equality in the long term.

While AWID's survey reflects the views of mostly registered feminist and women's rights groups, it is important to emphasize that feminist and women's rights organizations and movements are diverse. Focusing only on registered and well-resourced feminist and women's rights organizations negates the diversity of organizing needed to tackle the complex issues affecting women and girls lives. Therefore, AWID will expand its focus from looking only at the formal funding available to feminist and women's rights organization to include the notion of other resources that feminist and women's rights activists, advocates and movements employ to progress their agendas. These non-financial resources, which include political influence and community trust, must be taken into consideration when any funding streams or gender responsive budgeting (GRB) processes are designed and implemented.

Funding Sectors

In addition to the survey of feminist and women's rights organizations, AWID has conducted desk research to identify trends within various funding sectors and attempts to draw parallels between the survey findings and desk research analysis. The following analysis represents the most updated desk research on some of so-called 'traditional' funding sectors that have been supporting women's rights and gender equality in the last decade and more. These sectors are international NGOs, private foundations, women's funds, bilateral and multilateral donors, women's funds and individual philanthropists.

Bilateral and Multilateral Funding

Trends in bilateral and multilateral funding for gender equality and women's empowerment show that Official Development Assistance (ODA) is increasing, yet still falling behind on stated commitments.[10] Overall, ODA flows were stable in 2014, after reaching the highest level ever recorded in 2013.[11] Thus, in 2014, Development Assistance Committee (DAC) members provided a total of USD 135.2 billion in net ODA (slightly higher compared to the 2013 figure of 135.1 billion in net ODA).[12] Net ODA as a share of gross national income was 0.29 % on par with 2013,[13] but still falling far short of international commitments to 0.7 % of GNI by 2015. Overall, ODA has increased by 66 % in real terms since 2000, when the MDGs were agreed.[14] The year 2014 figures reiterated that aid to the poorest countries continued to fall, bilateral aid to the least-developed countries fell by 16 % in real terms to USD 25 billion, according to provisional data. Eventually, the annual survey on donor spending plans carried by the DAC of the OECD indicates that country-level aid to the poorest countries should recover over the next few years after several years of declines, in line with a pledge by DAC members in December 2014 to reverse the fall in aid to countries most in need.[15]

In 2014,[16] 5 of the 28 OECD-DAC member countries continue to exceed the United Nations (UN) longstanding target of keeping ODA at 0.7 % of Gross National Income, namely Denmark, Luxembourg, Norway, Sweden and the UK.[17] The Netherlands, once a solid member of this group, dropped out in 2012 owing to drastic cuts to the development aid budget.[18] Thirteen countries reported a rise in net ODA, with the biggest increases in Finland, Germany, Sweden and Switzerland. Fifteen DAC members reported lower ODA, with the biggest declines in Australia, Canada, France, Japan, Poland, Portugal and Spain.[19]

Regarding support to gender equality, the principal tool used by DAC members to track ODA allocated in support of gender equality is the DAC Gender Equality Policy Marker. Building on the outcomes obtained by applying the DAC Gender Equality Policy Marker, the analysis developed by the GENDERNET Secretariat and the OECD Working Party on Development Finance Statistics (WP-STAT) states that DAC members' aid flows in support of gender equality have tripled since the MDGs from USD 8 billion in 2002 to USD 24 billion in 2012.[20]

Esplen and O'Neill's chapter in this volume examines ODA in detail; however, it is noteworthy to highlight that detailed analysis of OECD-Statistics, specifically the data on *Aid projects targeting gender equality and women's empowerment* for 2013,[21] shows that only a small percentage (15.4 %) of total ODA allocated to gender equality goes to standalone programming with gender equality as a primary focus. The remaining went to projects that have gender equality as a significant objective or initiatives with a gender mainstreaming approach. In AWID's view, this is problematic, because numerous studies have shown that gender mainstreaming has very mixed results in terms of its effectiveness and does not always result in empowering women.[22]

In addition, the GENDERNET analysis of 2012 ODA figures[23] identified financing gaps in critical subject areas that would also apply to 2013 figures such as women's economic empowerment; women, peace and security or women's leadership and participation.[24]

Direct ODA to women's equality organizations and institutions has decreased since 2011, as per OECD DAC statistic data.[25] When looking specifically at funds dedicated to women's equality organizations and institutions specifically (code 15170),[26] the OECD DAC statistics show a new[27] decrease since 2011, from USD 529.3 million to USD 338.9 million in 2013 (showing a decrease of 36%). Countries with steady and sometimes drastic declines from 2011 to 2013 in their support to women's equality organizations and institutions include Denmark, the Netherlands, Spain and Sweden. Australia, Austria and South Korea have increased funding to women's equality organizations and institutions since 2011, while Norway has fluctuated in support over the three-year period. It is important to state that this support to women's equality organizations and institutions makes up a very small percentage of bilateral aid focused on gender equality and the empowerment of women. For example in 2013, while the total amount of bilateral aid targeting gender equality and women's empowerment reached USD 29.2 billion (in commitment), funding for women's CSOs and national ministries was of USD 338.9 million (in commitment).

Additionally, several donors describe[28] a decline in their financial support for women's ministries in recent years, citing frustration with the low capacity of these ministries and weak political will as contributing factors. As a result, agencies like Irish Aid have ceased to directly fund such ministries and are instead scaling up their engagement on gender equality with central ministries such as finance and planning along with sector ministries. While support to finance and planning ministries is important, this should not be at the expense of national women's machineries that play a critical role in promoting gender equality and the empowerment of women including through oversight of mainstream ministries.

On the other hand, several important new bilateral funds targeting feminist and women's rights organizations have been scaled up and renewed in recent years. For example, the Netherlands launched three substantial funds to support gender equality and women's rights. From 2008 to 2011,[29] the Dutch Ministry of Foreign Affairs created the largest-ever fund for gender equality, known as the MDG3 providing €82 million in support of gender equality and women's empowerment with 35 of the 45 grants awarded to non-governmental feminist and women's rights organizations. A second round of the fund, under a new name Funding Leadership Opportunities for Women (FLOW), was launched in 2011[30] and provided €83.7 million to support women's economic empowerment, political participation and peace and security (2012–15). Of the 30 organizations receiving funding under FLOW, 23 were feminist and women's rights organizations, networks or funds. By 31 December 2015, the Netherlands would have disbursed over €150 million on gender equality and women's rights through feminist and women's rights organizations.[31] In 2012, a third fund focusing on Sexual and Reproductive Health and Rights was launched with €125 million made available for the years 2013 to 2015, though in this case none of the 12 grants directly reached feminist and women's rights organizations.[32]

During the 69th Session of the United Nations General Assembly in 2014, the governments of Denmark and the Netherlands launched a new fund of €15 million, the Amplify Change Fund, to support small, grass-roots organizations defending sexual and reproductive health and rights.[33]

Other mechanisms to channel resources to feminist and women's rights organizations have been multilateral funds. For example, the MDG Achievement Fund was established in 2006 by Spain, with USD 90 million to 13 programmes under the Fund's Gender Thematic Window. Since then other governments, including Mexico, Norway, the Netherlands, Switzerland and Germany, have also made smaller contributions to this fund.[34] The fund is currently managed by UN Women, under the name of Fund for Gender Equality (FGE), and is responsible for its own fundraising to replenish the fund.[35] The FGE provides multi-year grants to support feminist and women's rights organizations and partnerships between NGOs and government agencies with two broad areas of focus, namely women's rights economic and political empowerment. Feminist and Women's organizations have received over USD 32 million (75 %) of the total resources disbursed by the FGE.[36] Given the high demand, the Fund has only been able to support 1.25 % of the proposals received, a decision has been made to limit the applicant base in line with its focus on national and local support to 'government and women's local, national or regional NGOs, excluding international NGOs'.[37] A second multi-lateral fund initiative is the UN Trust Fund to End Violence against Women. This continues to be an important source of funding for innovative projects combating violence against women around the world. Since it began operations in 1997, the UN Trust Fund has disbursed over $95 million through 368 grants in over 132 countries and territories.[38] The UN Trust Fund currently supports 77 programmes in 70 countries with a value of USD 55.5 million.[39] While the majority of grantees are NGOs, grants are also awarded to governments and UN Country Teams. Funding in recent years has decreased since peaking in 2008 when USD21 million was granted. In 2011, the Trust Fund awarded $17.1 million to 26 initiatives in 33 countries and territories.[40]

Other agencies, such as the Norwegian Agency for Development Cooperation (NORAD), have established dedicated gender equality funds or budget lines, with a grant scheme that supports international and regional women's rights organizations and networks. In addition to dedicated funds,[41] donors have strengthened the gender equality focus of more general civil society funding. For example, Irish Aid's civil society funding round in 2011 and 2012 included a specific call for proposals on gender equality and for 2011, 34 % of the funding approved was for gender equality. Irish Aid's funding for women's organizations almost tripled between 2006 and 2011. NORAD made gender impact assessments mandatory for all CSOs in both the application process and when reporting on use of funds. Furthermore, the Icelandic International Development Agency (ICEIDA) requires CSOs to address gender equality in all project proposals, while the Spanish Ministry of Foreign Affairs mandates that gender equality be an integral part of NGO funding agreements.

AWID's research 'Watering the Leaves Starving the Roots' (2013)[42] observed that the share of resources reaching feminist and women's rights organizations has more than doubled from close to 25 % in 2008 to over 64 % in 2011. In dollar terms, that has meant an increase from USD 130 million in 2008 to USD 263 million in 2011. However, it is important to highlight that although this is a very positive sign, the number of feminist and women's rights organizations that can apply and have access to these kind of resources is limited, given the significant institutional requirements these donors demand and the size of grants normally provided.

UN Funds have been keeping track of the supply and demand for funding and have found surprising results.[43] For example, in 2011 the Trust Fund received an exponential increase in funding requests estimated at $1.2 billion. Due to constrained resources, the Fund could only support 1.4 % of the total applications received. Similarly, the demand for grants in the first round of FGE applications far exceeded the available resources, with 1239 funding requests totalling $3 billion from 127 countries. The Fund could only support 1.2 % of proposals, and yet 50 % of applicants had viable and strong proposals. Another example are applications received by The Netherlands to FLOW: In response to a single call for proposals, a total of 238 applications were received requesting over €733 million. Thus, the available € 70 million was more than 10 times oversubscribed.

This mismatch between the supply of funding and grantee demand shows the great and increasing need for support for gender equality and women's rights and empowerment, but it is also a testament to the potential for impact and outreach that could be unleashed.[44]

The above trends and shifts are important because bilateral and multilateral funding continues to be a significant source of support for feminist and women's rights organizations. However, an analysis of these funding trends is incomplete if the changing political and economic influence of emerging economies is not brought to attention. South–South Cooperation (SSC) is growing and there is a need to better understand its principles of cooperation that are based on 'a manifestation of solidarity among peoples and countries of the South that contributes to their national well-being, their national and collective self-reliance and the attainment of internationally agreed development goals, including the Millennium Development Goals. The SSC agenda and SSC initiatives must be determined by the countries of the South, guided by the principles of respect for national sovereignty, national ownership and independence, equality, non-conditionality, non-interference in domestic affairs and mutual benefit'.[45] While there is insufficient monitoring of financial flows to determine trends yet, to live up to set principles SSC actors must systematically include feminist and women's rights organizations and other CSOs in the design and implementation of aid flows and the regular assessments that follow on programme implementation.

International Non-Governmental Organizations

The shifting role of INGOs on financing for women and girls is also important to note. INGOs are one of the traditional sources of funding for feminist and women's rights organizations, along with multilaterals, bilaterals and women's funds. However, the AWID survey found that feminist and women's rights organizations have reported a decline in funding from INGOs. Since 2005, the percentage of total income sourced from INGOs has halved from 14 % to 7 %.[46] Simultaneously, INGOs interest in women and girls has drastically increased in the past decade, with 63 % of partners in new partnerships for women and girls being INGOs.[47] Equally affected by the financial crisis stemming in 2008, many INGOs have shifted their strategy to conserve resources, including transitioning from grant-making to field implementation. This has led to INGOs competing with feminist and women's rights organizations, particularly at the country level, for resources and reducing the total pot of INGOs funds directly available for feminist and women's rights organizations.

Feminist and women's rights organizations find themselves increasingly competing with INGOs for resources despite their expertise and direct connection to work at the local level. Feminist and women's rights organizations express difficulty competing with INGOs who they deem to be 'more savvy' when it comes to working with donors.[48] '*INGOs compete for funding, resources and advocacy space in country. The space is getting crowded. Local NGOs find it difficult to compete with better equipped and resourced INGOs for profile and networking opportunities with donors…and therefore funds. They often do not know how to 'play the game' as well'* shares Womankind partner from Zambia, Women for Change.

Furthermore, INGOs are tapping into the opportunities presented by the presence of the private sector in development financing with their focus on 'investing in women and girls.' INGOs are entering into partnerships with private sector actors that are described as a 'win-win' for all parties involved. Businesses gain access to untapped markets and receive good publicity, while INGOs increase their resources and their potential to influence conversations in the increasingly powerful corporate sector. Beneficiaries of INGO programmes supposedly gain economic benefits with the involvement of the corporate sector through the influx of funding available for their development. For example, Proctor & Gamble (P&G), a multinational corporation with a line of personal care products including cosmetics and feminine hygiene, partners with Save the Children for aid projects around the world including providing P&G Always brand sanitary pads to girls.[49] The India arm of P&G works with Care International to promote education with a special emphasis on girls.

More INGOs are placing emphasis on women and girls, even if their primary mission is not focused solely on women and girls. For example, CARE International is a 60-year-old INGO that focuses on poverty reduction with programmes on economic development and emergency relief. In 2007, CARE International began placing special emphasis on women and girls in all of their efforts.[50] Similarly, Mercy Corps, an INGO working with communities affected by conflict and disaster, began integrating gender into all its operations in 2011 following a gender assessment of its work the prior year.[51] This increased emphasis by non-women's focused INGOs can be seen as an important advance by the feminist and women's rights movement in bringing women and girls' rights to the mainstream agenda. At the same time, INGOs must ensure the full engagement and involvement of feminist and women's rights organizations and movements when working on issues affecting women and girls in any context. Furthermore, the partnerships between INGOs and the private sector need careful scrutiny to determine if, in reality, they do address root causes of gender inequalities that are essential to advance the feminist agenda in development.

Finally, INGOs shifting roles are contributing to the 'corporatization of philanthropy and development.' INGOs are adopting the 'more efficient' business practices of for-profit businesses, which include building widely recognizable and trustworthy brand names. INGOs can now compare to the likes of Nike, Coke and McDonalds in terms of brand recognition.[52] Increased investment in branding is matched with increase in staff size and expenses, creating a cycle of dependency on corporate donors who are eager to partner with INGOs for the good publicity and increased role in development. In addition to 'corporate-style' branding, INGOs are incorporating business practices such as short-term, easy to measure outcomes in order to achieve 'realistic goals,' resulting in a wariness towards larger visions that require shifts in cultural patterns that are not simple to measure. These larger, but harder to measure visions, include the work that feminist and women's rights organizations typically engage in to address the complex societal structures that underline gender inequality, such as movement building and leadership development.

Women's Funds

Women's funds are independent foundations that provide support specifically to organizations advancing women's rights. In the past 20 plus years, women's funds have emerged as a key source of financing for feminist and women's rights organizations and their number has increased globally. AWID's research 'Watering the Leaves, Starving the Roots: The Status of Financing for Women's Rights Organizing and Gender Equality' found that 28 % of survey respondents in 2010 reported receiving financial support from women's funds, growing from 15 % that relied on women's fund as their main source of funding in 2007.[53] Women's funds have also grown with research showing that the median income of 42 women's funds has increased almost 60 % from 2005 to 2010.

Women's funds consistently support a large number of organizations that mainstream funders fail to reach. Such organizations are underfunded for a variety of reasons, including that they are grassroots, in many cases unregistered and working on controversial issues or issues not considered a priority by mainstream funders. Women's funds reach populations that are marginalized and provide responsive support.

Feminist and women's rights organizations report that support from women's funds tend to be more flexible, more available for core support to strengthen organizational capacity, with uncomplicated application and reporting procedures. Recognizing the significance of this funding mechanism, AWID conducted a survey with members of the International Network of Women's Funds. Of the 42 women's funds surveyed, 67 % provide core funding while 40 % provide multi-year grants. Women's funds are also appreciated for their willingness to support new and innovative ideas, and the trust they place in feminist and women's rights organizations to address issues on the ground through collective organizing.

Although the median income of 42 women's funds rose by 60 % within the span of five years, the collective financial assets are minimal when compared to other funding mechanisms. In 2010, 42 women's funds reported a collective income of $54.5 million USD. In comparison, the Ford Foundation alone had assets over $11 billion USD in 2012.[54] Collectively, women's funds cannot provide enough financial support to sustain the feminist and women's rights organizations and movements. In regard to the private and corporate sector's interest in women and girls, women's funds are playing diverse roles within that space. Several funds have been engaging with the corporate sector in various capacities, from receiving direct funding to engaging in collaborative initiatives. For example, the Global Fund for Women received funding from Nike as part of Nike's 'Grassroots Girls Initiative'.[55] Similarly, Fundo Elas in Brazil partnered with Chevron to raise awareness, within Chevron, of the needs of local communities before making investments.[56] Some women's funds, such as Mama Cash, are carefully assessing the field and engaging with other players through joint research and advocacy to deepening their own understanding of the new development financing landscape.[57] In all the cases, women's funds are not ignoring the new actors and seeing the importance in this historic moment to engage and potentially influence how large amounts of funding are allocated to affect the lives women and girls globally.

Private Foundations

AWID's research indicates moderate growth in private foundation support to feminist and women's rights organizations. Private foundations accounted for 15 % of total income of feminist and women's rights organizations worldwide in 2011, growing from 13 % in 2005. Private foundations are the second most common form of support for feminist and women's rights organizations, after bilateral and multilateral agencies.

Private foundations, along with most mainstream actors, have also increased their interest in women and girls. This interest has led to some increase in funding dedicated to women and girls; however, most of this new money can be attributed to a handful of 'mega-funders,' like the Bill & Melinda Gates Foundation, rather than an increase in funding across the board in all private foundations. Furthermore, a nuanced analysis of the increased funding reveals that much of this money is going toward large INGOs or other groups that are not specialized to work with women and girls. This means feminist and women's rights organizations, who have the strongest experience and skills to address women and girls rights, are not commonly recipients of this 'new' money, pointing to a lack of mainstream knowledge of feminist and women's rights organizations expertise regarding women and girls.

At the same time, private foundation champions for feminist and women's rights funding like the Ford Foundation, Oak Foundation and the Foundation for Just Society, among others, use their influence to advocate for more and better funding for feminist and women's rights organizing with other foundations. In so doing, these private foundations are now playing the role of bridge builders between new private sector actors and feminist and women's rights groups and movements. Thus, Oak Foundation has been investing a lot of resources into developing an engagement and communication strategy with private sector actors to bring more and better resources to women's rights. For example, the Oak Foundation commissioned Business Case for Women's Economic Empowerment: An Integrated Approach unpacking corporate interests in women's economic empowerment and offering an integrated approach solution to corporate actors to consider when engaging on issues of women's economic empowerment.[58]

The Role of the Private Sector in Funding Women and Girls

According to projections from a recent Devex report, established bilateral development aid is expected to decline in the coming decade, whereas corporate aid is expected to double or grow significantly. It is clear that corporate support of international development work (including work that involves women and girls) is by no means a short-term phenomenon. Within this realm are new actors from the private sector (including businesses, financial intermediaries, associations and workers and employers organizations) who are increasingly playing central roles in development financing and as partners for governments, NGOs and donors.

It is therefore very important to understand the vast diversity of the private sector and its engagement in development and philanthropy vis-à-vis its role in the economy. The private sector is not monolithic. Unlike other social movements, feminist and women's rights organizations and movements do not have a long history of engagement with the private sector. In order to understand the motivations and strategies of the private sector, AWID conducted a study 'New Money, New Actors, New Conversations' that aimed to understand the landscape of the corporate sector and the role they play in shaping the funding discourse. The study found that out of 170 initiatives focused on women and girls, over 60 % of actors identify as corporate sector actors. While $14.6 billion has been identified in new funding partnerships devoted to women and girls predominately from corporate actors, only 9 % of these initiatives work directly (or in partnership with) women's rights organizations. In terms of thematic preferences and focus areas of the 'new actors', 35 % focused on women's economic empowerment and entrepreneurship, 25 % on women's leadership and empowerment, 21 % on women and girl's education, followed by health for women and girls, specifically 19 % for public health, 18% for maternal health and 18 % for sexual and reproductive health and rights. While the thematic focus is largely aligned with priorities of feminist and women's rights organizations and movements, the approach is instrumentalist with a focus on investing in individual women rather than a collective approach that supports structural and systemic change. For example, within the highly preferred theme of education for women and girls, the majority of initiatives focus on individual scholarships and trainings for women and girls rather than changes in education systems or policies that negatively impact girls access to school and employment opportunities.

When looking at the strategies chosen by these actors, 44 % of support is allocated to training and technical assistance, followed by 31 % to in-kind services and contribution, with only 9 % going directly to feminist and women's rights organizations. While engaging with the private sector is complex, particularly due to the lack of transparency and public accountability, there is a strong and urgent need to expand funding for women's rights and gender equality, which may include tapping into the private sector. It is clear that private sector actors are important players in development financing and are shaping the funding environment and discourse. It is therefore imperative to ensure that new investments from the private sector reflect, and are informed by, feminist analysis and practice. Feminist and women's rights organizations and donor allies need to assess this changing funding context and figure out how best to engage with new actors while maintaining their transformational strategies. AWID has proposed a number of possibilities. Feminist and women's rights organizations need to understand the tremendous diversity among funders, and ask themselves: 'Who else is working with women and girls, and how can we work together?' Feminist and women's organizations can learn from their counterparts in the labour and other movements about when or if to engage with private actors. Feminist and women's rights organizations should challenge the current trend for short-term, quick-fix results and 'return on investments.'

What Happens When Feminist and Women's Rights Organizations Are Supported With Significant and Long-Term Funding?

The above analysis on funding trends for feminist and women's rights organizations demonstrates the lack of sustainable financing to drive sustainable change for women and girls. AWID continues this analysis as well as emphasizes where progress has been made and success achieved such as the MDG3 Fund. Between 2007 and 2011, the Fund disbursed a total of €82 million to support 45 projects focusing on gender equality and women's rights initiatives around the world. The Fund channelled much needed resources to over 3600 national, regional and international feminist and women's rights organizations, and funds. These organizations have in turn helped amplify the Fund's impact through several critical interventions. According to AWID's research,[59] feminist and women's rights organizations supported by the Dutch MDG3 Fund successfully reached 225 million people, including 65 million grassroots women in 165 countries and 15 regions of the world.

Just a few highlights of the Fund's aggregated results demonstrate the incredible reach, scale and impact grantees were able to achieve including:

- Strengthening 105,000 grassroots feminist and women's rights organizations and providing them with a wide array of new tools, manuals, surveys, knowledge products and other innovations for empowering women, strengthening state programmes, generating new data and information, and exposing new forms of gender-based violence. To cite just one example: the International Association of Women Judges in Tanzania created a new concept called 'sextortion' to describe the use of sexual coercion especially by public officials, and developed a tool to help women's groups to recognize and combat this practice and bring perpetrators to book.

- Influencing 46 National governments enabling them to strengthen their gender equality policies, and programmes, including 36 countries that were persuaded to ratify and adopt the newly approved Convention 189 on Domestic Work, adopted in 2011 as a result of the 'last mile' lobbying by grantees like Women in Informal Employment: Globalizing and Organizing (WIEGO) and Central American Women's Fund (FCAM).
- Influencing 14 different international policies, and laws to better advance women's rights, including crucial work towards the International Labour Organization passing a convention protecting the rights of Domestic Workers. This was a huge success for millions of domestic workers from around the world.[60]

In an effort to encourage other funders to embrace strategic funding mechanisms as well as to offer an accountability tool to the funding sectors AWID, in partnership with Instituto del Tercer Mundo (ITeM)/Social Watch, and a number of partners and funding allies, including UN Women, developed the *FundHer* Scorecard. The *FundHer* Scorecard is a benchmarking tool to assess the quality and quantity of gender equality financing of donors. Among its goals, the *FundHer* Scorecard aims at strengthening the delivery of more and better funding for transformative women's rights and gender equality work.

Conclusions

As the chapter starts from framing funding as political, gender-responsive budgeting and funding for women's rights and gender equality must have a clear political agenda connected to the long-lasting systemic changes to achieve women's rights and gender equality.

GRB must address the root systemic causes of gender inequalities. That also means that accountability systems must reflect the ways to 'calculate' collective impact and systemic changes that are long-term. For example, providing individual scholarships and loans is only going to have a lasting change beyond individuals benefiting from those investments if done in parallel and with full understanding of systemic levers that need to be pulled and addressed simultaneously.

AWID believes there is a role for each financing actor and individual agency to make strategic contribution toward a transformative agenda. However, this cannot happen without coordination among and within funding sectors. GRB if integrated into budgetary planning and programming of funding agencies could ensure on the one hand, that gender analysis is mainstreamed into their budgets; on the other hand, that resources are earmarked for gender equality and women's rights programmes including supporting feminist and women's rights organizing. Financing for Sustainable Development Goals (SDGs) will be successful not only if it ensures greater funding availability to grassroots local, national, regional and global feminist and women's rights organizations and movements but also if it integrates robust planning and accountability mechanisms for each player in development and across the financing modalities—GRB provide venues to explore on this direction. The gender indicator of the Busan Partnership Agreement Monitoring Framework that monitors 'the number of countries with systems that track and make public allocations for gender equality and women's empowerment' is an important step to reduce corruption, ensuring money actually reaches the ground, and to seeing what results aid and other sources actually makes to women's lives.

Funding mechanisms must reflect the diversity of organizing. For larger funds and mechanisms, working with other actors who are able to absorb large amounts and distribute them to the diverse movement allies is an important strategy to embrace. Women's funds should be explored as valuable partners to multilateral institutions, governments and bilateral institutions in reaching deeply to the grassroots groups as they are part of a larger ecosystem of feminist and women's rights organizing and well positioned at local, national, regional and global levels to distribute funds efficiently and thoughtfully.

Funding distribution should go beyond the trickle-down approach and include bold and unprecedented budget lines and funds created specifically to be channelled to and through feminist and women's rights organizations and movements. Simultaneously, feminist and women's rights organizations and movements must be part of the decision-making process for creation of the funds and distribution mechanisms emphasizing the importance of diversified funding mechanisms and expanded notion of what entails resources for successful strategies toward achieving the SDGs, especially women's rights and gender equality.

Notes

1. https://www.opendemocracy.net/5050/srilatha-batliwala/beyond-individual-stories-women-have-moved-mountains.
2. The understanding of private sector in this chapter can include every enterprise, from the huge multinational corporations (MNCs) such as Wal-Mart, Shell and General Motors, to large and small private enterprises that are indigenous to the countries where they operate. Adopted definition from: http://www.odi.org/sites/odi.org.uk/files/odi-assets/publications-opinion-files/7734.pdf. In some contexts, private sector interests in profit and at times nefarious role in rights violations, goes hand in hand with their corporate social responsibility initiatives, including corporate philanthropy, business value and development financing through partnerships with bilateral governments, INGOs, foundations and/or celebrities.
3. http://www.awid.org/Library/Watering-the-Leaves-Starving-the-Roots.
4. http://foreignminister.gov.au/speeches/Pages/2014/jb_sp_140618.aspx.
5. For more detailed information on survey results and methodology, see: Pittman, A. et al. 2012. "2011 AWID Global Survey 'Where Is The Money For Women's Rights?' Preliminary Research Results" AWID, Toronto, ON www.awid.org/Library/2011-AWID-Global-Survey-Where-is-the-Money-for-Women-s-Rights-Preliminary-Research-Results. Of note regarding the survey sample is that some of the feminist and women's rights organizations that have benefited from recent large funds such as the Dutch MDG3 Fund and the UN Fund for Gender Equality did *not* complete the survey. Nevertheless, our sizeable sample leaves us confident that the results present an accurate picture of the situation for femnist and women's organizations broadly speaking.
6. This analysis only includes data from the 645 organizations that reported income for each donor. Thirty-eight per cent of feminist and women's rights organizations mentioned individual donors, 37 % mentioned membership fees, and 29 % mentioned income- generating activities, as an income source.
7. Twenty-eight per cent of feminist and women's rights organizations mentioned women's funds as an income source; 13 % mentioned multilateral organizations and public and private foundations as an income source, and 11 % mentioned bilaterals, national governments, and INGOs each as income sources.
8. We use the mean percentage of donor funding that feminist and women's rights organizations received for particular issues, strategies, and populations as a proxy for donor project-specific giving in this sample.

9. Core support is flexible funding that can be used for a variety of expenses and is not only dedicated to project/programme funding.
10. Based on the OECD article "Aid to developing countries rebounds in 2013 to reach an all-time high": http://www.oecd.org/newsroom/aid-to-developing-countries-rebounds-in-2013-to-reach-an-all-time-high.htm.
11. From the OECD article "Development aid stable in 2014 but flows to poorest countries still falling": http://www.oecd.org/development/development-aid-stable-in-2014-but-flows-to-poorest-countries-still-falling.htm.
12. Ibid. 8.
13. Ibid. 8.
14. Ibid. 8.
15. Ibid. 8.
16. Ibid. 8.
17. The UK joined this group in 2013 and its commitment to continue meeting the UN 0.7 % target is shrined in law. See: http://www.actionaid.org.uk/blog/news/2015/03/10/amazing-news-about-the-07-aid-commitment.
18. Ibid. 4.
19. Ibid. 8.
20. Esplen, E. et Hedman, J. (2014). From ambition to results: Delivering on gender equality in donor institutions. OECD: Paris, France. Pgs. 24–25.
21. http://stats.oecd.org.
22. See for example: Sweetman, C. (2013) "Introduction" at *Gender & Development Journal* 20.3. Oxfam: Oxford, UK; http://www.tandfonline.com/doi/pdf/10.1080/13552074.2012.743266
23. Ibid. 12. Pg. 25.
24. Other chapters in this collection will examine these gaps in detail.
25. OECD Stats, Extracts Stats: Aid projects targeting gender equality and women's empowerment (CRS) – Code 15170 Women's Equality Institutions and Organizations, 2011 to 2013 data: http://stats.oecd.org.
26. It is important to highlight that these figures also include women's institutions, such as women's national machineries, and that they may actually be getting more funding than women's organizations due to better positioning and ability to absorb funding. Still national women's machineries have very limited funding in comparison to other state institutions.
27. The amounts were going down from $559.5 million in 2008 to $371.9 million in 2010 (a variation of 33.5 %), but then increased in 2011 with a commitment of $537.6 million.
28. Ibid. 12. Pg. 26.
29. Ibid. 12. Pg. 26.
30. Ibid. 12. Pg. 26.
31. Ibid. 12. Pg. 26.

32. http://www.government.nl/issues/development-cooperation/grant-programmes/sexual-and-reproductive-health-and-rights-fund
33. Liz Ford (September 2014). "Denmark and Netherlands launch fund for sexual health groups" at the Guardian: http://www.theguardian.com/global-development/2014/sep/23/denmark-netherlands-amplify-change-sexual-health.
34. Arutyunova, A. Et Clark, C. (2013). *Watering the leaves starving the roots: The status of financing for women's rights organizing and gender equality.* AWID: Cape Town, South Africa; Mexico City, Mexico; Toronto, Canada. Pg. 60.
35. See Fundraising Fact Sheet at http://www.unwomen.org/~/media/headquarters/attachments/sections/trust%20funds/fundgenderequality/fge-fundraisingfactsheet-en.ashx
36. Ibid. 28.
37. Ibid. 28. Pg. 62.
38. Source: UN Women – UN Trust Fund to End Violence Against Women webpage: http://www.unwomen.org/en/trust-funds/un-trust-fund-to-end-violence-against-women.
39. Ibid. 29.
40. Ibid. 28. Pg. 62.
41. Ibid. 12. Pg. 27.
42. Ibid. 28. Pg. 54.
43. Alpizar, L. (2012). Review theme: Evaluation of progress in the implementation of the agreed conclusions of CSW 52 on 'Financing for gender equality and the empowerment of women.' UN CSW: http://www.un.org/womenwatch/daw/csw/csw56/panels/panel-4-Alpizar.pdf.
44. Fund for Gender Equality Brochure. (2011). UN Women.
45. http://ssc.undp.org/content/ssc/about/what_is_ssc.html
46. Angelika Arutyunova, Cindy Clark *Watering the Leaves, Starving the Roots,* Association for Women's Rights in Development, 2013 http://awid.org/Library/Watering-the-Leaves-Starving-the-Roots
47. Miller, J., Arutyunova, A. Et Clark, C. (2013). *New Actors New Money New Conversations: A Mapping of Recent Initiatives for Women and Girls.* AWID: Cape Town, South Africa; Mexico City, Mexico; Toronto, Canada. Page 15.
48. Emily Esplen, *Leaders for change: why support women's rights organizations?* Womankind Worldwide, March 2013 http://www.womankind.org.uk/wp-content/uploads/downloads/2013/03/LeadersForChange-FINAL.pdf
49. http://www.savethechildren.org/site/c.8rKLIXMGIpI4E/b.9171611/k.8E35/Procter__Gamble.htm
50. http://www.care-international.org/about-us/history.aspx
51. https://www.mercycorps.org/sites/default/files/tsu_gender_external_1012_r2.pdf

52. 14 March 2014 *Not Just About the Money: Corporatization is Weakening Activism and Empowering Big Business* https://www.opendemocracy.net/transformation/genevieve-lebaron-peter-dauvergne/not-just-about-money-corporatization-is-weakening-a
53. http://www.awid.org/Library/Money-Watch-for-Women-s-Rights-Movements-and-Organizations-FundHer-Brief-2008
54. http://foundationcenter.org/findfunders/topfunders/top100assets.html
55. http://www.globalfundforwomen.org/news/publications
56. Miller, J., Arutyunova, A. Et Clark, C. (2013). *New Actors New Money New Conversations: A Mapping of Recent Initiatives for Women and Girls.* AWID: Cape Town, South Africa; Mexico City, Mexico; Toronto, Canada. Pg. 63.
57. Mama Cash collaborated with AWID on the action research: 'New Actors, new money, new conversations'
58. http://www.oakfnd.org/economicempowerment
59. Women moving mountains.
60. https://www.opendemocracy.net/5050/srilatha-batliwala/transformative-strategy-true-value-of-investing-in-women%E2%80%99s-rights

Bibliography

Alpizar, L. (2012). *Review theme: Evaluation of progress in the implementation of the agreed conclusions of CSW 52 on "Financing for gender equality and the empowerment of women"*. In UN CSW. http://www.unwomen.org/en/csw.

Arutyunova, A., & Clark, C. (2013). *Watering the leaves, starving the roots. The status of financing for women's rights organizing and gender equality.* Canada/Mexico/South Africa: AWID.

Australian Ministry or Foreign Affairs. (2014, June). Speech by Honourable Julie Bishop MP to the National Press Club.

Batliwala, S. (2013). A transformative strategy: The true value of investing in women's rights. In *Open Democracy - 50.50 Inclusive Democracy.* UK, www.opendemocracy.org.

Batliwala, S. (2013). Beyond individual stories: Women have moved mountains. In *Open Democracy - 50.50 Inclusive Democracy.* UK, www.opendemocracy.org.

Batliwala, S., Rosenhek, S., & Miller, J. (2013). *Women moving mountains. Collective impact of the Dutch MDG3 fund.* Canada/Mexico/South Africa: AWID.

Esplen, E. (2013). *Leaders for change: Why support women's rights organizations?* London: Womankind Worldwide.

Esplen, E., & Hedman, J. (2014). *From ambition to results: Delivering on gender equality in donor institutions.* France: OECD.

Ford, L. (2014). Denmark and Netherlands launch fund for sexual health groups. *The Guardian*. UK, www.theguardian.com.

Foundation Center, Top Funders - Top 100 U.S. Foundations by Asset/Size. www.foundationcenter.org.

Hopenhaym, F., Rabeer, N., & Carrasco, L. (2008). *Money watch for women's rights movements and organizations: FundHer brief 2008*. AWID: Canada/Mexico/South Africa.

Lebaron, G., & Dauvergne, P. (2014). Not just about the money: Corporatization is weakening activism and empowering big business. In *Open Democracy – Transformation*. UK. www.opendemocracy.org.

Mercy Corps. *Gender sector approach*. www.mercycorps.org.

Miller, J., Arutyunova, A., & Clark, C. (2013). *New actors new money New conversations: A mapping of recent initiatives for women and girls*. Canada/Mexico/South Africa: AWID.

Oak Foundation, Dalberg, ICRW et Witter Ventures. (2014). *The business case for women's economic empowerment: An integrated approach*. Switzerland: OAK Foundation.

OECD. (2014). *Aid to developing countries rebounds in 2013 to reach an all-time high*. OECD: France. www.oecd.org.

OECD. (2015). *Development aid stable in 2014 but flows to poorest countries still falling*. OECD: France. www.oecd.org.

OECD Statistics. (2011/2013). OECD: France. http://stats.oecd.org.

Pittman, A., Arutyunova, A., et al. (2012). *2011 AWID global survey 'Where is the money for women's rights?' Preliminary research results*. Canada/Mexico/South Africa: AWID.

Save the Children. Info on multi-stakeholder partnerships. www.savethechildren.org.

Sweetman, C. (2013). Introduction. In *Gender & Development Journal* 20.3. Oxfam: Oxford.

UN Women. (2011). *Fund for gender equality brochure*. www.unwomen.org.

UN Women: Fundraising fact sheet: Partnering for results, partnering for change: Investing in UN women's fund for gender equality. www.unwomen.org.

UN Women: UN trust fund to end violence against women. www.unwomen.org.

UNDP, What is South-South cooperation? In *United Nations Office for South-South cooperation*. http://ssc.undp.org/content/ssc.html.

Vesvrotte de, F. (2015). *Amazing news about the 0.7% aid commitment!*. ActionAid: UK. www.actionaid.org.uk.

CHAPTER 12

Climate Finance: Why Does It Matter for Women?

Mariama Williams

Introduction

Climate change and climate variability are already adversely affecting the lives of countless millions of men, women, boys and girls in Africa, Asia, the Caribbean, Latin America and the Pacific. Variability in rainfall patterns, rainfall shortage and droughts impact water resources, create dry wells, increase impurities in water and threaten food supplies and access to safe drinking water. On the other hand, increased intensity and frequency of rain that is associated with tropical storms and cyclones brings more water than can be reasonably managed in a specific time frame, resulting in overburdened ecosystems and stresses on bio-physical resources. Extreme weather events such as floods, cold spells, heat waves, storms and earthquakes affect the health and well-being of women, girls, boys and men in local communities and households directly and devastatingly. These events can also retard advancement in social and economic development. The Intergovernmental Panel on Climate Change's Fifth Assessment Report (AR5 2013) as well as its 'Special Report on Managing the Risks of Extreme Events and Disasters to Advance Climate Change

M. Williams (✉)
The South Centre, Geneva, Switzerland

© The Author(s) 2017

Z. Khan, N. Burn (eds.), *Financing for Gender Equality*,
DOI 10.1057/978-1-137-46101-8_12

Adaptation' (SREX) 2012 warns that many such events are to be expected in the future.

Science has attributed climate change to the global emissions of man-made greenhouse gases arising primarily from the long march to industrialization and growth of the now rich and industrialized countries of the EU, the USA, Australia, Canada, New Zealand and Japan. These countries have grown rich from utilizing fossil fuels, the transformation of rural ecosystem to urban cities and the exploitation of industrial agriculture. They have very high income, well-developed industries and infrastructures and can deploy a wide range of technologies without seriously burdening their economies. The developing world, long the major providers of natural resources, labour and land that helped to foster the industrialization of the rich countries, have not benefitted significantly from the transformation of these resources, and now must bear the brunt of the effects of a changing climate. The developing countries are also now the ones to sacrifice their growth potential in order to help to alter the trajectory of rising greenhouse gases and to deal with the reality of limited atmospheric space.

The injustice of climate change therefore lies in one evident fact: The impacts of climate change are real and are most urgently and most devastatingly felt in the developing countries and by the poorest women, men and children, who are the least responsible for creating or contributing to the factors giving rise to anthropogenic climate change.

Addressing climate change thus places on developed countries a central responsibility for addressing the man-made challenges to the atmosphere and also to provide financial and technological support for developing countries to adapt to the damaging effects of climate change, as well as to support the rapid transformation of developing countries' economies to a low carbon, clean energy development pathway. Ultimately, there is need for finance and other support for the losses and damages incurred by the women and men in the developing countries arising from the impacts of climate change generated events.

Fairness, equity and democracy, hence, lie at the heart of global climate change protection policy. But the issues of fairness, equity and democracy also have to do with issues of gender inequality and injustice and the marginalized and heightened vulnerability of indigenous men and women.

Extreme weather events, rising sea levels and threats to water and food production all have differential impacts on the lives of women and men. Women and men have different capability, opportunities, ownership and access to economic, social and technological resources that are needed to facilitate adapting to a changing climate, which adversely impacts the availability of food, fuel and water. Women, as a group, relative to men, as a group, have different possibilities for recovering from frequent and intensive periods of droughts, floods and hurricanes.

Women and children die disproportionately more than men from extreme weather events such as floods, hurricanes and storms (Neumayer and Plumper 2007).[1] The IPCC's AR4 notes that climate change is likely to directly impact children and pregnant women because they are particularly susceptible to vector and water-borne diseases, which will both intensify and increase with global warming. WHO (2011) argues that pregnant women are more susceptible and die from malaria and water borne diseases than the general population. IPCC AR5 notes that '(w)orldwide, mortality due to natural disasters, including droughts, floods and storms, is higher among women than men' (World Health Organization 2011; IPCC 2014).

Women, due to historical discrimination and biases in the labour markets, financial and credit markets, as well as cultural and social practices, have less assets, income and savings to deal with the loss and damages from extreme weather events. Climate change and climate variability impact the availability and the quality of water resources to communities in developing countries, particularly in the rural areas. Adapting to climate change and climate variability places increasing burden on women's and men's care and social reproduction work. In some countries, the effects of climate change also place women and girls at greater risks for bodily injury, rape and harassment when they must travel further and further away from home to secure household drinking water, fuel and food (Bridge 2008).

Climate strategies that call for radical emissions reductions and societal transformation will impact men and women differently. The strategies that underlie climate protection policy frameworks must tackle areas such as public transportation, the accessibility of individual, household and business to clean energy and their responsibilities for energy efficiency production and household goods, waste handling and consumption. Commitments to reduce emissions and transition to low carbon pathways that underlie developing countries' nationally appropriate mitigation actions (NAMAs) and now more comprehensively integrated under the framework of the Intended Nationally Determined Contributions (INDCs), which is key pillar of the recently adopted Paris Agreement (December 2015), all have implications at individual, household and firm levels and have different burden and benefits for men, women, female headed/male headed households, female and male farmers, and women and men owned and operated micro-small and medium enterprises (MSMEs).

The INDCs, which have been submitted by over 186 countries, cover all areas: adaptation, mitigation, finance, technology development and transfer and capacity building. These planned contributions by developing countries towards the global effort to address climate change are eventually to become nationally determined contribution. Their scope, coverage and planning processes will determine the pace and timing of national strategies for reducing greenhouse gases, for example, by switching increasingly to renewable energy and implementing forest conservation and management strategies for enhancing sinks and reservoirs of greenhouse gases. INDCs also include methodologies for assessing adaptation, capacity building and technological development and transfer needs of developing countries and their identified key economic actors. The INDCs, which set targets around each of the thematic areas identified, will also be the main instruments for mobilizing domestic and international flow of finance to support the implementation of climate change plans.

Ultimately, climate goals, priorities and the concomitant actions that are implemented to address the growing climate challenges concern the well-being, livelihood and lives of all citizens—women, men and children, across different socio-economic classes and life cycles. The preamble of Paris Agreement paragraph 7 exhorts Parties to the agreement, *'when taking action to address climate change (to) respect, promote and consider their respective obligations on human rights, the right to health, the rights of indigenous peoples, local communities, migrants, children, persons with disabilities and people in vulnerable situations and the right to development, as well as gender equality, empowerment of women and intergenerational equity.'*

Gender and the Pillars of Climate Change Protection and Development

Gender issues are important in climate protection policies, specifically in the design, implementation and financing of adaptation and mitigation strategies, for at least three main reasons:

1. Structural gender inequalities are affected by climate change, climate variability and the losses and damages these generate: The effects of extreme weather events as well as the long-term chronic

impact of climate change on water, agriculture and natural resources impact pre-existing structural gender inequalities. Crises of health and food systems and the measures implemented to mitigate it can enhance or worsen the situation for gender equality and women's social and economic empowerment.

2. Participation and Democracy: The gendered nature of the economic and financial architecture that dominates the responses to climate change has implications for the participation of men and women in decision-making and affects men's and women's lives in different ways. Hence, it is important that women as well as men have a voice in decision-making on climate change policy, especially around adaptation and mitigation strategies. A high degree of integration of women's and men's participation and systemic representation (agency) across all aspects of climate governance is essential to ensure the most fair, equitable and cost-effective solutions to the climate challenge.
3. Accountability and Monitoring: Monitoring the gendered outcomes of climate change policy responses is important for pin-pointing reforms of climate protect system so that adaptation and mitigation responses can promote gender equality, poverty eradication and sustainable development. Knowledge, experience, insights and capacities for contributing to the way forward require drawing on all the available resources to which a country has access in a climate constrained world. Women and Indigenous Peoples, as with other groups that have been historically marginalized, have knowledge, insights and practices that could be integrated in climate protection policies. They also need the upgrading of their knowledge and capacities for ensuring livelihoods, sustainable development and for contributing to local, national and planetary safety.

The need for climate policy to integrate gender concerns into its frameworks and programming is increasingly being recognized by Parties to the United Nations Framework Convention on Climate Change. The Conference of the Parties (COP) which is the supreme decision making body implementing the convention's provisions has been, through multiple piecemeal decisions over the years, intensifying actions on gender and climate change in the policy arena, since 2001 when it adopted the initial decision calling for gender balance in decision-making institutions of the Convention. This was followed in 2011 by the gender decision. The 20th Meeting of the Parties held in Lima, Peru, further strengthen this process by adopting the Lima Work Programme on Gender (Decision 18/CP.20) which seeks to both further advance the implementation of decisions 36/CP.7, 1/CP.16 and 23/CP.18 as well as to advance the integration of gender equality considerations into, and to facilitate, gender responsive climate change policy, in particular, with regard to further strengthening all activities related to adaptation and mitigation and technology.

Adaptation and mitigation activities impose heavy burdens not only on developing countries governments, but also on the businesses, families, households and individual men and women living within these countries.

Adaptation and Gender in Brief

The IPCC defines adaptation as 'adjustment in natural or human systems in response to actual or expected climate stimuli or their effects, which moderates harm or exploits beneficial opportunities.'[2] More simply, adaptation is the set of coping strategies undertaken by individual men, women and communities in response to a climate-related threat such as slow onset events (e.g., sea-level rise and ocean degradation) and/or extreme weather events (e.g., storms, hurricanes, etc.).

Adaptive activities (e.g., climate-proofing agriculture and ensuring food security, promoting water conservation and efficiency in its usage, pest and disease management and fire management) are critical to sustainable development. Adaptation efforts, which are daily issues for individual woman and man, families and households, are likely to require more resources than they currently have available. Though this impacts both men and women and male- and female-headed households, it is likely to be more acute for women and for female-headed households due to gender gaps in income and social and economic resources.

When governments and households must re-allocate expenditures on climate change adaptation measures, this may reduce both targeted (such as projects that improved health and educational outcome for girls and women) and non-targeted gender equality interventions (such as health clinics)[3] and poverty eradication spending[4] and budgeting. In addition, if climate change prompts resettlement and engenders decline crop yields, it may reduce household resources and their ability to meet their day-to-day functioning. The depth of these effects and women's and men's ability to respond with appropriate survival strategies will depend on how gender-sensitive poverty reduction strategies are integrated into adaptation and mitigation measures—whether the strategies function complementarily or are adversarial to each other.

Women are dynamic actors in projects and programmes particularly related to adaptation, such as crop and livestock selection, crop shifting and soil preservation, the use of traditional water harvesting techniques and the efficient use of water. Women, as the managers of household energy and water supplies, are adapting to the changing climate conditions. Women, as farmers and major producers of food, are also adopting production and growing practices that ensure food security, in spite of climate change (Perlata 2008; Damptey 2007).

Gender inequalities in socio-economic, political and cultural norms of adaptation were understated and under-recognized within the National Adaptation Programmes of Action (NAPAs), instruments designed for least developing countries to assess their adaptation priorities and needs. However, gender has been included as one of the ten guiding elements to be emphasized in both the NAPAs and the National Adaptation plans (NAPs)[5] (of developing countries initiated in the 2010 Cancun Adaptation Framework).[6] Annex II of a November 2011 Technical Paper on NAP produced by the Subsidiary Body on Implementation of the United Nation Framework Convention on Climate Change (UNFCCC) focused on the integration of gender-related considerations in identifying and implementing medium- and long-term adaptation activities. The Annex which cites numerous reports from the UN Commission on the Status of Women and the United Nations Entity for Gender equality and the Empowerment of Women (UN Women) argues that:

> *Integrating a gender perspective into medium-and long-term adaptation is therefore necessary to ensure that adaptation activities undertaken by the least developed countries (LDCs) will not exacerbate gender inequalities and will ensure women's equal participation in the decision-making and implementation phases of adaptation. It will lead to better adaptation and more resilient communities.*

More recently, the Paris Agreement in article 7 paragraph 5 acknowledges '*that adaptation action should follow a country-driven, gender-responsive, participatory and fully transparent approach…*'

Mitigation and Gender in Brief

In seeking to mitigate GHGs, the focus is on low-carbon, clean and efficient energy development, and the enhancement of both natural and man-made greenhouse gas sinks. While the former focuses on industrial production, energy generation and energy end use intensive sectors such as transportation, the latter revolves around a large number of activities such as agricultural production, deforestation, land use and land-use changes that are important for the lives and livelihoods of men and women in quite distinct ways. Mitigation strategies, though generally associated with technological interventions, are not gender or equity neutral.

Mitigation within the context of sustainable development can help to promote gender equity and women's empowerment by addressing at least four issues: (1) women's and men's energy needs and uses; (2) women's and men's employment and entrepreneurship—potential challenges and constraints in the agriculture, energy and power sectors; (3) incorporating women's and men's traditional knowledge and practices into mitigation strategies and policy frameworks; and (4) paying focused attention on ensuring gender equity in the use, conservation and management of forests.

Some mitigation actions, such as the provision of clean and modern energy services, save women's and men's time and lives and promote better health. However, other mitigation actions, such as those implemented to affect land use and land-use change, can shift the balance of economic and social resource distribution between women and men and among different communities and hence can exacerbate inequality. Mitigation strategies that focus on land use such as those that involve investment in land to produce agro-fuels and programme aimed at reducing deforestation and degradation from forests and so on, depending on how they are implemented, may displace communities and exacerbate loss of access to land for women. It may also exacerbate or create land-related conflicts that disenfranchise women and put women and girls at risk for gender-related violence.

As noted by Godfrey, the social dimensions of these international (or cross-border) 'land deals' are not recognized. There are also quite strong and negative gender dimensions which have even been less acknowledged and compensated for. These issues are real threats from the point of view of poor women and men and indigenous women and men (Godfrey 2011).

Mitigation, in as much as it focuses on large-scale, capital-intense energy, manufacturing and commercial activities, has not been seen as an area that is amenable to gender dynamics. Thus, there has been a blind spot with regard to the household sector in this area of climate change. However, this blind spot is being marginally transformed towards a greater appreciation of the role of the household, informal and community sectors in both creating mitigation factors and being areas for the proactive application of mitigation actions.

An important area where mitigation efforts can translate into immediate and direct benefits for women on multiple levels is the area of women's and men's cooking activities using traditional biomass and/or lighting with kerosene lamp in the developing world and its association with the production of black carbon (soot/smoke).[7] Black carbon, which is argued to contribute to about 18 % of global warming (Rosenthal 2009), is the likely number two leading contributor to global warming. The household sector in developing countries, which is still over-reliant on traditional unsustainable biomass and/or kerosene lamps, should therefore have increased importance in the mitigation strategies of developing countries.

Addressing black carbon will require paying greater attention to mitigation at the household level in order to reduce its release into the atmosphere. Reduction in black carbon emissions is now seen as a relatively cheap way to reduce global warming, as it can be accomplished by simply switching to solar and new energy efficient low (or none) soot cooking stoves (GHF 2009; Rosenthal 2009). As noted by researchers, solar or other forms of energy efficient cooker in 20 million homes at an approximate cost of $20 each will cause less smoke and use less fuel (Rosenthal 2009).

The renewable energy sector can produce employment and entrepreneurial activities in the areas of energy development, production and transportation. Here, gender issues arise in terms of 'employment equity and working conditions and women's participation in decision-making' (NORAD 2010). There is need for rapid and large-scale emersion and enrolment of women in skill building programmes in all levels of the six renewable sectors identified by the IPCC (solar, wind, hydro, geothermal, ocean and biomass and bioenergy). Though there is tremendous amount of research on the mitigation potentials of each of the sector, there is insufficient research on the gender dimension of these sectors as well as with regard to the petroleum and oil sector.

Gender Technology Development Transfer and in Brief

The development (or acquisition), deployment, diffusion and transfer of technology to control greenhouse gas emissions are critically important for both adaptation and mitigation in developing countries. Successful adaptation and mitigation of climate change in priority sectors such as agriculture, fishery, forestry, coastal zones and health require relevant adaptive technologies. The adoption of relevant technologies is also important for systemic observation, monitoring of climate variability and the prevention and protection against climate-related disasters at local, subnational and national levels.

In order to contribute to gender equality outcomes, technology development should focus on areas that help to ease women's time burden, scale up their economic activities and promote their human development. Examples include solar- or wind-powered water pumps for the drying of agricultural products, which in many developing countries is a female-dominated activity. Even as countries seek to upgrade to capital-intensive technologies (e.g., carbon capture and storage, nuclear energy, clean fossil fuel generation and biofuels), they should ensure that the technologies are appropriate to the needs of different social groups.

Access to technological resources goes hand in hand with capacity building to both enhance the use and application of the technology, and access to new equipment and knowledge helps to promote women's awareness, skill and resourcefulness with regard to adaptation and mitigation.

Technology transfer and cooperation are also linked to financing. It is important to focus such support on technology that is gender, social and development friendly and that protects the web of life and promotes ecological security. This includes paying particular attention to protecting traditional knowledge and seeking to improve and enhance its effectiveness through gender-sensitive approaches to traditional knowledge and gender-aware benefit sharing agreements. For example, rainwater harvesting, recharging of ground well and facilitating sustainable agriculture and development are critical to women's involvement in food production and food self-sufficiency. However, these areas tend to be time consuming and impose a heavy care burden on women and girls. Technological support would be beneficial in reducing women's time burden as well as increasing their productivity.

Feminists and gender advocates working within the context of the UNFCCC negotiating space, under the umbrella of the 'Women and Gender Constituency,' as well as at national levels, have been hard at work seeking to promote gender-sensitive, gender-responsive and gender equality climate governance policies around adaptation, mitigation and technology transfer and capacity building. These activities are targeted around at least five important pillars: (1) improving women's role in climate governance, through gender balance in representation and improved capacity building for climate negotiations for women; (2) improving women empowerment concerns and gender analysis in climate and related sciences, (3) programmes and trainings for enhancing the skill set of women to undertake adaptation and mitigation and related vulnerability assessments; (4) increasing women's participation in timely and strategic interventions around climate protection and building resilience and (5) ensuring adequate climate finance, that is publicly sourced, non-debt crating and easily accessible, to developing countries and community-based organizations in those countries; and ensuring gender equity in the flow of this finance.

The overarching goals of gender-responsive climate and development policy are to:

- Promote and ensure gender equitable results that improve the economic and social situation of men and women and promote women's empowerment.
- Improve the welfare impacts of adaptation and mitigation strategies on men and women in communities across the developing world.

This can be achieved by setting in place processes and mechanisms to:

- Improve the understanding of the primary, secondary, direct and indirect role and contributions of women and men in adaptation and mitigation.
- Show how adaptation and mitigation policies impact women's and men's multiple roles: as workers, producers, mother, care-giver and consumers (highlighting the differential constraints, challenges and opportunities of each gender in these areas).
- Ensure that climate protection policy has gender-based analytical components.
- Embedding climate-focused gender analytical tools (that are climate policy relevant) into global, regional and national climate protection policies.
- Ensure that climate change adaptation and mitigation policies, programmes and strategies aim to support the elimination of gender and other social gaps and promote women's and men's well-being.

However, in examining gender, adaptation and mitigation and technology development and transfer, it is also important to highlight the linkage to climate finance which is an important tool for leveraging greater participation of women in adaptation and mitigation projects and for promoting their access to environmentally sound and socially useful technologies. It is important to also consider climate finance because of the fiscal and budgetary implications of financing climate actions in developing countries. In the context of constrained climate finance flows, there is likely to be the potential of trade-offs between financing climate activities versus financing traditional economic and social development budgets (such as poverty eradication, targeted gender equality interventions and food security). This is increasingly so, if there is inadequate provision of climate finance at the global level.

Climate Finance: Distinctions, Principles, Scope and Quantum That Are Important for Gender Equitable Access

Climate change finance is distinct from regular development financing as it arises from, and the architecture supervising it is grounded in, the UNFCCC (UNFCCC 1992). At the heart of this Convention is the principle of equity and polluter pays. Hence, climate financing is an obligation on developed countries whose development path has led to the existing overhang of greenhouse gases in the atmosphere. The planet is committed to a path of decades of warming trends despite whatever present actions might be taken. According to the scientific literature, the impacts of this warming trend will be felt primarily and more acutely in developing countries, particularly those that are vulnerable to climate variability and change. Coordinated and collaborative actions and measures to cover the losses and damages incurred remain a global, regional, national and local imperative.

Climate finance is not simply ODA, which is voluntary stream of financing with varying motivations by donor countries. Climate finance is a global public good, which in the framework of the Convention, is a commitment made by Annex II Parties[8] (OECD countries) to provide finance, including for technology transfer to non-Annex I parties (developing countries) to compensate for a 'global public bad'—the accumulation of anthropogenic GHGs, which is contributing to the historic warming of the planet. A significant portion, about two-thirds, of accumulated stock of GHGs is the historical responsibility of developed countries (Annex I parties to the Convention). Hence, climate finance is defined, and the nature and principles of its flow are regulated by Article 4 of the UNFCCC, which stipulates the commitments of the Conventions Parties to act on climate change (specifically articles 4.3, 4.4 and 4.5).

The historical responsibility of Annex I Parties for climate change, in tandem with the polluter pay principle remains quite relevant in climate finance. Non-Annex I Parties (developing countries) still have significant challenges of poverty eradiation and millions of men, women and children living in their economies, who lack of access to essential services such as proper sanitation, access to water and modern energy services for climate finance. These are the hard realities behind the development of the principle of common but differentiated responsibility (CBDR), which has been an essential principle in international environmental governance since the Rio conference of 1992.

However, the applications of the CBDR and equity principles do not mean that developing countries have no responsibility to transform their economies to support the objectives of the Convention, they do. Developing countries, as they grow, are contributing to flow of GHG gases in the atmosphere.[9] Hence, they are increasingly taking more actions in their national economies to mitigate climate change, and under so-called market-based mechanisms, such as the Clean Development Mechanism (CDM), many developing countries have also contributed to the mitigation actions of the developed countries.

Climate finance, though highly touted to be one of the key deliverable of the Paris agreement, turned out to be one of the least significant provision in the agreement, which has weakened the responsibility of developed countries to provide new and additional climate finance for developing countries. Developed countries simply re-affirmed their promise to continue the flow of climate finance and to honour their commitment to a goal of mobilizing $100 billion per year by 2020 for developing countries. How this will play out eventually impacts on the lives of women and girls in these countries will be carefully monitored in the coming years.

Why Does Climate Finance Matter for Women?

Climate change finance presents new opportunities, challenges and constraints for women and men in developing countries. This is consistent with the IPCC's argument that climate change can create economic benefits as economic structures are re-designed to meet climate challenges. The opportunities at this point in time have not been greatly explored and depend to a large extent on the positive spill-overs from the presumed wider economic benefits associated with potentially increasing streams of financial and investment flows into adaptation and mitigation activities. This is likely to occur, it is argued, primarily through expenditures on infrastructure, equipment and buildings and on the deployment of clean, renewal and efficient energy technologies.

Climate finance matters for women on at least six grounds: (1) the under-recognition of women's roles and contribution to the two pillars of climate protection; (2) the potential trade-off between ODA for climate and ODA for social development activities; (3) women need assistance in climate proofing their employment/livelihoods and climate-proofing dwellings and so on; (4) women may be left behind in mitigation activities and related environmentally sound technology transfer and development; (5) women will need support accessing and absorbing greater flows of finance for climate-related challenges and (6) with ever warming trend and consequential increase in the frequency of extreme weather effects that increase the need for protection and recovery from the losses and damages that will accompany such events, female and male-headed households, women in the MSMSE sector and women's groups will require access to growing streams of climate change financing at global, regional and national levels.

Under-recognition of women's role and contribution to adaptation and mitigation may mean that significant flows of funds bypass women's projects and programme. In some cases, activities normally undertaken by women in order to secure their livelihoods and preserve natural resources also generate adaptation and mitigation outcomes. Such activities which include mixed and rain fed farming, agroforestry, rain water harvesting and re-charging well water are not well recognized in the global carbon trade market or are often overlooked by different groups of funders. Many women in fishing communities in countries such as Ghana and Senegal are undertaking adaptation and mitigation activities without access to credit or extension services (Perlato 2008).

Climate financing is also needed for the systematization of traditional and emerging indigenous adaptation and mitigation technologies within and across coastal, rural and peri-urban areas of developing countries.

But, the complex nature of the instruments of the various climate change funds and their complicated applications processes are discouraging even for many developing countries' governmental institutions. Women's and community groups, hence, have difficulties accessing such funds.

Women must also be concerned about climate finance due to the potential of trade-offs between financing climate activities versus financing traditional economic and social development budgets (such as poverty eradication and food security) which can arise if there is inadequate provision of climate finance at the global level. The OECD Development Assistance Committee Reporting Framework under its Rio Markers and other researchers such as OECD/Benn 2011 are beginning to track climate-relevant or climate-related ODA expenditures. Furthermore, the terms on which the climate finance is provided, if not in line with the Convention, can lead to the accumulation of debts as governments are forced to take loans (concessional or non-concessional) to finance climate change activities.

Finally, the financing of adaptation and mitigation are also increasingly competing for funds from development finance arena, ODA. Michaelow and Michaelow (2005) argue that there is no limitation on how much ODA can be diverted to climate activities. Brown et al. (2010) argue that re-orientation of ODA towards climate policy objective tends to move resources from education and health sectors in addition to the Aid for Trade policy area. They also point out that re-prioritizing aid from poverty and other social development objectives to climate may result in less aid flows to Africa, with aid shifting more towards South Asia, Latin America and the Middle East towards meeting projected future adaptation needs.

The Nature, Scope and Flow of Climate Finance

Under the article of the UNFCCC, developed countries committed to take the lead on mitigation and to provide finance and technological development and transfer to developing countries in order to help these countries meet their obligations under the Convention and to support their adaptation and mitigation actions. The Kyoto Protocol further quantified the nature of the commitment of developed countries to take mitigations actions to reduce the level of GHGs emitted into the atmosphere. However, there was no corresponding protocol or agreement quantifying the scale and scope of finance and technology transfer.

The UNFCCC did establish a financial mechanism (under article 11) and currently has two operating entities under its framework, the Global Environment Facility (GEF, since 1991) and the Green Climate Fund (GCF), established since 2012 and expected to start funding projects by 2016. At the same time, developed countries have also created their own bilateral climate financing mechanisms as well as contribute funds to multilateral entities, such as the World Bank and the network of regional development banks. This is allowed under (article 11.5 of) the Convention but was intended to be complementary to direct flows through the financial mechanism. Today, this bilateral and multilateral finance dwarfs the flow under the Convention. This is a problem for developing countries. Bilateral and World Bank type climate-related finance are not country-driven; they tend to have their own priorities and concerns, which may or may not align with the needs of the countries. In some cases, these flows can contribute to the accumulation of debts, since they may be in the form of loans or have co-financing requirements. Hence, the present flow of climate finance, as necessitated to meet the objective of the Convention, specifically to support developing countries adaptation and mitigation actions as well as technology transfer and development, is not sufficient.

Under the UNFCCC, article 4.3, climate finance was expected to meet specific requirements, including it should be *new* and *additional* (not divert from traditional ODA flows), adequate (to meet the needs of developing countries), predictable (also noted in article 11.3(d) and *primarily grants*. Hence, it should flow from public sources in developed countries, and not debt creating, particularly for adaptation activities.

IPCC fifth assessment report notes that there is *limited evidence and, high agreement)* that the total climate current finance, including bilateral and multilateral sources currently flowing to developing countries is estimated to be between US$39 and US$120 billion per year (2009, 2010, 2011 and 2012) and IPCC 2014 and UNFCCC 2014. Of this, public climate finance is estimated at US$35–US$49 billion (2011/2012 US$) (*medium confidence* IPCC 2014). Current dedicated climate resources from Annex II parties to Non-Annex I parties under the UNFCCC financial framework have been estimated at about $10 billion per year (2005–2010) and during the fast start finance period, 2010–2012 (IPCC 2014). This represents the combined total financing and investment flows available under the Global Environment Facility for financing adaptation and mitigation projects and programmes in developing countries.

However, there is widespread agreement that this is not sufficient to cover the scale and scope of required adaptation activities needed (conservatively estimated at $171 billion per year for adaptation) and to reduce carbon dioxide equivalent (CO2 eq) emissions by 25% below 2000 levels in 2030 by 2030 for $200–$210 billion per year for mitigation (UNFCCC 2008). Recent work by the International Energy Agency indicates that at least US$5 trillion additional investment is required by 2020 in the energy sector only, to limit warming to below 2 degrees Celsius (3.6 F), the global temperature guard rail agreed in 2010 (IEA 2013). Maintaining global temperature between 1.5 C and well below 2C degree is important for the lives and livelihoods of women, men and children in Africa, Asia and the Pacific, Latin America and the Caribbean regions of the world. In these areas, regional variation in temperature is known to exceeded the global average so a rise in global average temperature nearing to 2 degree (up to a factor of 1.5 for Africa). Hence 2C degrees will be really very hot for Africa (+3.5 C) and will cause untold devastation and suffering for the men and women living in these countries.

Under the Cancun (2010, COP15) agreement, developed countries committed to a goal of mobilizing $100 billion per year by 2020 from various sources, including public and private and innovative sources. It was hoped that significant part of this amount plus any additional flow of funds generated through innovative financing mechanisms should flow through the Green Climate Fund (GCF) established by the Cancun (2010, COP15) agreement and whose governing instrument was endorsed by the Durban, COP 17, 2011.

But now much of this is up in the air. Under the terms of the Paris Agreement and related decisions, there is no commitment by developed countries to a quantified amount of funding for climate change in developing countries. The Cancun pledge remains on the table, and there is a promise to implement this $100 billion per year through 2025. But beyond that, there is no further commitment for climate finance. At the same time, developing countries have assumed much more deeper and comprehensive obligation for both mitigation and adaptation than they had under the Convention. They are also expected to contribute to the mobilization of climate finance including through participating in wide variety of climate finance instrument such as export credit instruments, loans, loan guarantees and so on.

Serving Gender Needs and Priorities, Empowering Women?

It is not clear how much of the total of $10 billion-$62 billion, per year, 2000-2014[10], so far reported to have purportedly been spent on climate change actions in developing countries have supported women's empowerment and gender equality oriented projects and programmes in the areas of adaptation and mitigation. In the case of the approximately over $30 plus billion of fast start finance (2010–2012) reported to have been contributed by developed countries through various channels, there is wide spread disagreements about the actual amount of fresh (new and additional) monies it earmarked or disbursed. A few contributing countries, mainly Scandinavian countries, have specified portion of their fast start financing for gender equity projects and programmes. But, apart from ensuring gender equity with regard to the governance structure of the GCF, there has been no commitment to fund gender equality climate-related interventions, either through a specific set of sub funds or under the funding of adaptation or mitigation.

At the national level, no government has yet systematically included the topic of gender and climate change finance in their own national level budgeting and planning around climate change, though gender has been identified in a number of INDCs and NAPAs, the instrument through which least developing countries have pin-pointed their adaptation needs; nor is gender analysis incorporated into the emerging frameworks of the new NAPs (applicable to all developing countries), the Cancun Adaptation framework or to mitigation measures, such as the nationally appropriate mitigation actions (NAMAs) of developing countries.

Climate Finance, Gender Equality and Women's Empowerment

Historically, the participation of women's organizations within the UNFCCC framework has been weak. Women continue to be under-represented in boards, bodies and delegations attending the Conventions meetings.[11] Despite the fact that fairly early on (COP 7 2001, Decision 36/CP7), gender equality was recognized as important for adaptation and mitigation, it was not fully implemented. Women, as a group, did not have a significant organized presence at climate change policy gatherings until fairly recently. Though there were strong highly placed women in a number of delegations throughout the period of negotiations, including at Cancún (2010) and Durban (2011, COP 17 which saw a peak in women's leadership role[12]): the UNFCCC's Executive Secretary, Christiana Figueres; the President of COP17, Minister of International Relations and Cooperation, South Africa, Maite Nkoana-Mashabane; and outgoing COP President, Minister for Foreign Affairs, Mexico, Patricia Espinosa. Dessima Williams and Connie Connie Hedegaard were simultaneously lead negotiators for two of the very powerful groups of countries in the climate negotiations, the 40 plus members, Alliance of Small Island States, AOSIS and the European Union/European Commission, respectively.

At the Doha meeting, 2012, the Conference of the parties (COP) made yet another decision to improve the representation of women. With decision *23/CP.18 Promoting gender balance and improving the participation of women in UNFCCC negotiations and in the representation of Parties in bodies established pursuant to the Convention or the Kyoto Protocol*, the COP agreed to the goal of gender balance and the participation of women with a commitment to capacity building to ensure the full implementation of the decision. The decision also set in place process for its implementation through the work of the Secretariat and the subsidiaries bodies of the Convention as well as making allowance for gender to be standing item on the COP's agenda

Despite the representation of some women in key positions as previously highlighted,[13] climate change is male dominated in the climate science and policy communities. As noted by Boyd (2002), 'there is strong patriarchal underpinning of the sustainable development and climate change policy agenda, especially mitigation.' She also argues that 'western ideas of science and development are predominantly driven by "masculine" interest especially with regard to forestry, accounting, agriculture and policy making.' Ultimately, the predominant decision makers in many climate change institutional processes are men (bureaucrats, technical analysts, NGO representatives, extension workers and influential leaders at the community level) (Boyd 2002). According to Denton (Denton 2002), men are biased towards providing technical solutions to the climate change problem, and some men have little understanding of or regard for the concerns or interests of women (ibid). Thus, decision-making and policy formulation at environmental levels within conservation, protection and rehabilitation and environmental management follow predominantly male agendas and market-driven notions such as emissions reductions, fungibility and flexible mechanisms (Denton 2002:1; Boyd 2002).

This problem of women's under-representation in climate governance has prompted the call for more women's representation on the various commissions within the climate change policy environment (Dankelman 2002). But the problem is not simply numerical representation, which can be easily fixed, but rather the lack of integration of gender analysis and perspective into those contexts. This problem of the under-representation of women's voices, concerns and priorities permeates climate change financing mechanisms, instruments and processes. To this end, WEDO and the Global Gender and Climate Alliance (GGCA) with support from the government of Finland and Iceland have implemented the mechanism of the Women's Delegate Fund to help to increase gender diversity within the UNFCCC process. The programme has so far supported women delegates with an expanded agenda of training on technical issues, diplomacy, legal language, network and communications (WEDO 2012).

Women's Participating in Climate Finance

It is the case that women remain under-represented in financial decision-making within the UNFCCC's key finance-related bodies such as the GCF's Board (40 men and 8 women up until 2014) and the Standing Committee on Finance (16 men and 4 women), the Adaptation Committee (11 men and 4 women), the Adaptation Fund Board (24 men and 4 women) and the CDM (16 men and 4 women, in 2012), WEDO 2012 and UNFCCC 2013.

The under-representation of women and gender concerns in the funding priorities of the various climate change financing forums such as the Global Environment Facility, the Climate Investment Fund's (CIF's) and the GCF is partly due to lack of gender sensitization of male and female leaders and in part due to inadequate or no gender analysis and perspectives among women and men leaders within the negotiations process and ultimately in the management of those funds.

In a gender-friendly climate change world, there would likely be tremendous speculative for profit enterprises and employment/income generation opportunities equally, or equitably available for men and women. These opportunities would be generated by the flow of investments into plants and infrastructure development around clean energy and climate-proofing investment activities and likely as well by the continued growth of the carbon finance market. Unfortunately, this may not be the case, as in the current environment, most of the many of the high-valued/returns, high profit and high income activities are likely to be filled by men. These include positions in climate management, carbon financing, carbon risk management, construction and transport sectors.

It may also be the case that the same pre-existing gender-based constraints (such as inequality in property rights and chronic low income and low or zero savings) that created problems for women in the regular financial markets may also operate in the context of climate change financing. Such constraints are interlinked with discriminatory norms in the financial markets resulting in inefficiency in resource allocation.

A number of researchers (Perlata 2008; Schalatek 2009) in the area of gender and climate financing have argued that many of the financing mechanisms promoted have gendered inefficient outcomes in that they either (1) misallocate resources by funding projects and programmes that create personal and community damages and reduce access to existing natural resources, or (2) impact negatively on critical resources such as water, sewage and housing, thereby exacerbating social issues. In all cases, women are the ones to bear the brunt of the burden as the households adopt coping strategies to deal with declining access.

This has been the case for men and women and some rural communities with regard to forest and land resources. See for example, the case of Mount Elgon National Park, Uganda, where the Benet people were forcibly displaced from lands on which they had historically dwelled and for which many claim title holdings. The men and women were displaced and the land turned over to a foreign entity who had been issued carbon 'rights' for tree-planting projects. Similar issues, including 'land grabbing for bio fuel productions', face indigenous women and men in the Amazon region in Brazil and elsewhere.

Inefficiencies in the climate financing architecture, which impacts adaptation and mitigation financing, are problematic for gender equality and women's empowerment. Adaptation is important for supporting the life and livelihood of poor men and women in developing countries to cope with adverse weather events. If adaptation financing is driven by loans (and the policy conditionalities that usually accompany them), then that creates a problem in national government financing which may more negatively impact women. The last 20 years of structural adjustment, debt and financial crisis management have demonstrated conclusively that policy conditionalities have undesirable association with negative development, poverty reduction and gender equality impacts.

Historically, governments operating under tight budgetary constraints tended to trade-off gender equality and other social interventions in their budgeting decision-making in order to finance debt services. Secondly, as mitigation projects are large hydro power and high-efficiency coal plants, then there is less likelihood of women's project (both adaptation and mitigation) having significant access to this funding stream.

Perlata (2008), in examining gender and climate change financing in the Philippines, argues that the CDM 'manifest an inordinate reliance on market based solutions that excluded the poor.' This resulted from CDM processes being cumbersome and costly rendering small-scale projects with strong poverty alleviation impacts unviable and making it difficult for the poor to participate. Currently, the CDM is being reformed to mitigate some of its most negative social, gender dimensions and to improve the sustainable development impacts.

However, this does not have to be the case. Gender-sensitive resource allocation can lead to improved outcomes for women, if it increases women's access to credit and income and introduces technology that reduces their time burden. In addition, gender equality in access to resources can translate into productive gains and increased well-being for women as well as economic growth when these resources receive a market price. Current review and reform processes of the CDM, in addition to seeking to generate more positive sustainable development impacts as well as better geographic distribution, seem to be also focused on enhancing its gender dimensions and promoting more benefits for women.

At the present time, it is not clear to what extent climate change strategies and the financing of these impact gender equality and women's empowerment, positively or negatively. This is a matter for empirical verification through fund-specific, national and sectoral case studies. The imperative for undertaking a thorough review of such impacts is now, given that the negotiations for bolstering and re-girding the architecture of climate change finance are currently underway. An initial starting point in this direction is to de-mystify the subject matter by carefully examining the scope, composition and direction of financial and investment flows. This must be complemented by a careful analysis and tracking of the specific dynamics and inter-relationship between gender and climate change financing.

The UNFCCC, as the normative framework for climate change financing, provides more than an adequate basis for integrating a gender social equity and women's empowerment approach into climate change policy and its related financing. Subsequent decisions of the COP (2001, 2011 and the 2014 Lima Work Programme on Gender and climate Change) have and are contributing to enhancing the role and status of gender concerns into the Convention's governance framework. Yet more work needs to be done in integrating gender perspective into the various works of the substantive areas and bodies of the Conventions. At the same, the overall climate change financing architecture and governance system has no systematic, consistent and coherent institutional framework for promoting gender equitable outcomes and the empowerment of women, to which most of the member states have made binding commitments under the Convention for the Elimination of Discrimination Against Women (CEDAW) and other human rights oriented instruments.

It is also difficult to track how much of these funds and investments have flowed to gender-sensitive projects or programmes that promote gender equality outcomes. Social and gender impact assessments are critical to identifying improvements to adaptive capacity and resilience of vulnerable groups of men and women among and within countries. At present, however, these assessments are marginal to the distribution and utilization of flows of funds for climate change.

The CIFs[14] of the World Bank, the Adaptation Fund and the GCF (both under the UNFCCC), have both committed to integrate gender into their frameworks, and this work is ongoing.[15] The GEF is also mainstreaming gender in its operations. It is, however, not clear how much of funding stream is dedicated to women's project as a distinct group of actors.

Historically the Small Grants Programme (SGP) is the main fund of the Global Environment Facility that has gender as one of the main criteria underlying consideration of the approval of grants. The role of women and men is also central to the initial stages of the project conception, approval and implementation. Overall, the SGP documents the contribution of women to projects. In order to build women's capacity to access climate finance, the SGP also conducts 'proposal writing workshops' as well as 'accepts project proposals in local languages and in oral format,' thus increasing the opportunity for women to access climate finance. A gender specialist is required to be included in the voluntary national steering committee that makes decision on grants. By 2013, 26% of the SGP grants are targeted to women, and according to the GEF/UNDP, women participate in the implementation of many of its other non-gender equality targeted grant projects as member of local community. Indeed, some of its funded programmes (such as the training of women as solar engineers and support for tree planting) contributed to women's empowerment. A 2008 evaluation of the SGP, undertaken by both the Evaluation Units of the GEF and UNDP, found that women are a priority group for the SGP in almost all countries reviewed.[16] In Senegal, women are almost 60% of the SGP grantees.

The Adaptation Fund to date has been the premier funds supporting adaptation activities in developing countries. Since adaptation is critical to women's lives and livelihood, gender sensitization of this fund is quite important. Unfortunately, the AF did not start out with gender as a key variable in its operations. However, its 2011 Operational Policies and Guidelines flag the 'needs of the most vulnerable communities' as an aspect of its project criteria review (Decision B.14-15/1_2011). In expanding on the definition of vulnerable communities, women are included in the category of the vulnerable and there is a requirement for sex-disaggregated data for some indicators (GEF 2011; UNDP/GGCA 2011).

Until 2010, World Bank's CIFs key mitigation programmes, the Clean Technology Fund (CTF), the Forest Investment Programme (FIP) and the Special Renewable Energy Programme (SREP), lacked clear processes for accountability with regard to gender and social audits. Since then FIP has a dedicated mechanism to provide grants to Indigenous men and women and local communities to support their participation in FIP investment strategies, programmes and projects. However, a 2013 gender review of the CIF found that only one out of four investment plans referred to gender in the text and that a majority of the investment plans did not include gender indicators, nor did the majority of the IP mentioned national gender policies in any of the documentation.[17]

Unlike the other existing climate change fund, the GCF at its design included a mandate for fund-wide gender sensitization. The governing instrument of the GCF commits the board to 'taking gender sensitive approach in its funding for adaptation and mitigation' (section 1), calls for 'due consideration to be given to gender balance' in the selection of board members and takes 'into account geographic and gender balance in the staffing of the secretariat' as well as 'address gender aspects' in providing simplified and improved access to funding, including direct access. The gender sensitization process is currently underway, and the GCF is still implementing its business model to be ready for project operationalization and financing. However, like the other funds, the GCF, which has made a commitment to have a 50:50 balance in funding adaptation and mitigation, has no specific window for funding women's projects, either for adaptation or mitigation, thought it has a private sector facility.

Gender Biases and Asymmetries in Climate Finance

Since climate finance operates as a subset of the global finance market, where undeniably, gender discrimination and biases work to the disadvantage of women,[18] it is widely acknowledged that women are underserved in the global and national banking sectors and the financial markets, which has shunted them to the margin of finance, into micro finance. Hence, it can be expected that there will likewise be difficulties in ensuring that adequate amounts of climate finance flow towards women's projects and women's enterprises. But the imperative of climate change and the high cost of adaptation as well as the rising losses and damages associated with extreme weather events demand that women are not yet again shunted to the margins of climate finance.

Financial decision-making at the macro (policy) and meso (institutional and industry) levels affects the day-to-day realities of women as caretakers of home and community, as workers and as business owners. The Stiglitz Commission, which examined the nature of the financial crisis for the UN General Assembly in 2009, noted that democracy and participation require that the people whose lives are impacted by financial decisions have their voices, priorities and concerns reflected as part of decision-making. This is certainly the case for women and men in local and national communities. Currently, it is the male perspective that dominates decision-making in global finance; this is also the case with climate finance.

Climate finance and investment are expected to flow from developed countries, through a variety of instruments and mechanisms, to implement emission reduction or removal projects in the developing countries and to support adaptation activities. The financial mechanism and the set of evolving funds under the Convention as well as other multilateral funding sources are the means to secure the financing of adaptation and mitigation activities in developing countries. Significant portions of these flows have been conditioned on co-financing from national budgets, ODA or the regional development banks. The financial markets' actors and the private sector presently are involved in climate finance and are anticipated to play an even more increasingly greater role in both adaptation and mitigation finance. However, this is not without controversy. There are issues of how well the private sector, motivated by the maximization of profit, will fit with national climate change and development policies. Will the private sector gravitate towards adaptation activities, which are not so easily conducive to profit maximization? How will the private sector relate to serving and meeting the needs of women actors in community projects?

Adaptation financing is needed to provide gender equality interventions and promote women's empowerment. This is a two-way interchange. Gender equality and women's empowerment can enable better adaptive capacity, and adaptation activities can bolster women's empowerment, if done well. Better awareness and capacity also enable more effective and sustainable support for mitigation actions by men and women in communities. So from the point of view of gender, poverty eradication and human development, adaptation must promote development and development must promote adaptation. In the first case, adaptation promotes development by enhancing and protecting current achievements. It also establishes pillars for anticipating and responding to future climate events. In the second case, development promotes adaptation when it develops resilience to climate change, or when 'climate-change adaptation is mainstream(ed) within development activity' (Agarwala 2005, cited in IPCC 2007).

Potential Fiscal and Gender Budget Effects of Adaptation Finance

Adaptation financing instruments range from insurance products, fiscal resources, grants and levies and domestic national fiscal expenditures and in some cases ODA. Adaptation finance raises particular fiscal challenges given the marginalization of the financing of adaptation activities under taken in developing countries from external climate finance sources. Adaptation received only about 20% of the over $30 billion in fast start finance and less than about 10–15% of climate investment expenditures globally. As a result, many developing countries must finance adaptation activities from domestically generated fiscal revenues. Additionally, under the anticipated new climate regime, developing countries may have to ramp up climate resilient and adaptation planning and expenditures without the certainty of financing from developed countries. Thus, there will be even greater emphasis on the fiscal aspects of adaptation. Attention will need to be paid to the fiscal implications of climate change adaptation on poverty and gender-sensitive expenditures. Fiscal and financial management around adaptation may include budget contingences (both as ex post and ex ante financing) and the financing of reserve funds to deal with disaster risk management and climate proofing.

Climate Public Expenditure and Institutional Reviews (CPEIRs) are being developed (by the UNDP and the World Bank) to track and assess the linkages between national climate change policy and resource allocation of national public funds to climate policy objectives. To the extent that international climate finance flows do not meet the adaptation needs of some developing countries, the greater the extent to which budgetary allocations must be reallocated for climate priorities and institutional frameworks. Adaptation costs are defined as those due to climate change but additional to development, Bird et al., 2012. Hence, shortfall in adaptation funding from external sources might therefore evince a trade-off with other areas of the national budget and may have adverse impacts on gender equality interventions. Gender-responsive budgetary (GRB) analyses, therefore, need to be aware of the potential inter-linkages and challenges between climate change-related expenditures and fiscal policy and gender and social objectives.

Climate-related fiscally generated resources will impact government budgetary and expenditure patterns. There is certain to be some potential synerges and cross-fertilization with gender budgetary analyses. Connecting the two spheres of analysis can occur through the public expenditure reviews as well as through public expenditure and institutional review. The CPEIR adds public environmental expenditure review component and wrestles with identifying and classifying climate-related expenditures in the national budgetary process. GRB analyses will have to confront the challenges around the gender dimensions, if any, of such expenditures. GRB exercises in the future will need to be mindful of the specific pathways and how and to what extent climate-related new and additional incremental spending focused on scaling up the financing of climate priorities across sectors and economy-wide may act to either crowd-out, adversely impact or may work to positively reinforce gender equality and non-gender equality oriented expenditures.

Mitigation financing tends to focus on creating incentives for consumers, individuals, households and producers to reduce GHG emissions and to encourage the transition away from fossil-fuel-based production and consumption activities. Investments primarily flow into the seven key sectors identified by the IPCC as major contributors to the production and release of greenhouse gases: (1) energy, (2) transportation and its infrastructure, (3) residential and commercial buildings, (4) industry, (5) agriculture, (6) forestry and (7) waste management (IPCC 2007).[19] Within this framework, there are also investment flows to projects and activities aimed at preventing deforestation and supporting afforestation and reforestation.

The household sector also plays an important role in mitigation. Here, financing is needed for mitigation activities such as improving the availability and efficiency of energy to communities and households, including clean and health protecting cooking stoves, other household appliances, lighting and personal transport services. This type of financing may be small-scale and less profitable or less likely to attract pure market mechanisms. It is also the area most closely related to enabling the high-quality functioning of women and girls in least developing countries.

The main UNFCCC mitigation financing mechanism is the CDM, a market-based mechanism to support Annex I Parties fulfilling their emission reductions commitment by promoting emissions reduction projects implemented in developing countries. Ostensibly, the CDM has the dual objective of also supporting the sustainable development of developing countries. (It provides countries with emissions obligation a flexible way to meet part of their emissions reductions targets, under the Kyoto Protocol, through emission reduction (or emissions removal) projects in developing countries. Such projects earn certified emission reduction credits (CERs) that can be traded and sold.)

Mitigation finance and investment also flow through a variety of channels, such as the Global Environmental Facility, the World Bank and its collaborative network of regional banks and UN agencies. Private sector entities and meso level institutions such as foundations and international organizations also contribute to the flow of mitigation financing through the private markets. Increasingly, large commercial banks, hedge funds and institutional investors and key actors in the global capital markets are engaging in mitigation financing and related activities. The private sector plays a significant and growing role in mitigation financing through traditional forms of investments in clean energy as well as through activities in the carbon finance, offset and capital markets.

Potential Fiscal and Gender Budget Effects of Mitigation Finance

Like adaptation finance, there are clear fiscal aspects to financing mitigation activities in developing countries. Unlike adaptation, which tends to rely more on grant financing, mitigation financing leans more towards loans (low or highly concessional). Both the IMF and the World Bank have pointed out that '(f)iscal policy has a critical role to play in mitigating greenhouse gas emissions and raising revenues for climate finance, fiscal consolidation, and other purposes' (IMF 2012). In the context of the more ambitions mitigation actions that will be expected from developing countries under the Paris 2015 agreement, there will be need for fiscal expenditure vis a vis such activities as Feed-in-tariff programmes, investment subsidies for clean energy and energy efficient investment, tax credits and publicly support R&D. The extent to which strong demands are placed on fiscal policy for mitigation by developing countries will depend on the nature and scope of financing offered through the UNFCCC financing mechanisms as well as the price of carbon, the operation and function of carbon markets (nationally, regional and globally). Furthermore, the push towards the phasing out of fossil fuels subsidies, while it may relax constraints on government budget, through the elimination of the subsidies, may create higher costs for fuels for cooking, farming and so on, unless great care is taken to offset such untoward results. GRB analyses must also take these considerations on board.

Towards Gender-Sensitive and Gender-Responsive Climate and Development Policy

In the transition towards a gender-sensitive, woman-friendly climate change financing world, the negative attributes of global finance may also be muted or transformed. Consider the operating principle of 'no regrets' that is currently a topic of discussion in promoting resilience and climate-proofing development. The idea is that a set of projects may be considered for implementation, after cost and benefit analysis has been undertaken, even if it is doubtful that the anticipated climate event will occur. This is because these projects would of themselves generate net social benefits, even without the effects of climate change.

On the grounds of social net benefits, there can be targeted interventions by governments and funding institutions for the development of projects and programmes that seek to eliminate the high transaction costs that women and community groups may face in attempting to accessing and utilize the financing available within existing financing instruments. Such actions could include initiating the provision of financing to women's groups, women-owned entities and projects through special windows that entertain applications for specific types of gender-sensitive adaptation and mitigation projects, discounted premiums on insurance products and the subsidization of the administrative costs of registering projects developed by poor women.

Over time, women's access to credit should be mainstreamed in climate finance funds and instruments. This can be accomplished when climate finance mechanisms and instruments begin to incorporate gender-sensitive policies and guidelines into their management structure and into project design, implementation, evaluation and monitoring. It is only through such proactive efforts that the pernicious and pervasive issue of gender bias and segmentation can be eliminated. Additionally, a commercial entity could receive specifically targeted tax write-offs or subsidies for supporting gender-sensitive adaptation and mitigation projects. Likewise, national development banks with climate change portfolios may have a special gender window utilizing donor-sequestered contributions.

Where market-based mechanisms, such as the CDM and REDD+, are allowed to operate projects, there should be provisions built into project documents and so on that stipulate clearly the protection of women's access and or ownership of land and their access forest. Just compensation, structural and institutional changes will be needed, where necessary, including land reform that goes beyond western conceptions of property titles. In some cases, conventional land entitlement processes have been associated with further marginalization of women and the dispossession of families from land. Land reform must therefore be undertaken in a gender-sensitive consultative way involving men and women stakeholders in the community. It must also take into account different forms and dimensions of the existing inequities and accounting for both distributive and corrective justice. Thus, there has to be social and gender justice preconditions that must be settled prior to the operations of programmes under REDD and/or similar mechanisms.

There needs to be specific skills-upgrading and knowledge-building programmes geared towards women in order to enable more women to take advantage of climate change-related opportunities in the medium to long run. Such capacity building and skill development efforts should cut across the financing of the thematic areas of adaptation, mitigation technology transfer and financing. Capacity building efforts should focus on integrating women into all levels of mitigation actions, from rehabilitative work in home and commercial buildings to infrastructure to technical specialists in carbon risk management. Particular attention should also be paid by governments, project planners and implementers to building capacities or women to fully participate at all levels of carbon marketing financing instruments and mechanisms. This may mean that some of the funding streams associated with the Convention finance mechanism and bilateral as well as multilateral development banks may have to be sequestered or redirected towards gender-specific capacity building, education and awareness training.

To sum up, with regard to climate change and its financing, the engendering imperative is to ensure that the concerns and priorities of women, especially poor women, move to the centre stage of the financing agenda. The process of engendering must tackle the details and intricacies of specific agenda items as well as traverse the contours of the climate change financing regime with a particular focus and attention to its funds, their instruments and modalities. How are the financial resources generated, managed and distributed? Here, the concern is with the management of financial resources in terms of predictability and adequacy of public and complementary private flow of funds for gender equality and women's empowerment projects.

Another concern is with the nature of the distributional impacts with regard to adaptation and mitigation mechanisms such as the Adaptation Fund, the CDM and the reduced emissions from degradation and deforestation (REDD+) and the carbon market. With REDD+, the concern is with the effectiveness, efficiency and transparency, especially with regard to the criteria of funding mechanisms and formal and informal barriers to entry and exit in the private climate change financing market. It is important to ferret out the nature of the eligibility criteria—to what extent they are facilitative of women, especially poor women's participation or are they barriers to entry.

Within the scope and framework of the Adaptation Fund Board, which was established in Bali 2007 to supervise and manage the Adaptation Fund,[20] governments have accepted that all parties must have ownership and decision-making power. Within this context, it is well accepted that 'skewedness or lack of representation' has implications for 'the prioritization and quality of projects selected, given the weak understanding of issues that underlie developing countries and their concerns' (TERI p.10). However, these principles have not yet been applied to gender equality issues or to the claims of indigenous people.

As noted above, the GCF, which is widely heralded as the world's only dedicated climate change financing fund, is in the process of operationalizing its mandate from its governing instrument to operationalize a fund wide gender-sensitization process. This process has involved consultations and outreach with gender experts and women and gender activists from a wide range of organizations in the UNFCCC's 'women and gender constituency.' However, as yet there is no indication that the GCF will decide on a gender window or a similar mechanism to ensure gender equality in its disbursement of fund. Currently, it seems that it will rely on its network of implementing entities and executing entities, who have been the traditional ones operating in the GEF and the CIFs orbit.

Unfortunately, the Paris Agreement did not do much to advance the issue of gender and climate finance. Though gender advocate worked hard to integrate gender references into the text, particularly in the mitigation and the finance sections, these were dropped in the final text adopted. Hence by its neglect of gender issues, in its key operational domains, the Paris Agreement has taken a step backward from the gender progressive stance of the governing instrument of the Green Climate Fund. It seemingly did not recognizing the critical importance of ensuring new, predictable and adequate flow of funds towards policies, programmes and projects that promote gender equality and women's empowerment. This is so despite the recognition that climate policy must pay attention to gender equality and women's concerns. However, the stipulation on gender responsive adaptation in article 7 and gender response capacity building in article 11 can help to provide helpful bases for pushing for more funds to be distributed to women's projects and for gender equality climate and sustainable development related interventions.

Some critical questions that should be at the heart of the GCF and other climate funds' decision-making should include:

> What kinds of adaptation readiness or capacity building programs and projects are needed for women owned and operated business distinct from male owned businesses?
>
> Who are the normal targets of adaptation and mitigation capacity building and technical assistance?
>
> To what extent are the needs, priorities and concerns of micro, SME's and women entrepreneurs taken into account into the design, planning and implementation of adaptation and mitigation projects and programs?

Answering the above questions will point to the kinds of supportive policies at the Fund level as well as to national and sector levels that are important for creating enabling conditions for women and men to adapt to climate change and to deal with loss and damage due to extreme weather events. This should include mechanisms to promote more gender-sensitive expenditure allocations for skill development, skill upgrading, day care and family assistance.

Notes

1. The recent Fifth IPCC Assessment Report (AR 5) note that while there is this high propensity of harm to women from extreme weather events, it varies regionally. The IPCC highlights that in the USA, China and Vietnam, men seem to be at greater risk of death following flooding. In the latter two cases, men died due to rural farming and search and risk and protection of fields during flooding. It further noted that, while the Paris 2003 heat wave

led to 'excess mortality among females overall, but there were more excess deaths among men in the working age span (25–64)'. These deaths, it is argued, were linked to differential exposure to heat in occupation settings such as working outdoors, Feuillet et al. (2006) cited in IPCC 2014.

2. IPCC glossary.
3. Targeted gender equality interventions refer to programmes and projects that directly reduce gender inequality and empower women. These include programmes or projects geared to improving educational outcomes for girls and women, and gender mainstreaming activities such as gender training and gender focal points in sector ministries. Targeted non-gender inequality interventions are projects and programmes that are directed at improving social development but which have spill over effects (work synergistically) on gender equality. Examples of non-targeted gender equality interventions are the construction of feeder and rural roads, health clinics and water services, UN Millennium Project (2005).
4. MDG3-emphasized poverty sectors include: education, health, rural development, slum upgrading, water, sanitation and energy, UN Millennium Project (2005).
5. NAP is the instrument used for developing countries as whole to assess their adaptation needs since 2010.
6. The ten guiding elements listed are as follows: (1) A participatory approach involving stakeholders; (2) a multidisciplinary approach; (3) a complementary approach that builds on existing plans and programmes; (4) sustainable development; (5) gender equity; (6) a country-driven approach; (7) sound environmental management;(8) cost-effectiveness; (9) simplicity; (10) and flexibility, based on country-specific circumstances (UNFCC FCCC/TP/2011/7).
7. The IPCC (2007) glossary defines black carbon as the '**o**perationally defined species based on measurement of light absorption and chemical reactivity and/or thermal stability; (it) consists of soot, charcoal, and/or possible light-absorbing refractory organic matter.' In the developed countries, the main source of black carbon are diesel fuels. But in the developing countries, it is produced from the burning of wood, animal dung, vegetable oil and other biomass fuels. V. Ramanathan and Greg Carmichael found that 'black carbon soot, from burning wood and other biomass, cooking with solid fuels, and diesel exhaust has a warming effect in the atmosphere three to four times greater than prevailing estimates' (Nature Geoscience 1, 221–227, March 24, 2008). According to Ramanathan and Carmichael, *black carbon* emissions arising from: (1) 'cooking with biofuels such as wood, dung and crop residue,' 20% of the total, (2) 'fossil fuel combustion (diesel and coal),' 40% of the total, and (3) 'open biomass burning (associated with deforestation and crop residue burning),' 40% of the total. They argue that 'soot and

other forms of black carbon could have as much as 60 percent of the current global warming effect of carbon dioxide.' Ramanathan and Carmichael also argue that 'over 400,000 annual fatalities among women and children are attributed to smoke inhalation during indoor cooking,' especially in Asia. The IPCC (2007) defines black carbon as the 'operationally defined species based on measurement of light absorption and chemical reactivity and/or thermal stability; (it) consists of soot, charcoal, and/or possible light-absorbing refractory organic matter.'

8. The distinction between countries under the UNFCCC is not between developed and developing countries, per se, but rather about historical responsibility for the problem of climate change. Hence, the key distinction is between Annex I parties (those with historical responsibility for climate change) and Non-Annex I the developing countries as a group who have made the least contribution to the accumulation of the stock of GHGs into the atmosphere. Annex I parties also include the countries of Eastern Europe and the former USSR network of countries, and Annex II parties, the rich OECD countries of Europe, North America, Australia and Japan, who have commitment for providing climate finance and technology transfer and development to the developing countries. This categorization between AI and NAI is at the heart of the contestations around CBDR, equity and the push for a new climate agreement. Annex I countries want to do away with the annexes, what they now term 'outdated' bifurcation. While some of the substantive issues and the best way to address global warming and keep temperature below 2 C is a real concern, it is undeniable that countries such as the USS and the EU also seek to escape from their commitments (under article 4 of the Convention) for providing finance and technology transfer to the developing countries.
9. This reality was recognized, acknowledged and provided for in the Convention.
10. The figures for 2013 and 2014 which were reported in OECD/CPI report OECD/CPI Report, *Climate Finance in 2013–14 and the USD 100 Billion goal* October 2015 are highly contested by many climate finance expert.
11. For example, the Adaptation Committee, the Adaptation Fund Board, the Consultative group of experts on National Communications, the Executive board of the Clean Development Mechanism, the Least Development Country Fund and the Technology Executive Committee.
12. For example, the Executive Secretary of the UNFCCC is female, and in 2010–2012, a trio of women leaders dominated the COP meetings: In addition to the ES of the UNFCCC, in both the host countries leadership of the COP (Mexico, 2010) and (South Africa, 2011), Foreign Ministers were women. This dynamics shifted back to male leadership since 2012 (Qatar), 2013 (Poland) and 2015 (Peru). The Paris COP21 (2015), though dominated by French Minister of Foreign Affairs and International Development,

Laurent Fabius also had the strong presence of Laurence Tubiana, French Ambassador responsible for climate change negotiations and Special Representative for the 2015 Paris Climate Conference and Ségolène Royal, the French Minister of Ecology, Sustainable Development and Energy.

13. See note 12, above.
14. The CIF is a $8.1 billion set of four funds dedicated to piloting low-emissions and climate-resilient development in developing countries: (1) the Clean Technology Fund ($5.5) billion, (2) the Pilot Program for Climate Resilience (PPCR), $1.2 billion, (3) the Forest Investment Programme (FIP), $785 million and (4) the Scaling Up Renewable Energy (SREP) in Low Income Countries Program, $796 million.
15. The GCF is the first climate fund to mandate the integration of gender perspectives from the very outset of its operations. Its Governing Instrument (GI) recognizes the importance of mainstreaming gender into GCF financing; it thus has five references to gender: paragraphs 3, 11, 21, 31 and 71. The GI's objectives and guiding principles stipulate that the fund will maximize the impact of its funding for adaptation and mitigation while *taking a gender-sensitive approach*. As of November 2015, the Fund has formally adopted a gender policy and interim gender action plan.
http://gcfund.net/fileadmin/00_customer/documents/pdf/GCF-governing_instrument-120521-block-LY.pdf.
http://www.gcfund.org/fileadmin/00_customer/documents/MOB201503-9th/10_-_Gender_Policy_and_Action_Plan_20150304_fin.pdf.
The CIF has been mainstreaming gender into its programmes. It had a gender review of its programme in 2013 and has a gender action plan for 2015–2016, The *CIF Gender Action Plan FY15-16*, approved in June 2014.
16. Of the 22 country strategy reviews, only one did not consider women to be a priority target group. The report also points out that in some countries, local socio-cultural factors may constraint women's participation, while in others, their participation may be in roles to contribute little to their empowerment (GEF 2008). About 15% the third operation phase of the SPG grants explicitly target indigenous people (GEF 2008).
17. The two exceptions in both cases were Chile and the Philippines, who both use gender indicators partially, p.63 IUCN 2014.
18. The global financial architecture and its governance, which has been in place since at least the post-war period, are highly gendered. They are so in terms of the principles, aims, practices and knowledge base underlying decision-making (Lethbridge 2012) as well as in terms of the outcomes of the policies implemented. The operation of the financial system impacts pre-existing structural gender inequalities and can enhance or worsen the situation for gender equality and women's social and economic empower-

ment (Antonopolous 2009, World Bank PREM and Young et al 2009 and 2010).

In exploring the gendered nature of the global financial markets, four specific forms of gender biases have implications for the efficacy and efficiency of climate change financing (van Staveren 2002). According to van Staveren, these gender biases are:

(i) Under-representation of women in financial decision-making;
(ii) Increased gender gaps in the economic positions of women and men;
(iii) Inefficient resource allocation in financial markets due to gender discrimination and
(iv) Gender-based instability of financial markets.

For more in-depth discussion of how these related to climate finance please, see Williams 2015, forthcoming.

19. The IPCC identified seven key sectors (arranged according to their relative percentage contribution to greenhouse gas release into the atmosphere); they include: energy sources (25.9%), industry (19.4%), forestry (17.4%), agriculture (13.5%), transport (13.1%), residential and commercial buildings (7.9%) and waste management (2.8%) (IPCC 2007).
20. The Adaptation Fund has been established by the Parties to the Kyoto Protocol of the UN Framework Convention on Climate Change to finance concrete adaptation projects and programmes in developing Countries that are Parties to the Kyoto Protocol. http://www.adaptation-fund.org.

Bibliography

Ackerman, F. (2009). *Financing for climate investments.* Washington, DC: Inter-Governmental Group of Twenty-Four (G-24).

Agarwala, S., 2005: Putting climate change in the development mainstream: introduction and framework. *Bridge Over Troubled Waters: Linking Climate Change and Development.* S. Agrawala, Ed., OECD, Paris, 23–43.

Antonopoulos, R. (2009, May). *The current economic and financial crisis: A gender perspective* (Working paper No. 562). New York: The Levy Economics Institute of Bard College.

Bird, N., Beloe, T., Hedger, M., Lee, J., Nicholson, K., O'Donnell, K., & Steele, P. (2012). DRAFT. The Climate Public Expenditure and Institutional Review (CPEIR): Developing a methodology to review climate policy, institutions and expenditure. UNDP/CDDE/ODI.

Boyd, E. (2002). The Noel Kempff project in Bolivia: Gender, power and decision making in climate mitigation. In R. Masika (Ed.), *Gender, development and climate change.* Oxford: Oxfam Publishing. *Gender and Development Journal, 10*(2).

Bridge. (2008). *Gender and climate change: Mapping the linkages—A scoping study on knowledge and gaps.* Sussex: Institute of Development Studies University of Sussex(IDS).

Climate Investment Funds. (2010, October 29). Strategic environment, social and gender assessment of the climate investment funds. SCF/TFC.6/Inf.2. http://www.realclimateeconomics.org/equity_global_distribution.html

Climate Investment Funds. (2013). Gender review of CIF. Prepared by Global Gender Office of the International Union for Conservation of Nature—IUCN. Lorena Aguilar, Francois Rogers, Rebeccca Pearl-Martinez, Itza Castaneda, Andrea athanas and Jackeline Siles North–south Agenda for Environmental Justice. January 14, 2009 Ottawa, Ontario.

Damptey (2007). Climate change and Womens Livelihood. Paper presented during the National Forum on Climate Change, Accra, Ghana.

Dankelman, I. (2002). Climate change: Learning from gender analysis and women's experience of organizing for sustainable development. In R. Masika (Ed.), *Gender, development and climate change*. Oxford: Oxfam Publishing.

Denton, F. (2002). Climate change vulnerability, impacts, and adaptation: Why does gender matter? *Gender and Development, 10*(2), 10–20.

Durban (2011) is also not a publication but the 17th meeting of the parties. Should read: Durban (2011, COP 17)

Fouillet, A., Rey, G., Laurent, F., Pavillon, G., Bellec, S., Guihenneuc-Jouyaux, C., Clavel, J., Jougla, E., & Hémon, D. (2006). Excess mortality related to the August 2003 heat wave in France. *International Archives of Occupational & Environmental Health, 80*(1), 16–24.

GEF. (2011). *Gender mainstreaming*. Washington, DC. http://www.thegef.org/gef/OPS5.

Gender Action Heinrich Böll Foundation. (2009). *Doubling the damage: World Bank climate investment funds undermine climate and gender justice*. Washington, DC.

GHF (2009). Climate Change - The Anatomy of a Silent Crisis: Climate Change Human Impacts Report. Geneva: Global Human Forum.

GGCA UNDP. (2010). *Adaptation fund exploring the gender dimensions of climate finance mechanisms*. New York: UNDP.

Godfrey, S. (2011). Conference report for Euro/Africa cross networking meeting on the global crisis. The financialization of natural resources.

Grown, C., Bahadur, C., Handbury, J., & Elson, D. (2006). *The financial requirements of achieving gender equality and women's empowerment*. The World Bank April 2006 (Levy Economics Institute working paper No. 467). New York: Levy Economics Institute.

Harris, R., Schalatek, L., Eggerts, E., Strohmeier, H., Wanjiru, L., Gore, T., Raczek, T., & Eddy, N. (2012). *Gender and the green climate fund: From principles to operationalization*. http://www.gender-climate.org/Content/Docs/Publications/BM1_Gender_GCF_2-pager_FINAL_21Aug2012.pdf

Hellmuth, M. E., Osgood, D. E., Hess, U., Moorhead, A., & Bhojwani, H. (Eds.). (2009). *Index insurance and climate risk: Prospects for development and disaster management* (Climate and society No. 2). New York: International Research Institute for Climate and Society (IRI), Columbia University.

Inter-governmental Panel on Climate Change (IPCC). (2007). Climate Change 2007: Mitigation. In B. Metz, O. R. Davidson, P. R. Bosch, R. Dave, & L. A. Meyer (Eds.), *Contribution of working group iii to the fourth assessment report of the Intergovernmental Panel on Climate Change* (XXX pp). Cambridge/New York: Cambridge University Press.

Inter-governmental Panel on Climate Change (IPCC). (2012). Managing the risks of extreme events and disasters to advance climate change adaptation. In C. B. Field, V. Barros, T. F. Stocker, D. Qin, D. J. Dokken, K. L. Ebi, M. D. Mastrandrea, K. J. Mach, G.-K. Plattner, S. K. Allen, M. Tignor, & P. M. Midgley (Eds.), *A special report of working groups I and II of the Intergovernmental Panel on Climate Change* (p. 582). Cambridge/New York: Cambridge University Press.

Inter-governmental Panel on Climate Change (IPCC). (2013). Summary for policymakers. In T. F. Stocker, D. Qin, G.-K. Plattner, M. Tignor, S. K. Allen, J. Boschung, A. Nauels, Y. Xia, V. Bex, & P. M. Midgley (Eds.), *Climate change 2013: The physical science basis. Contribution of working Group I to the fifth assessment report of the Intergovernmental Panel on Climate Change.* Cambridge: Cambridge University Press.

International Energy Agency (IEA). (2012). *Energy technology perspectives 2012: Pathways to a clean energy system* (p. 1). Paris: OECD/IEA. http://www.iea.org/Textbase/npsum/ETP2012SUM.pdf

International Energy Agency (IEA). (2013). *World Energy Outlook* (*WEO-2013*). Paris: IEA/OECD.

IMF (2012). IMF Work on Fiscal Policy and Climate Change. http://www.imf.org/external/np/seminars/eng/2012/rio/pdf/fiscal.pdf

IPCC, 2014: Climate Change 2014: Synthesis Report. Contribution of Working Groups I, II and III to the Fifth Assessment Report of the Intergovernmental Panel on Climate Change [Core Writing Team, R. K. Pachauri and L. A. Meyer (eds)]. IPCC, Geneva, Switzerland, p. 151.

Lethbridge, J. (2012). *Impact of the global economic crisis and austerity measures on women. A report commissioned by Public Services International (PSI) Public Services International Research Unit.* PSIRU, Business School, University of Greenwich, London: University of Greenwich. www.psiru.org.

Michaelowa, A., & Michaelowa, K. (2005). *Climate or development: Is ODA diverted from its original purpose?* Paper No. 2 by the HWWI Research Programme International Climate Policy. http://www.hwwi.org/uploads/tx_wilpubdb/HWWI_Research_Paper_2.pdf

Neumayer, E. & Plumper, T. (2007). *The gendered nature of natural disasters: The impact of catastrophic events on the gender gap in life expectancy, 1981–2002*, London School of Economics London School of Economics and Political Science with University of Essex and Max-Planck Institute of Economics. London: LSE.

NORAD (2010). Progress Report—Gender Mainstreaming in Norad's Energy Programme. Norway: Leusdem, Energia.

Perlata, A. (2008). *Gender and climate change finance - A case study from the Philippines.* New York: Women Environment and Development (WEDO).

Rosenthal (2009). Third World Soot is Target in Climate Fight. 16 April. www.nytimes.com/2009/04/16/science/earth/16degree.html (accessed 4 Jan 2012).

Schalatek, L. (2009). *Gender and climate finance: Double mainstreaming for sustainable development. Heinrich Böll Foundation.* Berlin: HBF.

TERI. (2008). *Adaptation financing.*TERI viewpoint paper 6. The Energy and Resources Institute (TERI) www.teriin.org. http://www.realclimateeconomics.org/equity_global_distribution.html.

UN Millennium Project (2005). Taking Action: Achieving Gender Equality and Empowering Women, Report prepared by the Taskforce on Education and Gender Equality, UNDP, Earthscan: London and Virginia.

United Nations Framework for Climate Change. (2013). *Report on gender composition note by the secretariat.* Bonn: United Nations Framework Convention.

UNFCCC 1992. *The United Nations Framework Convention on Climate Change.* UNFCCC secretariat.

UNFCCC (2008). *Investment and Financial Flows to Address Climate Change.* An Update. FCCC/TP/2008/276. Bonn: UNFCCC Secretariat.

UNFCCC (2013). *Biennial Assessment and Overview of Climate Finance Flows Standing Committee on Finance.* UNFCCC Secretariat.

UNFCCC (2013). *Biennial Assessment and Overview of Climate Finance Flows Standing Committee on Finance.* UNFCCC Secretariat.

WEDO. (2012) *Women's participation in the UNFCCC 2008–2012.* New York: Women's Environment and Development Organisation.

Williams, M. (2015). *Gender and climate change finance: Coming out of the margin.* Routledge: London and Newyork.

WHO (2011). Gender, Climate Change and Health. Geneva: WHO.

World Bank. (2009, March 6). *Women in 33 countries highly vulnerable to financial crisis effects* (Press Release No: 2009/245/PREM), Washington, DC: The World Bank.

World Bank (2011). Climate change and fiscal policy: A report for APEC. Washington, DC. https://openknowledge.worldbank.org/handle/10986/2734. License: Creative Common Attribution CC BY 3.0.

Young, B. (2002). *The gender dimensions of the global financial architecture conference: Gender budgets, financial markets, financing for development.* Berlin: Heinrich-Boell-Foundation.

Young, B., & Schuberth, H. (2010). *The global financial meltdown and the impact of financial governance* (Garnet Policy Brief Number 10).

Index

Note: Page numbers followed by "n" refer to notes.

© The Author(s) 2017

Z. Khan, N. Burn (eds.), *Financing for Gender Equality,*
DOI 10.1057/978-1-137-46101-8

T

CPSIA information can be obtained
at www.ICGtesting.com
Printed in the USA
LVHW082258170319
610985LV00009B/64/P

9 781137 461001